Yes, The World Is Round

Sailing in the Wake of Early Explorers And History Makers

Part I
~ England to Fiji ~

Yes, The World Is Round

Sailing in the Wake of Early Explorers And History Makers

Part I
~ England to Fiji ~

DONNA HILL

Yes, The World Is Round, Part I

© 2018 by Donna Hill

All rights reserved. No part of this book may be used or reproduced in any manner whatsoever without written permission except in the case of brief quotations embodied in critical articles and reviews. For information, address *admin@oriolepublishing.com*.

Oriole Publishing, Toronto

Permission to reprint lyrics The Cliffs of Baccalieu, composer Jack Withers; Morning Music Ltd., Mississauga, Ont.

Grateful acknowledgment is made for the permission to reproduce the world chart by Nautical North, Sarasota, U.S.A. To Steve Callahan, author of Adrift; Ballantine Books, 1996, for the quote used in the introduction to Chapter 5. To Sail Magazine Re: "Daniel's Bay Lost". And to all authors in this century and past, who gifted us with accounts of explorations by land and by sea.

Cover: Damonza
Interior design: Typeflow

Library and Archives Canada Cataloguing In Publications
Hill, Donna -author

ISBN 978-0-9950579-4-4 (Part I, paperback)
ISBN 978-0-9950579-1-3 (Part I, electronic book)
ISBN 978-09950579-2-0 (Part II, paperback)
ISBN 978-0-9950579-3-7 (Part II, electronic book)

Non fiction

For Jennifer and David

*Be proud of your smallest accomplishments,
learn to forgive, be kind to others,
love, be loved, live life to the fullest....*

CLIFFS OF BACCALIEU
Jack Withers (1899–1964)

We were bound home in October
from the shores of Labrador
Tryin` to head a bad nor`easter and snow too
But the winds swept down upon us
makin` day as dark as night
Just before we made the land off Baccalieu.

O we tried to clear the island as we
brought her further south
As the wind from out the north east stronger blew
'Till our lookout soon he shouted
and there lay dead ahead
Through the snow squalls loomed the cliffs of Baccalieu.

And `twas hard down by the tiller as
we struggled with the sheets
Tryin` our best to haul them in a foot or two
`Till our decks so sharply titled we
could hardly keep our feet
As we hauled her from the rocks of Baccalieu.

O the combers beat her under and
I thought she`d never rise
And our mainboom it was bending nigh in two
With her lee rails three foot under
and two hands at the wheel
Sure we hauled her from the rocks of Baccalieu.

To leeward was the island and to innard was the gale
And the blinding sleet would cut you thru` and thru
But our hearts were beating gladly
for no longer could we gaze
Down to leeward at the Cliffs of Baccalieu.

CONTENTS

What's in a Name	*iii*
Acknowledgements	*v*
Chart	*vi*
Preface	*xi*

1. **Toughening Up: England to the Mediterranean** — 1
   - *London, Channel Islands* — 5
   - *England's South Coast, Iberian Coast* — 24
   - *Gibraltar* — 61
   - *The Mediterranean* — 68

2. **Leaving the Mediterranean** — 75
   - *Spain* — 79
   - *Majorca, Return to Gibraltar* — 92
   - *Gibraltar to Canary Islands* — 102
   - *Canary Islands: Lanzarote, Gran Canaria* — 108

3. **Crossing The Atlantic Ocean** — 113
   - *Preparation* — 117
   - *Days Leading Up to Departure* — 125
   - *Crossing the Atlantic Ocean* — 132

4. **End of the First Leg** — 157
   - *Sailing the Windward Islands* — 161
   - *Leaving the Grenadines* — 195
   - *Antigua and Barbuda* — 202
   - *Nevis* — 215
   - *Homeward* — 229

5. Embracing the New Lifestyle ... 245
   Antigua to Aruba ... 249
   Aruba to the San Blas Islands ... 256
   Transiting the Panama Canal ... 272
   Panama City, Passage to the Galápagos Islands ... 285
   The Galápagos Islands ... 295

6. Leaving the New World ... 315
   Crossing the Pacific Ocean ... 319
   French Polynesia ... 341
   Tuamotu Atolls ... 370
   A Reef Takes Another ... 385
   Tahiti, Bora Bora ... 390
   Cook Islands (Rarotonga), Niue, Tonga ... 415

7. Heading South ... 461
   Fiji, the Cannibal Isles: Musket Cove ... 465
   Passage to New Zealand ... 491
   New Zealand ... 507
   Fiji—Second Time Around ... 546
   Leaving Musket Cove ... 567

Afterword ... 573

Ports, Anchorages ... 577

Mileage ... 585

Players in the Story ... 587

Selected Bibliography ... 589

Credits ... 598

Indices ... 607

WHAT'S IN A NAME

In the late 70's Donna and I lived in Newfoundland and sailed out of the Royal Newfoundland Yacht Club on Conception Bay, near St. John's. The annual summer pilgrimage for cruising sailors was to Bonivista Bay with its stunning islands, anchorages and numerous sightings of humpback whales. While the destination was a prize, the 120 mile passage from Conception Bay was acknowledged to be challenging as it involved navigating two headlands and three bays. These bodies of water were exposed to the perils of North Atlantic weather and often shrouded in fog. The most discussed part of the passage, both prior and in reflection, was the infamous five mile stretch of Baccalieu Tickle, a channel between the Bay de Verde Peninsula and Baccalieu Island. This is where Conception Bay, Trinity Bay, and the North Atlantic converge. This rush of water squeezing through a five mile strait can create unpredictable and wild sea conditions. Twenty ships and two hundred lives have been lost here.

Luckily, our three transits were relatively uneventful, other than an iceberg or two and mating whales that we needed to give way to. The aura and reputation of Baccalieu Tickle well captures the rugged and wild beauty that is sailing in Newfoundland. When we moved back 'up along', we wanted to bring a part of that with us and hence our boat name, *Baccalieu III*.

The name Baccalieu is an amalgamation of French, Portuguese and Spanish words for codfish. Early explorers referred to Newfoundland as Baccalaos or Los Baccaloos.

MIKE HILL

ACKNOWLEDGEMENTS

I AM MOST grateful to those who helped sail *Baccalieu III* around the world. Meeting us in remote countries and isolated islands required effort. These blue water veterans, who I think of as the 'Salty Six', brought sailing know-how, laughter and companionship to our passages.

Andy Jones, Arthur English, Bob Medland, Brian Smith, Mike Rose, Ray Graham, if I could carve your names into *Baccalieu III's* mast I would.

After reading my 'newsletters', my brother-in-law Doug Hill, recognized my potential to write this book. I am grateful for his confidence. Thanks also to those who encouraged me during my writing: Joanne Bee, Mary Anne Parkinson, Thelma Tamaki, Trish Innanen, Susan Mackenzie, Nancy Davidson, Andy and Jo Jones, Arthur and Barbara English and Bob and Sally Medland. A special thanks to Bob Medland for copy editing the book.

Thanks to John McNeil for helping edit the manuscript with lawyer-like precision. Prior to crossing the Pacific Ocean, I wrote the words—"We were embarking on a worldly experience we knew we would never forget and hoped we would never regret." With cross examination manner, John responded with, "I don't know how you could have known this, you hadn't experienced it yet." Hence, I rewrote the sentence. Sadly, John passed away before the manuscript was published.

Oyster Yacht's Customer Service Aftersales deserves recognition for replying promptly during *Baccalieu III's* mechanical setbacks. Helpful information was received within hours and sometimes within minutes of our inquiries. Parts were sourced and sent to upcoming destinations. Support continued while I researched and wrote this book.

Before leaving home, we initiated another support system. It included someone to deal with important mail, banking issues and numerous other important matters. Our good friend Manuela Uribe took care of these details. She paid bills, informed us of important news and even supervised house construction. She tracked down a hard-to-find Slovenia burgee which, when the time came, we mistakenly hung from the halyard upside down!

While we were offshore and unable to order mechanical parts, Manuela sourced the equipment and arranged for delivery.

She was also our family's second heartbeat. Our two grown children could count on her. Take for example in 2004, when David lost his passport before he was to join us in Antigua. Manuela drove him to a Toronto suburb where she had organized a reference to sign the passport renewal documents. She then took him to the government office where the passport was issued. Due to her efforts, we spent Christmas together with our son.

I leave the best for last.

Thanks to my husband Mike, who helped edit my manuscript. Three words often sufficed for my usage of four words.

Throughout our around-the-world journey, Mike morphed from savvy business executive to Navigator, weather professional, autohelm specialist, computer techno whiz, generator expert, refrigerator repairman, diesel mechanic, electrician, toilet repair guru, not to mention the hours spent with our infamous outboard engine. Mike ran the boat with intelligence, care and caution, instilling in me the confidence that each critical decision had been weighed carefully for both safety of the crew and the yacht.

In a perfect world, first mates and captains would be bound by trust and love.

Mike and I shared a perfect world.

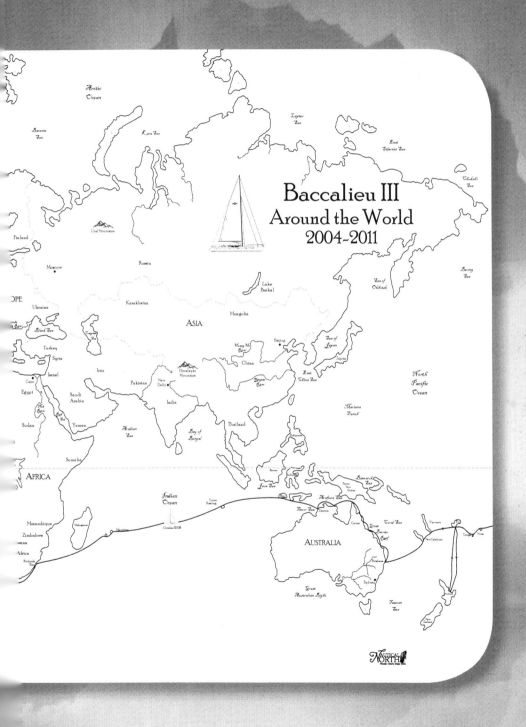

PREFACE

THE TRUTH IS I was never fond of water; I was one of the few kids who never learned to swim in my hometown's swimming hole and years later, I experienced the worst case of sea sickness while on the *Chi-Cheemaun* ferry crossing from Tobermory to Manitoulin Island on Lake Huron. Despite my aversion to it, water became a huge part of my life.

The following pages are an account of the five years we spent visiting far off places, primarily by water. Within that five year period, we explored 36 countries, some of which I had never heard of, others so remote as to be accessible only by sea.

The fact that we used the oceans as world highways, using the same means of travel as past trading vessels, whaling ships and plundering privateers is part of the reason our journey was often fraught with setbacks, unforeseen challenges and pain. And the fact that the journey was carried out by a married couple who are still married, is one of the great accomplishments of the voyage.

My greatest wish is that you could have been there, that you could have witnessed the moon expanding as it rose from the horizon, while on the same evening the sun set in an array of pink hues off the bow. I wish that you could have seen as I did, the luminescent sparkle in the white foam of the sea while rushing dolphins raced alongside us during night passages. I wish you could have been there when we dove to over a hundred feet to witness a school of small fish blinking their fiery little lanterns in the dark of the hold of a ship and the times we shared the same waters with some of the largest shark species in the world.

We didn't have to depend on only the sea to find adventure, I could have easily been killed when I fell from boulders during a hike in French Polynesia or looked down upon an active volcano in Vanuatu. Our hearts nearly stopped when we were challenged by a mother elephant while in South Africa.

To have looked out over the Great Barrier Reef where Captain Cook once stood while searching for a passage was inspiring.

Sailing the routes of the great tea clipper ships was a true adventure, as was visiting South Pacific Islands that were once stripped of sandalwood by the 18th century sea captains for trade to China.

Our adventure took us through the Torres Strait, one of the windiest places in the world, discovered in the early 1600s by an explorer who failed to locate Australia even though he and his crew were sailing only a few miles north of it.

In Panama we were allowed to walk the lands of the Kuna Indian as long as we were gone by sunset. Months later we were greeted by a small nambas tribe on remote, mysterious Malekula Island where still today, pigs are used as currency and cannibalism is still part of rituals.

Part of the excitement of this adventure stems from the fact we had never planned to circumnavigate the world; we just one day found ourselves in Australia and had to somehow get back home. At the time we were neither highly skilled racers nor experienced offshore yachtsmen, but simply sailors seeking adventure.

In time, we found there were Brazilian carnivals to experience, New Zealand glaciers to climb, lagoons of the Tuamotus to explore. Before our voyage, I thought Tuamotu was the name of a Japanese wrestler. I thought when people spoke the word Vanautu they were saying, "Van wants to." I often wondered who Van was. Vanuatu is a small country in the South Pacific.

Truly I have the greatest desire to have you stand beside me in the Wessel Islands, to experience the loneliness I felt in those solitary windblown islands that can only be accessed by sea, to get startled when a kangaroo jumps from the bushes, or to wonder whether it really was a sea crocodile that had made that indentation in the grasses we were walking through.

I wish you could have been there when we visited the Cook Islands, Tonga, Bora Bora and Bali. When we stepped onto the black lava islands of the Galápagos, shared a rugby game with the Fijians, sat between two Vanuatu chiefs in a native village, ate iguana, crocodile and kangaroo. I could have used your support when I was bitten by so many leeches, my blood dripped in small pools onto the floor.

There were times too when I wished you could have taken a watch or two, and suffered with me while we sailed the notoriously rough Indian Ocean and Cape of Good Hope. That is the real reason I have written this book. So you could be there.

1

Toughening Up
~England to the Mediterranean~

**London,
Channel Islands**

**England's South Coast,
Iberian Coast**
Spain, Portugal

Gibraltar

The Mediterranean
Spain: Balearic Islands

*Life is either a great
adventure or nothing*

Helen Keller

LONDON, CHANNEL ISLANDS

The river sweats
Oil and Tar
The barges drift
With the turning tide
Red sails
Wide
To leeward, swing on the heavy spar
The barges wash
Drifting logs
Down Greenwich Reach
Past the Isle off Dogs

The Waste Land
The Fire Sermon
T.S. Eliot

There are far more interesting places to visit in England than Ipswich even though historic figures including, Henry VIII, Nelson, Darwin and Dickens have walked its streets. Nevertheless, Ipswich is where we started what was to turn into a five-year adventure.

Ipswich is home to Oyster Marine, where we took possession of an Oyster 56, a cutter rig sailboat. We christened her *Baccalieu (bac-a-loo) III*.

It was June 8th 2004, one of the few dates I would be able to recite in the upcoming five years, because quite frankly, no one needs to know what day it is when sailing. It's permissible to let one day merge with another without ever knowing whether its Monday or Friday.

The idea of purchasing a new boat and sailing offshore had commenced with my husband's retirement. Months of sourcing equipment and electronics had provided Mike with a new focus.

When the boat was finally completed, we were ready for some real adventure. We had the perfect boat. Now, all we needed to do was to point her bow to wherever we wanted to go.

The town of Ipswich lies 69 miles (111 kilometres) northeast of London on an estuary of the Orwell River, a short distance from the North Sea.

Not having concrete plans at the time of leaving, we had no idea where the boat might take us or where we might take the boat. Whether we were in control of her or her of us, would not be determined until weeks later.

For the first few months we experienced a steep learning curve, but the Mediterranean seemed like a good place to aim for and if we really wanted to think big, we might sail to the Canary Islands and then cross the Atlantic to the Caribbean. We could then sail north to the United States where we would leave the boat for a spell. Maybe for good.

Spending so much time sailing offshore was new to us. Maybe it wouldn't suit us.

OUR INAUGURAL VOYAGE was an 11-hour sail to London. Six hours of that was spent motoring up the famous Thames River. The entire river measures approximately 210 miles (338 kilometres).

The truth is I don't recall a great deal of what there was to see on that short passage. Sailing the new boat required concentration on maneuvers that had never been required on previously owned boats. Working the sheets for the first time was like learning to walk; every step had to be thought through before taking the next. I felt like I had never sailed before. I even injured myself. I was holding the outhaul with my left hand and let off the rope clutch before placing the sheet around the winch. The result was the sheet ripped across my hand causing a severe friction burn. The entire palm and fingers of my hand turned pinker than a new born piglet in about half the time it takes to take a breath. Swelling followed.

Fortunately, I'm one of those people who prepare for emergencies that are likely never going to happen. So even though this was the first time we had left the dock, I already had ice packs cooling in the freezer. A few days later, when I visited a London hospital, the nurse said I had done all the right things and she was impressed with my bandaging. But it was those ice packs that saved me from being unable to use the hand the following days.

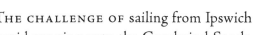

THE CHALLENGE OF sailing from Ipswich to London is to avoid running onto the Goodwind Sands, a line of shoals that lie at the entrance to the Strait of Dover. We also needed to time our approach to the River Thames at low or ebb tide to avoid adverse currents.

One of the first indications we were sailing far from home was the difference in the buoyage system. The International Association of Lighthouse Authorities (IALA) allows two buoy systems throughout the world. Each of the systems is opposite of the other.

When one sails upstream in North, Central and South America, Japan, Korea and the Philippines, red buoys mark the starboard (right side) of channels; green buoys mark the port (left side). This is System B.

In the rest of the world, while travelling upstream or in the direction of the floodtide, the buoyage system is green on the starboard, red to port. This is system A.

These two completely opposite systems developed in the late 1800s, when an attempt was made by certain countries to mark channels with similar colours. Black can buoys were placed on the port hand and red conical buoys were placed on the starboard hand. Since red markings were and are still used today to mark the port side of harbour entrances, when electric lights were introduced, some European countries placed red lights on the port side to conform with the red lights marking the port side of harbour entrances. But on the other side of the world, red lights were placed on the red starboard hand buoys.

As recently as 1976, there were more than thirty different buoyage systems in use worldwide, many of these systems having rules in complete conflict with one another. Conferences, conventions, the Geneva Convention, the League of Nations, and finally the International Association of Lighthouse Authorities, and the International Hydrographic Organization (IHO) tried their hand at establishing a single universal system. The conclusion? That it couldn't be done.

THERE IS NOTHING beautiful about the entrance to the Thames River. I was surprised at that. It's one of the greatest rivers in the world. The opportunity to travel up the river to where once beat the heart of all of England, a river that once supported a city of two thousand barges, is exciting.

Part way up the Thames, around Greenwich, ten massive steel, submerged flood gates straddle the river. Resembling a row of miniature Sydney Opera Houses, each floodgate reaches five stories high, allowing thruways as wide as the opening of the lift on the Tower Bridge which is located further up river. These are the Thames Barriers, moveable flood barriers that protect central London from flooding caused by tidal and storm surges such as what took place in 1928, when water poured over the Thames Embankment and drowned several people; thousands more lost their homes. The barriers are sometimes called the eighth wonder of the world. The barriers are equipped with navigational lights to indicate which of the ten gates you are to use when travelling the river.

There are not many moorings along the river for pleasure craft because in summer the piers are reserved for commercial tourist boats and waterbuses. Although private marinas exist, they are situated behind locks and therefore accessible only at certain hours and mostly by reservation. The Thames is a tidal river rising and falling as much as 8 metres (26 feet) between high tide and low tide.

To berth our boat at St. Katharine Docks just steps away from Tower Bridge we needed to enter a small lock accessible from two hours before high water to one and a half hours after, making timing essential if we didn't want to spend hours tied to a mooring outside the gate.

When we arrived to the lock, it was only the second time Mike had ever maneuvered the boat in a marina. And though he guided the boat into the lock like a master seaman, he almost decapitated an innocent bystander with our overhanging dinghy as we pulled out of the lock.

Our previous boat had been twelve feet (three and a half metres) shorter; *Baccalieu III* was 56 feet (17 metres) with another three feet of dinghy hanging off the stern. The extra length was going to take a little getting used to.

WHILE IN LONDON, I was in a happy state of shock. There were so many attractions to be seen: the National Art Gallery, the British Museum and the Victoria and Albert, just to name a few.

The entire city burst with excitement: crowds hurried down stairs to the Underground, black cabs whisked passengers over brick and cobblestone streets, double decker tourist buses announced famous sites: Buckingham Palace, Tower of London and Westminster Abbey.

From the marina, we could walk to Trafalgar Square, Covent Garden and to a multitude of theatres. Each morning we woke to the beauty of Tower Bridge, which sometimes opened for boat traffic when a moveable link would lift like an elegant extended ballerina's leg.

St. Katharine Docks was once a commercial harbour surrounded by six-story warehouses that stored international goods: rubber from Brazil, sugar from Jamaica, tea from Ceylon. Skippers took part in round trip passages from ports like Buenos Aires, Melbourne and Singapore. Their ship's keels were too deep to pull alongside the dock so they unloaded their merchandise onto London barges. The barges would then deliver the imported goods to the port's warehouses. By the 1930s, a hundred thousand men were employed at the docks.

St. Katharine Docks was constructed in 1928 to provide ships with a dock to tie to. The docks allowed freight to be directly transported from the ship to the warehouse by crane. This helped eliminate pilfering when the dock was used for valuable cargo such as ivory, spices, marble, ostrich feathers and tortoiseshell. Today, many of the warehouses are apartment complexes, and are named to reflect the cargo that was once stored here: Ivory House, Indigo House and Marble Quay. Bars, cafés and restaurants surround the small, locked marina and people often sit sunning themselves at small bistro tables while sipping early morning espressos and reading newspapers.

It seemed as though we couldn't turn around without bumping into history. Even St. Katharine Docks had been named after a medieval hospital, formerly part of the site. The hospital had derived its name from a pagan king's daughter who, after converting to Christianity, refused to make sacrifices to the emperor's gods and consequently met her fate on a spiked, breaking wheel.

London was so exciting.

FROM St. Katharine Docks, we visited the Tate Modern, took walks past the Houses of Parliament, the London Dungeon, and even a World War II Royal Navy battleship that was anchored in the river. Just by wandering down side streets one could find places of interest. For instance, the Savoy Theatre (1881) has a sign that indicates it was the first public building in the world to be lit by electricity, and a patent sewer ventilating lamp that was installed on Carting Lane in the 1880s is still in operation today, using methane gas trapped in a dome from the sewers below. Locals call the short street, 'Farting Lane'.

One afternoon we sought out Canadian friends who were living and working on the south side of Tower Bridge in the restored area of Shad Thames where Butler's Wharf, a massive brick Victorian warehouse complex, at one time housed the largest tea warehouse in the world. It has since been converted into restaurants, offices and apartments criss-crossed by narrow cobbled, and brick streets, and replica steel gangway footbridges. Tucked into secluded crannies, where buildings were decorated with cornices, parapets, arches and iron pilasters, bars, coffee shops and specialty shops lined intertwining streets. We shared a meal at a small Italian restaurant where one of the waiters unexpectedly broke into song with Puccini's "Nessun dorma", right at our table.

Perhaps it was being a tourist in far off places that was the best part of offshore sailing. We might never want to move on from here.

By walking forty-five minutes from where *Baccalieu III*

was docked, enjoying the scenery of the Thames Embankment, a park-like stretch of land that lies several miles along the River Thames, we could be in Covent Garden a piazza once frequented by slum dwellers and now a tourist area full of boutiques. In Covent Garden, small restaurants and kiosks are sheltered beneath a grand, glass-domed building, where licensed mimes perform, jugglers toss an impossible number of paraphernalia into the air and riders weave in and out on unicycles. Classical music might waft up from the open-air lower level where the courtyard is reserved for classical musicians who are often well-known professionals.

Built in 1830, the domed structure once provided a permanent market space for what began as a vegetable and fruit market but ultimately transformed into a place where one could buy exotic goods. Not only exotic goods from around the world, but exotic favours. So popular were these services that a directory of prostitutes of Georgian London, a sort of guidebook called *Harris's List of Covent Garden Ladies* (1757–1795), was published. The list provided biographical details of the 'Ladies', including descriptions of physical characteristics, personality and, sexual specialties. Over thirty-eight years, the guidebook sold over a quarter of a million copies.

In the centre of London, Trafalgar Square is an enormous open public meeting place where locals might catch a ray of sunshine during a lunch break or rally during political demonstrations. The Square also plays homage to several figures in British history.

A statue commemorating one of England's national heroes, Admiral Horatio Nelson, towers atop a granite column in the centre of the square. Lying at the base of the column are four bronze lions made from recycled cannons taken from the French Fleet.

TAKING one of the waterbuses down the Thames, we arrived at longitude 0°0'0 W, latitude 51°28'38 N, Greenwich, where we visited the National Maritime Museum and Royal Conservatory. All world time is measured relative to Greenwich Mean Time (GMT), while all *places* on Earth are noted with latitude, (distance north or south of the equator), and longitude, (distance east or west of the Greenwich Meridian).

Up until the 18th century, sailors had no way of knowing their longitude; no way to determine how far east or west they were located while at sea. Even Christopher Columbus who was a professional astronomer and Navigator, relied on the size of ocean swells, samples he took from the seabed, and what he saw floating in the water, to calculate whether there was land ahead.

While touring the museum and observatory, we learned that a sightseeing telescope, used to measure moon and stars, led to the invention of the sextant which makes use of these measurements. The sextant is an accurate navigational aid used when the sun, moon and stars are visible and today some sailors use it recreationally. But in the 18th century, ships depended on clear skies to navigate and would often drift off course when it was cloudy.

In the early 1700s, when a British Royal Navy ship ran aground costing 2,000 seamen their lives, scientists were galvanized to invent an accurate time piece that would improve navigation. This new timepiece not only had to be accurate, but had to be able to withstand the motion of the sea. In the 1730s, John Harrison invented this type of clock, the marine chronometer, and here at the Maritime Museum, the first chronometer is on display and running.

In the middle of the 18th century, twenty-five countries decided that all calculations would be centered in Greenwich and each day would begin at midnight. It was a Canadian representative who pointed out that seventy-two percent of the world's commerce at that time depended on the sea, and sea charts should use Greenwich as the prime meridian, (0 degrees longitude). Hence, the longitudinal co-ordinate of Greenwich is 0 degrees. It's where the east meets the west, and you can stand with one foot in the west while the other is planted in the east.

Up until the 19th century, cities kept independent time by using a sundial. When the sun crossed a city's north-south longitudinal line, it was said to be noon. But because every city is located at a different degree, each city had a different time for noon. When the railway network was developed, eighty different stations kept their own time and passengers travelling long distances would need to change their clocks up to twenty times in order to make connections.

Today, sea going vessels get their longitude and latitude co-ordinates from a U.S. Global Positioning System (GPS). Onboard *Baccalieu III*, we carried paper charts to back up the GPS. The boat was also equipped with a compass.

IN dry dock at the Greenwich Museum is the clipper ship, the *Cutty Sark*. Built around the time that steam driven ships came into use, and the Suez Canal was under construction, the *Cutty Sark* experienced a short career in the China tea trade from 1870 to 1887. Because the first teas to arrive in port sold for higher prices than shipments that followed, and because the crew of the winning ship received financial reward, clipper captains did everything in their power to load their ships and leave the Chinese ports as quickly as possible. Often clippers would leave a port at the same time, racing neck and neck as they headed back to London's ports. With the lack of sophisticated communication, no one in London knew which ship was to arrive first until one was sighted turning into the mouth of the River Thames. Then, telegrams were hastily sent from Western Union offices, newspapers would report the name of the vessel or vessels nearing port, and onlookers, including tea tasters, would rush to the docks to watch as the ships arrived.

With the opening of the Suez Canal, and subsequently steamships monopolizing the tea trade, the owners of the *Cutty Sark* turned their attentions to trading wool with Australia. For ten years, the *Cutty Sark* held the fastest recorded transit time of sixty-seven days between Britain and Australia, a rhumbline of 10,550 nautical miles.

AT THE TIME, I had no idea that so much of what we saw and learned during our time in London would be meaningful to me throughout the following five years of our travel. I never imagined while standing in front of a glass case displaying Nelson's uniform, blood soaked around the little hole where a sharpshooter, aboard the ship *Redoubtable* had shot and killed him, that someday we would be visiting the shores of Gibraltar, where his beloved troops laid his body following his death. Nor did we foresee that one day, not only would we sail with Sir Francis Chichester's, *Gipsy Moth IV*, a boat that, in 1967, had set the record for the quickest trip around the world of any small vessel, but that we would help with her rescue from a reef in the South Pacific. *Gipsy Moth* was almost in ruins when we saw her in Greenwich.

TOURING London was fabulous. From debtors' prison to Buckingham Palace, I couldn't get enough. But I knew that we would need to take leave of this place, venture out to sail to unknown places and though stumble along the way, we would eventually take control of a new lifestyle.

Due to gale force winds in the English Channel, our plans to leave London were delayed, allowing us to spend extra days familiarizing ourselves with onboard electronics, and various technical systems, and gave us time to methodically organize and stow our gear. You might not think it possible to lose an item while living in only 48 square metres (157 square feet) of space, but since everything is stored in closed lockers, behind or under seat cushions and floor boards, we documented every item we put away: whale gulper kit — forward berth starboard, duckbill valve kit — forward berth port. From max prop grease nipples to steering cables and refrigerator compressor controls, we stocked over £1,000 worth of spare parts.

We had yet to work the davits, stainless arms extending from the stern like prongs on a fork lift truck meant not just for knocking people and pylons from docks, but for securing the inflatable dinghy while we were travelling. We used a mechanical system whereby we used two winch handles to crank it into place and then secured it. One day while cranking it up, one of the winch handles went into a free spin severely smashing Mike on the back of his hand. Out came the ice again. Then I scorched my arm while using the oven, one of many scars I was to collect on our voyage. I came to think of the scars as marks of achievement. I could eventually turn out some pretty good baking from an oven while travelling over knock-about seas and heeling at an angle suited more to a kite than a cook. I discovered what a galley maid really needs is a pair of oven gloves that extend to the elbows, and maybe a leather facemask too. One time while underway, I set spilled grease from a roast afire when I pulled the oven door open.

THREE WEEKS LATER we left London on a high tide. High winds had left the channel choppy, but now it was almost windless as we motored seventy nautical miles to Ramsgate.

The following day we were up early making our way towards Brighton when we sailed past the massive, chalky White Cliffs of Dover. Peaking like elongated stainless shields, at heights of 91 metres (300 feet), they have stood in the face of potential invaders for centuries as they are nearest to continental Europe at the narrowest passage of the English Channel.

The distances between our destinations gradually got longer. We needed ten hours to arrive in Brighton, and when we did arrive, Mike nearly knocked the bow pulpit off the boat while docking. But who was I to criticize? I had yet to even attempt one.

We were headed towards the Solent, a thirty-mile strait separating the Isle of Wight from mainland England when the computer running our navigation system began to malfunction. Sailing in the Solent is a complex world of double high tides, eddies, tide lines, spring streams, currents, sailing traffic and high-speed ferries. Fortunately, we could replace the computer with a spare laptop which acted as back-up in times of breakdowns.

For the next eleven hours, we pushed through sturdy thirty-five knot winds. We were totally knackered by the time we arrived outside of Yarmouth. With its picturesque deep harbour, Yarmouth is one of the jewels of the coastline. But we never even got a glimpse of the bay because we learned upon our approach that there was no available dock space. Instead, we were forced to moor outside the harbour in the unrelenting wind.

Picking up a mooring can be challenging at the best of times. The helmsman needs to bring the bow alongside a ball about the size of a beach ball while another crewmember reaches to pick up a line attached to the ball using a long handled boat hook. The boat hook is an indispensable tool on a boat. It can be used to pick up mooring lines, snag a hat that has blown from a crewmember's head, or retrieve dragging fenders that haven't been tied on properly. I have even heard of those who have hooked their dogs by the straps of their dog-sized life vests after the dogs have slipped overboard. And it's an essential instrument when picking up mooring buoys. When you need a boat hook, you need a boat hook.

Outside Yarmouth that evening the wind was not letting up and the current remained devilish. I was down on my knees, my body squeezed between life line and deck, stretching for all I was worth, with only a small handle in my hand to guide the hook to its target. I kept touching the floating mooring line with the end of the hook, but the line repeatedly would move out of my reach. Then I hooked it. Now I had to keep hold of it and pull it onboard, but it continued to pull away from me due thanks to the wind and the current. I was like an anchor line in a storm, stretched to capacity.

While I was holding on to about three inches of the handle, the current suddenly carried the mooring ball beneath the bow along with the hook end of my boat hook, and I couldn't detach it. Now the handle was under pressure against my hand and I felt as though I was trying to pry out a slab of buried rock with a crow bar. The boat hook was wrenched out of my hand.

I walked to the back of the boat and confessed my loss of the hook to my captain and then got out the wooden handled deck brush from the stern locker and walked it to the bow. The current was still running against us and Mike pushed the engine into revs it had never seen before. It was, after all, going to get dark soon. I managed to hook the line with the deck brush, pulled it onboard and held onto it like it was my only link to life. Mike came forward to help pull it in hand over hand. Swept by the current, the boat immediately backed away putting distance between us and the ball, but with determination we managed to pull the rope in far enough to slide it through the chock and onto a cleat. And that's when disaster struck. The rope rode over the back of Mike's hand, pinning his flesh to the chock. Thirty-tons of boat, sixty thousand pounds pressed down on his trapped hand!

No one heard him swear but me. At first, his curse words were loud, but then they fell to mere whispers of pain. I had never heard such language from him. And there was nothing I could do but wait for the boat to swing with the wind when the rope would, we hoped, slide from his hand. In time, that's what happened. The line slipped from his hand, leaving the hand severely bruised but miraculously needing nothing more than an icepack.

As it was necessary to leave England within a certain period of time in order to avoid paying VAT (Value Added Tax) on our new boat, we prepared to leave the country in the morning. We took the dinghy into the port of Yarmouth to drop a customs form into a box supplied for early risers and then headed for the Channel Islands, a mere 90 nm across the English Channel, Mike still with a pack of ice secured to his hand. When we returned, we would reenter the country as visitors. This little maneuver of leaving England briefly would allow us to stay in the country for several months without paying VAT.

Preparing to cross those mere ninety miles of Channel was an exercise in understanding tide tables. We would need to deal with three tides before landing. And even though riding an ebb tide out of the Solent would give us extra knots of speed, we still wouldn't be able to escape a turning of the tide. Tide conditions upon arrival are also important because at a possible 27 feet (8 metres), the tides here are some of the highest in the British Isles. If our timing was good, we might ride an ebb tide down to St. Peter Port or alternately, we could get it wrong and go nowhere for quite some time.

Freighter traffic in the English Channel Traffic Separation System (TSS) has two staggered lanes positioned two miles apart for ships moving in opposite directions. Ships run up these lanes at speeds of more than fifteen knots, twenty-four hours a day and a yacht crossing from England to France has four lanes to cross while large ships speed by every seven to eight minutes in each of the four lanes. Yachts are strongly discouraged, from using the monitored lanes and fines are levied against those who ignore the rules. We were required to cross the four lanes at a perilous right-angle.

THE passage to the Channel Islands gave us time for thought. In the few short weeks we had owned the boat, we had sustained more injuries than we had in our past thirty years of sailing. We determined this was due to the fact we were sailing a much larger, heavier boat, equipped with far more powerful equipment. Our winches were electric, which didn't offer quite the feel for sheet tension that one had in a manual system. The sails were larger, and more powerful. It was a lot of boat.

It all came down to, when we made a mistake, it was going to be big. It was going to cost us flesh or money.

THE weather remained somewhat dreary. The three chalky grey, towering stacks off the northwest coast of the Isle of Wight were probably quite beautiful in sunshine against a backdrop of blue sky. The coastline here is dramatic. Separated by a narrow broken peninsula, the water swirls and foams, crashing into the bases of three long-toothed, limestone pillars. An extension of the chalky cliffs onshore, the pillars protrude from the churning sea and have been aptly christened The Needles. This is where the English Channel meets the Solent, the body of water that separates the mainland from the Isle of Wight. The Solent has always been a navigational hazard to ships. Even after a lighthouse was installed in the late 1700s, it was often obscured by sea fogs. Ships' sailing for the Dutch East India Company in the early 1600s and 18th century frigates loaded with personal fortunes, went down here. Today, memories of these wrecks are evoked when gold coins are swept onto the beach and found by beachcombers.

A new and taller lighthouse equipped with a helicopter pad eventually replaced the original where a lighthouse keeper, known as a 'wickie' tended the light and lens until 1994.

THE CHANNEL ISLANDS are British dependencies, although they are not part of the United Kingdom. French and English are the island's official languages but several dialects, originating from the time of the Normans, are also spoken. The islands have their own currency and they are only partly in the European Union. We needed to clear customs once we arrived.

The approaching coastline of steep cliffs and rocky shoreline does not offer much in the way of anchorages but a vivid, white lighthouse identified the entrance to the harbour while behind it numerous chimneys poked skyward from 13th century Cornet Castle, built to protect the islands and St. Peter Port from invasion. The islands were originally settled by the Vikings and the French, and right beneath us, as we ran through the mouth of the harbour, an ancient Roman ship had been discovered in 1984 near where it went down in the year AD 280. When the ship was raised, pottery from Algeria and Spain was found in the hold.

As we followed the buoyed channel into St. Peter Port, we were immediately intercepted by the harbour master's dinghy. We were instructed to tie up to a floating pontoon in the Pool, part of St. Peter Port Marina. Beyond this area is a second marina where boats with shallower keels can tie to concrete walls, although access is strictly regulated to two and a half hours before or following high tide.

The depth in this inner marina, is controlled by the natural tide. When the tide is at its lowest, there can be a drop of 8 metres (27 feet), leaving the marina with so little water that those boats lashed to the concrete wall end up standing high and dry on their keels. Boats tied like this look as if they are hanging off the wall on tethers. Owners tie up here when the bottoms of their boats need cleaning or mechanical work is to be carried out on the hull or props. It appeared to be nature's way of co-operating with sailors.

The Channel Islands are divided into two bailiwicks, the Bailiwick of Guernsey and the Bailiwick of Jersey representing two of the largest islands and their districts.

The larger of the two islands is Guernsey, which offers long days of sunshine and therefore attracts an onslaught of annual tourists.

Guernsey's capital, St. Peter Port has an old European flavour. Rising steeply from the harbour are pink and blue tinged granite buildings, once private homes that have been converted to shops and boutiques. Cafés and restaurants, historical town markets and art galleries can be found along the uneven, cobbled streets that are connected by nearly vertical stone stairways. Arriving here felt like docking in the middle of a 17th century city. Up until the early 20th century, the language spoken here was Guernésiais. Most people speak English now but the local accent is very distinct and unusual.

It was here that Victor Hugo wrote Les Misérables and where the strain of Guernsey cow is thought to have been refined, because there have been virtually no other breeds of cattle imported to the island since 1820.

The island measures only 14 by 8 kilometres (9 by 5 miles), and in 1950, 400 farmers kept two thousand cows. Today there are approximately twenty farms keeping sixteen hundred cows. However, in 1950 a Guernsey cow would have produced approximately three thousand litres (793 US gal/659 Imp. gal) of milk per year whereas today, on average, a single cow might produce six thousand litres (1,585 US/1,319 Imp. gal). Some cows produce as much as twelve thousand litres (3,170 US gal/2,640 Imp. gal).

The Jersey cow on the other hand, originates from the Isle of Jersey and the town of St. Helier celebrates this fact with four life-sized bronze Jersey cattle sculptures standing around a drinking trough in the middle of town. There was a time during the middle 1700s when cattle were shipped from Normandy to Jersey to be fattened on rich pastureland before being shipped to England under the name of Alderney cattle, thus escaping excise duty for foreign countries. Laws were put into effect to stop the practice consequently assisting in keeping the breed's purity of fine, small bone structure and docile manner. Elsie,* the doe eyed beauty that appeared on Borden's Eagle brand Sweetened Condensed Milk, was a Jersey.

---

* Elsie, a caricature of a Jersey cow portrayed on Borden labels, first appeared in Borden adds in 1938. The cartoon-like face went on to become one of the most recognized icons in the world. The caricature has been updated, but Elsie's face is still used on certain dairy product labels.

ENGLAND'S SOUTH COAST, IBERIAN COAST

SPAIN, PORTUGAL

WE RETURNED TO Cowes on the Isle of Wight. During race week, the small town of Cowes, is the place to be seen, much like Louisville, when the Kentucky Derby is held in the United States. To many, Cowes is believed to be the home of yachting.

Sailing events such as Cowes Week and the Fastnet Race, which starts in Cowes, are some of the most successfully organized regattas and races in the world. Just sailing into the same harbour where glorified yachts *Britannia*, *America* and *Velsheda*,* to name only a few, had passed before, was exhilarating.

We had come to Cowes to take part in an Oyster Regatta, an organized event for a group of sailboat owners who share a love of the sport, and have the same make of yacht. Often the yachts are customized with carbon fibre masts, full batten mainsails, cruising chutes, spinnakers, shoal keels or full keels. A total of forty-two Oysters had come together for what was sure to be a fun-filled week.

---

* HMY *Britannia*, a 37 m (121 ft.) gaff-rigged cutter, built for the Prince of Wales (HRH Albert Edward—Edward VII) in 1893, won 231 races and took another 129 flags.

America, 101 ft. (31 m) schooner, sailing for the New York Yacht Club, won the America's Cup in 1851.

Velsheda, a J-Class yacht built in 1933 in Hampshire. By the late '30s, *Velsheda* represented the most advanced technical design in spars, rigging, sails and deck gear. Her masts were constructed of aluminum, made by bending plates and riveting them together.

Oyster Regattas are well organized functions that include parties, social dinners and, most importantly, an opportunity to put our cruise-designed yachts through a week of racing. Although it was July, high winds, cool temperatures and familiar English dampness had us bound head to foot in fleece and foul weather gear. It was one of the coldest July weeks on record.

Since sailing the Solent, I believe that anyone who can race in that body of water under the conditions sailors experienced that week, can sail almost anywhere in the world. Sailing in conditions of double high tides pushing currents through a fifteen mile long passage of coastline that tapers from twenty-one to three miles and winds of thirty-five to forty knots, seemed to replicate sailing across a flood dam in a gale. All that week, we dealt with winds in the high thirties, which were a challenge while sailing a new boat. When it began to blow into the forties, the races were cancelled. Lucky us, as even behind the concrete protective enclosure of the marina, the wind was merciless to skippers maneuvering their boats in and out of the docks, which all the while made for great entertainment for those already safely tied up. One of our approaches was made even more harrowing when the engine's hand throttle separated from the pedestal upon our approach to the concrete wall.

During the Oyster races, two local men, who were experienced Solent sailors, joined us aboard *Baccalieu III* to help sail her while sharing their knowledge of local winds, currents and water depth. Their knowledge of depth became vitally important when on tacks directing us towards shore, we would drive the boat within mere feet of it while submitting to orders of, "Hold your course! Hold your course!" so that we might squeeze the last seconds out of a sail full of wind. Our accomplished sailing friends were calling the tacks, and exhilarating tacks they were! I placed my entire faith in them, as if I were a machine and they the operators, and I would hold the course they demanded until even I, when ducking to look beneath the sail, would catch sight of a few tufts of grass rather than water underneath the Yankee.

We weren't the only ones pushing the limits. We learned that two other boats had miscalculated and driven their boats aground. But besides sharpening our racing skills, we learned much about how *Baccalieu III* responded in heavy winds and maneuvered in close quarters during those few exuberant days of racing. Thanks to our local sailing friends and Mike and me, (two free thinkers who allowed their brand new boat to be put through paces we didn't know she was capable of), we ended the Cowes regatta with a fourth and fifth place in two of the races along with a scar on *Baccalieu III's* eyebrow resulting from a too tightly winched Yankee sheet. Years later I would still look at that scar fondly, remembering the great times we had with no regrets over the disfiguration. You can't win if you don't play your best.

One of the races directed the Oyster fleet towards Portsmouth located on Portsea Island just off the south coast of England, the hub from which the British Royal Navy controlled the seas for over five hundred years. By 1813, one hundred and thirty thousand men made up Britain's navy. As it was difficult to obtain enough men to man the entire British navy with volunteers, (the sailing ship HMS *Victory* carried 850 crew), press-gangs scoured the countryside, yanking men from villages, cities, farms, from families that relied on them, pressing them into the navy where they often spent the rest of their lives aboard a ship.[*]

Nelson's ship, the HMS *Victory* lays in Portsmouth as a museum ship, reportedly in much the same condition as when

---

[*] By year 1811, there were approximately 1,019 ships servicing the British Royal Navy.

she led the victory over the combined French and Spanish fleet at the Battle of Trafalgar in 1805. She carried one hundred iron forged guns weighing up to three tons each and stowed thirty-five tons of gun powder with which to fire them. She was one of the largest ships of her time and her collection of twenty-seven sails allowed her to be one of the fastest ships on the seas. In calm conditions, she required a team of four to steer her, and during rough conditions, a team of eight. Several teams were engaged to lift her anchor which often took up to twelve hours.

She was built from the timber of six thousand trees.

PRIOR TO ARRIVING in Portsmouth, I had made the decision that I would master the art of docking *Baccalieu III*; guide her into and out of docks as well as any master seaman. I suggested we take turns in order that I would have the opportunity to work the boat in all conditions and it happened to be my turn when we needed to pull away from a tight docking in Portsmouth. Even though the circumstances called for expert handling I insisted on taking my turn. I figured the sooner I jumped into a challenging situation, the sooner I would learn how to handle it. These experiences however, didn't come without my heart beating like a drum roll.

We were rafted to another Oyster yacht alongside a concrete wall where boats were squished together in a sort of well, made even smaller by boats rafted to one another. It was a tight spot for an expert much less a novice to maneuver in even while using the engine and bow thruster as a team. As I had little feel for the workings of either and didn't even know which side of the thruster to activate, my team was more like two politicians in a debate. But the only time one gets such practice is when in tight spaces, and it just happened I had inherited a situation with an audience.

I had docked the boat for the first time a few days prior after returning from one of the races in Cowes, and on one occasion had also steered her away from the dock. Neither maneuver had been pretty, but the hull was no worse from the experience. I'm not so sure that I could say the same for Mike who had to watch me. Now a whole gang of us were all tied up, cozy-like, ready to leave at the same time, requiring *Baccalieu III* to be one of the first to peel away in order to make room for others to get out. Every skipper, crewmate and passenger was either untying lines or looking on while waiting for us to take our leave. Once I was on the wheel that day I'll admit no boat was safe. I over gunned the engine and pressed the bow thruster into action like it was NASA's newest rocket booster. I wouldn't be surprised if witnesses to my departure still talk today about the crazy lady who threatened to test their insurance policies. But it all turned out for the good and I continued to insist on my turn at the wheel. In time, I became skillful in handling the boat. However, I could never calm my adrenalin boosted heartbeat which often seemed, in these circumstances, to be in full throttle.

But in fact, sometimes docking the boat was the far easier maneuver to undertake. Sailing into Portsmouth Harbour is an example. This large natural harbour is frequented with numerous private yachts, some of which insist on keeping their sails up as long as possible while entering the restricted harbour-mouth, although rules state they must be running their engines while sailing in. According to seamen's rules-of-the-road, those using engine power must shoulder the responsibility of keeping distant from any with sails up even though they choose to flop around in fluky winds in tides that flow with nearly five knots of current. In addition to private traffic, there are the Isle of Wight ferries, cross-Channel ferries and ferries to Spain.

Cargo ships also use the harbour as do small fishing vessels and it is documented that one can expect to see a ship using the harbour entrance every five minutes. Also frequenting the harbour is the British Navy, where one might find anything from a stealth trimaran to an aircraft carrier or nuclear submarine running up your kazoo. Because of the naval connections here, the harbour master is known as the Queen's Harbour Master (QHM). Staff from the QHM is often seen shepherding small pleasure craft in and out of the entrance just to make sure they don't cause any calamities within the harbour that might slow down commercial vessels.

Vessels over 20 metres (65 feet), are required to enter and leave Portsmouth Harbour in the main channel and must have permission from the QHM to do so. The tides run fast through the harbour mouth and cross-tides do their best to throw boats off course. Add to that a bit of wind and swell from a passing ship and you can find yourself in a sort of localized storm. When entering the channel small boats do not enter on the starboard side of the channel as they do at most other ports. All small boats are required to keep to port on entry, and keep outside the line of red buoys until past the last one. Of course, you can't steer too far to port as you need to leave room for the outbound vessels and there is also a sandbank you can run into if you wander too far.

Perhaps this is why they say Portsmouth Harbour is one of the most exciting harbours in the UK. Its bustling nature is enough to make you want to get out to sea.

THE historic Portsmouth Dockyards is the home of the Royal Navy. The *Mary Rose*, the flagship of King Henry VIII, was raised in 1982 from where she was sunk by a French invasion fleet just outside of Portsmouth Harbour in 1545. Nearly four hundred men drowned when the ship was sunk. The ship was one of the earliest ships to carry heavy guns. She is the only 16th century warship on display anywhere in the world. Also located at the Portsmouth Dockyards is the Trafalgar Sail Exhibition which displays a battle-scarred sail from a ship that had fought in the Battle of Trafalgar.

THE OYSTER REGATTA wound up with a dinner and awards-giving at the Royal Yacht Squadron, located in Cowes. The Royal Yacht Squadron was founded in 1815 and today, many of the club's early traditions are still followed. For instance, only men are allowed to be members. Partners or spouses, referred to as 'LAMs' by the members, must use a side door rather than enter the club through the front door. Women and children have a separate dining room. But women can join their husbands in the formal dining room when a couple wishes to eat together.

The ladies don't mind keeping with these traditions. In England, traditions play an important role in everyday life.

SKIPPERS attending the Oyster Rally received formal invitations to the awards-giving event. Each skipper's name was printed on the invitation and read like the one that was issued to Mike:

> MIKE HILL ESQ. BACCALIEU III
> THE FLAG OFFICERS AND MEMBERS OF THE
> ROYAL YACHT SQUADRON HAVE MUCH PLEASURE
> IN INVITING M. HILL ESQ. TO BE HONORARY
> MEMBER FROM 6TH TO 10TH JULY '04.

ACCOMPANYING the invitation was a miniature hand booklet of navy linen cradling cream coloured pages. The booklet offered a short history of the castle and mentioned that the Royal Yacht Squadron had purchased the Castle from the Crown in 1917. Prince Philip had been Commodore in

1964. The handbook stated that the purpose of the booklet was for "gentle guidance and encouragement". It outlined the required dress: clean and tidy clothes until 1900. Men are required to wear a jacket and tie in the Members Dining Room. Ladies should wear a skirt. After 1900 hours, a reefer jacket or jacket and tie, suit or yachting suit is required dress for the men. The ladies are required to wear a skirt or dress or dark trouser suit. Children under the age of eight are not permitted in the Castle but they are welcomed on the lawn. Children between the ages of eight to fifteen years are limited to the Ladies Room and Changing Rooms for Lunch and Tea.

A BUFFET dinner offered by the Royal Yacht Squadron was not held inside the Castle but in a new airy Pavilion on the property just west of it.

One of the members with whom we sat at dinner invited us to tour the Castle. This was a real honour. Receiving the invitation was like getting an invitation to look inside the Queen's palace. Only this was better. After all, Admiral Sir Thomas Hardy, Nelson's captain during the Battle of Trafalgar, had headed the list of naval members when in 1815, the club was simply referred to as the 'Yacht Club'.

Our member friend led us to the Member's Dining Room where portraits of former commodores, painted by period artists, hung on dark paneled walls. Throughout the club, portraits of Earls and Dukes, including the Duke of Edinburgh, hung beneath high ceilings. Paintings, by famous marine artist W.J. Huggins (1781–1845), depicting full-rigged sailing ships in gusty winds, suggested the club had been a place where sailors had gathered for centuries.

Our host escorted us to the oak lined library furnished with wing backed chairs and fine, old exotic rugs. Shelves stacked to the ceiling held original volumes of historical accounts like 'The Life of Nelson', 'Napoléon Chronicles' and 'Churchill'.

Just being in the same room with this treasury of books, made my body tingle. I was even allowed to touch and turn their pages.

We were honoured to be asked to sign the guest registry. The Royal Yacht Squadron is one of the most prestigious clubs in the world.

The nucleus of this all-important sailing club is located in a small castle built by Henry VIII in 1539 to help defend England against attacks from French forces. It was feared the Isle of Wight might be taken by the enemy and the advantage of its strategic position used to conquer England.

The flag staff used by the Squadron is the mast from the cutter racing yacht, *Bloodhound*, whose owner sailed to Mauritius in 1769 to observe the transit of Venus at the same time Captain Cook visited Tahiti to document the same event. Months later, we would make note of these very place names in our own ship's log.

IT WAS TIME to take leave of the banquets and social parties and head out on our own. We were ready for adventure and longed for warmer weather. We needed to head south.

The next three days we sailed along the south coast of England, making stops in Dartmouth, Plymouth and Falmouth. To break up the nine hour trip to Dartmouth, we planned a leisurely night stop in an anchorage outside of Poole. Two miles out from the anchorage we heard the easy-to-distinguish twin blade swoosh of a helicopter. We often sailed with a helmsmen's bimini erected over part of the cockpit. We preferred this partial bimini arrangement rather than the customary full bimini because it offered visual access to the sails. But while the canopy shaded us from the sun, it prevented us from seeing directly overhead.

We paid little attention as the sound of interrupted

helicopter chop came nearer. When the noise appeared to be stationary and the surface water on the port side fanned out in miniature cyclone fashion, we looked out from under the bimini and saw a chunky red British Coastguard Recovery helicopter hovered thirty metres (ninety feet) overhead. I grabbed my camera.

As I looked through the view finder, I saw a helmeted man dressed in a red survival suit, kneeling at the edge of the opened door. He was holding a large placard with the number 72. We determined that the number was meant to instruct us to tune our VHF radio to channel 72.

The communications operator identified the aircraft and asked if we would be interested in taking part in a training exercise. We agreed.

At the time of our interaction, we were under engine power and flying the mainsail. The radio operator instructed us not to deviate from our present course; they would drop a line to our aft deck. We were ordered not to attach the line to the boat. Mike and I had trained for rescue situations, and understood that by attaching a rescue line dropped from a helicopter, the aircraft could be yanked from the air. But when the line landed on the back deck, we had to fight the urge to tie it off because tying off lines is an instinctive thing for sailors to do.

During boat construction, we had purposely left the port side of *Baccalieu III* free of aerials and communication equipment that might interfere during an air rescue. All rescue helicopters approach from the port side. That day, during the exercise, the pilot had ideal conditions for maneuvering the helicopter and lowering the rescuer. But it doesn't take a great deal of unsettled sea to make a boat ride 6 metres (20 feet) from crest to trough and cause a boat to roll. Even this rescue practice required precision flying skills.

Our part in the exercise was to hold the line taut after

the free end landed on the deck. "Tighter!" the radio operator demanded. When the line's tension met the necessary standards, a rescuer shackled his harness to the line, left the aircraft and slid down to our aft deck.

Once on deck he disengaged his harness and greeted us with a handshake. Acknowledging our Canadian flag, he asked what we were doing so far from home. Following a short chat he reattached his shackle to the line, radioed his crew mates and was hoisted back to the aircraft. With a wave goodbye, we continued to our anchorage where we spent the night before sailing to Dartmouth.

"So nice of the British to stop by," I said to Mike. "What a shame we didn't have tea and crumpets ready."

To approach a harbour under sail, a harbour that has been used by sailors for hundreds of years, where rock formations and cliffs have stood for millions, is exciting. I feel the excitement in my chest, like something in there wants out. This must be the feeling of adventure, of dealing with the unexpected, of discovery. Entering unfamiliar harbours hidden behind blind entries where winds and currents often cause steering challenges, is exhilarating.

Approaching Dartmouth must have been frightening for early mariners. From the sea, the harbour is hidden among daunting cliffs that run uninterrupted for miles. The coast is strewn with outlaying rocks: The Blackstone, The Mewstone, The Cat Stone, The Verticals.

Leaving the green conical Castle Ledge buoy to starboard, the entrance begins to open; Dartmouth Castle is to the west, Kingswear Castle to the east. In early times, the castles operated a defensive chain across the opening to block enemy ships from entering.

As one enters, swinging to port, then to starboard, the

main harbour of Dartmouth opens up as if arriving to a secret harbour. Once through the passage, we were surprised to see that the harbour was so large. Brightly painted houses line the hillsides surrounding the bay. Dartmouth Harbour is almost a replica of our own St. John's port in Newfoundland. No wonder so many who emigrated from Dartmouth felt at home when they arrived in the Canadian seaport.

Plymouth lies twenty-two miles west of Dartmouth and is where the *Mayflower* left for America, in 1620. One hundred and forty-eight years later, Captain James Cook left Plymouth aboard the ship *Endeavour*. He and his crew of eighty-five were heading for Tahiti. His mission was to observe the transit of Venus as it passed on a rare occasion in front of the sun in order to measure the distance of the earth from the sun. During that same voyage, Cook discovered terra Australis incognito (the unknown land) and claimed it for Britain.

Plymouth offered some excitement for us too. A partially submerged vessel resembling an oversized surfboard passed us on its way out to sea. We joked about its appearance. But the surfboard turned out to be a partially submerged submarine. A uniformed officer stood on its deck not far above the waterline. We learned that the vessel was in fact a member of the Royal Navy Submarine Service sometimes referred to as the 'Silent Service'. Plymouth is the main refitting base for Royal Navy nuclear submarines and the base for seven of the Trafalgar class nuclear powered hunter-killer submarines. In retrospect, the funny looking surfboard should have commanded a little more of our respect!

WE PULLED INTO Falmouth just thirty-five miles west of Plymouth. Falmouth was the last British port we visited before sailing *Baccalieu III* on her first offshore passage: six hundred miles across the Bay of Biscay.

Although this was *Baccalieu III's* first offshore passage, Mike and I had crewed on two trans-Atlantic passages. Our first trans-Atlantic passage was a boat delivery from Bermuda to Portugal and included a stopover in the Azores. During the second trans-Atlantic passage, we sailed from the Canary Islands to St. Lucia, Caribbean. While on the latter crossing and while taking part in the 2002 Atlantic Rally for Cruisers (ARC) we learned how vulnerable sailors are at sea, even on fair weather days. While en route, we received a distress call from one of two brothers sailing *Toutazimut*, a Formasa 51. The caller was frantic. His brother had been hit by the boom and had fallen overboard. Phillip had been wearing a secured safety harness and was attached to the boat. But the caller was unable to get him back onboard. Sadly, Phillip succumbed while tied to the boat. He was buried at sea.

We realized commanding our own boat demanded even more responsibility than taking part as crewmembers. Mike was well versed in navigating, having behind him several years of Great Lakes sailing. As well, he had recently acquired his Yachtmaster Offshore qualification* from the International Yachtmaster Training facility in Fort Lauderdale, Florida.

On board he had me, someone who was incapable of even crossing Lake Ontario without feeling at least lethargic, but most often grimly ill. I have, during my sailing career, experienced such severe motion confusion that my tongue has gone numb, my mouth dry, my head achy and my body nearly paralyzed. I have even become seriously discombobulated while travelling on the *Queen Elizabeth II*, a trans-Atlantic ocean liner weighing over 150,000 tons!

Nevertheless, I had no intention of letting sea sickness command my life. In an effort to discover whether I could

---

* Yachtmaster Offshore certification allows the holder to be Master aboard a 200 gross ton vessel, 150 miles offshore.

ever master long passages I had signed on for the above mentioned voyages. On the first passage from Bermuda to Portugal, I spent my first three days in a state of complete nausea. Other than those times when I stood watch, I sat alone at the stern gazing at the only stable focal point—the sterling-edged horizon—waiting for my seasickness to pass. I had thoughts about how I could have been instead, satisfying my wish to experience Wimbledon. But we had turned down the gift of tickets to gain experience. In what? "Puking"? I thought remorsefully.

Besides proving that we could survive the sea, we had each taken courses in maintaining diesel engines. We were both certified SSB (single sideband) radio operators. I also held a certification from Wilderness First Responder. I had taken navigation courses but I had never exercised the knowledge at any great length.

BEFORE LEAVING FALMOUTH, we welcomed aboard a good sailing friend from Vancouver Island. Ray would accompany us across the Bay of Biscay and sail the coast of Portugal and Spain with us.

We left Falmouth with a good forecast. Winds were predicted to be northwest and light, perhaps lighter than what we would dial up if we could, but our timing was good. It was early July and the most violent storms generally take place in August and September. But the Bay of Biscay can be nasty anytime of the year.

The continental shelf extends into the bay creating large bodies of shallow water that can cause the Bay to be rough. We headed far out to sea to avoid the steepening swell. There was little wind and we complained about the choppy seas.

The route across the Bay is well travelled by commercial ships, and while crossing traffic lanes, we kept out of the way of oil tankers, grain freighters, and super tankers cruising at speeds of up to twenty knots.

We were to learn much about crossing shipping lanes in the upcoming years, but the lesson we learned here, was to never assume you have time to cross the bow of an oncoming freighter. We came far closer to an advancing freighter than we had calculated.

With a watchful eye and the help of the radar screen, we tracked cargo ships, fishing vessels and oncoming yachts day and night. In daylight, the naked eye can spot ships at approximately six nautical miles. During dark hours, navigation lights can be seen from approximately eight nautical miles. A yacht under 20 metres (65 feet) however, might not be spotted by ships until within three miles. Often they're not detected at all.

Navigation lights indicate the type of vessel; whether a vessel is a freighter, a high-speed ferry, fishing vessel or a towing vessel. The lights even announce how far behind the vessel the tow is located. Reading navigation lights allows one to distinguish which direction the vessel is travelling and whether a vessel is under engine power or sail power. We got lots of practice reading navigation lights on that passage.

We sighted our first dolphins while crossing the Bay. We even spotted a whale and another submarine. Each evening we had an unobstructed view of the setting sun which never failed to colour this new world of ours in a warm orangey glow.

Weather conditions were ideal except for the lack of wind. Then one morning the Cíes Islands (Baiona Islands) appeared off our bow. They were blanketed in a light mist and looked more like a mirage than distant land formations. The sighting of them signified that we had travelled five hundred and thirty-three miles. It had been an easy passage. A piece of cake I said.

But perhaps I was a little too cocky. When we attempted to leave the dock at our next port, we neglected to untie one of the lines from a post. Nothing could have made us feel more foolish.

Sailing down the Galicia coastline and arriving in Baiona (Bayona), was a double thrill. Baiona was the first port we arrived to in Continental Europe. It was also the first day in weeks that we could replace our fleeces with T-shirts and shorts.

From the sea, an immense towering statue of the Virgin Mary, Santa María de Afuera dominates the crest of an almost vertical hill. The statue greets mariners with outstretched arms in an offering of Christian welcome. The massive statue is mostly hewn from rock, (other than her molded face and hands), and stands at the end of fourteen Stations to the Cross. Devoted Roman Catholics climb the hill on Fridays during Lent stopping at each station to meditate the sufferings of Christ while asking forgiveness. It was not until a few days later when we walked the steep uneven path that we discovered inside the hollowed structure, a narrow spiral staircase circling within the statue itself. At the top, cradled in the palm of her one hand, lay a miniature sailing ship that we could walk out onto. The ship was even fitted with lifelines to protect visitors who stepped onto her deck.

As we entered the harbour, similar designed houses, reflecting 1950 architecture, towered above us on the hillsides. Like giant steps, one higher than the other, the elevated buildings offered each apartment clear views of the bay below. The protective stone walls of a fort wrapped around the most seaward part of the peninsula. By the time we were to finish this voyage we would see more forts than most historians.

A call to the marina prompted a meet and greet orange dinghy to rendezvous with *Baccalieu III* at the mouth of the bay. The dinghy driver, who spoke with a thick Spanish accent, directed us to the marina where we would also find the customs office.

The marina is located at the base of a small historic town. Narrow streets, resembling alleyways and constructed of smooth irregular stones, intertwined like secret passages. Apartment buildings constructed of granite block, created near perpetual shade to the cool, damp cafés, bars, and collections of souvenir shops. Overhead clotheslines, crisscrossing streets, held lacy underwear. The sound of clinking china drifted from an open window. An elderly lady sitting on her small balcony observed the town she once knew of fish mongers, sail makers and ship's chandleries. Today, glass blowers and potters blend the new world with the old.

It was in Baiona that we discovered the joys of eating tapas, small side dishes meant to be shared from a Spanish menu: crusty bread, cheese, salad, sea food, soup, fish, fried peppers, fried sardines, mussels in vinegar and oil, so many to choose from. It was a great way to explore the country's delicacies.

In the evening we walked the streets in search of a restaurant for dinner stopping occasionally to admire enticing baskets of lobsters, shellfish, and colourful, locally grown vegetables displayed outside restaurant doors as if prepared for the cover of an epicurean magazine. This was a world of fresh squid and mussels and cod empanadillas. Aromas of chorizo, sausages and ribs from street barbeques provoked our appetites. Waiters in knee length white aprons stood in doorways beckoning tourists with promises of succulent meals. At least that's what we presumed they were saying.

I confess that I speak only one language. My punishment is to feel a degree of discomfort when visiting countries whose native language is not English. For one thing I fear getting lost. Could I remember for instance, when I wanted to return to the marina that I had walked up Calle de Diego

Carmona to Rúa de Ventura Misa then turned left onto Calle de la Carabel La Pinta? Fat chance.

We walked almost vertical streets to reach the level of the city's dominating fortress, Monterreal. Turning towards the headland we marched towards the sea in the direction of the fort and walked two kilometres more to round the lengthy fortifications still standing with original gateways and sentry towers which offer views of mountainous Northern Portugal and the Cíes Islands.

From the fortification, rugged coastlines with crashing white surf jutted in and out below us. Beaches strewn with soft grainy sand and scantily dressed sunbathers presented a modern world against a back drop of fortresses and ancient cathedrals. From our vantage point we caught sight of *Baccalieu III* looking ever so minute while swinging on her mooring among a fleet of international yachts. Baiona is a favourite landfall for cruisers crossing the Atlantic, yachts travelling from northern Europe to the south Atlantic or bound for exotic countries along the shores of the Mediterranean Sea.

Since the 1960s, part of the fortress has been used as a *parador*, a chain of state run luxury hotels designed to enhance the inside of historical buildings such as fortifications, castles and monasteries. Inside this beautifully renovated portion of fort, overstuffed armchairs beckoned us to sit for a drink in a comfortable lounge while overlooking a garden courtyard with bubbling fountain. After sitting our weary behinds down on those luxuriously plush couches, waiters were as courteous to us as they were to their more formally dressed guests.

It was here in the small town of Baiona in 1493, that residents of Europe welcomed Christopher Columbus' return from his voyage of discovery.

Italian born Columbus, along with one of his sons aboard the *Santa María*, plus two additional square rigged caravels, the *Niña* and the *Pinta*, had set out from Spain in search of new territory across the great unknown waters of the Atlantic Ocean. It was a time in which scurvy disease, resulting from a lack of vitamin C, was thought to be caused by excessive exposure to salty air.*

In fact, it was a crewmember on the *Pinta* that first spotted the New World and again the *Pinta* which first returned to this Spanish port several months before Columbus arrived. The *Santa María*, the ship Christopher Columbus commanded, was the slowest of the three. It was also the *Pinta*, with torn sails and a weathered, sickly crew, that arrived with the news of a discovery that would change their world forever: among the gold stocks, parrots, tomatoes, tobacco and two Indians onboard, the captain of the *Pinta*, Martín Alonso Pinzón is credited with transporting the bacteria responsible for syphilis to the world.

In celebration of the New World discovery, a replica of the 20 metre (65 foot) *Pinta* is displayed in the Port of Baiona. The original *Pinta* had carried twenty-six crewmembers, an assortment of carpentry tools, weapons and enough provisions that enabled them to stay at sea for months at a time. And you can be sure the crew would not have been wearing the lightweight breathable Gill offshore foul weather gear with vapour, moisture resistant interior that we wear today. In fact it was not until the 20th century that these comfortable, waterproof fabrics were developed. John Guzzwell† for instance, wore a British Columbia Indian sweater knitted from raw wool while

---

* Between the 16th and 18th centuries, it is estimated that scurvy killed two million sailors. Due to experiments lead by a British physician (James Lind) in 1747, Captain Cook, in preparation for sailing around the world, loaded his ship HMS *Endeavour*, with a large quantity of sauerkraut. He instructed his crew to eat fruits while ashore and sauerkraut when at sea. Cook never lost a single sailor to scurvy.

† John Guzzwell, sailed, *Trekka*, a homebuilt 20-foot (6 metre) yawl, around the world in 1955-1959. At the time, it was the smallest vessel to ever circumnavigate.

aboard *Tzu Hang* when he and the Smeetons* attempted to sail around Cape Horn in 1957. Wool readily soaks up moisture. Miles kept his head warm with a wool sock and attempted to keep one of his hands dry by wrapping the hand that wasn't being used for steering in a plastic bag.

A HIRED CAB drove us across the countryside to the city of Santiago de Compostela, the capital of the province of Galicia on the northwestern Iberian Peninsula. As early as the 9th century, since the discovery of what is believed to be the remains of St. James the Apostle and the transport of those remains to the Cathedral of Santiago de Compostela, pilgrims have trekked hundreds of miles to reenact the delivery of St. James' body from Jerusalem. Once they've arrived, the faithful pray for forgiveness under the cathedral's grand vaulted arches and in her numerous chapels. The remains of St. James the Apostle were in fact the reason the city developed where it did, and now, Santiago de Compostela is a holy city on par with Jerusalem and Rome.

A cornucopia of Baroque, Romanesque, Gothic, Renaissance and Neoclassical are centuries of design left by artists in golden filigree, frescoes, stained glass windows, sculptures and carvings of stone that have merged to make up this magnificent cathedral. Outside, courtyards encapsulated by thick, grey, arched walls, domes and steeples on multi level roofs, house figures of evangelists, prophets and elders tucked into architectural corners, some thrusting forth crosses and staffs while fountains trickle in plazas spread broad for the purpose of holding thousands who have for eons, come from miles to

---

* Circumnavigators, Miles and Beryl Smeeton, made three attempts to round Cape Horn in their 46-foot (14 metre) ketch, *Tzu Hang*. Pitchpoling on the first attempt (1956), and rolling on the second, (1957), *Tzu Hang* successfully rounded the Cape in 1968. The Smeetons are recipients of numerous sailing awards.

pray, ask forgiveness and recharge their faith. This is a meeting place for saints and sinners.

The Camino de Santiago (The Way of the Saints), is more than a thousand years old. Each person, from teenager to septuagenarian, joins the trail for personal reasons: deaths, renewal of faith or simply the accomplishment of the physical and mental challenge the trail demands. From people who wish to claim worthiness to those who expect holy visions, they all share the same destination—the Cathedral of Santiago de Compostela.

To guide them, spread across hundreds of European miles, small yellow signs indicate the way to Compostela. But before embarking on their journey, each pilgrim secures a 'passport', to identify them as Christians en route to the cathedral. Possession of the passports offers reductions on lodging in *refugios* as well, it confirms they have travelled the required miles. The passports must be stamped at each stopover. In order to receive a *credencial* of the journey, one must walk 100 kilometres (62 mi.) or cycle 200 kilometres (124 mi.), but many walk much further; some nearly 1,287 kilometres (800 miles), depending on where they begin their journey. Through rolling wheat fields, pasturelands, meadows, vineyards, woodlots, to the top of steep hills, over Pyrenees mountain passes, through villages lying at summits, and miles and miles of hot, paved roads, they trek to their destination wearing backpacks. The less hurried stop in cities and hamlets to attend mass or vespers, bathe in public unisex showers if they are lucky enough to find one, and at the end of the day plunk their aching muscles and blistered feet onto bunk beds that rate anywhere from clean to disgusting.

Upon arriving in Santiago de Compostela, the hikers take their last steps across an extensive, grand open square where huge bell towers scrape against a blue, cloudless sky. Entrance is through a set of immense, black, wrought iron gates to a quadruple set of massively wide-spread steps where figures of David and Solomon look down upon the final footsteps of their journey. A granite façade adorned with clusters of prophets bids them welcome as they enter a medieval, darkened portico suggesting purgatory. Here, a marble figure of Saint James stands above a tree, its roots now imprinted with indentations where centuries of pilgrims have stopped to pray and pressed their fingertips into the marble.

In one of the several chapels, a gold crucifix, dated 874, is believed to contain a piece of the True Cross, the actual cross upon which Christ was slain. And in a little silver coffer beneath the altar, set back in a dimly lit grotto, are the bones of Saint James the Apostle. This is why they come here. Can there be any place holier outside of Jerusalem? And when arriving at the Cathedral Compostela after ten to thirty days of 100, 200 or 800 miles of walking, many will enter to hear the hum of low conversation. Sitting on an immense stone floor with feet still pressed into hiking boots, a scattering of tired bodies await mass. Then all falls quiet when the priests appear. Sins are forgiven through prayers while clouds of incense escape the golden *botafumerio*.

WE joined a long lineup of pilgrims and tourists who had congregated with patience in a secluded courtyard swallowed by towering walls of grey concrete detailed again with carved saints and holy men tucked into every eave, fascia, stone window sash and door treatment as if holiness depended on them being there.

The visitors were waiting to enter the cathedral from the rear for the opportunity to climb a set of scaffold-like stairs so they could touch and caress the bejeweled bust of St. James the Apostle, the patron saint of Spain. The two tiered altar of intricately carved and stacked gold columns, each rich and glistening with golden painted friezes, boasted ornaments so dense with gilt paint that they sparkled rich metallic-orange in the subdued lighting. We filed past, moving solemnly as visitors reached out to embrace, pressed their lips against and ran palms across the back of St. James' head as if it held a life enhancing gift.

OVER THE NEXT few days we continued sailing south making short day passages of sixty, seventy, eighty nautical miles. Sailing parallel to the rocky cliffs of the coastline, we continued to move in and out of fog patches where westerly Atlantic winds traditionally blow in cold towards the warmth of the mainland.

Taking down the Spanish courtesy flag we ran up the Portuguese red and green following our arrival into Portuguese waters. In time, we would hoist dozens of these courtesy flags, each representing the country we were about to visit.

The Atlantic coast of Portugal offers little for the sailor who wishes to anchor but we found marinas in the coastal towns of Leixões, Cascais, Sines and Lagos.

APPROXIMATELY fifteen miles out to sea, smoke stacks came into view signaling the approach to the Leixões marina (Porto Marina Atlântico). Leixões is a large manmade industrial harbour protected by lengthy break walls. Here heavy cranes and container-park gantries are capable of handling Panamax container ships 294 metres (965 feet) long. Fishing boats barrel by with throttles full forward leaving no question this is a working man's harbour where pleasure yachts need to move aside. But the attraction to come here is it takes only thirty minutes by bus to travel to one of the oldest cities in Europe, Porto (Oporto) best known for the excellent port wines that are developed there. The city of Porto is centered on the Douro River (River of Gold) but there is no major harbour and neither comfortable mooring nor docking facilities available.

Porto is a modern city and beyond this lies century old architecture. Walls covered in tiles, façades running with garlands and arches with decorative balusters still remain of the old city. Narrow brick laid streets flow with alleyways so narrow balconies almost touch. Convents and churches and a customs house stand on the very sites where they stood five hundred years ago. Much as it was in medieval times, access through the old town is by steep cobbled streets along slender five story houses roofed in red terracotta rustic tiles. High above narrow streets running almost vertically down to the Douro River, women still reach out of apartment windows to hang damp laundry on clotheslines.

Praça da Ribeira, located at river level, where bustling markets of imported worldly goods once boomed with successful trade and commerce as far back as the Roman 4th century, is the location of a medieval market square. Now surrounded by restaurants, cafés and patio bars it offers the picture perfect view of the metal arched expansion bridge, Arrábida, once the longest arch in the world. Lying beneath the elegant bridge, along the river, single masted Rabelo shipping vessels which in years past delivered crushed grapes to the port cellars now float in retired elegance, their gigantic white sails advertising famous port wineries of Cockburn, Croft, Graham, and Sandeman. In the days of Rabelo shipping the pine constructed boats equipped with single broad sail, a flat keel for manipulating jagged rapids and vast rudder for steering, would have left the Douro Valley one hundred and thirty kilometres (eighty miles) distant to sweep downstream by fast running currents towards Porto's cellars in Gaia. Standing towards the scooped stern of his vessel, the captain stood on a platform towering over his freight of eight barrels, two across end to end. Gripping a long wooden rudder with calloused hands he maneuvered his boat through shallows, around rocks and over rapids. Leaving air space in the almost full barrels enabled possible retrieval if one should break away.

Sailing homeward and while battling upstream, a crew of four needed three days to forge the most difficult white water torrents. Yoked oxen on adjacent pathways, dragged the small working boats while assisting them through the rapids and back to the port cellars.

We walked across the bridge away from the city to Cais de Gaia, a less touristy area. This part of the city is where the country's name comes from. Not from the famous wines, but from the Roman harbour named, Portus Cale (Port of Cale) which in time became Portucale or Portugal.

Here, locals sit at sidewalk cafés along the river to order glasses of wine and lunches of *feijoada*, a typical Portuguese stew of meat and white beans. Dried cured hams, known as *presunto*, often hang from ceilings behind bars in restaurants.

Beyond the city, on the hills bordering Cais de Gaia, green leafy vines shape the landscape. The steeper hills allow for more space between the vines where in the autumn, workers trample the awkward slopes, bags slung over shoulders, ready to hold the handpicked grapes much in the way they have for centuries.

The wine lodges of the Douro Valley were originally established in the 17th century by English wine tradesmen who found it difficult to secure Bordeaux wines while Britain and France were at war. After successfully moving Napoléon's army out of Portugal, property was offered to British generals in reward. The climate in this northern part of Portugal offers ideal conditions for the production of wine grapes and famous wine companies such as Cockburn, Croft, and Dow have established successful wineries in the area. The grapes are either macerated by foot or by today's modern machinery in local villages. They are then transported by trucks to Porto to be aged in casks for making into port. Port wine differs from table wine in that it is fortified with the neutral grape spirit, aguardente vinica, halting fermentation and leaving more sugar while boosting the alcohol content. Most often served as a dessert wine, port is usually a mixture of wines from several different years.

Like many of the wineries, Graham's Port Wine Lodge offers tours including the opportunity to taste test the three main types of port: Ruby, Tawny and Vintage. Each type has a distinct taste of its own. Vintage port has been aged the longest with some being aged over a hundred years. The ageing process continues even after this type has been bottled.

As we entered the Graham cellar the scents of sweet smelling alcohol and oak barrels mixed with high humidity, combined with the coolness of the dimly lit cellar. Some say the oak barrels are as old as the lodges themselves. When the barrels have outlived their usefulness for port production, they are shipped to Scotland where they are lent to quarter whiskey.

It is possible to visit one cellar after the other but walking down those hills can be a little more complex than when hoofing it up sober.

Touring the city on foot, we climbed the 225 steps of the St. Clérgios Church Tower (Church of the Clergy) built in 1754. Standing 76 metres (249 feet) high it had once been used by seaman as a navigational guide when entering the Cais da Ribeira.

The Igreja de São Francisco, (Church of Saint Francis) 1244, is the best example of Gothic architecture in Porto. The small church offers a glimpse into the opulence once bestowed on religious buildings of that period. It is as if walking into the centre of an intricately carved gold nugget; chiseled arches, elaborate altarpieces, scenes from the Bible carved in such detail that if they had not been covered in gold, one would be in awe of the talented woodcarvers. Gold painted cathedral ceilings, walls, pillars; window frames so densely covered in ornate Baroque gilt I felt smothered in a glitter of topaz orange gaudiness.

Beneath the church lay the dead, the once hopeful leaders of Christianity that longed to live forever in a heaven of everlasting holiness. Up until 1839, cemeteries did not exist in Porto and in order that the hierarchy of state and church could lie close to saints and God, burials took place beneath the church. To view their final resting place, we descended a subterranean stairway to find a dimly lit passageway leading to damp underground catacombs beneath the church. Lying in the Ossario, containers holding diminutive bodies lay stretched across shelves lining bleak, damp stone walls. Here, nearer the holiness they had sought most of their lives, they lie in peace with a thousand other human bones. Left to rot beneath the church, the resulting odour of putrid, decaying bodies must have nearly been unbearable to those attending the church in the times of burial.

As long as we had been in Europe, our stomachs had never quite become accustomed to late night dining that was traditional in Portugal for everyone including young families. So it was with some trepidation that we set out one evening in a small fishing village outside of Matosinhos, to find a restaurant that would feed us an early dinner.

It was a rather dreary little village with the fronts of small stone cottages sitting shoulder to shoulder bordering stone laid streets, their front doors opening directly onto cobbled roads where pedestrians and the occasional car shared the same narrow space. This was a working man's town, a village born on the backs of fishermen where today is like many years of yesterdays. Stone construction colours the town grey leaving the rugged look of the village to reflect the hearty nature of those whose workplace is the sea.

There were no baskets of crustaceans to beckon us, no waiters in white aprons, not even signage advertising restaurants. It was not a place one should expect to find English spoken. There were few people to be seen and we could walk the streets three abreast hardly ever having to step aside for a car.

We came upon a slightly opened door ajar to what appeared might be a restaurant although if so, appeared to be a gloomy little thing. A few old wooden tables with a compliment of chairs sat on a well-worn floor. The room was entirely empty of patrons which did not surprise us as our clocks read just past six-thirty. The proprietor indicated we should go away and come back at eight o'clock. We returned an hour later as we tried to comply with what was expected of us. When we entered the same dark interior of the restaurant there was no sign that we were expected. The middle-aged proprietor with whom we had previously communicated appeared, somewhat frantic with our return, but graciously sat us at a table and immediately set to scurrying about his kitchen. He must have been alone except for perhaps a cook somewhere in the back.

He quickly set our table and proceeded to serve us our meal, a meal, which as it developed, was one we would likely never forget.

There never was a menu that night; food just appeared at our table beginning with eight appetizers and a flask of red house wine. Throughout the course of the dinner our table remained in abundance with local delicacies, the main course being of stewed rabbit.

Dinner ended with three desserts, all presented to our table in their entireties for us to serve ourselves. This was followed by a tot of homemade digestive liquor. It took us two hours to savour all the tantalizing flavours that burst forth from that home cooked meal and not until we were about to leave did his first Portuguese customers begin to arrive. We later learned that the restaurant frequently attracted connoisseurs from the nearby city of Porto, city folk who were willing to make the drive to experience what we had just stumbled onto by chance.

It wasn't until the following day we realized Portugal keeps the same time clock as Britain. Consequently the country runs an hour behind Spanish time which means we had inconsiderately returned to the restaurant at six-thirty rather than seven-thirty.

If we had appeared uncooperative in returning at the proper time the proprietor showed no annoyance and we couldn't have been treated better. We certainly could not have been fed better. We left feeling ready to hibernate for the rest of the season.

WHILE HEADING TOWARDS the port of Cascais on a twenty hour passage, the windswept headland of Cabo da Roca, the most westerly point in mainland Europe, was somewhere far off to our port. Again, we sailed through foggy patches and constant mist until nearing Cascais when the fog lifted and dodging fishing nets became a full time job for spotter and helmsman. The weather leant itself well to continuous standing on cockpit seats as we peered over the canvas dodger letting sea breezes brush our faces. Tied to an assortment of small floating bottles, milk bottles, translucent pop bottles, the prerequisite for markers seemed to be that the bottle floated, not that it could be easily seen. Nets lie in wait of not only unsuspecting fish but inattentive boat propellers.

One never knows what obstacles might await behind a breakwater until you blindly round the end of it, but pulling into Cascais Marina (Marina de Cascais) was a refreshing surprise. Rounding the corner was like driving onto a football field. The harbour was so spacious that one could partake in choreography of pirouettes; swing ones bow in a series of figure eights without ever coming near another boat. Constructed to berth six hundred and fifty yachts within its inner harbour, lift-out cranes sit ready to handle mega racing yachts that arrive here to participate in various world racing championships. But it was expensive, outrageously expensive; overnight berthing costs for *Baccalieu III* was €71 ($100 US) a night while the simple chore of washing clothes in local Laundromat machines demanded €5 per load. The good thing was that a Jumbo supermarket was only a ten minute walk from the marina, although we needed a taxi to help get us home with all our provisions.

Cascais is a British holiday enclave of bars, shops and restaurants. A traditional Portuguese dish served in restaurants is bacalhau, a meal consisting of salted codfish, onions and potatoes. Our yacht's name *Baccalieu* is derived from the word bacalhau.

Palm trees, strung along the wharf, swayed and rustled with a casual elegance. In the evening, we watched the orange glow of the sun brighten the hues of the reds, yellows and blues of the small local fishing boats tied nearby. The old town was once protected by several small 17th century fortresses. In 1588, the Spanish Armada, the largest naval fleet ever to exist until the Second World War, left this harbour to sail towards its doomed fate at the hands of the British navy. For centuries the defeat of the Spanish Armada was thought to have been due to the superiority of the British navy but in time, the examination of cannon balls discovered at the bottom of the North Sea has indicated the cannon balls were not all of the same size. It has been suggested that perhaps the Spanish ships had not been equipped with the appropriately sized cannon ball for the guns they carried, and were subsequently unable to return fire on the English ships that attacked them. With that, the Spanish Armada had no choice but to retreat, and in doing so were swept northward in high winds where they were to meet their fate against the rocks of northern Scotland.

WE took a local bus north to the town of Sintra forty minutes from Cascais. Nearby Lisbon, (Lisboa), located only 30 kilometres (18 miles) from Sintra, was for centuries, the home of Portugal's monarchs. Royalty often travelled to Sintra to escape the heat of the city. Ornate palaces designed in Gothic, Mudéjar (Moorish), Manueline, and Renaissance styles, are hidden behind walled gardens. These grand homes with domed ceilings, spacious banquet halls and kitchens that one time fed up to a thousand guests, are owned today by Portugal's wealthy.

Seventeenth century ambiance is brought to life by the horse drawn carriages that carry tourists throughout the winding streets of the little town. Most tourists ride buses to the top of a steep hill to tour Palácio Nacional da Pena (Pena National Palace), a UNESCO (United Nations Educational, Scientific and Cultural Organization) World Heritage site. Instead, we embarked on some much needed exercise and set out to walk to the castle. The steep uphill road ran among scenery of thickly forested vegetation and for a few minutes we enjoyed the walk. But unknown to us, the hill twisted and turned to become a trek of lengthy mountain variety and while panting and feeling at times we were about to succumb with elevation fatigue, we were passed by numerous air conditioned buses filled with far more savvy tourists than we.

Palácio Nacional da Pena stands on one of the rocky peaks of the Serra de Sintra, (Serra Mountains). Almost as if floating among sky, it dominates its surroundings like a medieval Disney castle and can be seen as far away as Lisbon on a clear day. For centuries a monk's monastery, it fell into ruin but was later brought to life by the German husband of the then-reigning queen, Maria II, King Consort Dom Fernando II (1816–1885). In contrast to the common castle of dingy grey variety, Castelo da Pena is unique. Although constructed with a series of architectural turrets, ramparts, domes and the expected drawbridge, the whimsical thinking of Fernando II demanded his summer palace be painted in pastel shades of yellows and pinks. Almost entirely built on a summit of rock at a height of 1,500 metres (4,900 feet), walks taken outside around the windblown turrets are located so near the edge of the rock-face as to be cliff hangers. Terraces and courtyards accompanied by sundials and cannons, one of which had been automated to fire every day at noon even in early times, share a panoramic view of wooded hills and extensive parkland where King Fernando ordered several species of trees to be planted from distant lands: North America sequoia, western red cedar, cypress, magnolia, Chinese ginkgo, trees from Japan, ferns from Australia and New Zealand. With a somewhat fanciful exterior which in fact, is off the chart in most people's imaginations, the entranceway includes a stone carved grotesque looking statue staring down upon visitors from the archway. This eerie looking chimera, sharing medieval features similar to a gargoyle, along with the outrageous colours of the exterior, suggests that the castle's interior is weirdly decorated. But the interior is extravagantly adorned with Victorian and Edwardian furnishings, ornaments, works of art and priceless porcelains just as the royal family left them when in 1910 Queen Amélia foresaw the inevitable fall of the monarchy and realized it was time to leave.

Before sailing away from Cascais for the small town of Sines, seventy-five miles south, we both determined we were in need of a haircut. It was to be our first since we had left home.

There are some things that instill more fear in me than sailing oceans, and getting a bad haircut is one.

By the time I had left home, the same hair stylist had come to my home for ten years. But now I had no choice but to expand my horizons, experience a real salon, allow a stranger to cut and clip freely as she saw fit.

I walked into the first hair salon I came to, gave the stylist the universal clip, clip sign with index and middle finger and sat in her chair.

No one in the salon spoke English. Gesturing with my hands, I enunciated in a clear, slow manner, "I–want–an–easy–to–care–for–hairstyle." Her face took on a quizzical expression. Cocking her head, she replied "Como um cordeiro?" "Yes," I said, not knowing what the words meant, "Como um cordeiro."

With eyebrows raised, she gave a quick, startled glance at one of her peers, shrugged her shoulders and began cutting.

I should have known from that bewildered look that she shot towards her co-worker that something wasn't right.

The following day, while sporting a sheered-kind of hairstyle, I learned that 'como um cordeiro' means 'like a lamb'.

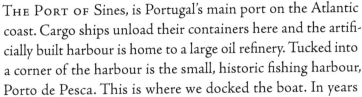

The Port of Sines, is Portugal's main port on the Atlantic coast. Cargo ships unload their containers here and the artificially built harbour is home to a large oil refinery. Tucked into a corner of the harbour is the small, historic fishing harbour, Porto de Pesca. This is where we docked the boat. In years past, when cod fish were plentiful, Portuguese fishing trawlers left here to fish off Newfoundland's Grand Banks.

A quiet, pleasant town, Sines sits on an escarpment

overlooking a sandy beach bay dominated by red tiled roofs and simply designed white painted homes. Far from the tourist trail, Sines proudly displays a statue of home born Vasco da Gama (1469–1524), the first European to reach India by sea. By sailing the route to the Indies, da Gama showed the way for new and exciting trade. Depicting the swordsman in knee britches with sword stashed in belt, the statue displays da Gama with knee length cape spread across severely squared shoulders of a bearded man. The Cross of the Order of Christ hangs about his neck as though wearing this insignia of Christianity bestows upon him forgiveness from his heinous crimes.*

Looking every bit a powerful seaman, the statue gazes towards the Atlantic in remembrance of a time when it was thought that serpents and sea dragons awaited ships sailing miles from home-ports in exploration. In Robin Knox-Johnston's *The Cape of Good Hope, A Maritime History*, the author notes it took da Gama one hundred and sixty-one days to complete the passage from the Cape of Good Hope to Portugal (5,232 nm) when his ship would have averaged 1.4 knots of speed.

JUST TWENTY-ONE MILES south of Sines lay the port of Lagos. This large harbour is a popular stopover for yachts sailing the Iberian Peninsula coast, and was a port of call even before Vasco da Gama's time. Where fishermen once anchored their small fishing vessels and rowed ashore to spread nets to dry, a modern harbour of spacious docks now

---

* After da Gama returned from defending Portuguese colonies in 1492, he left again on a second expedition with 20 well-armed ships in preparation for conflict with the Muslims. In one case he waited for a ship to return from Mecca, a Muslim trading and religious center. After his men overtook the ship and seized merchandise, they locked 380 passengers in the hold and set fire to the ship killing all men, women and children.

exists. Beaches, bars, restaurants and hotels continue to attract the sea traveller as it did even in Nelson's time when following a stopover in his ship *Victory*, he sailed away not only with provisions but ripe stories of voluptuous women and bottomless drink. Numerous tales are told of other well-travelled seaman who arrived in the harbour: Henry the Navigator and Sir Francis Drake (who apparently tried unsuccessfully to raid the town), and Christopher Columbus whose life was saved, as locals recount, from a nearby sinking ship. And it was from here that Vasco da Gama set sail in 1499 to discover Brazil. The harbour is thought to be as important to the Age of Discovery as Cape Canaveral is to space exploration.

Steeped in history of explorers and slave trading, the city merges with the modern world while still displaying centuries of past architecture.

Within walking distance of the yacht basin, the pedestrian friendly old city attracts swarms of European tourists to roam cobbled alleyways enhanced with terracotta potted flowers, iron balconies and centuries of worn, hand painted blue mosaic tiles. Cascades of lavender tinted bougainvillea spill over the stone walls of the city's fortress.

In narrow back streets, where locals sip daily cups of minute but strong coffee, plastic patio tables packed the esplanades so densely we needed to weave in and out among the chairs to navigate past those who were patronizing the restaurants. As evening approached, we enjoyed a wandering street musician whose aged fingers fluttered across the board of a billowing accordion while his little dog perched on a shelf above the instrument beneath his chin. Street buskers, practicing the ancient arts of sword swallowing and fire eating, entertained us while we ate. Ice cream vendors, located on nearly every corner, added to the holiday atmosphere in the near perfect summer evening air.

While walking to find a chandlery, we discovered the

fishermen's bay where residents work in modern warehouse buildings repairing marine engines and fishing equipment. Looking through the retractable door of one of these concrete floored gigantic garages, we caught sight of rows of long picnic benches where people sat shoulder to shoulder eating lunch. We walked in, paid for two meals and slid into vacant spots on one of the benches. A meal of all-you-can-eat fresh barbequed sardines was the lunch of the day and we watched as those beside us placed a sardine onto a piece of bread, slid the upper side of the fish off, ate it, lifted out the bone, ate the second half and continued with each fish in this manner until all were gone. Only then, was the piece of bread, now soaked in fish oils, savoured.

Not far from the marina, a new building houses a market place where vendors sell fresh garden vegetables and freshly caught fish. Small grocery stores stocked with dry goods were also within walking distance. When I shopped, I took several strong canvas bags so as to avoid having to handle twice as many plastic bags. I found it easier to walk with shoulder bags touting the weight rather than six thin plastic handles digging into my fingers. That day I had two hanging off each shoulder and another two in each hand while I trudged back to the boat like an overburdened pack mule.

It was summer and our son David, who was a university student, had joined us in Lagos during his school break. He brought with him a friend who had never sailed before. Perhaps there was an opportunity here, I contemplated. Mark would never know the difference if we told him he had to stand all the night shifts, now would he?

Before leaving port, we gave the boys a few days to adjust to their new time zone then we left the marina to spend the night at anchor before embarking on a 130 nm overnight trip. Mike and I had learned that leaving a dock to spend the night in an anchorage before a lengthy sail helped us with mental and physical transitions of going to sea. We hoped the exercise would do the same for the boys.

When we got underway David teamed up with his Dad while Mark worked with me for standing night watches. Around 0200, Mark and I had found ourselves approaching an area crowded with commercial fishing boats. Clouds had buried the moon making for a dark night and tracking several unpredictable fishing vessels can be a nail biting experience. Longliners let out fishing lines reaching up to 60 miles (100 kilometres). Main lines hold between 2,500 and 3,000 hooks. The vessel steams between ten to eleven knots in any direction while the line pays out. It takes five to six hours to set a line and another eleven hours to haul it in. When a large fish is detected on the line, the vessel turns towards the fish. This erratic steering practice and the white brilliance from commercial spot lights for illuminating decks, can create confusion to oncoming traffic. It was a serious job keeping out of the way of fishing boats and away from their nets. Avoiding freighter traffic is much easier. Freighters travel in relatively straight lines.

Just before dawn broke, a high powered light suddenly appeared in the distance heading towards our bow. It was not showing on the radar screen and I was concerned about its identification and its intention. It continued to move closer and I could not determine how to avoid it because it almost seemed to follow us. But where the black sea meets the black sky, our world is not divided and the light that caused me so much concern was an airplane with landing lights preparing to land at a local airport!

GIBRALTAR

EMBARKING ON A NEW LIFESTYLE

THE FOLLOWING DAY we headed towards Gibraltar, a mighty monolith even as it first peaked from the horizon far out to sea. Bleak but righteous, it stands as a bold cornerstone to one of the most important passages throughout history as it plunges seaward with sheer ruggedness, a ruggedness that carries its theme right to the heart of its interior.

A British territory, the rock is located at the southern end of the Iberian Peninsula at the entrance to the Mediterranean Sea. A narrow rocky isthmus on the north end connects it to Spain.

As mighty as it looks, Gib, (as it is referred to locally), only covers an area of just over 6 square kilometres (2.6 square miles). Most of its real estate is piled onto itself in continuous rugged elevations. A towering mass of unattractive limestone and shale, it is one of the most densely populated areas in the world, even though it lacks a source of inland fresh water, natural resources or even arable land. It's a wonder any country ever fought over it, but they did, due to the fact it towers over a highway of water and whoever owned the tower, controlled the highway.

Surprisingly, the rocky giant is self-sufficient. Approximately ten percent of the seventy thousand ships that pass through the Strait annually, stop there for refueling. As well, offshore banking, several internet gambling companies and tourism keeps the economy healthy. With that, Spain has never given up wanting to regain ownership. Having controlled the piece of rock for two and a half centuries after yanking it from the Moors, Spain ceded the territory to Britain through a treaty signed at the end of the War of the Spanish Succession (1701–1714). However, hostility continued between Britain and Spain and three more years of fighting sent a slew of cannon fire into the little city crumbling almost everything of historical importance, and is why, today, the city is difficult to place in any period of history at all. While lacking the inspiration of youth, it also lacks the sophistication of old.

But the 'Rock' remains an important gateway to the Atlantic Ocean and the merchant rich Mediterranean and like a good diamond, holds its value. Having the Royal Navy docked there during the Falklands War (1982), was undeniably of great importance to Britain.

Although many who work in Gibraltar commute from their homes in Spain due to Gib's high real estate costs, Gibraltarians have no interest in allowing the land to revert back to Spanish ownership. They have not forgotten or forgiven history when the Spanish military general, Franco, in 1969 closed the border between Gibraltar and Spain in an attempt to strangle it into submission resulting in local Gibraltarians having to overcome threatening starvation. But for the assistance of Britain, the outcome could have been disastrous. With this came loyalty to the Crown, but even prior to Franco, when Lord Nelson's body was carried to shore at Rosia Harbour, after being hit by a sniper's bullet during the Battle of Trafalgar, Gibraltarians felt something of importance to Britain. Here, on this small plot of rock, this great man had lain dead while waiting to be submerged and preserved in a barrel of cognac before embarking one last time for his homeward journey to London. He lies now in St. Paul's Cathedral.

Two promontories, one on each side of the Strait, one in North Africa, the other, the rock of Gibraltar, were once thought, according to Greek mythology, to be the Gates of Hercules. Travelling to the end of the Mediterranean Sea, the promontories posed as a gate in which sailors were warned not to go beyond, because to proceed into the ocean was to travel into the unknown where one could well face unmerciful dangers that waited within its depths. Centuries of Greek mythology stewed hauntingly in the heads of sailors: the Sirens, sea-nymphs who enticed sailors to hurl themselves into the sea; Poseidon's stormy oceans; and Cyclopes, man-eating giants who were thought to reside in the Sicilian islands. Other legends told of wide gaping mouth monsters, ugly shapes vying horns, some adorned with human faces and sea wolfs that could live in water as well as on land. Even in Captain Cook's time sailors were more afraid of what they might encounter from the sea than sailing off the edge of the world and still, by the early 19th century, giant octopuses with tentacles encompassing ships were depicted in paintings, much of it artist driven and the rest from yarns spun from incorrect accounts of sightings.

From just outside the old city's walls, Marina Bay offered dockage where boat owners had set up permanent residency, erecting dock barbeques, carpentry tables and thick gang planks creating a quayside lifestyle with inexpensive dockage. Within a short distance of the marina a thick stone archway, once the city's fortified wall, leads to a parade square surrounded by stone buildings of garrison style and proportions, now business offices and a few boutiques.

There is a difference between old and quaint. The main street of Gibraltar, simply put—is old. Lined with tired, dark dingy stores, several of which are dedicated to the selling of duty free tobacco, perfumes and liquors, one litre of spirits sells for a mere £5. Adolescents can legally drink alcohol at the age of sixteen.

On our walk towards the base station of the cable car that

takes tourists to the top of the rock, narrow slab headstones stand erect beneath the shade of low hanging tree branches. In the small, damp cemetery renamed *Trafalgar Cemetery*, a few lie buried here after falling during earlier sea battles or succumbing to disease. Only two of those buried in the moss stained graveyard had died of wounds during the Battle of Trafalgar. Others were buried in unmarked graves north of here and many had been buried at sea. One headstone appeared without a name:

1798–1814

DIED OF WOUNDS

LATE HIS MAJESTY'S SHIP COLOSSUS

HE RECEIVED IN THE GLORIOUS

BATTLE OF TRAFALGAR, AGED 20

Nineteenth century fortifications are as much part of Gibraltar as trees are to Toronto. Casemates, bastions and cannons still lie in their strategic positions, while gun batteries from the Second World War, intertwine with a network of tunnels higher on the mountain.

The Siege Tunnels were carved out by the Merchant Marine to defend Gibraltar from the mainland during the Great Siege of 1779 to 1783, when Spain and France attempted to take the city from Britain. The original purpose of the tunnels was to get cannon fire on the northern face of the rock known as the Notch. Originally the tunnel was only 25 metres (82 feet) in length, but by the end of World War II, the tunnels had reached a winding distance of over 48 kilometres (30 miles).

St Michael's Cave, was used for lodging soldiers, storing ammunitions, water and oil. Other caves lead to exits in the cliff face where British gunners would have stood guard over their cannons. Cathedral Cave, with its long passages and gigantic caverns, is a chamber of St. Michael's Cave and is the part we explored. Due to the discovery of two Neanderthal skulls *Homo neanderthalensis*, in Gibraltar and a prehistoric painting in one of the caves, it is believed that primeval man sought shelter in the cave around 40,000 BC. So deep are the caves that the ancient Greeks believed them to be the Gates of Hades, an entrance to the Underworld, "where the dead might rest, but not in peace."

It was an unusually clear day when we reached the top of the mountain by cable car and there, spread before us, was the Costa del Sol, (Sun Coast), where we would soon be making headway as we turned our boat eastward into the Mediterranean Sea.

At the top, where we exited from the cable car, families of monkeys walked a narrow stone ledge turning about freely with expert balance, some with babies clutching to their underbellies. Boldly displaying shiny pink, bald backsides, their curious, expressive faces do not indicate they are truly outrageous thieves who stop at nothing to secure an edible tidbit. Posted signs beg tourists not to feed them but many cannot resist and find the little beggars searching their handbags after having undone fasteners and zippers. While spotting a visitor taking a food bar from his pocket, one monkey, in his determined quest for food, jumped off the roof of a car, bounced off the head of an unsuspecting bystander, dropped to the shoulder of the man holding the food and tore it from his grasp. A second monkey scaled the man's pant leg in hopes of beating the other monkey to the prize.

The darlings are in fact not monkeys but originate from a family of Barbary macaque, known as Barbary or Rock apes *Macacus inus*. Gibraltar is home to the only population of these apes in the whole of Europe, encouraging some to remark, "Lucky for the rest of Europe." The small-sized apes often break into hotel rooms, scavenge garbage bins and sometimes terrorize sunbathers at beaches. However, having lived there for centuries, the tailless colony consisting of approximately two hundred, is a national symbol of Gibraltar. Their origin had been baffling to biologists and thought at first to have arrived with the Moors (711–1492) when tribes travelled from Africa, but in later years it was suggested they were introduced by British sailors who had collected them on their travels. That's when the myth was born: that Gibraltar would cease to be British if the apes no longer made their home there. The myth was taken so seriously by Winston Churchill during the Second World War that, as the population dwindled, (aggressive apes kill rivals and soldiers might have used them for target practice), Churchill ordered the importation of more apes and to guarantee their well-being, he instituted a health care plan in which the monkeys have for years received food and medical care from the local hospital.

DNA screening has proven the monkeys are of Moroccan or Algerian origin.

RUNNING BETWEEN NORTH Africa and Europe, the Strait of Gibraltar links the North Atlantic Ocean and the Mediterranean Sea. Up to three hundred ships pass through the 8 mile (13 km) wide Strait every day heading for the Suez Canal or delivering goods to the twenty-one surrounding countries. On the chart, separation zones divide shipping lanes in east and west directions which translates into a super highway with an imaginary median down the centre. Crossing this super highway at right angles, are ferry boats running from Tangiers and Ceuta.

At the western end of the entrance, where boats enter from the Atlantic Ocean, a natural sill over the ocean floor prevents water from the Mediterranean Sea from totally escaping, subsequently slowing water from the Atlantic to freely flow inwards. Consequently the tidal range in the Mediterranean is greatly reduced and because of the natural high evaporation rate and low rain fall in the Mediterranean, the sea has a higher ratio of salinity than the Atlantic Ocean. What this meant to me, was that I could finally float. Born with a butt like a wrecking ball, my bottom heads south as soon as it hits water. It was quite a treat for me to lie on my back and float like an unconcerned preening sea otter.

THE MEDITERRANEAN

SPAIN: BALEARIC ISLANDS

Nudity is a form of dress
John Berger

Leaving Gibraltar, our first Mediterranean stop was the Spanish city of Estepona located in the most westerly part of the Costa del Sol.

When arriving in each new Spanish port, before being issued a berth, visiting yachts are required to first visit the local harbourmaster's dock where information is documented regarding last port of call, next destination planned, passports, details of gross tonnage, engine power and other facts concerning the boat that couldn't possibly be of interest or use to anyone. By the end of our travels, Mike had filled out what seemed to be hundreds of these documents.

The trick when arriving in a Spanish port is not to arrive between two and four o'clock in the afternoon as the Spanish close most businesses during that time to enjoy a siesta. Following a lengthy trip, we might find ourselves waiting for hours at the immigration dock to clear customs in order to procure a berth.

In the Mediterranean, we most often backed the boat into the assigned space between two boats with room not much wider than our own. Sometimes we needed to ease the stern in while pushing others aside. However, in the Estepona Marina, there were docks, and they had been constructed to accommodate yachts far larger than ours. Here we shared a dock with a 21 metre (70 foot) power yacht which towered over us like an apartment building over a bungalow. The power boat's deck reached halfway up our mast, obliterating everything on our starboard side including light. I could very easily experience neck strain while talking with a crewmember standing on his third deck looking down at me. One day he confessed the yacht he ran burned 300 litres (66 Imp./79 US gallons) of fuel per hour and confided that as far as he was concerned, a sailboat was the way to go.

We took a bus to Marbella, one of those picture perfect resort towns where I wondered if anyone real might actually live there. And the answer was no, only the rich and famous, who drive their Ferraris and Bentleys down the Golden Mile to Puerto Banus, to shop in designer boutiques and mix with other people of obscene wealth in bars and world famous restaurants.

We were relieved that our decision to dock in Estepona had saved us from extreme embarrassment as the total length of *Baccalieu III* could hardly compete with the tenders strapped to the decks of 30 m (100 ft.) luxury yachts. Fitted with wine cellars, swimming pools and enough underwater lighting to make Jacques Cousteau think he had discovered a new planet, these yachts float like miniature Dubai's while crews rub perfectly shiny stainless railings in a futile attempt to improve on perfection.

While in Estepona, Mark and David attended a bull fight at the Plaza de Toros, a '70s concrete structure holding sixteen fights a year. They were small bulls they killed, and not much interested in charging a flailing red cape, reported the boys.[*]

---

[*] Before obtaining stardom, which most never do, a matador makes less money than a waiter.

During prestigious bull fights, bulls used in the ring are those bred explicitly for the fight, trained to be fearless in the hopes they will replicate the wild traits of the Iberian bull. Bullfighting is linked not only to the Roman Circus where men fought wild beasts in amphitheaters, but to Spanish warfare. Because Spain had an overabundance of wild boars, they offered soldiers a way of keeping sharp for battle. Moorish cavaliers also fought on horseback, killing the bulls with spears, with the exercise eventually turning into public entertainment. Just as common among Spanish families as playing hockey is among North Americans, there have been various Spanish Kings and Queens who have wished to end the spectacle but met with little success.

Bull fighting in some areas of Spain is losing ground because government funding for the national past-time continues to face cutbacks. One province recently passed laws forbidding bull fighting all together, and during summer months bullrings are often used as concert venues.

However, in the evenings, local television stations run replays of the final moments of the bloody killing of the bulls. Like watching the best part of a hockey game, the sports network runs highlights of each bull as it is pummeled with spears and drops to its death. One after the other they can fall to the ground right in your own living room and not even stain your carpet.

Other fun events in which to participate with the bulls include running from them on cobbled streets during the internationally known *Encierro*, 'running of the bulls' and taking part in *Bou Embolat*, where bulls are encouraged to run while adorned with flaming wax balls on their horns.

JUST EIGHTEEN MILES to the east is the city of Benalmádena. Mark left us to fly home here while David and I travelled inland to the city of Granada to tour Calat Alhambra, a

Moorish citadel and castle. Mike had been there before and therefore remained onboard to clean the blocks and fittings on the lifelines. Also on his list was to resolve the blocked toilet in the aft head.

ALHAMBRA is the only intact medieval Muslim palace in existence and the most visited site in all of Europe. Eight thousand people per day pass through the gates, each purchasing a ticket marked with a specific entry time.

In AD 714, Muslim armies conquered Spain and continued to rule the country for the next eight hundred years. During this period, they far surpassed the rest of the world in science and mathematics, which is demonstrated in their exquisitely detailed architecture. In the 13th century, the Moors erected Arabian palaces and a fortress, which came to be known as Alhambra (the Red One, to reflect the reddish colour of the nearby mountains). The palace was erected on one of the Sierra Nevada Mountains following which a supporting city was built surrounding it. Alhambra consists of three palaces, one for the ruler, another for his family and a third palace to house the elite guard responsible for protecting the nearly twenty-six acres they sit on.

The structure began as a 9th century citadel but became more developed in the 14th century during which time the Nasrid Kings (Arab Muslim) ruled the Kingdom of Granada. Alhambra sits on a hill surrounded by valleys, ravines and the Alhama River that intertwines along the base of them. Red clay fortifications surround several buildings including gardens, reflection pools, fountains, numerous turrets and watch towers, all constructed for various rulers who conquered it throughout the centuries including Charles V (1527) who built a Christian palace within the Alhambra in celebration of his grandparents, the Catholic Monarchs who conquered it from the Muslims.

The result is buildings of contrasting architecture and art forms that have been in a process of restoration for over a hundred years.

Constructed in grand scale, it encompasses Roman-like architecture in its halls and courts that include 42 metre (140 foot) dimensions with soaring domes.

The most outstanding features are the decorated ceilings and walls intricately sculpted with molded plaster, stone, wood carvings and patterned tiles. Applied horizontally in what appears to be perfectly straight lines, the hand carved geometric patterns are either decorative friezes or scripts recounting stories that appear so dense with writings, the walls and ceilings resemble wall paper. Each room retells a poetic story with molded plaster script in either Gothic or Arabic language. The palaces, constructed with marble columns, turrets, courts, large halls and arches are unlike 19th century castles where furnishings and heavy draperies are often the focus of beauty. This instead is a palace of remarkable art form where the simplicity of space enhances outstanding, elaborate workmanship of past artisans.

We decided to spend the night anchored in a nearby bay. A lighthouse marked the entrance. We motored through a narrow channel of protruding rocks that extended submerged into the passageway. We appreciated the fact that we had made our arrival in daylight and would not need to navigate the dangerous passage in darkness.

We dropped anchor in the vacant picturesque bay and were surrounded by cliffs supporting terra cotta roofed houses, each appearing to balance carelessly on rocky slopes cascading towards the bay in giant plateaued steps. Cream coloured sand shouldered the shoreline with tiny beach pebbles where waves rolled lackadaisically to shore.

This was a real find.

Soon after dropping anchor, I noticed the isolated beach was dotted with a small number of people. I reached for the binoculars.

"Cripes", I said turning to Mike, "They're naked!"

"What have we sailed into? Have we interrupted a groupie thing? Do you think it's alright if we stay here?"

After coming to terms with the fact we had dropped anchor off a nudist beach and determined we would take only one peak through the binoculars for not more than five minutes each, we decided to stay. Then, while scanning the beach with the use of binoculars, we saw a small boat leave shore. Rowed by four men in naked splendor, the boat set course towards *Baccalieu III*. I quickly put the binoculars down, tucking them under a cushion.

We could hear the rowers singing and laughing while directing their little boat towards us. Why were they coming to our boat? Was I really going to be faced with having a conversation with what resembled a couple of skinned rabbits? All these questions and more flew through my head. All I really knew was they were coming closer and it concerned me what they might say to us.

At least we knew they weren't carrying concealed weapons.

As it turned out, they were not coming to our boat either. They were just out joy riding in their little craft, getting in touch with nature. Letting their skin absorb the sun's rays and feel the cool winds sweep over their nakedness.

In time, darkness fell and the beach became deserted. It was a pleasant evening and we basked in the fact that we had the anchorage all to ourselves. Waves continued to roll gently to shore with that unmistakable relaxing swoosh of lightly rushing water over beach sand creating the same steady, rhythmic sound effects thousands of people pay money for to aid them with sleep.

When we went to bed, a gentle breeze blew through the open hatches adding to the perfect evening.

During the night, the wind changed direction, blowing waves into the bay. In time our utopia was invaded by large ocean swells.

Now we knew why we were the only boat there.

We tried ignoring the gentle rolls but found it similar to hearing a tap drip. We lay awake waiting for the next irritation, then the next, while attempting to disregard the motion. The swells built, then increased in tempo and by 0130 we were almost rocked out of bed. We got up to examine the deteriorating situation.

With each roll, we could feel the bow yank hard on the anchor chain and we recognized the anchor could be pulled from its hold setting us free to drift onto the rocky shore. Our great find had now become dangerous.

We stayed on watch, waiting, hoping the wind would take another turn and blow the swells from the bay but by 0400 the conditions worsened and we lifted anchor.

Two blinking lights sat on the submerged rocks on either side of the channel. We pointed the boat towards the lights and headed out into the moonless night steering around the rocks we remembered seeing the evening before. The lighthouse guided us around the point.*

---

* Each coastal light has a different character (light pattern). One light might flash every three seconds, others every 60 seconds while others flash in groups of twos, threes or fours repeating at regular intervals. The length in which the light flashes also varies. Light characteristics are noted on charts in abbreviation such as Fl (flashing), F (fixed). Other information noted is the range in which the light is visible, the height above chart datum, and the cycle in which the light osculates such as 15s (15 seconds) or 10s (10 seconds).

2

Leaving the Mediterranean

Spain

Majorca, Return to Gibraltar

Gibraltar to Canary Islands

Canary Islands
Lanzarote, Gran Canaria

There is nothing like lying flat on your back on the deck, alone except for the helmsman aft at the wheel, silence except for the lapping of the sea against the side of the ship. At that time you can be equal to Ulysses and brother to him.

Errol Flynn

SPAIN

When you travel, remember that a foreign country is not designed to make you comfortable. It is designed to make its own people comfortable.
CLIFTON FADIMAN

*T*IENDAS, SHOPS IN Spain, open between nine-thirty to one-thirty, and four-thirty to seven-thirty in the afternoon. That was very difficult for me to keep in mind when I needed to shop or visit an office. It seemed the oddest thing that the whole country would take a nap at the same time and in midday.

Carrefours are the exception, and shopping at one was heavenly. But shopping in a Hypermarket was even better. For someone who's been away from stores for weeks at a time, other than village markets, a Hypermarket is a city wonder. Such a grand display of merchandise under one roof instills a feeling you've rediscovered a lost civilization. Clothes, footwear, garden plants, bicycles, hardware, furniture, electrical appliances, DVD's, toys—everything a regular person needs. It was all there. Some stores had up to forty check outs. By the time I got there I wanted to hug it. Just put my arms around the whole store. Being there was like an injection of speed, a shopping fix for a person out of touch.

As for variety, there were more sausages hanging in their delis than you could eat in a year; chorizo, blood, Polish, Turkish, some flavoured with spicy paprika others savory pimento, air dried hard or cured soft. The cheese counters could fill a gym. And so many varieties of long life milk. I think Spanish cows must empty their udders straight into tetra boxes.

Apparently the British, who flock to Spain's great beaches, cannot do without their English sausages and steak and kidney pies because the freezers were full of these British specialties. No wonder the stores are so large, with German muesli, French cheeses, Italian canned tomatoes, British marmite and lamb from New Zealand filling their shelves, they cater to the whole of Europe and beyond. But I couldn't find good whole wheat or all grain breads. Making bread with certain European flour is like baking with dust. It made me appreciate Canada's great Western grown wheat.

More challenging was purchasing weeks of provisions without Spanish language skills. For months afterwards, I was opening cans of goods that sort of resembled the pictures on the label but mostly didn't. The surprise contents often required me to make quick changes to meal plans.

Shoe stores in Spain were alluring. Never have I seen so many sexy styles. Walking down the Carrer Sant Miquel in Palma is like shopping in one long shoe store. Women in Spain love shoes and shoes are good value here due to the designers not being as well-known as Italian designers. The problem is the shoes are not meant to be worn, at least not on my feet. They're designed to make you look sexy and guaranteed to make you at least four inches taller. Admittedly, that was a boost I could have used. When I went to a store to purchase a pair of boat sandals they directed me to a shoe with a peep-toe front hanging with tassels on a strappy high heel.

This is the place to be a podiatrist.

IN Spain, dining out is a timely experience because choosing when you eat is important. There is a narrow window for the serving of all meals, and if you do not learn what they are, you end up eating in substandard, touristy places.

A typical breakfast in Spain might include a *café con leche*— strong coffee with hot, frothy milk, sweet rolls or toast with jam or mild cheese.

The midday meal is the largest meal of the day and often includes multiple courses. It's no wonder they need to take a two to three hour siesta.

The siesta is a tradition that dates back centuries when most people worked outdoors in agriculture and the noonday rest was necessary to escape the hot afternoon sun. When the temperature dropped in the evening, workers returned to the fields.

Dinner is much lighter than the midday meal, and is rarely eaten before nine o'clock and often as late as eleven o'clock. I wouldn't have done well if born Spanish, since most don't go to bed much before midnight. During summer and holidays, entire families might not turn in until three or four in the morning because after dinner, Spaniards continue to socialize in neighbourhood cafés and taverns. If you're in a bar before ten o'clock, you'll probably be drinking alone.

One of my favourite meals to share with friends is *paella*, a saffron seasoned dish of rice and seafood. I got the recipe for the meal from a cookbook that I purchased while travelling in Spain. I make the paella in a large flat pan on the stove and when finished, take the pan straight to the table for everyone to serve themselves. I make it only when I can obtain fresh seafood but originally paella was made by field workers who cooked on an open fire eating directly from the pan after gathering snails to add to the dish. On special occasions, it might contain duck or rabbit, but it never included seafood.

One of the most important words to know in the Spanish language is *cerveza*—beer. It's not unusual to purchase a local beer for the price of just one to three Euros and they arrive at your table mightily cold. Among others, there is Cruzcampo, a refreshingly light tasting lager, several varieties under the San Miguel label and Alhambra Mezquita (Mosque), a strong pale lager that some think was named Mezquita to deliberately cause offence to Muslims. Bars and restaurants serve an assortment of tapas. They were sometimes offered free when we ordered a drink at a restaurant patio or bar. If they came gratis, they were often finger foods, such as a cocktail onion skewered on a tooth pick with an olive, or a basket of bread with cheese.

We left Benalmádena and headed for Almerimar. Sailing past rocky ledges and plateaus of dry sloping hillsides, the landscape resembled more a sea of plastic than anything from nature.

Invernaderos, plastic covered greenhouses, which are used to grow vegetables, cover every available mountainous plateau making this part of Spain look as if trapped inside an assortment of Ziploc bags. The once dry and useless plains have now been converted into one of the richest vegetable markets in Europe, nurtured by underwater streams originating hundreds of miles from the melted snow of the Pyrenees Mountains.

We shoehorned the boat into a dock space in Almerimar Marina. At first glance, there appeared to be no space whatsoever, but with dock boys calling instructions in thick Spanish accents while arms flailed above their heads to encourage us, we continued in reverse. Miraculously, like parting of the waters, boats on either side reluctantly moved aside until we were wedged in like ham and cheese in a sandwich.

We stayed there four days, just chilling out, although 'chilling' is hardly the word for spending time in such a hot, humid climate. We frequented the local restaurants, sampling local delicacies of *escabeche*, marinated fish and *pringá*, mixtures of cured sausages or beef slow-cooked until the meat falls from the bones.

ONE evening it rained, the first rain we had seen since leaving England. We welcomed the downpour, it would help in washing the salt from the boat, but when we rose the next morning, we were shocked to see that *Baccalieu III* resembled a gaudy pink lawn ornament. Rain had transported red dust from the Sahara Dessert, part of the sixty to two hundred million tons of dust carried away from the desert each year by the wind. Like a light blanket, dust lay over the entire surface of the boat, and we would find it in every crevice, clutch and piece of mechanical gear on deck.

DAVID was leaving from our next stop, Aguadulce. Before he left, we drove through the countryside rich with olive orchards and orange groves. Acres and acres of vineyards line hillsides. Some of the best wines in the world come from Spain.

In the north, where the topography takes a dramatic change and becomes the Tabernas Desert, the driest part of Europe, movie set crews have constructed mock cavalry forts and Mexican towns to shoot spaghetti westerns like Sergio Leone's 1966, The Good Bad and the Ugly. The public can watch while a group of cowboy actors throw saloon chairs, smash liquor bottles and ride their steeds in speedy gallops through the town.

CONTINUING TO SAIL eastward, we headed towards the Spanish Balearic Islands (Islas Baleares), an archipelago located fifty miles from Spain's mainland coast. The islands are diverse, being both mountainous and flat, and offer numerous bays and inlets in which to anchor. Our goal was to reach one of the largest islands of the archipelago, Majorca (Mallorca).

After thirty hours of sailing, we pulled into Ibiza, (114 nm west of Majorca). The trip had been good, with calm seas and a quarter moon to accompany us. Although freighters and fishing boats had been numerous, tracking them helped pass the monotony of the night watch.

We arrived early morning, went straight into Cala Jolanda, anchored and spent a peaceful day catching up on sleep. To our chagrin, it rained Sahara dust again that night. Decks, coach roof, boom, were all lightly dusted with pink tinged powder. Sheets and lines were dirtied to a salmon colour and it even invaded the interior through opened hatches while we slept. The following day, I noticed Mike had a little puddle of the pink sitting in an indentation of his ear, probably having settled there while he slept.

In spite of the red rain we stayed an extra day. Dusty winds span thousands of miles and are impossible to outrun so there was no sense trying to escape their deposits. We settled in, enjoying water temperatures of 27°C (80°F) despite the fact we had been warned to watch for jelly fish, whose stings can cause painful itching, nausea and even muscle spasms. We had witnessed the effects of a sting once while scuba diving when a diver's mask had been completely obliterated by one of the milky white gelatinous creatures. Fortunately, I had a container of *Accent*, (MSG) which when sprinkled on the affected area almost immediately relieved the victim's pain. Undetectable jelly fish sting hundreds of swimmers every year along the coasts of Ibiza. In an attempt to control the problem, authorities have organized a fleet of fishing boats to patrol the shores where, using satellite imagery to locate the transparent fish, the fleet scoops them up using nets, then market the spoils as protein-rich fertilizer.

That evening around midnight a short thunderstorm brought more red sludge followed by strong winds. We stayed on watch and could detect a person walking in and out of the illumination of an oil lamp onboard the boat in front of us, a 30 metre (100 foot) wooden Alden. We felt assured that someone onboard the boat directly off our bow, was on watch during the inclement weather.

As the night progressed, the wind continued to drive across the cliffs funneling into the small bay below with increased intensity. Our wind instrument indicated several forty to forty-five knot gusts blowing through the anchorage.

Suddenly, the Alden broke loose from its anchor hold and fell back on us with the speed of a freight train. We watched helplessly as sixty tons of wood and lead slammed into our bow. The Alden's extended boom caught our spinnaker halyard laying his stern to our broadside. We could read the words, *Sea Gypsie*.

Sea Gypsie slowly slid down the side of our hull only to get caught up in one of the other shrouds where it was again held fast. Then the halyard snapped under pressure, freeing *Sea Gypsie's* hull to bounce off our teak cap rail gouging pieces of wood from it as it moved down the side. *Sea Gypsie's* lengthy boom then caught our pole's topping lift and once more she was held tight alongside while the hulls jounced against each other in the swells. The wind continued to howl. Mike and I needed to shout even to communicate to each other.

The hulls continued to gyrate grinding against one another in uncontrollable motions. Then, stretched to its limit, the pole lift snapped, releasing *Sea Gypsie's* boom, but only for it to get caught within seconds on our stainless high-tech rigging.

This was a real concern; if the shrouds tore loose, it could result in our mast collapsing.

There was little we could do but watch as *Sea Gypsie* rose and fell against *Baccalieu III*'s hull while tangled within the shrouds. Mike turned on the motor and eased *Baccalieu III* forward in hopes of assisting the anchor with the excess load it was carrying. If the anchor gave way, both yachts would be swept into the rocks within seconds.

In time, the wind and swells juggled the schooner free from its entanglement, but as she moved along, her massive old wooden boom immediately caught our port Yankee sheet, stretching it to capacity and allowing *Sea Gypsie* to move aft towards the cockpit where, if we had wanted to, we could have stepped into their cockpit. The destructive boom tore into our dodger ripping through the canvas until it landed, crushed in our cockpit. The stainless supports narrowly missed our heads in their collapse.

With our Yankee sheet holding the Alden prisoner, I crawled under the crumpled canvas in an attempt to free it from the winch while staying free of any possible recoiling lines. If the sheet broke while I was under there, I might end up missing a face.

Suddenly with no help from me, the sheet gave way under pressure allowing *Sea Gypsie* to drift free.

Surprisingly, our anchor had held both boats throughout the ordeal. If nothing else, we can lay claim to the title, 'anchor champions of the year!' We quickly surveyed the damage, retrieved the flying halyards, cleaned up the mess, tied down the remains of the canvas dodger and prepared for an emergency exit if weather conditions worsened.

The schooner got under control, left the bay and returned to anchor once again in front of us!

The wind continued to gust. It was 0300.

The following morning the skipper of *Sea Gypsie* came to

speak with us, offering apologies and insurance papers. He reported he was a paid skipper with paying guests on board. His guests certainly got more than they had bargained for. I suspect they all thought they were going to die.

That same day we moved the boat ten miles east to an adjacent bay. We were in need of some new scenery.

Formentera is a privately owned island but public access is allowed for the pleasure of walking along a beach of swirling white sands. Several small boats arrived early and threw out light day anchors so passengers could swim and enjoy the short stretch of intimate beach. But instead of enjoying our new anchorage, we found ourselves constantly surveying other boaters' anchoring techniques, especially those in front of us. By the looks of some, if the wind came up, we might possibly see some chaos again.

DURING the night, the wind picked up and changed direction — the perfect recipe for lifting out anchors. Mike was up checking to see if boats remained in the same location they had been when we had gone to bed. He was good at that, sleeping lightly enough to hear wind conditions.

That night he had to wake me from a deep sleep. Two boats had dragged and were dropping their anchors a second time. We consulted the chart to plan an emergency exit. There were two navigational lights. One flashing nine times every fifteen seconds marking an island. The second light was constant and it marked the rocks. The lighthouse with its rotating brilliant flash of light marked a third point. If we had to leave, we would steer towards the flashing light keeping the constant light to our starboard.

We decided to take turns on watch, Mike took the first one. I lay down on the settee and left my shoes on. My life jacket was in easy reach. I could be up the stairs within seconds if he called.

Later that night while taking my watch, I thought back to the years of anchoring on Lake Ontario, Georgian Bay and the North Channel.

Those were peaceful times, serene evenings under a canopy of stars. It meant dinners in the cockpit and good night sleeps with the kids aboard. Something was wrong with this Spanish recreational anchoring; it was more of an ordeal than a pleasure. We had anchored five times in two days since arriving in Spain, and each time we had bopped around like a canoe in a wave pool. Half the boat resembled a wounded war veteran, and I wasn't getting my beauty sleep.

In the morning, we decided to stay one more day. It was a pleasant anchorage, at least during daytime. It offered quiet and a view of a white sand beach. Most visitors on the beach appeared to be Spanish with brown toned skin, but there were others, like us, who were pasty white. Then there were others still who appeared to have skin tones of mysterious grey.

We took the dinghy ashore to discover the grey looking physiques were naked bodies smeared with something that made them resemble the walking dead. Some looked pretty darn good even in their 'dead' state. I got a good look because I was wearing dark sun glasses. I normally wouldn't think of talking to anyone who was naked, but there were others on the beach wearing bathing suits, skimpy as they were and only narrowly in the category of bathing suits.

A man, who was wearing one of those little Speedo elastic band things, informed us that the naked grey-looking sunbathers had recently come from a nearby natural sulphur pool. To reach it, he directed us to walk towards a distant lone palm tree keeping it in sight as we navigated through a labyrinth of flat dunes, shrubs and dead end paths. Following those directions, we eventually came upon one pathetic looking little mud puddle in a field full of scrub brush. We looked at each other; "Do you think this is it? This is what people come here for?"

For centuries foreigners from all backgrounds: aristocrats, the bourgeoisie, Poles, Austrians, Croatians, Serbs, Lithuanians, Russians, Jews, visitors from all across Europe, have paid untold amounts of money to splash themselves with health giving waters, sit in medicinal pools with life extending capabilities and drink minerals offering promises of ageless skin. And right here before us was a small but totally free opportunity to try one of Mother Nature's miracle sulphur baths. It was a rare opportunity to douse ourselves with a homeopathic treatment of detoxifying slime. I wondered if it helped to release tension. We could sure use some tension releasing.

"This doesn't appear to be very hygienic," I said to Mike as I lay wriggling on my back in the creamy pool of crud. "It looks like a good way to spread diseases to me." Then I realized—you don't lie in it, you fool. You cup the stuff in your hands and smear it over the length of your body like you're frosting yourself with Betty Crocker chocolate buttercream.

Gratefully, none of those Spanish exhibitionists back on the beach returned for another medicinal smear while I was lolling in their priceless find. No one caught me with my derriere wallowing, sunken and smooshed, into the very clay they would someday return to and lovingly caress over their faces and other cherished bodily parts.

THE NEXT ISLAND in the archipelago is Ibiza. One of the island's largest cities, Ibiza Town, is well known for another kind of wildlife. During the day, women in one piece bathing suits (bottoms only), lay stretched out on sun soaked beaches while bare chested men cruise the shores, scanning the bevy of topless sunseekers. This is the party capital of the Mediterranean and a place where men learn to be sweet, seductive and sensual because that's what gets them the results. Then at night, parties and nightclubs bring them all together when they learn how well they have done. Ibiza Town is all about results.

With all the opportunities to get out and have some fun we had in fact been in port two days and not seen a bloody thing but the inside of the boat. It was maintenance time. Among a host of other accomplished duties we changed the oil in the generator. But for some reason the oil kept escaping from the engine case and we filled one container after the other in an attempt to contain it. We mopped up what we spilled but in doing so we spread it even further afield. Before we knew it the pool of slippery goo spread to four to five times the area. Then ten times. There's no limit how far oil can go.

It was also laundry day and I had several loads to do in my small washing machine. I ran clothes lines all over the fore and aft decks twisting the lines around forestays, backstays and shrouds. I had more laundry than lines but the unimpeded sun and good strong breeze made short work of the drying process. By the time my third wash load was done, the first was ready to take off the line.

The following morning was another maintenance day but we took time out to go into Ibiza Town. The streets are narrow, lined with souvenir shops and upbeat clothing stores filled with items that only the tall, slim and gorgeous can wear.

Already my hair was in need of a cut. This time I sat before a very attractive girl in her early twenties. I think most of Ibiza is in their early twenties. Apparently she knew how to cut hair only one way—Punk style. As I left the salon she kindly instructed me to use lots of gel. "Thanks," I said, "That should do it." Then I noticed an opened book located at the front of the salon. It was her portfolio of hair styles — page after page of spiked hairdos. She must have wondered what the heck a woman in her fifties was doing sitting in her chair.

Had I seen the collection of pictures before entering, I would have avoided looking like a member of the Sex Pistols.* All I needed to complete the look were some fishnet stockings and a spiked dog collar!

---

* The Sex Pistols were an English rock group that embraced florescent coloured hair, patched leather jackets, stud and safety pin piercings. The group formed in London, England and lasted about three years from 1975 to 1978.

MAJORCA, RETURN TO GIBRALTAR

The sea, vast and wild as it is, bears thus the waste and wrecks of human art to its remotest shore. There is no telling what it may not vomit up.
HENRY DAVID THOREAU
(1855–1865)

IT WAS EARLY September when we arrived in Palma, Majorca. Stretching above city walls, a Gothic sandstone cathedral dominates the hill it stands on while overlooking the port. Constructed with an immensely high nave, it exudes holiness for all to see for miles around.

If boat repairs are needed, Palma is the place to be. And we had a long list of them.

With dock space for nearly a thousand boats and a lift-out with a hundred and fifty ton capacity, Real Club Náutico attracts yachts from every part of the world even though dockage fees were a scandalous €113 ($160 US) per night for a boat *Baccalieu III's* length.

Container ships and cruise ships arrive here for repairs and tune-ups. Deep wells fitted with giant lift cranes accommodate most privately owned cruising boats, even super yachts.

We were there to have our collision damage surveyed. A rigging inspection was also needed. The boat was in its first year of ownership and an Oyster Customer Care representative met with us.

While waiting for the riggers and surveyors we washed the decks and polished the stainless. The ocean's salt is corrosive. Stainless parts left to rust, can weaken and break. Salt got into everything: turnbuckles, shackles, swages and snaps, lifelines and pelican hooks, spar tangs and fairleads. From miniature sized split rings and cotter pins to hefty winches and davits, each piece needed to be cleaned of rust and protected with polish. They all played a role in our safety or the workings of the boat.

We removed the sheets from the sails to soak them in fabric softener then rinsed them to remove the accumulation of salt crystals. We took good care of our boat but I sometimes wondered who owned who. The Avon inflatable dinghy needed a serious scrub but no matter how much time we spent cleaning it, I always thought it resembled a homeless piece of rubber. The two stroke Yamaha engine benefited from a change of oil and new spark plugs.

We wiped down the fine grained, cherry wood walls and indoor teak parquet flooring. We cleaned and lubed the heads, washed the windows, defrosted the fridge and freezer, rinsed the holding tanks, pickled the watermaker and changed the oil in the Seafresh high-pressure pump. A haul out allowed us to have the bottom repainted and anodes replaced.

I was quickly learning why cruising is referred to as 'Maintenance in exotic places'.

FROM REAL CLUB Náutico we could walk to the promenade. Lined with clubs and restaurants, it was all easily available to anyone staying in the marina. Designer clothes, duty free perfumes and good restaurants draw visitors to the cosmopolitan city. In the evening, the chic swarm into all night bars after mopeding from local nudist beaches. But the charm of the old city is the history it reveals and moving throughout the streets we couldn't help but become immersed. From Roman ruins to Moorish/Arab baths and Christian influences, the past came alive.

Massive trees lined streets dotted with tapas restaurants and charming cafés. Sidewalk patios overflowed with chattering patrons. Outdoor town squares hidden among tangles of streets and century old buildings offered benches for those not in a hurry. A knife sharpener sat shaded beneath the sprawl of a huge fig tree anchored by twisted, convoluting buttress. Historic monuments, churches, museums, art galleries and boutiques sold pottery and hand painted tiles. Miniature ceramic Jesuses and Virgin Marys were for sale everywhere.

WE STAYED THREE weeks in Palma. As our most easterly Mediterranean destination, it served a twofold purpose. Boat repairs included replacing a length of solid teak cap rail, a section of the Reikman Yankee head foil, a bent stainless stanchion and a new custom dodger to replace the torn one when the hundred foot Alden tore it from its supports. The other reason we were in Palma, the one for which we had planned, was to participate in the Palma Oyster Regatta.

After welcoming friends from Toronto, we set off in the direction of Cabrera Island (Goat Island), twenty-one miles south of Palma.

Cabrera Island is an uninhabited small piece of land dominated by mountains, scrub-covered hills and bare, steep rock. There is only one narrow entrance into its large, protective anchorage. A crumbling, medieval castle situated on the brink of a headland is hardly noticeable when entering but it was formerly used to guard against the invasion of Barbary pirates in the 16th century. The island has no substantial grazing land and lacks a source of fresh water but its close proximity to Majorca deemed it important during times of frequent invasions.

The island was a perfect venue for an Oyster fleet regatta. Towering hills wrapped around us offering a private and serene setting. Clear, still waters allowed for swimming among fish we could detect twenty-five feet below. A restaurant ship, the *Barca Samba*, arrived from Palma to provide us with food, drink and a place for merriment.

The island, however, stands in remembrance of thousands of French prisoners who died there.

When the care and lodging of defeated French prisoners from the famed Battle of Trafalgar (1805), became too costly in southwestern Spain, the prisoners were transported to the island of Cabrera. It is estimated between 3,500 to 5,000 prisoners perished on the island. Many died of starvation. Now, somewhere within a pine forest high on one of the hills, a stubby obelisk stands engraved with a single date — 1847*. It is all that exists of the prisoners who had been imprisoned there during the Napoleonic War (1803–1815).

WHEN THE RALLY came to an end, we bid our friends goodbye and headed the boat westward, back towards Gibraltar. We crossed the 0° line of longitude and were suddenly sailing in the Western Hemisphere again.

Sailing just fifteen miles off the coast, shore lights accompanied us on our nighttime journey. The night was cool and I added a fleece and pair of gloves during watches. A small bird, migrating to a warmer climate, flew under our dodger away

---

* In 1836, approximately 400 survivors of Cabrera Island, most too ill to work or live normal lives, applied to the National Assembly for recognition of their sufferings and for aid. Their request was denied. In 1847, the Prince of Joinville, son of King Louise-Philippe, brought his naval squadron to Majorca. While there, he visited the island of Cabrera and determined to raise a monument to his lost countrymen.

from the cool winds. Within hours, another landed on the foredeck to huddle next to the toe rail.

As we neared Gibraltar our VHF radio became busy with radio operator announcements from high concentrations of freighter traffic. We would meet some of them in our approach when we sailed through the Strait of Gibraltar where we would again enter the Atlantic Ocean.

Around this time, we received our first Satellite security phone call. It reported semi-submerged containers had broken away from a container ship and were lost overboard during heavy seas.

Each day five to six million containers cross oceans aboard ships. Every year more than ten thousand containers are reported fallen overboard. The containers might contain anything from 17,000 hockey gloves to 80,000 pairs of Nike shoes, as had been lost, mid-Pacific, in 1990. In 2014, the Danish flagged-ship *Svendborg Maersk*, lost five hundred and twenty containers while crossing the Bay of Biscay during hurricane force winds. Waves were reported to be 9 metres (30 feet). It was the largest single load of containers to ever fall from any ship. Eighty-five percent of the containers were empty. Loaded containers carried fourteen tons of cigarettes. Weeks after the incident, containers were seen floating in the English Channel (one washed ashore), others were spotted floating in the sea of Cherbourg, France.

WE stopped in Espalmador and left early the next morning hoping to reach Gibraltar, two hundred and forty miles distant, within two days. The plan was to take on provisions along the way in Almerimar.

Travelling westward, each evening we sailed towards the warm glow of the setting sun. It seemed to balance on a thin line then disappear as if suddenly being swallowed. I often sat with my eyes glued to it, hoping not to burn my eye balls out while straining to see the optical phenomenon known as the 'green flash', an occurence of refracted light: high light frequency (green/blue light) curves more than low frequency (red/orange) light. The blue/green light remains visible after the red/orange light has been obstructed by the curvature of the earth.

We had never seen green hues illuminate from a setting sun but in the upcoming five years we would have hundreds of chances to watch for its appearance. But this night only dolphins entertained us, their silver bodies bounding over the water like little dancers, ducking and shooting across the sea in front of our bow.

When night fell, a new moon joined a legion of stars leaving it a coal black night. Even the waves that broke over the bow were engulfed in darkness. When the largest waves smashed against the hull, I knew from the aftermath of rushing, sizzling water charging up the deck, it would only be seconds before I felt the sting of salt on my face.

The wind was stronger than predicted and we were taking it on the nose. The boat bucked like a bronco.

The seas steepened heaving the bow even further out of the water. As if having its support pulled from under it, the hull fell into trough after trough only to rise again on the next heightened sea. This went on all night while tons of water rolled up the deck coming to abrupt end on the windshield. Whack! I spent my shifts unsuccessfully dodging spray and watching the radar screen. Mike's watches were no better. But we were not alone. We were crossing some of the busiest shipping lanes in the world.

We would have liked to have headed further off shore but a ship, off to our port, was bucking the same seas and had reduced her speed, trapping us about a mile off shore.

The wind speed instrument reported winds had increased and now indicated they were blowing to above thirty. Spray began to fly off the bow more forcibly. It was constant now. Each oncoming wave engulfed the bow then rolled up the deck breaking against the dodger window with such force it shot straight into the air. Sea water rained down on whoever was on watch.

We were not making much headway and we realized we would not reach Almerimar before dark. If we arrived after dark, it would not be possible to navigate Almerimar's tricky, shallow entrance.

In a last effort to make an improvement, we turned inland to where we hoped to fine coastal thermal winds and calmer seas. When that didn't materialize Mike went below to study the pilot book and chart again. His stomach must be made of cast iron I thought. The chart indicated there was a bay in the lee of Cabo de Gata. It wasn't mentioned in the pilot book and we would be taking a chance going there. Perhaps the bottom was rocky or the bay didn't offer protection from the elements or maybe the entrance was dangerous to navigate.

Only a couple of hours of daylight remained and our alternative was to spend another night bucking high winds and steep seas.

We headed towards the headland.

It was about 1600 when we arrived outside the bay. A separation of the hills along the coast revealed an entrance. Cautiously, we steered through. The bay was surrounded by more steep hills but the same thirty-five knot winds swept through a rocky cleavage into the anchorage. We pointed the bow into the wind and dropped the anchor. The anchor took hold immediately. The bay was large and the wind funneling through the gulches helped to lay the water flat.

It's hard to explain the feeling of getting out of a rough sea; to suddenly feel a flat sea beneath your feet. Magically, a certain peace came over me as if walking into a house out of a blizzard.

During our passage, the engine had experienced a series of coughing spells, perhaps a sign that it was burning dirty bottom fuel from the stirred up fuel tanks. For a while, we were looking at the possibility of not having any power at all. But we solved the problem by switching fuel lines and now anchored, we had the opportunity to change the dirty fuel filter and top it up with clean diesel.

The diesel container we carried for such top-ups was in the lazarette at the stern. We had just retrieved it when we were interrupted by a SAT phone call. We left the container on deck to take the call. The container blew over in the wind, leaked through a faulty screw top and saturated the aft deck with diesel.

Thirty hours tired, the last thing we needed was to be immersed in the rigors of a diesel cleanup.

The following day, blue skies hinted we should be underway. But both weather faxes and the gusts that blasted through a deep open gorge in the hillsides, carried a message of unfriendly seas beyond the cape. We hiked to the top of the surrounding hillsides to see westward-bound sailboats struggling to make headway. We were not at all tempted to give up our pleasant anchorage. Instead, we trekked along a narrow pathway trampled carelessly in the side of desert-dry cliffs towering above a wild and windblown Mediterranean coast below. We felt smug to be hiking in warm sunshine while witnessing strong winds pile whitecaps onto the sea.

We spent two days in this beautiful bay waiting out the weather. This is where we celebrated Canadian Thanksgiving. We had much to be thankful for.

I cooked a chicken in the pressure cooker and served it with sides of mashed potatoes, carrots and gravy. It wasn't the young, stuffed gobbler we were used to eating back home, and I had not seen cranberries since leaving Canada, but it was tasty and a good feast. Sometimes a lesser meal can be more appreciated than a grand one simply because of the circumstances.

We made a run for it on the third day, arriving in Almerimar, our provisioning destination, five hours later. We went through our usual 'landing in port' routine which was never a small job for the two of us. Fenders and dock lines were secured to the boat in preparation for landing at the harbourmaster's dock. Then when we moved the boat to the assigned berth, we often needed to move the fenders and lines to the opposite side. Four dock lines, including a mooring bow line were readied before backing in. To protect the stern lines from wearing on concrete wharves, stainless steel chains were shackled to the lines. The dinghy was lowered in order to rig up the passerelle (gang plank) which is an art in itself for two people to manage. If the berth was subject to surges, we added dockline snubbers. Frequently, after arrival and plugging the electrical cord into Spanish shore receptacles, we discovered the boat was receiving reversed polarity requiring the plug on the electrical cord to be rewired. If our plumbing didn't fit the shore water connection, one of us needed to trudge back to the office to borrow a local sized fitting for our hose. These inconsistencies, while visiting marinas along the Costa del Sol, happened over and over again. No standard fitting ever existed on anything, even in Spanish terms.

After we were settled, and all of the above completed, we learned everything in Almerimar was closed for a three day local holiday.

Spain has so many holidays that locals can't even give you a straight answer when asked how many are celebrated. Each city and town celebrates local saints as well as national saints, national culture, local culture, national feast days, local feast days, fiestas and carnivals. In August, when most Spanish take vacations, numerous shops and businesses close for the entire month. To the traveller, all this can be a nightmare, especially when you need to take on provisions.

We had obviously bedded the team down in the wrong port.

We left the following morning without provisions.

IN Sotogrande, our next stop, unseasonable southwest winds kept us in port two days. When we got the chance, we inched our way towards Gibraltar where we joined other boats waiting for favourable weather to the Canary Islands.

For six days we sat protected in Queens Quay Marina while fierce weather patterns stirred up the Atlantic Ocean. It was hard to believe that forty-five knot winds were kicking up just outside the door of our placid marina. According to the weather faxes, it appeared day seven would be the time we could leave. But more headwinds were in the forecast and the weather window for the passage was only four or five days.

As the day approached, sailors from across Europe spoke of little else than of weather. A buzz ran through the marina of shared information. Everyone was anticipating getting away from dock.

Several sailors talked of forming groups and proceeded to set up radio times to communicate while en route. We were to be part of a fleet but when the time came, we were the only boat ready and we left alone. This would be our first offshore passage with just the two of us.

Given the preceding days of high winds it wasn't surprising that we were soon met by sizable Atlantic swells.

GIBRALTAR TO CANARY ISLANDS

*You will find whatever you need under
everything that you don't need in the
furthest reaches of any storage area
if you know which compartment
to look into in the first place.*

AUTHOR UNKNOWN

BEFORE LEAVING GIBRALTAR we upgraded our fishing gear. We visited a fishing supply store and described what type of trolling we wanted to engage in. We only wanted to catch small sized fish. Large species would be difficult to get onboard and handling them could be dangerous. The owner suggested a new pole, some fancy lures and a heavy duty line.

Shortly after leaving Gib, we slipped the new carbon pole from its plastic case and fixed it to the new rod holder we had attached to the stanchions. One of the expensive lures that was meant to sink without the help of weight, bobbed along the surface, creating a greater likelihood of attracting sea birds than a fish. When we pulled it in, the finish had not held up well. Its iridescent colours looked as though it already had gone through a few long toothed battles.

Within fifteen minutes the rod holder wobbled furiously and the grip fell from the rod handle into the water.

Fishing was not turning out to be one of our fortes.

NINE hours out of Gibraltar, we initiated our watch system. I went to bed. It was power boat weather and it looked as though we had a night of motoring ahead of us. That usually meant good napping. But ten minutes after I was down, Mike reported the transmission fluid had leaked from the engine and we needed to shut it down to find the source.

With a freighter coming up on our stern and a fishing fleet straight ahead, we drifted in confused seas without wind or power. It was nearly dark. We donned life jackets, grabbed flashlights and made our way across the aft deck in rolling seas. We dug out the spare fluid from under an assortment of lines, fenders and sails from the lazarette locker.

The 'engine room' was well over 38°C (100°F) when we crammed our torsos together to bend over the hot engine while trying to protect our arms from burns. Rolling around in an overheated cabin, with the smell of diesel fuel isn't one of my favourite tasks, even if it is with a loved one.

We cleaned up the spill, replaced the transmission fluid with our last container and hoped that the leak was caused by a screw cap not properly seated. If fuel continued to escape, we would lose the use of the engine and need to return to Gibraltar under sail. We checked the engine room hourly for escaping fluid but tightening the screw cap seemed to have rectified the problem.

On the second day, I was having an afternoon sleep when I was woken by the sound of a freighter's warning blast. I jumped out of bed to find Mike sitting at the navigation station looking rather blasé about the threatening signal.

"Is that blast for us?" I asked, panic stricken.

"What blast?"

"That freighter's horn!," I yelled.

He looked back at me blankly.

"Freighter's horn?" he asked softly.

"Yes! Freighter's horn!" I repeated anxiously.

Casually he turned and climbed the stairs.

Honestly, sometimes he moved like he was wearing ankle weights. I was freaking out that some freighter was about to knock us into marine history and he was doing the stairs like he was knee deep in mud.

Once in the cockpit, he took a 360° scan of an empty ocean. He returned to the salon giving me that blank, irritating look of his. He actually cocked his head like I was daft.

"I don't see anything," he calmly reported.

That calmness of his really irritated me sometimes. And you know what I wanted to do with that little smirk.

OK, OK, maybe I had been dreaming. Had my life become so focused on life aboard a boat that I was now dreaming of threatening ships?

As we proceeded down the coast of Africa, sailing thirty to sixty miles off shore, I noted the name, Casablanca on the chart. How exotic was that? I thought. And we were so close!

I couldn't believe I was so near to this fascinating continent. I had spent hours when I was young studying Africa; that far off land of naked breasts, nose bones and loin cloths depicted in my parents' *National Geographic* magazines. And there I was. So close.

We considered making a stop to visit an African port, but sailor VHF chat informed us the coast was ill equipped to handle yachts and somewhat unfriendly to strangers.

Two hours before the sun disappeared below the horizon, a pod of dolphins joined us to play in our bow wake, entertaining us with their game of 'dodge the ship'. Like silver torpedoes they charged at the bow to rebound playfully to the surface. And then as quickly as they had come, they left.

An hour later they returned, or their cousins did, recharged to jump even greater heights while jet streaming through the evening's tangerine, sun-painted waves. Their visits always made me feel as if I too were part of the ocean and I almost felt as wild and carefree as they were.

On the fourth day, the outline of the Canary Islands, (Islas Canarias) came into view. I knew from experience not to get too eager about sighting land. It could take us hours to catch up to the horizon. A few weeks earlier, while approaching Gibraltar, the mountain had loomed in the distance under a hazy mass. It had taken hours before this great giant had grown out of the sea, and then more time for us to reach it. I could have sworn the rough outline of rock had been backing away from us.

Just off the northwest coast of mainland Africa, the Island of Dogs, named later Canary Islands (Canarias), was named for neither birds nor canines but for what is thought to have been a species of Monk Seals. The archipelago sits only sixty-two miles off Africa's northwestern coast.

Graciosa Island (Islas Graciosa), the smallest of the inhabited Canary Islands, is a quiet and serene islet attracting little tourism. Located only fifteen minutes from its parent island, Lanzarote, and separated by narrows, El Rio Strait, it lies tucked away like an undiscovered jewel. Defined by red rugged cliffs and desert-like sand, the Strait lead us into Playa Francesca, where we dropped anchor. Dog-tired and exasperated when the anchor wouldn't catch, we moved around the corner into the sheltered cove of Bahia del Salado just off the low, desert-like scrubland of Graciosa Island.

WE woke before dawn to the *putt putt* of a single piston diesel. A barrage of Spanish dialogue beckoned me to the porthole. I spotted two men in a small, open fishing tug heading out to sea. I immediately imagined the pocket-sized tug tossing in rough seas and was glad I wasn't part of their adventure.

Perhaps they weren't going far I thought. Often old fishermen here, armed with only pole and line, direct their open crafts towards sea moistened rocks, where peering through glass boxes, they search for *vieja* (parrot fish).

Graciosa Island is small. Most residents live modest lives in the village of Caleta del Sebo. Not much more than desert sand and bare volcanic rock, the island has been protected from grand schemes of development and hasn't changed much in years.

Low motel-like boxy square bungalows stood facing sand strewn streets. White-washed and trimmed either blue or green, front doors opened to postage sized fronts where a single sparse-looking cactus or chunky, terra cotta pot added bits of simple ornamentation. Uncluttered and clean, nothing was out of place. Suggesting a vacant Mexican village on the verge of a shootout, I wouldn't have been surprised to see bounty hunter, Clint Eastwood* squinting from beneath a leather Stetson, Toscano cigar between his teeth and a burgundy coloured poncho thrown over his shoulder revealing a holstered colt 45.

It wasn't until the second day that we saw any form of life in the village when a woman swept sand in front of her bungalow erasing imprints of wandering footsteps. Further down the street, three children kicked a soccer ball.

The rest of the island is compacted, wind resistant sand except for rugged, paved fields of contorted black magma. Long, vacant beaches, swept by continuous sea breezes, almost always lay under clear, blue Canary Island skies. Sprinkled with glittering basalt and quartz, they shine like a covering of sea salt and pepper.

No vehicles are allowed on the island except for a few old Land Rovers.

---

* Clint Eastwood starred in a film series known as The Man with No Name. Director, Sergio Leone, released the first of the spaghetti western trilogy, A Fist Full of Dollars in 1964.

THE few small docks, adjacent to the village, offered no amenities for the disheveled sailboats that used them. The lack of water or electricity seemed to have no effect on the decision to live there. Walking into town with plastic containers was part of the lifestyle just as were the cockeyed canopies jerry-rigged over cockpits and the empty water cans strewn in disarray across decks. Solar panels sucked up sun energy and wind generators whirled at high speeds manufacturing battery power.

There is no need for amenities if the focus is to escape the rest of the world.

Everything on the island seemed undersized. Even the old fishermen were of slight stature. Miniature rowboats held only a single person with light fishing tackle and an outing's small catch. At the end of the day, weathered scarred fishermen helped carry each other's run-abouts up the beach safe distance from incoming tides. They loaded their Styrofoam coolers into wheelbarrows then pushed catches over sucking sand towards a pickup truck at the end of the harbour. Sheltered by straw hats and baggy pants, they gathered to have their catches weighed. Standing among fish permeated air, they stood drawing on cigarettes discussing the day's catch and learning of news from the mainland.

CANARY ISLANDS: LANZAROTE, GRAN CANARIA

The most beautiful thing we can experience is the mysterious
ALBERT EINSTEIN

MARINA RUBICÓN, ON the island of Lanzarote, lays just fifty nautical miles around the corner from Graciosa. The marina reception pontoon, usually an office located at the very far reaches of everything, was instead, located next to a bar offering a chance to sip an arrival beer before tying to your appointed slip. Like so many of the Spanish marinas we visited, Marina Rubicón was new construction where far more money had been invested than would ever be seen in return. There were waterfront restaurants, alcoves for future shops and boutiques awaiting vendors. Just up the hill, the Hotel Volcan, a five star hotel, sported a lobby of real volcanic rock resembling the inside of a volcano. Massive areas of cut stone plazas and walkways in and around amenities and future conveniences presented an upscale marina lifestyle.

So pristine and picture perfect is the island of Lanzarote one might think the small island had been architecturally planned from the beginning of time. But nature had a big hand in setting the tone when, in the mid-1930s six years of spewing and sputtering sent the insides of a hundred volcanoes to flood numerous valleys and flow across plains, filling in salt marshes as liquid lava raced towards the sea. When cooled, the topography mirrored much of what had taken place in the early 1700s, leaving more expansive fields of cooled, rugged black lava.

Years later, when the island witnessed an increasing number of visitors seeking the easy-to-reach land of sunshine and beaches, César Manrique a famous Spanish artist and architect who had incorporated a collapsed lava tube into the build of his own home, played a crucial role in planning and designing the island by merging an inhospitable feature of nature with tourist infrastructure. His designs include a café imbedded in lava and a concert hall located in a walkable lava tunnel.

Strict development regulations followed, demanding that houses be whitewashed with a limited assortment of trim colours. Even garbage bins were designed not to compete with the landscape. Billboards were not allowed and buildings were permitted to be no higher than a palm tree. But when tourism became a major influence on the economy, greed overcame respect and a corrupt government has since been charged with tendering illegal building permits for several high rise hotels constructed along the island's coasts.

The only island in the world to receive the distinguished classification of UNESCO's biosphere site, now teeters on the brink of losing the prestigious award.

NATURE on the island appears as Earth in its infancy. Not long ago fertile plains and villages existed. Now a twisting black gravel road crunches beneath the tires of tour buses while they steer around volcanic cones, craters and grotesquely shaped hardened lava drippings. So much lava spewed from surrounding mountains that the flow added 8 km (5 mi.) to the coastline, some of it sculpting monumental sized cliffs.

Hot sink holes under volcanic pressure still shoot steam to great heights. A restaurant cooks lunch for tourists over one of the open pits where dried brush ignites immediately on contact with the heat in one of the holes.

Although vegetation is scarce, the gritty volcanic plains allow for the growth of vegetables and wine grapes. But it is necessary to dig foot-diameter craters for every newly planted piece of vegetation. In a land that receives only 13 cm (5.5 in.) of rain a year, the lava stones piled around each plant help to retain dew that might lightly wet the plants in the evening.

While travelling down a country road in the northern part of the island, we came across a small sign hanging carelessly from a rugged lava outcrop, a sign as innocent as any child's attempt to announce a sale of lemonade.

Skewered letters on a weathered board called our attention to the fact we had reached Cueva de los Verdes, the longest volcanic tunnel in the world.

An eruption of Monte Corona, four thousand years ago, flowed towards the ocean, covering seven kilometres (four miles). Flows of lava cool first from the top forming crusty surface layers, while the magma below flows freely, creating numerous underground galleries and caves.

Island residents once used the caves to hide from pirates and African slave traders. Years later, families sought protection again when they attempted to escape lava flows from another volcanic explosion.

Following a tour guide, we entered the tunnel where rapidly flowing lava had collapsed the surface. Crudely sculpted steps, wide enough for a single entry, lead us into the interior of the tunnel.

Nothing creates the ambience of adventure and mystery better than a small dimly lit entrance purportedly leading to the bowels of the earth. Depths have always been intriguing: *Twenty Thousand Leagues Under the Sea,*[*] cosmic journeys into the infinite universe, black holes, bottomless lakes and

---

[*] *Twenty Thousand Leagues Under the Sea* — A classic science fiction novel by French writer, Jules Verne. The book was published in 1870. A movie by the same name, *20,000 Leagues Under the Sea*, was produced by Walt Disney in 1954.

fiery volcanic caldrons summon the more adventurous to go deeper.

Slowly, we proceeded downwards navigating around tightly formed turns to reach caverns Cabeza del Monstruo (The Monster's Head), La Cripta (The Crypt), and Horno del Diablo (The Devil's Furnace). Light was subdued but the air surprisingly warm. The low ceiling of the twisted path required us at times bend at the waist to avoid hitting our heads. At the end of the path we entered a vast cavern where liquid lava had years before squeezed around mountainous bellies of grey rock and dripped from oozing ceilings.

Cathedral ceiling heights soared to second and third levels where gaping cavities and tunnels lead even further into dark, gloomy unknowns.

As we climbed makeshift steps to an upper level, we were cautioned to stay alert where ledges fell away to bottomless pits.

Progressing along a second tunnel, we entered caverns where soft lighting dramatically enhanced reliefs and textures of oxidized iron reds, soft hues of ochre and glittery sparkles of salt deposits. One of the caverns was used as an auditorium where the Visual Music Festival of Lanzarote holds concerts throughout the year. Surely musicians do not have to drag their oboes and double basses through narrow passages over uneven floors we wondered, but apparently they do.

It was Halloween on our last night in Marina Rubicón. We had no idea what the Druid celebration night might mean in a Spanish marina, but following a North American calendar, we placed a lit pumpkin on our coach roof and purchased a few treats. You can find children in almost every large marina, children spending some or perhaps all of their youth travelling the world by sea with their parents. Later that night we were pleasantly surprised to hear the tap, tap, tap of little fists on our hull. "Trick or treat," they yelled.

WE LEFT LANZAROTE around 1700 for an overnight trip to Las Palmas. A gentle breeze blew across the stern filling our sails. Sailing downwind often causes me to feel ill, especially in light airs and choppy seas. Typically, we wallowed from side to side and I spent my shift sitting in the companionway hoping to stave off sea sickness while taking breaths of the fresh ocean air. Lightning flashes quivered among a blanket of clouds like an old fluorescent bulb.

It was a quiet evening and an opportunity for me to reflect on the purpose of our travel to the largest of the Canary Islands, Gran Canaria. It was there we would welcome our friends from Canada who would help us to sail the trans-Atlantic passage. Our plan was to join a rally, the Atlantic Rally for Cruisers an annual event enabling cruising yachts to set sail in company and end their crossing at the same point. At the time, it was the largest trans-oceanic sailing event in the world.

3

Crossing The Atlantic Ocean

Preparation
Days Leading up to Departure
Crossing the Atlantic Ocean

Crossing an ocean in a small yacht is a bit like living your life backwards. At the beginning you die, then you get fitter and younger, and then when you arrive you have an orgasmic celebration and the idea that life is just beginning.

Douglas Graeme

PREPARATION

*Before anything else preparation
is the key to success*
ALEXANDER GRAHAM BELL

AFTER FIVE HUNDRED years there's not much improvement to be made on the classic trade route Christopher Columbus used when searching for India. The idea is to sail south, find the tradewinds and let them blow you west. But it's best not to leave the Canary Islands before late November in order to avoid any lagging hurricanes that might still be hovering in and around Caribbean waters. The winter tradewinds will just be developing. Just the thought of sixteen to twenty days of sailing downwind is enough to make me nauseous.

WE had sailed with the ARC fleet two years previously, crewing for another skipper. This year, as owners and skipper of our own boat, it was our responsibility to provide a safe passage. Our mission would be to sail as quickly as possible, avoid bad weather, feed and water five people for sixteen to twenty days, avoid injury and keep the crew happy. Mutiny can be so nasty.

We needed to prepare for storms as well as light winds that would extend our passage. Emergency provisions included canned food in the event the refrigeration and freezer failed and bottled water if we lost water making capabilities. Our desalinating watermaker had the ability to produce 100 litres

(21 Imp./26 US gallons) per hour using power from the generator. To back it up, we carried one litre of bottled drinking water per person per day totaling approximately 100 litres. Ray, who had returned to sail across the Atlantic, suggested if we were so concerned about running out of water, why not drink the wine and save the water?

We carried sixty cans of sodas, seventy-two cans of beer, twenty litres of UHT milk, ten litres of juice and three bottles of champagne to help celebrate special occasions; our shipmates had no problem thinking of reasons to celebrate.

My galley was equipped with a three burner, gimbaled stove including oven, microwave, a spacious freezer, a refrigerator that was easy to access and a breadmaker. I had chosen a three burner stove to accommodate using a large pot for cooking pasta and lobster. With such a galley, I would be hard pressed to find an excuse not to provide good meals.

The cockpit table was equipped with a refrigerated compartment that we used to stock beverages. This allowed me to take control of the refrigerator and for the most part, keep those pesky seamen from crushing the more delicate produce in the refrigerator or holding the door open for great lengths of time because they couldn't find what they had not put back in the original spot in the first place. There was no guessing here, I was the warrior woman of the galley — Amazon Donna.

Fresh produce and a variety of meals was a priority and without a grocery store just around the corner I knew it would be a challenge. I needed to know every ingredient I was to use and for me to have that information, I planned every meal, two meals a day for twenty days. Not that I would follow the menu plan, but I would know what I was capable of making.

Breakfast was a get your own cereal, fruit, and yogurt, although at times, I would bake muffins, cinnamon rolls and breakfast bars which I thought would be appreciated since the cereal we provided was high in fibre, and, to some, would taste like cattle fodder. I felt one of my jobs was to keep my boys regular.

Preparation was paramount and I made several dry mixes to make baking possible in rough conditions, at the same time simplifying galley clean up. Corn bread mixes, muffins, hot roll mixes, bread mixes, cookies and loaf mixes, and stove top stuffing for the pressure cooked roast chicken. I froze cheese stuffed potatoes to accompany the roast beef, pastry to make quiche, precooked lasagna, and cooked chicken that I could use to make chicken enchiladas, Caribbean banana pasta, soups and salads. Humus freezes well and by the time Happy Hour rolls around, everyone is ready for a snack whether it's smoked salmon on crackers or simply a bowl of nuts.

Our freezer was stocked with forty-two chicken breasts, twenty-five chicken thighs, five pounds of ground beef, six pounds of sliced beef, five pounds of thickly sliced good quality steak, a beef tenderloin and a pot roast. Five pork chops, a three pound pork rolled loin, a leg of lamb and five salmon steaks. You would have thought we were headed for the northern waters of the Qikiqtaaluk Region in the Canadian territory of Nanuavut rather than the sunny Caribbean.

In order to locate any of these animal parts, I organized the freezer by placing the beef, poultry, pork, and lamb into large coloured shopping bags I had purchased at a dollar store. A different coloured bag for red meat, chicken and fish, with each package of meat colour coded so that I could distinguish it at a glance. The red sticker indicated five chicken breasts, the blue sticker indicated four to a package and so on. This may appear to be unnecessary work but I knew that the less time I spent standing on my head inside the freezer, I would be a happier cook. The irony was that the condensation that formed on the bags before getting them into the freezer glued everything together the size of a slaughtered hog, resulting in having to unload almost the entire freezer the first time I dug in. After separating the frozen mass, the plan worked perfectly. I listed everything in a book that went into the freezer and crossed off what I used. At least that was my intention. Whether I followed through with my own plan or not, the meat was at least packaged and vacuum packed with the number of pieces I might need for the dish I was going to prepare.

I should have been awarded the Order of Efficiency.

This was far more meat than we would need to cross the Atlantic Ocean but I wanted to keep those carnivore-loving male creatures onboard content,* and the Canary Islands was an excellent place to stock up. Once landed in the Caribbean, we would be at the mercy of the food available in the islands including their tough, scrawny chickens.

I made a list of storage compartments: behind the settee, forward, under the seats, indicating port and starboard, and a floor layout plan of the bilge space available, numbering the floor boards while listing the items we stored under them. We placed plastic baskets and shallow kitty litter trays in the spaces available in the bilge which held many of our fruits and vegetables and bottled drinks.

Not ever having been much of a sandwich eater, I preferred to serve an onion, cheese and smoked salmon pie, a rice and vegetable salad served with Indonesian peanut dressing, tortellini salad with wasabi dressing, or maybe a pressure cooked salmon soufflé or cold seafood mousse made with a fresh caught Dorado for lunch.

A soup pot is one of my favourite lunches and leftovers are often featured in my stew-like concoctions.

---

* In the 18th and early 19th centuries, seamen aboard Royal Naval vessels were issued one pound of bread and a gallon of beer per day. In addition, a meagre supply of salted meat, dried pease (peas) and oatmeal were divvied out to each man.

WITH long distance cruising, it's sometimes the little things that make a big difference; a side dish of tempura, a Popsicle on a hot afternoon, or a dish of homemade ice cream at the end of a rough day.

When I finally had my grocery list completed, I had two long pages of provisions to find in a well-stocked store but where all labels were printed in Spanish: beberechos, alemjas, ventresca de atun! What were these things? I could have easily bought cat food and not known.

The El Corte Inglés advertised available translators but I was not the only one provisioning and it took me hours by myself to decipher the packaging resulting in buying items that were not what I thought they were. Whole canned tomatoes turned out to be pureed and when the rinse water in the washing machine started to foam, I realized I had purchased liquid soap rather than liquid rinse. The simplest items we find at home were sometimes not available. Pickles, chocolate cake mixes, peanut butter, canned salmon, powdered Gatorade, chocolate chips, and frozen concentrated juices were some that I never found. Breakfast cereal was almost nonexistent except for small boxes of a German brand of muesli that would have been exceptionally costly for my stocking purposes. Luckily we still had a good amount of cereal that we had purchased in Spain and it was free of weevils, one of the perils of storing dry cereals and flour for long periods in warm conditions.

IN preparation for mechanical failure, we had stocked spare parts to replace and repair bilge pumps, fridge and freezer pumps, vacuum pumps, watermaker pumps and air con pumps. We had plumbing spares, winch and sail repair kits, toilet kits and rigging kits, engine and generator parts, impellers, fan belts, and anodes. Holding tank filters, fuel, oil and racor filters were all organized and labeled and we recorded where they could be found.

Hydraulic rig cutters, a powerful tool that can be used to cut away the rod rigging supporting the mast, was stored in an easy-to-reach cupboard. In the event of a dismasting, a swinging mast can hole a boat and cause it to sink.

Our safety equipment was extensive. Two throwing lines with floats plus a Jon Buoy Recovery Module, an inflatable life ring equipped with apparatus allowing for an out-of-water lift were attached to the stern rail in readiness of 'man overboard'. A six man liferaft fitted with parachute flares, high energy food rations, simple fishing equipment, drinking water and other supplies to meet emergency needs. A 'ditch' bag, a bright yellow valise we kept near the companionway, was filled with necessities needed to survive several days in the six man liferaft. The bag contained six thermal blankets, a Swiss army knife, flares, rubber liferaft patches, flashlight and extra batteries, sun screen, edible power bars, vitamins, sugar, Gravol capsules, plastic bags, hand bearing compass, First Aid Kit, a submersible hand held VHF radio with extra battery, and a hand held watermaker. Drinking saltwater results in the shrinkage of human cells and can result in death.

Instructions for these pieces of equipment were enclosed in a plastic bag. I added a pair of reading glasses. I also included toothpaste and brushes. I figured the taste of toothpaste might be the one thing that could bring normalcy to an otherwise dire situation.

The ditch bag included an EPIRB (Emergency Position Indicating Radio Beacon) which when triggered sends a signal indicating the location of the registered EPIRB to ground-based rescue authorities. Information such as type of vessel, make and length, are included at time of registering the EPIRB. After receiving an SOS signal from an EPIRB, the ground station alerts Mission Control Center which in turn notifies the Coast Guard or Air Force

Rescue Coordination Center nearest to the vessel's location. The apparatus, which works with an orbiting satellite system, resembles a large flashlight. GPS enabled EPIRBS can determine the position of a vessel within accuracy of 50 metres (164 feet).

A second EPIRB was mounted near the companionway. If abandoning ship, this EPIRB was to be unclipped from its wall mount and taken to the liferaft along with the ditch bag.

Our emergency supplies included two medical kits. One kit was stocked with household Band-Aids, skin preparations, a clinical thermometer and medications for colds and gastrointestinal upsets. The second kit, included antibiotics, prescription painkillers and trauma supplies such as wound dressings and immobilizing splints. Syringes, intravenous supplies, scalpel and blades were available in the event remote medical care facilities were not equipped with sterile instruments. I knew how to use the blood pressure cup and stethoscope.

Aids for navigation, included Admiralty Charts and cruising guides for Caribbean waters. Internet was not available without great cost and we eventually accumulated a small library of cruising guides, pilot books, books on world routes, weather, radio and satellite communications and practical information such as formalities when entering countries. Repair manuals covered pumps, engines, motors, furling gear, winches, refrigeration and electronics. When away from shore, self-sufficiency is crucial.

The boat was well equipped and we wore life vests with personal strobe lights and used tethers to secure ourselves to well anchored pad eyes during night hours and rough conditions.

Before our sailing friends arrived, they had already received an informative document outlining what would be supplied such as life jackets, toiletries, towels etc. Also included was a summary of *Baccalieu III's* rules regarding personal safety regulations and the drinking of alcohol.

When crewmembers arrived, each was instructed where to locate and how to use lifesaving equipment, radios, phones, fire extinguishers, and emergency tiller. They were asked to read a booklet designed to assist them in carrying out emergency procedures. The booklet with red cover, was stored in the navigation table. It contained the following:

- ~ How to activate search & rescue using the VHF, SSB, SAT C, satellite phone and EPIRB.
- ~ Boat identification including *Baccalieu* spelled in NATO phonetic alphabet.
- ~ How to activate the masthead strobe light.
- ~ How to call a Mayday, Pan Pan.
- ~ Man overboard procedures.
- ~ Illustrations how to use life saving equipment including how to launch and board the life raft.
- ~ Search and rescue patterns to locate man overboard.
- ~ Locations of bilge pumps; what to do when an alarm sounds (indicating high water levels); locating a manual hand pump.
- ~ A diagram to locate thru-hulls.
- ~ How to steer using auto pilot control, (if steering cable was severed).
- ~ Location of emergency tiller.
- ~ How to use smoke flares, rocket flares and hand-held flares.
- ~ What to do in the event of a demasting (where to locate hydraulic rig cutters, how to rig a VHF antenna etc.).
- ~ Locating portable GPS and spare laptop in case of navigation computer failure.

DAYS LEADING UP TO DEPARTURE

*One cannot think well, love well,
sleep well, if one has not dined well*
VIRGINIA WOOLF
ESSAY, WOMEN AND FICTION
FORUM 1929

THE DOCKS FILLED quickly with boats arriving daily from Europe. Two hundred and twenty-four sailboats would make up this year's ARC fleet. Each participant had their own reasons for joining. There were those returning to North America with new boats they had purchased in Europe. Others were embarking on around-the-world adventures. Most participants however, just wanted to experience an Atlantic Ocean crossing. Something they could check off their bucket list. Fifteen boats would have children aboard; one child would be turning one year old on the day of departure. A seventy-one year old father would crew for his son in a double handed crossing aboard a Warrior 40. A recently married couple decided to spend their honeymoon double handing a Westerly Oceanlord 48. The Douglas family, including their eight year old daughter, decided to move aboard their Prout Escale 39 catamaran to experience some adventure following the father's recovery from a near fatal medical problem. People came from all walks of life but hardly anyone ever spoke of former occupations. Love of the sea was our bond.

Several boat builders were represented in the fleet; Beneteau, Bavaria, Hallberg Rassy, Swan, Oyster, Faar, one Moody, and a host of yachts I wasn't familiar with. There was also a division of SuperMaxi yachts, ready for some serious racing. The average size boat was 14.50 metres (47.57 feet).

THE CRUISING BOATS had tied stern-to to the dock. With aft cockpits facing in the same direction, the arrangement offered as much sociability as a tailgate party. Country flags flew from sterns like an international convention; tri colours of Germany, the coat of arms of Spain, crosses of Norway, the five stars of Australia's Southern Cross, the United States, Finland, Belgium, Sweden, Great Britain, British Virgin Islands, Ireland, Italy, Portugal and a slew of others.

We immediately felt connected with our new neighbours knowing we would be comrades at sea. We had, after all, come for the same purpose; we were almost of the same blood.

As we passed each other on the docks that week, sharing local information that might be helpful with preparations, drifters continued to cruise docks in hopes of finding a ride to the Caribbean. A young Canadian couple, who were attracted to their country flag flying from our stern, approached us. We could not offer them passage but we welcomed them into our lives for the short period we were at dock, and offered them a few hours' work to help them earn some money.

During the official opening, those who owned code signal flags ran lines of the small flags from the top of their masts to the sterns of their boats. Flapping like a swarm of brightly coloured butterflies, the flags fluttered ceremoniously over the more serious preparations taking place below. Battleship flags, pennants, burgees, house flags, anything that could be run up a halyard waved in the breezes until the entire marina was an autumn of colour rippling in the wind.

Four days before we were to leave, all those taking part in the ARC joined together to form a parade. We followed a local band around the marina while we all marched and danced proudly behind our national flags. Twenty-five countries were represented in the ARC, but we were the only boat to fly a Canadian ensign.

As part of the celebration, ARC participants prepared for the Don Pedro's annual dinghy race, a race fraught with sabotage against anything that could be overloaded with passengers and remain afloat. Costumed participants manned long range squirt guns and tossed water balloons from small boats. Dinghies were rammed and capsized while concoctions of peanut butter and brews of mud sought out the enemy. Fine displays of seamanship!

A WEEK before the Rally started, crews and friends began to arrive. The population in the marina grew in leaps. Duffle bags rolled in thunking tones down wooden walkways piling up in front of boats. Newly arrived city slickers were easy to identify with their brisk gait and recently cut hair styles. Suddenly, evenings that had just days before been quiet, were now interrupted by music and languages from around the world.

Ray from Vancouver Island and Arthur and Bob from Toronto, all competent sailors, joined us for the crossing. Overnight, our two person world became five and soon, soft sided luggage overwhelmed our salon. The head pumps pumped more frequently and the coffee cups multiplied in the sink.

Then I discovered there were no restaurants within walking distance of the marina and as a result, preparing dinners for five suddenly became part of the daily routine. Provisions that were meant for the passage were consumed and I began to worry as I had forgotten to figure in that five people would need to eat the week before we left.

Morning chatter, uncommon on the two person boat, filled the air with news from home; politics, world crisis, weather and updates about friends and families. The overwhelming camaraderie was a jolt to our system. We had suddenly become a group rather than a couple.

THE ARC organization offered seminars in First Aid at Sea, Offshore Emergencies, Provisioning, Navigation and Weather. Dinners and cocktail parties had been organized where we met other cruisers. It was nice to be able to put faces to the voices we would hear later over the radio. After attending the functions, we walked home. Hundreds of code flags blew aloft flapping and snapping crisp beats in the warm brisk tradewinds. You couldn't help but feel excitement while walking down the docks.

IT RAINS TWO weeks a year in Las Palmas and three of those days took place while we were tied to the dock. We used the time for indoor chores and to track down fresh produce that we wanted to load nearer the departure date. Purchasing from a farmers market allowed us to avoid buying previously chilled produce which will rot more quickly when stored at room temperature after having been refrigerated. We wanted them fresh from the ground so that they could be stored under the floor boards next to the bilge.

The covered farmers market had long counters stocked with orchard fresh fruits, homemade jams, butters, breads, fresh farm eggs and herbs. But Arthur and I hardly had a chance to look around before a vendor approached us with an offer to take us to the cellar where the freshest produce was stored.

You can be sure I would never have ventured to the basement storage rooms alone, but with Arthur, I had no reservations about following the seller down crude concrete stairs where a cool climate met us at the bottom. A roughly finished corridor lead past several large root cellars piled with potatoes, pineapples, melons, kiwis, oranges and cabbages. I was surprised to see crates overflowing with apples.

The vendor offered to deliver the produce, not only to the marina, but right to the stern of our boat the day before we were to depart.

Arthur and I set about to hand select every one of the thirty-two tomatoes, numerous lemons, oranges, zucchini, radishes and braids of garlic bulbs. Pineapples, kiwis, melons, apples, ginger, squash, cabbage, onions, potatoes and carrots would eventually find their way into our bilges, while the more delicate produce such as lemons, beans, asparagus, zucchini, broccoli, lettuce, radishes, cucumbers, bok choy and leeks would be stored in the refrigerator beside the oil covered chopped parsley and basil I had stored in jars.

When the vegetables and fruits were delivered to the boat, we washed most of them in a solution of water and bleach to eliminate insects, then let them dry a short time in the sun, turning each piece to allow for complete drying. En route, I would check the produce frequently and use what had ripened. To back up the fresh groceries, I stocked a few packages of frozen peas and corn. There was however, very little frozen produce to be found in the Canary Islands.

LEADING UP TO departure day the marina became a lively city of dutifully focused sailors. With only a few days left, a young woman walked the docks offering to cut hair and trim beards. Groceries delivered in cardboard boxes were unloaded on deck so as not to carry cockroaches or their eggs below. Once washed and dried, produce was taken below for storage in net hammocks or under floor boards. Never having provisioned for an extended passage before, the whole procedure was an experiment of trial and error.

A stalk of green bananas was hung from the bimini and emergency water containers, some half-filled to allow them to float were placed in the lazarette. The containers would need to be thrown overboard and then retrieved from the water if the crew were to escape to the liferaft. The Oyster 'After Sales' team was on hand to check rigging, steering and engine mechanics. They offered advice on where to look for halyard abrasion and how to minimize it.

ARC officials visited each boat checking for proper safety equipment and suggested we add a second life ring as well as identify all life jackets with the vessel's name in the event of a drowning. In this way, if the body was recovered, Coastguard officials would know which boat it belonged to.

Guidelines for the Rally were set out in a handbook. In the Cruising Division the use of engines was permitted although each sailing vessel was required to sail across both starting and finishing lines. Each boat would need to document engine hours. A time penalty for those hours would be applied after arriving in St. Lucia. Upon arrival at the finish, it would be mandatory that each member of the crew sign a declaration stating the hours travelled under power.

Prizes would be given for best placed yacht on corrected time, line honours (best elapsed time without the use of an engine,) and even a bottle of champagne for first across the line after reaching St. Lucia.

Four days before leaving port we celebrated my 57th birthday. The boys decorated the boat with coloured rope lights and even gave me gifts! Mike arranged dinner in a renovated house in the old city. To this day, the boys still talk about the venue; the Spanish ambience of small tables scattered over a dimly lit brick-laid courtyard under a sky of twinkling stars. At the far end of a highly polished bar, a handsomely dressed waiter drew a long bladed knife across a bone-in Jamón Serrano lying in a stand-alone Jamónero rack. Placing the paper thin slices of smoked ham on plates, he served them with glasses of Sangrias and Spanish wine before a cuisine of soups and freshly made paella dishes.

CROSSING THE ATLANTIC OCEAN

*Twenty years from now you will
be more disappointed by the things
you didn't do than by the ones
you did so throw off the bowlines.
Sail away from the safe harbor.
Catch the tradewinds in your
sails. Explore. Dream. Discover.*

Mark Twain

TRADEWINDS IN THIS part of the Atlantic Ocean are normally driven by an Azores high-pressure system. Unusual weather patterns in 2004 had weakened the high-pressure system resulting in light tradewinds along the normal route to the Caribbean. Yachts were advised to sail as far south as the Cape Verde Islands in the quest to find better wind conditions. This would add an additional two hundred miles to the normal 2,700 nm passage.

THE FOLLOWING IS my diary while crossing the Atlantic Ocean. Days are noted from 1200 to 1200 (noon to noon) the following day. The mileage covering a twenty-four hour period, is noted beside the day. Anything less than a hundred and seventy-five miles is considered slow with a boat the size of *Baccalieu III*.

DEPARTURE day—November 21, 2004—160 nm

Before departure, every boat displays a flurry of activity. Sheets are run down decks and wound around winches. Life-saving jacklines are attached, blocks and shackles snapped into place, anchors lashed and tenders hoisted, covered and secured. Winch handles, binoculars and sailing knives come out of storage. Ports and hatches are dogged down tightly. Everything below is secured in lockers, under seat cushions or stuck anywhere they will stay in place. Crews, who had purchased more provisions than their boats could hold, leave the excess stacked on the docks. Hitch hikers ranging from certified yacht masters to never-having-sailed-before and still hoping to find last minute passages to the Caribbean, continue to pace the docks. Dock gossip tells of crewmembers drinking their night-before jitters away. Our last minute thoughts before leaving are with the owner of *Tallulah of Falmouth* who, while in the process of provisioning his boat, fell between his boat and the dock and was admitted to an Intensive Care Unit last night.

OUR start time is 1300. The racing division, with super yacht racers the likes of *Sojana*, (35 metres/115 feet) and *Leopard of London* (30 metres/100 feet), take the starting line twenty minutes before us. *Leopard* apparently has a specialized swimmer onboard—a pet gold fish.

Before leaving the dock, I took a seasick tablet.

One hundred and eighty-eight boats have been divided into three groups according to cruising division, RORC IRC racing division and multi hulls. Each yacht has been issued a handicap. We are in the Rally's cruising division, but telling most sailors that 200 boats travelling to the same destination is not a race is like telling a pack of dogs there's no need to get to the dinner bowl first.

The start line is between a navy ship and an anchored power cruiser. Minutes before the cruising division is to start, everyone tunes into their VHF radios for warning signals and countdown. The stop watches are on.

Although each division has been subdivided into fleets of approximately twenty, all one hundred and fifty cruising yachts are out on the playing field at the same time. Light airs have demanded that each boat remain close to the starting line resulting in a mass of jumbled sails and hulls pointing in every direction. The boats appear to be one gigantic confused fleet. While crews hang off forestays to peer around large genoas, helmsmen are aware their tacks will be slow and cumbersome in the light breeze that is prevalent. We sail in close proximity to each other, taking our chances.

Competitive spirits shift into first gear and many cruisers forget they are participating in a rally rather than a race with a finish line almost 3,000 nautical miles away. Other than avoiding collisions, the firing of the gun was the most exciting part of the start. All our bows were pointed towards the starting line, but we were almost motionless. We learned later that some yachts took two hours to reach the start line.

After five hours of light airs and travelling only a few miles, we decide to motor and take a penalty; in hindsight we agreed we should have turned the motor on as soon as our bow was over the line. An hour and a half out, winds fill in from the northeast and we throw up the cruising spinnaker in an ocean of short jumbled seas. Soon evening was upon us and we break our first rule. Never fly the chute (spinnaker) after dusk. The sail is huge and if we have a problem with it, the consequences will be major. Working at night is not only more difficult but dangerous for crewmembers. It's hard, however, to shut down our only hope of making any significant headway and we keep it flying throughout the night.

By midnight our fleet had dispersed and we saw only the

occasional navigation light on the horizon. By early morning, two race boats, light in tonnage flying enormous sails and previously caught in light airs, trucked past us as if we were standing still. We envied their speed.

At 0400 the wind unexpectedly gusts to 25 knots and we suddenly take off like a bullet. But 25 knots of wind is a dangerous amount of wind to handle while flying the spinnaker and we proceed to take down. In the takedown the sheet gets away from us, falls into the water and winds around under the bow, preventing the take down. Metres of sail continue to collapse and reopen in its half-doused state like a giant lung. This opening and closing causes stress on the sheets and hardware and the sail itself. It took us an hour to rectify the situation and when we pulled out the Yankee to replace the spinnaker, we discovered the Yankee's halyard was wrapped around the fore guy preventing it from being hoisted. This is no doubt the doing of the night demons.

Finally, with all problems ironed out, the beauty of the night came alive. *Baccalieu III* slices silently through the water parting the white, salty sea foam that rolls alongside. Like diamonds rolling out of a velvet bag in a James Bond movie, a sparkling of phosphorescence tumbles in the foam.

ROUTING to St. Lucia is not difficult. A few hundred years ago, tradition dictated "ships sail south until the butter melts" then turn west. Although *Baccalieu III* is equipped with modern technology, our challenge is still to find the wind while staying out of reach of unsuitable weather. To help us accomplish this, we download GRIB files containing weather data and use a professional weather service who will keep us informed of changing weather patterns. Captain and Navigator, Mike studies the GRIB files in detail.

At the time of leaving, we were advised the crossing would not be a fast one. The more direct route, following the rhumb line is attractive due to what looked like good tradewinds, but by Friday, a mid-Atlantic gale may suppress the tradewinds and bring strong headwinds to those who take that course. We take a more southerly route, one which heads towards the Cape Verde Islands.

It's a game with Mother Nature.

DAY 2 — 186 nm

Today, we headed the boat more westerly to take advantage of a steady, 10 knot breeze.

With five onboard, we divide the 24 hours into four hour shifts. Two share a watch while a third is on standby. This format gives each crewmember six hours per day off, but the off hours disappear with navigation duties, radio time, cooking, cleanup, naps and, when all hands are needed on deck for spinnaker changes, some will miss their downtime altogether.

We seldom see all five of us at one time except during the sail changes, Happy Hour and dinner. Everyone is adjusting to interrupted sleep due to motion and middle of the night sail changes.

Light airs provide their own dangers and we attach the preventer to the mainsail to limit an unexpected swing of the boom across the cockpit. An accidental gybe could cause severe damage to the equipment besides sweep someone off the deck or kill them outright on contact. The winds are so light we've had to attach a pole to the Yankee sail to keep it in play. We're also flying the diminutive sized staysail; anything that will catch some breeze we put into use.

We sometimes hear from our sister yachts and share problems, fishing stories and locations. Other times they are out of range and we wait until evening when we download the division's positions and compare notes as to how far others have travelled.

We caught *Baccalieu III's* first fish today; a small Dorado or Maui Maui. The species has a sloped forehead and the body is of beautiful iridescent greens and blues. At least it was beautiful before it died when the colour quickly drained from it turning it grey. The disappearance of its colours definitely dramatized its death.

In order to not have to wrestle with squirming fish on an unstable deck we make a quick kill by spraying inexpensive vodka into the gills. While the fish lay waiting to be filleted, Bob remarked, "The fish looks dead drunk!"

Sunset always brings out the best in dolphin play, and our 8 knots of speed was merely puppy play to the two dozen that joined us tonight. Bursting with energy, they accelerated well beyond our boat speed while darting among each other and the oncoming bow. They provide us with great entertainment.

With a bright moon illuminating our run, we swooshed along until the moon disappeared and left us in the dark. Bob and I were on duty when we spotted what appeared to be an empty container ship approaching from the stern. Under power at 10 knots, it slowly approached in a direction that would see it cross our bow at what we determined would be an unsafe distance. We reefed the Yankee to reduce speed with the intention of allowing it to pass. Unexpectedly, the ship did not pass us but slowed, matching our speed. This was a highly unusual occurrence and it caused us some concern. The ship was not showing proper navigational lights and it hovered less than a mile off our starboard beam. It made no response to our radio call.

The ship continued to keep pace with *Baccalieu III* while we continued under reduced speed and to make observations with binoculars. The night was dark and she continued to sit off our beam lurking without making contact. This was very odd indeed.

This part of the Atlantic does not hold a reputation for having pirates, but we watched intently for high powered dinghies racing towards us occupied by armed men who might force themselves aboard. Other than two navigational lights, one white and the second red, the ship remained in darkness.

After several anxious minutes, the ship moved forward, crossed our bow and continued with its mysterious mission. The ship had displayed unusual behaviour but the night progressed without incident and the following day my biggest problem was wrestling a package of chicken from the freezer where it had frozen together with a bundle of other food creating a small iceberg.

Day 3 — 186 nm

Everyone is getting into the swing of things now, feeling comfortable standing watches and handling the motion. We now see more of each other during daytime hours.

Our ship mates all come from sailing backgrounds and are such fun to have onboard. Easy going travellers filled with wit and humour, they each help to make every day enjoyable.

This evening we celebrated crossing the Tropic of Cancer. We are now officially in the tropics!

Day 4 — 157 nm

Ray, our fishing expert, caught a second Dorado today, a two serving size this time. We are hoping to catch another so that we can have fish for dinner tonight. But we lost our vodka spritzer overboard after it rolled off the stern following the spray-of-death we dosed that last unfortunate with. We still have half a bottle of vodka left in the cupboard but I have threatened to use the precious rum if they lose another bottle of our cheap alcohol. The incident reminded us that everything, including the fishermen, need to be tethered to the boat.

By early afternoon, it sounded as if we would get another chance at dinner when the fishing rod began to chatter in its holder. Three of us sprang into action to land the beast and the rod was handed to me so that I might experience my first catch at sea. There was so much drag, I found it challenging to even turn the handle of the reel. But determined to do it myself, I struggled with the load until I managed to pull it from the water. I couldn't believe it! Hanging off my lure was an ordinary piece of green plastic sheeting, perhaps part of a garbage bag. It was surprising how much effort was required to pull in that simple piece of material.

Tonight we broke the 'no flying the spinnaker after dusk', rule again. We had accomplished very low mileage throughout the day and using the sail appears to be our only hope of moving.

Day 5 — 157 nm

We received a World Cruising weather advisory suggesting that all boats sail as far south as possible to avoid upcoming strong southeast winds. Due to some good navigating and weather diagnosis, we are presently situated in an appropriate position to avoid the high winds. But other boats to the northeast may run straight into the winds and we hope they can ride south in time to avoid any unpleasantries.

I did a vegetable check today and noticed signs of deterioration already in both the carrots and the fennel.

It was late afternoon when the line spun out from the fishing reel again. Three of us hastily stepped across the aft deck when the rod was handed to me in hopes that I might land something more interesting than a plastic bag. It took a great effort but I reeled the fish closer and closer while we all watched it dart back and forth across the surface. It was of good size and we were sure to eat fresh fish that night. Then suddenly the reel jammed and we stood there watching helplessly while our dinner fought for its freedom. Then the 60 pound test line broke and not only did the fish escape but it took the lure with it.

Ray made sushi tonight to accompany the Dorado that he caught yesterday. The evening is perfect for cockpit dining and tonight the moon shimmers on the water like crackled silver on an antique platter. Cumulus clouds reflect the moonlight providing us with just enough light to see by. Only the nearest stars can be seen sparkling through parted clouds while a gentle wind blows over the sea offering a smooth flat ride. Being on watch on such a night is a gift.

At 0200 I complete my shift and write an entry into the log book. "Approaching four strobe lights." I note that we are approximately 800 miles off shore. (I never did determine the source of the strobe lights).

EARLY this morning the nearly full moon was still sending beams to our bow when the sun rose with warm brassy reflections off our stern. The warm day gave us two more Dorados. One got lucky and went back to grow up, the other went to the refrigerator.

DAY 6 — 169 nm

Pace has been slow; light winds prevail demanding we gybe the chute several times throughout the day. I like to do foredeck work but today, when we were gybing the sail, the mainsheet shackle came detached from the top and fell to the deck narrowly missing my head.

Our total mileage by the end of the crossing should be around 3,000 nm. We held a celebration dinner this evening in recognition of breaking into the 19° latitude with just under 2,000 nm to go.

Mike and Ray treated us to a pepper-crusted beef tenderloin dinner. It was a special treat for me to not have to prepare a meal.

DAY 7 — 127 nm

The last 24 hours has been the slowest yet and we have not seen so much as a navigation light from any other boat for two days. Even the VHF and SSB radios have fallen silent. The occasional sea bird has been spotted and flying fish land on the deck at night.

We celebrated again; this time having sailed 1,000 nm of the Atlantic crossing. Mike is good at thinking of anything to celebrate! Those who were off watch, viewed a movie while eating dinner.

TONIGHT the full moon is smothered in grey clouds but still illuminates the night like a light bulb through an opaque lampshade. Occasionally it finds a hole in the clouds, sending a beam to spotlight the green, white and blues of the labouring spinnaker hovering over the foredeck. The water is calm but we would gladly trade it for some wind and matching seas. The forecast however, advises we can expect several more days of light winds. We have at times used the engine but we realize this cannot be a long term solution. Our fuel capacity will take us between 800 to 1,000 miles. In these conditions, the chute is our most valued sail.

DAY 8 — 127 nm

Another day of travelling a mere 127 nm! Surely even sea turtles move faster than this.

The temperature is getting warmer and we are presented with the problem of staying comfortable, especially at night when our cabins are hot and humid. Opening a port might mean taking a wave, perhaps soaking a bed that would never fully dry. Most often electric fans and dorade vents are our only weapons against heat. We use the air conditioner when the generator charges the batteries which might take up to ninety minutes. If you are lucky enough to be attempting to sleep at this time you get to revel in a cool climate. But shortly after the air is turned off it takes no time for the interior of the boat to warm up again.

One morning, Ray reported he had found it to be unbearably hot in his room the previous night. After investigating, he discovered he had kicked a comforter up against his air conditioner outlet while someone had tied the spinnaker bag over his cowl vent, his only source of outdoor air!

DURING the past few days we have experienced minor problems. A foot of sea water discovered in the engine room was determined to have come from a slow leak through a hose clamp on the water separator to the generator. The second problem occurred when the generator shut down. Lying on their stomachs, Arthur and Mike peered into the bilge to discover the main water intake was sucking air, consequently drying out the impeller. They have remedied the air leakage and replaced the impeller with our last spare impeller.

DAY 9 — 137 nm

We've been flying the chute day and night. So much for rules. Having travelled 1,450 nm, we crossed our halfway point today, at least according to the rhumb line. It's a wonder that we have even gone this far but things are looking up — we added an additional 10 nm to our daily mileage today! Yea! We celebrated our successful crossing of the halfway point with a pork loin roast and a bottle of champagne.

We are taking single watches now while a standby person rests below.

DAY 10 — 166 nm

This morning we woke up to Saint Andrews day. As patron saint of Scotland you can be sure Saint Andrew never intended to offer a day of celebration to a bunch of Canadians crossing the Atlantic. But it shows how far our crewmates will go to find any excuse for festivities. Suddenly, appearing on our aft deck was our friend Bob danc'in' a Scottish jig dressed in a Tam o' Shanter, a red wig, and a green towel about his waist. Just to make sure we had our Saint Andrew's day celebration fully documented, we each posed for pictures while wearing the full head of red hair topped with Tam o' Shanter. Looking more a red headed harlot than anything representative of a distinguished Scotsman, mine will haunt me for the rest of my days.

"How many Canaries can a Scotsman put under his kilt?" asks Ray. "It depends on the size of the perch!"

DAY 11 — 134 nm

Today we congratulated ourselves for choosing the southern route and making the most of the light airs we have been wretchedly saddled with. Playing the sails in light conditions is like tuning a fine engine. Only a skilled player can get the most out of either one.

With too many sluggish days already gone by, Arthur, while venting his frustrations over the lack of wind, looked skyward, and while clenching his fists good humouredly yelled, "Is that all you have? Give us all you've got!"

I figure he's the main reason I have the following to report:

Firstly, our fishing reel jammed, and just when Ray was pulling in what could have been several tasty meals. On inspection, the gear to the rod was found to be stripped beyond repair and we will no longer be able to enjoy a pastime of fishing. Then at 0500 this morning, while still engulfed in darkness and with only one man on watch, the spinnaker halyard chaffed through letting metres and metres of collapsed spinnaker cloth, accompanied with attached sheets and guys, fall into the ocean. Bob was on duty and called for help. We bounded up the stairs to find him clutching one of the spinnaker sheets for dear life. Dragging alongside, drowning with gallons of water trapped within its folds, the spinnaker had all but disappeared beneath the sea. Having the mind of a good sailor, Arthur immediately let off the mainsail to slow the boat. The wind and current however, continued to push the hull forward making recovery difficult.

Saturated with gallons of water, the drowning sail streamlined like a piece of flat, tricoloured streaked toffee alongside the boat; its now darkened colours reminding us it once offered elegant, efficient power to our way of travel. All hands were on deck and each gave all they had to pull it in metre by heavy, sluggish metre. A soggy portion of the sail, swept behind the boat, and as we pulled it onboard over the stern, it glued itself to the dinghy like a piece of snug fitting polyethylene shrink wrap. Managing to grasp only small bits at a time, we tugged at the rest of it hoping to release it from where it had caught beneath the boat around the keel. The sail inevitably tore and, we found later, after inspecting it, tears appeared in several places rendering it useless for flying again during the passage.

With the sheets and halyard still attached to the sail, one of the dragging lines had draped over the upper lifeline placing excessive pressure on the lifeline and connecting hardware. A second line had wound around the propeller shaft several feet underwater and we had no way of seeing how badly it was tangled. I often carried a Leatherman, a multi-tool with knife, in my pocket. The spinnaker lines were pulling so tightly something had to give and we had no choice but to cut them to avoid further damage to other equipment.

When the sun rose and offered enough light to work in, Mike suited up in scuba equipment. His mission was to free the lines from around the propeller shaft. Two safety lines were attached to his scuba apparatus; one to avoid losing him and a second line to help direct him as needed. Arthur stood nearby, rigged in a self-made harness, in case an emergency arose while

Mike was in the water. Even though the wind was light, and sea conditions as good as anyone could wish for while carrying out emergency measures, Mike was unable to overcome the forces of the ocean, which caused him to drift away from the intended work site. Not until he was in the water and near the underside of the hull could he appreciate the true danger of the situation. From one perspective, our boat was riding mild swells, from another, the rise and plummeting of *Baccalieu III's* 60,000 pounds into almost invisible troughs, created hazardous conditions for a diver. It was too risky to work beneath the boat and the operation to visit the sight of the shaft was aborted. However, before climbing out, he managed to reach the streaming, submerged lines and free them. Had he not been able to accomplish that task, we would have in time, been approaching shore, unable to use the motor.

Later today, after having dried the sail, we stuffed its cheerful, but sorry, fabric into its bag and secured it to the foredeck. This was a sad moment indeed. There is no question we all felt deflated, even depressed over our loss. The chute had been our main supply of power while contending with the overall presence of light airs. It had been the main reason we had made any significant mileage whatsoever. Now, left only with white sails, our pace has severely slowed.

We still have well over 1,000 miles to go.

We heard a call for medical assistance over the VHF radio from a boat to the north of us. It was *Tallulah of Falmouth* whose owner was still in hospital due to his fall that ruptured his kidney when he fell from the dock in Las Palmas. His yacht, now in the hands of another skipper, was calling with yet another emergency; a crewmember had a heavy insulated freezer top come down on his finger.

The call for assistance made us realize, that even though there had been several opportunities for personal injury onboard *Baccalieu III*, we have had none. Losing the spinnaker suddenly becomes only a minor annoyance.

DAY 12 — 161 nm, December 2nd

I noted the date to suggest some kind of normalcy in our lives.

Last night, Arthur made a beef stroganoff dinner and today the boys gave me a gift of free time. They stood watch during one of my shifts to give me an extended time off. What a thoughtful bunch of guys.

DAY 13 — 170 nm

We celebrated having only 1,000 nm left to go with a celebratory lunch and in late afternoon we watched the DVD, Brave Heart. It seems like an odd thing to be able to do — watch a movie while sailing!

We received a Pan Pan (call for emergency assistance) from *King's Legend*, a Swan 65 (20 metres), located a few hours northwest. They have a crewmember with an exposed bone injury and were looking for assistance. We responded with an offer of medical supplies and prescription pain killers, but their real need was to locate a doctor somewhere afloat. When they were unsuccessful, they rerouted to Barbados where professional assistance is available and if necessary, international flights.

WE have been motoring since yesterday evening. We see squalls all around us but we have experienced only a small amount of rain. Tonight we enjoyed a brilliant red, glowing sunset predicting good winds for tomorrow, "Red sky at night, sailor's delight." We will be eagerly waiting.

EARLY morning brought rain followed by 15 knot winds that soon swept the sea into a liveliness we hadn't seen since we had left the Canaries. A mere 15 knots of wind but what a difference it made! For as far as we could see white crested waves surrounded us like little energetic armies.

Finally, we were reveling in some good speed. Then suddenly, the exhilarating speed came to an abrupt end. The clew of the mainsail pulled away from the sail. Two webbing straps joining the clew to the clew-plate severed clean through causing the third to stress and rip apart. This resulted in losing the attachment that held the sail to the boom. Ironically, we now had the wind, but were minus another sail.

Sailing under Yankee alone left the boat unbalanced. The surrounding swells tossed the boat about even more. Someone left the coffee pot unattended on the counter and it fell to the floor. It was filled with coffee!

If we were to go anywhere, we desperately needed the mainsail. Pooling our thoughts, we decided to drill three holes into the reinforced portion of the clew, insert three shackles, finish the job with whipping line and then reattach the outhaul. It proved to be an effective fix.

THERE was no moon when I took my midnight watch that night. Mars flickered red behind me in a sky smothered in brilliant stars. Many fell like fireworks. Occasionally I caught sight of a satellite. There is nothing as beautiful as a night such as this.

I caught sight of a tiny light flickering in the distance. It must be a masthead light. Then suddenly, a much larger light appeared straight off the stern. It took me by surprise and I wondered how I could think myself a responsible watch keeper and yet, let a ship get so near before noticing. But it turned out to be not a ship at all, but the moon lifting from the horizon. Even in its infancy, it overwhelmed the dark horizon. I watched as its girth expanded to gigantic proportions in dramatic ceremony. In no time it spilled tints of tangerine across the water in a wide, shimmering path. Its brilliance was so powerful, it obliterated the dazzling scattering of stars. Oddly enough, tonight I resented its intrusion because the stars had soothed me like a dose of spirits. But stars or no stars, Andrea Bocelli continued to sing love songs in my ear, helping to suspend me in a world outside of this one.

Then suddenly a tap on my shoulder startled me. It was Mike reporting for watch duty.

DAY 14 — 161 nm

The wind comes and goes, testing the newly shackled mainsail. It appears to be holding well.

We have 700 nm to go before landfall in St. Lucia. I took stock of the food supplies today and we are down to our last fresh fruits and vegetables. Surprisingly the tomatoes have lasted outside the refrigerator in the continuous hot conditions. Even the small tasty Canary Island oranges are as sweet as ever but the bananas seemed to suddenly ripen one day then turn to mush the next. The carrots let me down long ago. I hope everyone likes cabbage, I have lots of it.

The fuel gauge indicates we have used 400 litres of diesel. The boat should be lighter, and lighter should mean faster but we continue to make water to keep the tanks at emergency reserve levels. Five people taking showers and hand washing their clothes, is taxing on the system, but the watermaker has no problems keeping up with our demands. Several days ago, a chartered boat with 14 paying guests aboard, reported their watermaker had failed. They were rationing and saving their remaining fresh water for drinking. When they needed to shower they took salt water deck showers. We offered to rendezvous and make a transfer of water but the skipper declined. In reality, we could have not made much of a difference to the needs of 14 people.

Day 15 — 163 nm

We have wind! This feels good. Everyone in radio contact is chatty now because their approach to land will take place in a matter of a few days. They are excited with the prospects of landfall and happy to have someone new to talk with. Even a radio watchman on a container ship was happy to chat.

Five hundred miles to go and another excuse to celebrate with champagne and brunch. We spotted our first seagull. Land is out there somewhere.

Day 16 — 176 nm

Two years ago while sailing the ARC, it had taken us 16 days to reach St. Lucia. I think of this because today is our 16th day on passage and where are we? Three hundred and fifty miles from our destination — a good 2 days away at the speed we are going.

This passage has been fraught with far lighter winds than the last trans-Atlantic crossing. We've worked hard to generate miles out of weak winds. But our sailing, friends are keen and content, even though it has almost been impossible to sleep the past 48 hours. Short, rough seas cause uncomfortable conditions and we struggle to stabilize our bodies while lying down. I stuff pillows and blankets around myself but they hardly have any effect at all.

Day 17 — 170 nm

Without a spinnaker, our night sailing is far less tense but sadly, far slower.

Day 18 — December 7th — Arrival Day-177 nm

The tradewinds have finally shown up. Better late than never I guess. Winds blowing 18 to 20 knots enable us to make a steady headway of 8 to 9 knots under poled Yankee and mainsail. I think we could easily do a 200 mile day today, but who needs it now? We're coming down the home stretch with only 140 nm to go. We spent so many days putting along and now we're sailing like a vixen!

AT 0713 local time we charge the finish line on a reefed port tack with 30 degrees of heel.

After 18 days at sea, covering 2,900 nm, out of sight of others for most of the time, five boats converge at the finish line. On the radio within minutes of each other, we announce our estimated arrival times to the ARC officials, giving them a heads up that it was time to ready the rum punches. Incredible as it seems, one of our sister ships that had taken a different routing from ours, arrived almost at the same time.

A welcome committee of ARC officials was on the dock to celebrate our arrival holding a tray of breakfast rum punches and baskets of local fruits. Tired from shifts that had congealed into long, wakeful hours, some were filled with adrenalin spirit while others felt subdued with calm reality that a long voyage had come to an end.

Baccalieu III's passage time: 17 days, 22 hours, 13 minutes, 20 seconds. We had placed 9th out of 21 in our class. The record for the fastest ARC crossing by a cruising yacht belongs to a 60 foot (18 metre) British boat that sailed the Atlantic in 2003 in 11 days, 13 hours.

SEVERAL yachts had arrived before us. But even *Sojana*, the SuperMaxi Faar 115 had also been affected by light winds, her hopes dashed of setting a new course record when she sailed the passage in twelve days, five hours and forty-five seconds. On the other hand, *Ciao* the Moody 39 (12 m) with the one year old child onboard arrived several days later having taken twenty-two days to complete the passage.

We went straight to the bar, sat on seats that didn't move and enjoyed conversation with those we had heard during

SSB radio net time. Then we mustered our last bit of energy to wash down the boat and bed down gear that would not be used in the upcoming weeks while cruising the Caribbean. By afternoon, the wakeful hours caught up with us and we realized the true meaning of crashing. Deep sleep at last!

IT WAS GREAT to be on land again and we weren't the only people to feel exhilaration from the accomplishment of the crossing. Boats continued to arrive throughout the week and the bar and Rodney Bay's two small restaurants took on a daily festive atmosphere with Happy Hour taking place at all hours of the day. Local entrepreneurs happily converged on new arrivals offering services for boat washing, mechanical repairs, and laundry services. The young hair stylist we had seen walking the docks in Las Palmas had arrived in St. Lucia and was again offering services of hair cutting and beard trimming. Placing one of our round fenders on the dock, Mike and I took turns balancing, while clumps of hair fell through the wooden planks to the water. I figured this was about as low as I could get in the hair styling world, but through conversation we learned she had been a hair stylist in her home country of Scotland where she had owned her own business before setting out on this lifetime adventure of sailing. In the end, she rectified all the bad that had been previously done during my Ibiza spike episode and I walked away with a first class haircut.

RODNEY BAY LOCATED on the north end of St. Lucia is a small harbour that sleeps most of the year until almost two hundred ARC boats arrive each December. Reveling in the sudden increase in population, a local baker sells croissants and bread as fast as he can bake them while customs officers wade through a host of passports and papers that was as trying for them as it was for the newly arrived yachtsman.

In 2004 there was no such thing as a standard procedure for clearing customs in the Caribbean. In St. Lucia, yachts were officially treated as commercial shipping and shared the same rules. Even to sail from the island of Grenada to the island of Carriacou, a mere twelve miles, one needed to obtain a permit from customs. Each time a boat moved to a new anchoring spot, even when staying within the country, customs dictated that you inform them of the move. When customs were not within easy reach, a yacht was legally required to sail back to an official customs office before travelling to a new destination. If one followed the proper procedures, it could take several days just to leave one island and get to the adjacent one. Other nation islands shared this same bureaucratic nightmare. Recently, some islands made cruising easier by allowing a yacht to sail anywhere within its waters after the initial check-in. Only when leaving the nation's waters would the yacht be required to check out.

However, in 2004, when a yacht cleared into St. Lucia, one would be required to state which anchorages they intended to visit and in some cases indicate what days they planned to be there. It's not a wonder Caribbean custom officials were often cranky. Many sailors travelling within the islands don't have a plan but instead go where the wind blows them. Besides that, a mooring fee of $25 EC ($9 US) per day was charged along with the fee for the written permits. Some anchorages were part of a national park where overnight mooring fees would be applicable on top of the mooring fee already paid. The whole shemozzle was a nightmare and many boaters just nixed the whole thing and took their chances.

OVER the next few days the last of the ARC boats arrived, some pleasantly surprised to find their families standing on the dock having flown to St. Lucia from their home countries to welcome them in. Some had been at sea for over twenty-five days. *Lady Menai*, an Oyster 435, (43 ft./13 m) and *Autumn Breeze*, a Fred Parker Ketch, (47 ft./14 m), took twenty-eight days. Although arriving too late for prize giving, each boat received a Pusser's Rum Survival Kit, the prize allotted for the last yachts to cross the finish line.

The docks were abuzz as sailors continued to share stories of torn sails, snapped rigging, a leak in a keel fastening, a problem with a skeg and the wear and tear of chafed lines. One owner reported sacrificing his thongs for chafe protectors and joking, made it quite clear that it was *his* sandals, not his wife's underwear he had used for the repair. Accounts of sleepless nights, fish that got away and accidents that nearly happened made hilarious stories that kept everyone entertained for hours. And then there was the disclosure of necessary inventions. Like the drinks concocted aboard, *Between the Sheets*: 'Chafed Screwdriver' and the 'Volvo 237' in honour of their trusty engine that took them through the periods of wind draught. The skipper of the Moody 39 (12 m) reported how his spinnaker pole had repeatedly come detached from the mast and finally, one day, he said, rather enlightened, the whole track peeled away putting an end to his frustrations of having to repeatedly fix the darn thing.

Stories of unfavourable weather abounded; squalls, bruising night winds, rock and roll seas. The crew onboard a steel hulled De Vries Lentsch 38 (11.5 m) experienced several hours of torrential rain accompanied by forked lighting. When they couldn't think of anything better to do, they all went below, to bed for six hours!

One crushed finger and a broken elbow was the tally of injuries for the passage of 188 yachts. There had, however, been some close calls. When the skipper of *Cat Taloo*, working on the foredeck without lifejacket or harness, was hit in the eye with the spinnaker pole during an accidental jibe, he neither fell overboard nor lost the use of his eye. On a more serious note the racing Yacht *Auliana II*, a Faurby 424 (42 ft./13 m) lost its rudder while just seventy miles southwest of Gran Canaria. A radio call to the Spanish Maritime Rescue Service, Salvamento Maritima, brought a tug to the stricken yacht, whereupon a tow was attempted. But as seas and winds continued to build, and cleats continued to pull away from the yacht's deck, the all-German crew had to be evacuated, and the yacht left to drift, after being fitted with a Yellowbrick Iridium satellite tracker which would allow for it to be monitored and hopefully recovered.

On another yacht, a crewmember fell from the scoop of a racing boat while cleaning a dirty fuel filter. He was reported to have had the sense before completing his fall, to throw the filter back onboard, which was a good thing, since it was the only one they had. However, without the filter installed in the motor and due to the challenges of locating any victim in the sea, it took his crewmates three hours before locating him and getting him back onboard.

It was of interest to learn much later, that a Westerly Oceanlord 41 (12 m) belonging to the British Offshore Sailing School that makes the Atlantic crossing on an annual basis, had a similar experience to ours involving a coastal freighter shadowing their yacht. I am certain it had to be the same ship.

According to the magazine, *Yachting World*, *Ocean Wanderer* announced their concern about the ship over the ARC radio network which in turn was passed to Falmouth Coastguard. Falmouth MRCC (Maritime Rescue Coordination Centre) put out an all ships bulletin announcing a possible piracy situation.

Drama followed. Fearful they were about to be boarded by pirates, *Ocean Wanderer* tested the cargo ship's intentions by carrying out a one eighty degree turn. The ship continued to follow them. It was nighttime and as the ship bore round, *Ocean Wanderer* slipped by the freighter while keeping so near to the ship's hull, that the ship would be unable to pick her up on its radar screen. It was then, that crewmembers aboard *Ocean Wanderer*, saw the ship sweep the water with searchlights. *Ocean Wanderer* headed in the opposite direction of what they thought the ship would expect them to travel, keeping their stern positioned to the ship, consequently offering a smaller target for the ship's radar. Nothing further developed of the situation.

On a lighter note, a young couple double handing the smallest boat in the ARC, a Norwegian Comfort 30 (9 m), became engaged during the crossing despite losing their boom which forced them to travel much of the passage while flying not much more than a small headsail. Only three days out of Las Palmas, their boom suffered extensive damage and they jury rigged a temporary repair. But soon after, the boom completely snapped in half. After repairing it a third time, it was later lost during a squall. After twenty-two days at sea with rigging problems, both Karl and Hedda exclaimed, "We loved it out there." Karl said he had planned to ask Hedda to marry him while en route so had left shore prepared with an engagement ring. (Probably with money he should have spent purchasing a sturdier boat!)

The most prestigious award, Spirit of the ARC went to a father and daughter team aboard *Asolare*, an Amel Super Maramu 2000 (53 ft./16 m). It would be several months later while sailing Australia's reef infested waters that we would hear again of this newly built yacht. Sadly it would not be good news.

AFTER a few hours of rest, we set about to prepare our dinghy for excursions. The boys lowered it from the davits then tied it alongside *Baccalieu III* in order to refasten the steering cables to the dinghy's engine. Following the completion of the work, Mike was standing in the dinghy ready for a test drive when he pulled the start cord. Unexpectedly, the dinghy charged forward in full throttle sending the bow straight into the air while standing it on its stern. Within seconds, Mike was sent into orbit flying over the engine while the propeller blades whizzed and slashed at full speed. While on his unexpected flight, somehow he had the good sense to reach down and grab the stop-cord, killing the engine in time to prevent a serious injury. He escaped a second hazard, when landing in the water, he narrowly missed hitting a concrete post. Lucky as he was to miss serious injury it can't be ignored that he had landed in a grunge of sewage polluted waters!

This dinghy motor was to become the bane of our existence. Twice, it had almost caused serious injury. While on the island of Cabrera in the Balearic Islands, we had just finished an Oyster Rally dinner and had returned to our dinghy after dark. Mike and I were sitting in the dinghy when our friend John took a step from the dock to the dinghy. Mike attempted to start the 'playful' outboard motor but due to a malfunctioning, the motor only had two speeds; off and eight knots. The dinghy took off as if boosted by a nuclear missile leaving John's foot mid-air. Instead of his foot landing on the solid floor of the boat, John took one giant step into the water, fully clothed of course. After returning to *Baccalieu III*, we needed to rinse and hang not only his clothes, but all his paper money on clothes pins.

4

End of the First Leg

Sailing the Windward Islands

Leaving the Grenadines

Antigua and Barbuda

Nevis

Homeward

Visual surprise is natural in the Caribbean; it comes with the landscape, and faced with its beauty, the sigh of History dissolves.

Derek Walcott

SAILING THE WINDWARD ISLANDS

Bad luck makes good stories
BERNARD EVSLIN

AFTER ARRIVING IN St. Lucia, our friends returned to their homes on Vancouver Island and Toronto. Or Toronna, as we from the big city call it. We now sat at dock in a quieter boat. But we really missed them, the laughter, their camaraderie. Gosh it seemed awfully quiet. Had we lived like this before?

I wondered what the men were reporting to their spouses and friends back home. Would Bob mention that a portion of his bed got soaked by a fresh water leak in the forward cabin? Ray for certain would cry about the fishing reel breaking down; for a fisherman the caliber of Ray to be without a rod in the middle of the Atlantic Ocean would be like staring down at a Kobe beef steak caked in a smoky char, seared and broiled in a 1600 degree oven, but with no teeth to chew it. Arthur for sure would be reporting that we wouldn't let him have a second glass of wine at dinner. That's what he said he missed most on the trip, that and his wife of course.

ST. LUCIA IS part of the Windward Islands, which stretch from Dominica south to Grenada. Located between St. Lucia and Grenada are a string of islands called St. Vincent and the Grenadines.

Winter tradewinds of fifteen to twenty-five knots blow consistently across these islands. The weather forecast for the entire five months rarely varies and can be summed up as "winds NE to SE from 15 to 25 knots accompanied by gusts and sometimes rain." A cruising sailor's dream.

WE began exploring the Caribbean in a minivan. It was the last organized event of the ARC and we were about to tour St. Lucia. Although twenty people had signed up for the tour, the van arrived with seating for fifteen. This was our introduction to the Caribbean, how things work here.

Just when we thought the vehicle was full, the driver flipped folding seats into the aisle and we sat wall to wall in the non-air conditioned van leaving the two tourist guides to stand with their heads jammed against the ceiling. Our load was lightened, when some of the tourists thought the bus was unsafe and they disembarked. Seat belt parts were visible but no two parts were compatible. This was a bus tailored to Caribbean living.

The winding, pot holed road took us across the island where people struggle to make a living, each family doing what they can to make a dollar. Vendors set up stands along roadways offering wood carvings and T-shirts, vegetables, St. Lucian bananas and their own version of takeout homemade fried chicken.

Stepping off the bus for a tour of the local rum factory we were met with aromas of burnt sugar and yeast. Large open pools of fermenting sugar emitted heavy yeast smells that had overly sensitive tourists holding their noses. Polished brass stills showed pure, clear alcohol on its' way to be blended, coloured with caramel and then aged at least three years in casks before bottling.

We sampled several flavoured rums; coconut rum, peanut rum, lime rum, ginger rum, rum that was advertised to be 'pistol strengthening' and rum guaranteed to act as an aphrodisiac. It's this blatant disrespect for modesty that we loved about the Caribbean. A road sign cautioning motorists approaching a speed bump, read, "Hump Here" and one of the water taxi services is named Orgasm Boat Tours. A local mix of English and Patois* languages, do not necessarily combine for grammatically correct sentences, but they surely get the message across. "Trespassers will be violated" and "Trespassers will be shot" are pretty clear what the owners want to convey.

Arriving back to the marina, hot and sweaty, we just had time for a shower before heading out to the west end of the island to the fishing village of Anse La Raye, where every Friday night a fish fry takes place on the main street fronting the sea.

At first glance, the village looked like a movie set, but the small unpainted shacks lining the street, some with worn miniature ginger bread gables, was home for local fishermen and their families. One and two room shacks sat along a dirt street separating the fish gutting tables from the houses while ocean waves beat the shore just beyond the tables.

That night, the fishermen were off duty and the wives worked the makeshift barbeques full of clawless lobsters and fish steaming in foil. Sizzling red snapper, lobster, lambi (conch) and fried hot cakes filled the air with tempting aromas while most of the husbands, with beer in hand, were huddled in a 'male only' zone at the far end of the street. The only two men working that evening were two senior members sitting on inverted pails in front of a short legged barbeque charring corn on the cob. West Indian music, a blend of calypso and soca, blared

---

* Patois is a mix of languages. Following the defeat of the Arawaks and Caribs, (Amerindian peoples indigenous to the Caribbean), both the French and the English laid claim to the island. St. Lucia changed ownership several times. When the sugarcane industry developed, African slaves arrived on the island. Following the abolishment of the African slave trade (1807), East Indians came as indentured servants. The British acquired St. Lucia permanently in 1834.

from stereo speakers the size of small buildings while three local men, danced alone seemingly lost in some sort of trance. Scrawny looking dogs, and one that had lost a leg, roamed the streets looking for tidbits. If owners had front steps, they sat on them, others slouched in unpainted doorways watching the cheerful white visitors enjoy their meals of seafood. At the far end of town, a six year old attempted to cuddle with his unhappy looking mother sitting on their wooden step, but she hardly took notice. In time, her husband sauntered from the male end of town delivering a bottle of beer when the young boy settled between her legs as if he had done this many times before. She offered him sips from the beer bottle probably hoping that he would fall asleep and leave her alone. Behind us, five children standing on the shore partially hidden by fishing nets, appeared to be in possession of a glass of punch and together embracing the naughty experience.

The drive home was dark and dangerous as cars and trucks passed on blind curves and headlights fell upon untethered cattle standing on the shoulder, knees locked into sleeping mode. We sped past the same little house that had displayed fried chicken in a glass covered box earlier that afternoon and I wondered if they were the same pieces for sale now. Our driver seemed to have not drunk too much while waiting for us with his taxi buddies and we arrived safely back to the marina.

WITH THE CHALLENGE of crossing the ocean complete, my state of mind seemed to change. Not that I missed the rigorous schedule, the completion just left me feeling empty. This was obviously a transitional phase, one I hadn't expected. I felt without purpose. And without the opportunity to exercise, I was putting on weight. This boating life style demanded something different of me. I would need to find a balance.

We left the marina to anchor just outside in the bay. We

threw open all the hatches, allowing the tradewinds to blow from stem to stern, which was a real treat after having been docked in a stuffy marina. We were only at anchor a short time when the boat boys visited offering their pick-up and drop off laundry service. Boat boys are entrepreneurial men trying to catch a piece of the transient market sailing through their territory. They arrive in brightly painted motor boats with names like, Zoro, Lucky Charm, Gangst*r, and No Problem. Many sailors think them a nuisance, but since I was new to Caribbean cruising life, I initially applauded them for their ingenuity and hard work. In a few weeks I would be like the others and wish they would leave us alone.

I knew it was close to Christmas because the boat behind us at the marina had a small brightly lit Christmas tree on their bow. Cruising hardly requires a timepiece or a calendar in order to navigate a regular day or week. We didn't even have a traditional brass marine clock with matching barometer hanging on our bulkhead. The weather was no indication of what time of year it was, but the locals call the constant tradewinds, Christmas Winds. Did I miss our traditional Christmas season? I missed getting together with friends and family, I missed the festive outdoor lights and I missed the change of seasons. But I did not miss the shopping or wrapping of what seemed like a hundred presents and when I thought of the pace the Christmas season demands, it seemed frightful. I thought of our friend who was frantically searching for an Air Brush Tattoo kit for her daughter and I did not wish in any way, to be in her shoes.

ONE day while at anchor, we heard a thudding crash a short distance off our beam. Looking out we saw that a 12 metre (40 foot) yacht had rammed into the boat adjacent to us at anchor. Apparently the offending boat was racing and had failed to keep watch beneath their flying genoa and ran under full sail into the stern of the anchored sailboat. Lying at anchor seems to be a dangerous pastime.

Having had a similar experience in Spain, we offered to be witnesses to the victimized boat, *Anna Caram*. The owners were appreciative but reported that the people on the offending boat, *Alchemy*, were very apologetic and obliging. The following day *Anna Caram* had something different to report, the owners of *Alchemy* were no longer being so friendly and were suddenly reluctant to talk. Mike and I were well acquainted with this type of situation since being involved in a lengthy Spanish lawsuit pertaining to our accident in the Mediterranean. The owner of the classic 1929 wooden Alden which had struck *Baccalieu III* that night, later made claims of hurricane strength winds that escalated the occurrence to "an act of God". Insurance companies don't cover God's acts and consequently there was little room for claims. However, according to the Beaufort Wind Scale, forty to forty-five knots has never been hurricane strength. At the end of the day we settled for fifty percent of the damages as, is often the case, the lawyer's fees were soon going to exceed the amount of the claim.

We had a great sail to Marigot Bay and I had wished the trip had been longer than nine miles. Several friends had reported the beauty of the small mangrove lined bay, but also told of the boat boys who had unceasingly pestered them, dissuading many from ever visiting again. Vendors, Lincoln, Lucky Seven and Vision, row out to visiting sailboats in rafts, broken down paddle boats or hand paddled surf boards with similar offers of fruit, necklaces and cheap ornaments. But the award for most original transport belongs to Gerald who putts around in a small wooden powercraft flying every country's flag he can get his hands on. Since he already had a Canadian one, we figured ours was probably safe from joining his display.

One morning a rather destitute looking man with a face

that told the story of a hard life approached the boat with a fender he claimed was ours. He had saved it from floating out to sea he stated. At the time we were tied to a dock and the boat had not moved so much as an inch. I replied that I did not think it could be ours. "Oh yes," he said, "It's definitely yours." Inspecting our fenders, I discovered we were in fact, missing one. We had been duped by the oldest game in town; untie a fender at night and sell it back at first light.

I reluctantly offered him five EC to get it back; the fender was worth far more than that and we could never replace it in St. Lucia. The incident made us realize cruising in this part of the world required different security measures than we had used in Canada or Europe. We were to learn the bigger game is to steal dinghies at night, then return them to the owners the following day, minus the motor for a finder's fee. And if the owner needed a motor, the dinghy thieves could certainly be relied upon to find one to sell.

The following day was Christmas Eve and we drove to St. Lucia airport to meet our son David. Driving through the country, we passed carcasses of freshly killed beef hanging from makeshift roadside stands. Our taxi driver informed us beef, stewed with vegetables, was the traditional Christmas dinner. In preparation, St. Lucians kill their cattle just prior to the festive day and then hack the required pieces off at their customer's request. At one stand I remarked on what long sausages they made. I was informed I was looking at entrails. Afraid to learn what they used them for, I didn't ask.

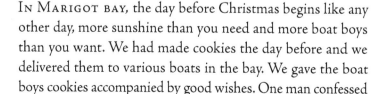

IN MARIGOT BAY, the day before Christmas begins like any other day, more sunshine than you need and more boat boys than you want. We had made cookies the day before and we delivered them to various boats in the bay. We gave the boat boys cookies accompanied by good wishes. One man confessed it was the first Christmas gift he had ever received. That evening, we celebrated Christmas Eve with dinner at Marigot Bay's Rainforest Café, an open air, thatched roof restaurant with highly polished tables of crosscut mangrove. The restaurant is stilted just inches above the water. Customers arrive by either water taxi or in their own dinghies to a weathered dock highlighted by turquoise tinged underwater lighting

That same day we moved to an anchorage near Soufrière on the west coast of St. Lucia. Boat boys roared out in their runabouts to intercept us as we arrived. One offered to usher us to a mooring where he helped tie our mooring line to the ball. When we realized the ball was too near to shore, he led us to a second ball where he attached the line again. Because the bay was small, we passed him a stern line to tie us to shore. This would allow more boats to use the other mooring balls.

It's not that we couldn't handle the lines ourselves, but it's understood the locals control the moorings. Visitors are expected to co-operate. This is how the men attempt to make a living. I draw the line, however, when someone is waiting on a dock to take my dinghy painter for a fee when I can easily step ashore with it myself.

After tying us to shore, the mooring keeper insisted on charging us double for the two tie ups. We were the only boat in the bay in an isolated area where locals had a reputation for boarding boats after dark. We paid the highly inflated fee. We decided not to hike the Pitons, a UNESCO World Heritage site because we didn't feel it was safe to leave the boat unattended. It's quite a simple matter to break the locks on most boats. In the future, we would bypass the areas that held poor reputations.

It was not long before a second man, who showed obvious signs of intoxication, paddled out on a surf board with the offer to sell fresh coconuts. He introduced himself as the one who would be untying us in the morning (when he would expect a fee for the service). But the following morning at 0700, when we were ready to cast off, there was no one around. Mike swam to shore and untied the stern line. We felt as if we were running from a parking lot without making payment, but it seemed pretty safe to assume we wouldn't see any of the locals that early in the morning.

MUSTIQUE IS A unique island located in the Grenadines. The island is privately owned and has been developed for the rich who seek to live an ordinary lifestyle without the interruption or invasion of fans or paparazzi. Mick Jagger holds an annual beach barbeque for residents two days after Christmas. Jagger has also been known to dress as an elf to accompany Charles Basil, owner of Basil's Bar, when Basil dons a Santa's costume to hand out gifts in the local village. At the time of writing, Mick Jagger held the position of chairman of the board at Mustique's forty student Primary School.

Like many of the islands, Mustique had originally been inhabited by Arawak and Carib Indians, but as Europeans arrived, populations died either of Old World diseases, defending their land, or from harsh treatment during enslavement. During the struggle between the British and the French, a small fort was erected on the top of the west hill.

Sugarcane was grown on the island during the 18th and early 19th centuries. When the demand for sugar decreased, the island was abandoned and returned to its natural state of dense scrubland. In 1958, Colin Tennant, a British Lord and Scotsman, purchased Mustique from the British Commonwealth for £45,000. He raised cotton and mutton and in time established a small economy that supported the local people in the village of Lovell, a town which still exists today.

In developing the island with a school, hotel, police station, customs house and post office, he began to build residences around the island. Tennant convinced the government of St. Vincent and the Grenadines of which Mustique is part, to offer tax free status to foreign property owners. When he presented Princess Margaret with a gift of ten acres as a wedding gift, the foundation was laid for a prestigious island offering seclusion for the rich and famous.

It wasn't luxury that attracted the wealthy, but the opportunity to be themselves, to be freer than they would ever be allowed to be in their real world, full of rules of etiquette and codes of behavior. Princess Margaret lived there when her marriage to Lord Snowden ended. Queen Elizabeth and Prince Philip visited her on their yacht, *Britannia*. One such visit was during the Queen's Silver Jubilee year (1977) when Colin Tennant organized a banquet for the Queen at his hotel, a converted 18th century cotton warehouse and the only hotel on the island.

Tennant died in August 2010. Erected in his memory is a bronze statue, the work of the queen's sculptor, Philip Jackson.

The Mustique Company (founded by Colin Tennant) continues to act as the custodian of the island. The company had entered into an agreement with St. Vincent to allow the construction of a maximum of one hundred and forty residences. The island would be open to visitors, the agreement said, but would adhere to a strict policy to protect it from exploitation. Today homeowners, such as Mick Jagger and David Bowie are dedicated to limiting development and protecting the environment.

The island is mercifully free of boat boys, and arriving in Mustique is like shaking loose from a grand annoyance. There are not even beach vendors. Everyone on the island is employed. There are no high rise hotels or golf courses. The beaches are pristine, and on some, you can often be the only one standing on the fine white sand, either wading into the warm and placid waters on the west shore or watching sizable rollers crash onto the seashore open to the prevailing winds. That's why people such as Brian Adams, Shania Twain and Tommy Hilfiger, all have homes there.

Several styles of Villas, which rent for weekly sums of $7,000 US to $45,000 US, suit every rich person's taste. From the minds of famous architects and landscape designers, unique creations flow around lush gardens, waterfalls, lily ponds and infinity pools. Many have been featured in *Architectural Digest*. Construction for the homes draws from the island's own resources as well as from exotic imports of precious woods and antique marbles. The homes are diverse in architecture and reflect Balinese, Tuscan and Mediterranean styles. A Moorish Castle design dominates the hillsides of the island's western coast. From contemporary interiors to African accents, from *Gamalan*, a Balinese one bedroom honeymooner's villa to *Shogun's* Japanese influenced villa with accommodations for up to ten guests, one can rent beach front or commanding two hundred and seventy degree views.

A SMALL informal airport is available for small planes. They arrive from over a hill to land on the short runway cut through a portion of heavily treed, flat stretch of land. The island's shallow, undulating valleys have been established as a natural reserve, where land turtles are often seen munching grass, oblivious to pedestrians and light road traffic. Kawasaki mules similar to golf carts, are the main form of transportation on the island, allowing the roads to remain narrow and fun to explore. A mule adventure might lead you down a dirt road that dead-ends or onto sandy tracks through the bush where you might find a spectacular deserted beach or a view from a hillside that takes your breath away. Nine beaches are said to surround the island and it would be a summer's worth of work to locate them all since there is no signage.

Hundreds of pink pearl coloured conch shells stacked

along Britannia Bay's waterfront act as a breakwater to the shoreline where fishermen bring catches of tuna and conch to be cleaned. Not far from this breakwater, two brightly coloured boutiques sell quality clothing and tourist keepsakes, and a small, but well-stocked grocery store sells provisions at the price of gold.

Basil's Bar, a conglomeration of large unpainted thatched roof shacks, claims to be the most famous beach bar in the Caribbean. It stands on stilts among swaying palm trees while an azure ocean gently rolls onto a beach of pale sand. Passing over a flat shallow reef, the sea swishes with a hush that is probably the world's most perfect sound while long legged sea birds pick at marine organisms left by a receding tide. And it all takes place a few feet below a room full of open windows where you can sit at tables while smelling the fresh scent of the sea.

Basil Charles, the son of a West Indian Fisherman, and owner of Basil's Bar, fell into a lifestyle of high society after a car accident nearly killed him but instead claimed just one of his kidneys. At the time of the accident, while working as a car mechanic on the adjacent island of St. Vincent, Basil was rescued by Hugo Money-Coutts, the son of Lord Latymer and former director of Coutts & co., an exclusive private bank in London, UK.

Following a year in hospital, Basil and a friend decided to travel the short distance to Mustique to seek a possible living there. By the time Basil arrived on the island, Colin Tennant had already established an inviting life for various royals and hoity-toits.

Coincidently, Hugo Money-Coutts, the man who had saved Basil's life, was a friend and business partner of Colin Tennant. At the time, Tennant was looking for a bartender for his boutique hotel, the Cotton House, and he hired Basil for the job. Basil suddenly found himself flung from the life of a mechanic to being caught up in the middle of visiting royals and uppercrust. He was such a success that Tennant put him in charge of an open air pavilion, next to the water's edge, in Britannia Bay where the bar still remains today. Tennant suggested the bar be named Basil's Bar.*

WE visited Basil's Bar during one of the weekly Wednesday night Pig Roast and Jump Ups when a pig turns slowly on a spit for hours in preparation for its appearance at the buffet table while a live band knocks out some rockin' dance tunes. On regular nights, visitors order off a menu offering anything from lobster to burgers.

On those nights, a DJ can be found behind a glass booth spinning music from a disc, while a mix of visiting islanders, owners of multimillion dollar winter homes, and renters of exclusive villas, share the same casual bar with lowly yacht owners and the charter boat crowd.

THE Firefly hotel and restaurant sits on a hill overlooking Britannia Bay. It was one of the first houses to be built during Tennant's time and has retained its casual appearance. It sits among a thick forest of trees on the side of a luscious green cliff. You might see Johnny Depp sitting at the bar, or Courtney Love, but if you appear to rubberneck in the slightest way, or look like you might have a camera in your pocket, you will be shown the door faster than you can yell, "Help!"

The small, intimate hotel offers luxurious rooms with spectacular views for $1,000 US a night. The hotel gets its name 'Firefly' from the gentle movement of masthead lights swinging through a dark night while anchored in Britannia Bay below. It is the most romantic spot I have ever been for dinner.

---

* For years, Basil shared a home on the island with European nobility. Such was his esteem, that in 2011 he received an invitation to Prince William and Catherine Middleton's wedding.

A MULE taxi picked us up at the dock where we had buzzed in with our dinghy.

We were driven up the hill to the restaurant where inside, two Gucci clad lovers sat cuddled in the middle of an overstuffed, oversized L-shaped sofa. Bar stools invited us to sit at either the white baby grand piano or the small bamboo bar. The waiters, dressed in white shirts and black tuxedoes, added real class to the place. While grooving to music, shaking and stirring drinks, they made easy conversation, recounting how to prepare the delicious, paper-thin sliced, roasted coconut meat they had set out in small bowls for nibbling. They failed to mention, however, the difficulty of slicing the coconut meat once it is pried from the shell. Although challenging, I have finally mastered it, and find these little roasted slices deliver such a powerful punch of flavour that they are worth all the hand cramping and discomfort the job demands.

Sitting at the bar, sipping local Carib beers and champagne cocktails, we placed our dinner order while watching the smartly dressed waiters make up the Firefly's specialty: A concoction of coconut cream, two kinds of rum, fresh papaya and a sprinkling of nutmeg. When our dinner was ready, we were ushered to our table where we could gaze down on the moonlit anchorage to watch the 'fireflies' dance.

THE following day, we received an e-mail from someone in Cambodia who was a friend of our daughter Jennifer. She was working as a dive instructor in Thailand. The note was short and to the point. "Jennifer is fine. Things are hectic, but there is no need for concern."

We had no idea what he was talking about and our e-mail got no response. We began to worry.

It was raining and we washed down the boat while waiting for a clear spell to go ashore for fresh baked croissants at the Sweetie Pie Bakery. Aside from the sweet aroma of breads, donuts and coffee cakes, a second attraction to the bakery is the availability of one hundred and fifty different reproduced newspapers visitors can purchase. If an order is placed the day before, you can be reading a copy of your favourite newspaper the next morning. To a yachting crowd who has been away from home and deprived of the internet for a lengthy time, this is a near miracle.

The bakery is so small there is only room enough for four people at a time to stand inside the bakery. As we waited beside the aluminum shelf pantry case, filled with plain and chocolate-stuffed croissants and raisin buns, people ahead of us were already reading the headlines from their newspapers. Gasps of disbelief were heard as they turned pages full of pictures depicting a recent disaster.

As we soon discovered, the images showed a tsunami* that had swept Thailand, where our daughter had been working. We returned to the boat to call her from our SAT phone. We were surprised when Jennifer answered her phone. We didn't expect to reach her on the first try. She was standing on the beach where her dive boat had just minutes before landed. She had been leading a group of twenty-two divers in the Similan Islands an hour and half from Khao Lak, one of the villages that had suffered the most damage. Upon arriving to shore, the divers were uncertain what had happened. The tsunami had swept the beach clean of anything recognizable. Fishing boats and a navy ship had been tossed out of the water to where they now sat, several metres inshore. The diving tourists were looking to her for answers. How could they get to their hotels? Did their hotels still exist? Where should they go?

---

* In 2004, the day after Christmas, Thailand and Indonesia experienced the strongest earthquake in the world since the early sixties. 1,000 kilometres (621 miles) of fault line had broken away from the northern Island of Sumatra with the result the tsunami had killed thousands in India, Indonesia, Sri Lanka, and Thailand.

Our daughter's voice bore the sounds of fear, urgency and confusion. She couldn't talk now, she said. There was too much going on. She wasn't sure what had happened. Our conversation was short but at least we knew she was alive. Some days later we were able to be in touch with her again to learn that she was staying with friends in Phuket.

THE DAY BEFORE New Year's, we left Mustique to head for the Tobago Cays which a National Park travel guide describes as "a small group of deserted islands." The islands were perhaps uninhabited, but the anchorage did not reflect this fact, as we dropped anchor among fifty other boats already bobbing in the blue green, crystal clear waters of the southern Grenadines. Admittedly it was New Year's Eve, and the Cays provided a destination for many to celebrate the coming of the New Year, but the Cays are the most visited area in the Caribbean. Yachts from as far away as Finland and Norway were anchored, although most were chartered catamarans from local companies whose patrons had come to spend holiday time in the most serene, "unspoiled waters of the Caribbean." There is no question the water here is magnificently clear, displaying the refracting colours of a treasured diamond. With the bow of your boat facing seaward, there is nothing between you and Africa except a local four mile long reef and thousands of miles of sea. You can watch squalls move uninhibited across the horizon, clouds compound into vertical pyramids and stars glitter so brightly at night you might feel as if you are suspended in a darkened planetarium. Here in the Cays, the sun rises early and if you get up early enough, you can watch it climb its way into the sky. You don't come here to watch sunsets; you come here to watch a new day be born.

Just as much a part of the Cays as the rising sun and turquoise waters are the boat vendors from neighbouring islands.

The Cays are 'Boat Vendor Central' and a swarm of them travel daily from nearby Union Island, bringing fresh baked croissants, ice, T-shirts, handmade jewelry, fish and lobster. Each vendor is known for a particular item. But boaters can order whatever is to be had from local ports and a vendor will deliver it to you the following day for a fee.

At one time boat vendors fought among themselves over who had the right to approach an incoming yacht, but they are now better organized and no longer converge on a boat before it is securely anchored. But as soon as you drop anchor off the bow and begin to walk back to the cockpit, the first one will be there, tied alongside with offers of saleable goods. Mr. Fabulous, Mr. Quality or Seckie on his boat *Velocity* and of course, Engine—aboard his boat *Free Spirit* or the runabout *Desparado*, who we have seen during every one of our visits. Some boat vendors might have their hair knotted into dreadlocks, or wear Rastafarian crochet hats. Others might proudly display a gold front tooth. But whatever their signature, they have all been sharing this workplace for years. This is the way they feed their families, put food on the table and send their kids to school in the required school uniforms. They work hard during the sailing season, spending most of their days bopping up and down in their open runabouts in all weather conditions; driving rain, bullet hard winds, salty spray and sun so hot you'd think they might combust sitting out there in their open boats.

The boat boys worked long hours on New Year's Eve, hoping to sell last minute meals of fish and lobster from their runabouts. As the day began to fade, we continued to hear their Yamaha engines hum through the darkness and I wondered how they missed colliding with each other without the aid of navigation lights.

For New Year's Eve, David and I made sushi. Then we all enjoyed a glass of celebratory champagne and a steak dinner which was a rare treat aboard *Baccalieu III*. Good beef had been difficult to find. Chicken was the safer choice if purchased from a large grocery store, which we seldom came upon. But chewing on locally raised chicken so tough they appeared to have done push-ups all their life was not very satisfying.

The clock ticked on towards midnight and the evening was a continuous celebration of fog horns and flares as each international boat recognized the celebrated time in their country's time zone. In the distance, we caught sight of a spectacular fireworks display that originated at a nearby resort. Rockets shot into the darkness, bursting into trails of sparks, while glittering sprays of silver rain tumbled in cascades of colourful stars. We had the best seats in the house.

New Year's Eve is a time when we recount our personal highlights from the past year; sorrows as well as accomplishments. For Mike and I, sailing seven thousand miles during the past seven months was the most significant. Our new lifestyle had become so ingrained, I could hardly remember what my life was like before. Learning to handle a large boat had been a steep learning curve, not to mention having to adjust being together twenty-four-seven in a limited amount of space. Our priorities had drastically changed; clothes took a back seat to almost everything. I went for weeks without using makeup and seldom used the hair dryer. What excited me now was a good chandlery, and I would often find myself scanning grocery marts for items I hadn't seen for a while. Like a good detective, I was always alert. Finding food and sundry items was serious business. Mike often had his eye out for engine oil, and was constantly comparing prices that could vary drastically. Having clean bed-sheets was almost as rewarding as having a shower after a few rough days on a long passage. I would lie on our bed, engrossed in the fresh scent of sea air impregnated on the clean bed sheets, after they had dried on a line, strung across the deck.

Provisioning and planning meals was challenging. I never knew what I might find at the next stop. I learned to go with the flow and substitute, revise and re-invent. Quite often I didn't recognize the kinds of fish for sale or the fruits or even the vegetables; what were callaloo or cassava root? I had no idea how to cook them. I cleaned and filleted fish and cooked struggling lobsters. Thank goodness I didn't have to pluck any hens! Although I rinsed the produce in sea water before bringing it inside to rid it of any insects, it wasn't unusual to find creepy crawlies in newly purchased dried goods. These needed to be disposed of and the item put back on the shopping list for the next stop. I read that when you become a REAL cruiser, you simply pick out the bugs or microwave them and appreciate the additional protein. I wasn't there yet.

One thing I learned: cruising was not a holiday but a lifestyle.

WE LEFT THE Cays and dropped anchor in a bay at Union Island, just nine miles away. Chatham Bay edged by a lengthy beach of soft white sand, lies at the foot of densely wooded hills. Wind gusted over the hillsides but the bay offered a protected anchorage and the boat sat flat and quiet. This side of Union Island was uninhabited.

When the sun vanished below the horizon, we climbed into our dinghy, attached the portable red and green navigation light to our bow, and headed into the blackened night, pointing the bow towards shore. Earlier in the day, we had scouted the shoreline and surrounding waters for buoys and other interferences.

We drove the dinghy close to the beach because earlier, when we had climbed out of the dinghy to go to shore, we had stepped into chest deep water. We killed the motor, jumped out, and waited for successive incoming waves to help boost the rubber boat as far up the beach as we could drag it. The beach was in darkness now except for a single flickering light coming from a shack owned by a man nicknamed Shark Attack.

Shack, as he is called by his friends, began his entrepreneurial business several years earlier, when the beach had no road access. On a whim that he might make money from visiting boats, he began his business by loading up his runabout with provisions in Clifton Harbour, then transporting them to the beach in Chatham Bay. While rounding the headland he would often be met with rough water or squalls that soaked him and his supplies. The piece of land he chose to set up his barbeque was owned by a family who had never developed it. Here, a few metres back from the shoreline, he erected a small shack where he sold slightly chilled beers from a semi useless cooler along with a few souvenirs. During the day, Shack would visit anchored boats in his runabout, offering to prepare barbequed fish dinners on shore in the evening. He made a reputation for himself by serving good food combined with a unique experience. Boaters began to seek him out.

The glow of hot coals burned out back where Shack was heating up his grill for our lobster and fish dinners. He appeared out of the darkness, his eyes and brilliant white teeth his only discernible features, and directed us to a rough-hewn picnic table beneath an Indian almond tree. A nail, tapped into the trunk of the large broad leafed tree, offered a place where he hung a second lantern before vanishing again into darkness. We set our bottle of wine on the turquoise painted table. My legs hung freely above the sand while we sipped our beverage from plastic glasses we had brought with us.

Shack returned with plates of clawless lobster and grilled king mackerel. Faded, worn bowls held cabbage slaw and a mixture of rice and peas. I only wished I had room in my stomach to eat everything that he served.

We did not see him again until we had finished our memorable meal. We paid, and he helped drag our dinghy back into the water. We set off to locate *Baccalieu III* concealed in nighttime blackness.

The next morning, we moved around to the other side of the island just off Clifton Village. With no one anchored in front us, we had an uninterrupted view of open water. The beauty of a clipper ship sailing past under full canvas* almost made us forget we were located in the main yachting hub of the southern Grenadines. Just metres behind us, a multitude of sailboats and catamarans were jockeying for limited space; dropping their anchors too near to each other. But that was the reality of this small bay. When several boats visited, they were forced to anchor in close quarters.

Not only were we too close to several other boats, but because the small bay is riddled with its own interior reefs, we had a reef off the bow and a reef off the stern. Nearby lay a semi-submerged catamaran that had been holed when grounding on a collection of coral.

Shortly after our arrival, Buhda, one of the local boat boys, pulled alongside selling bread and fruit, and offered to fetch gasoline for our dinghy. As is the case on most of the islands in the Grenadines, there are few marina facilities. Just a few days before, Mike had trekked into a town on one of the other islands to fill a portable fuel tank. Obtaining gasoline or diesel can be challenging in the Grenadines.

Later that afternoon, David and I took the dinghy into

---

* Canvas—a word used to refer to sails. By the end of the 15th century, sails were being made from the hemp plant, *Cannabis sativa*. 'Canvas' is the Dutch pronunciation of the word Cannibis.

a small dock on the edge of town. Unable to find the route into town, we mistakenly walked through a stretch of residential backyards where children laughingly encouraged a herd of goats to run towards us. We searched until we found a roughly laid concrete road leading into the town.

Stores backed onto the water's edge confirming the owners put no value on the view of the bay. The buildings were dismal and most sold similar items: canned goods, inexpensive aluminum cookware and white flour packaged in transparent bags. I was pleased to find the dry goods sold in see-through bags. The last flour I had purchased was infested with weevils and had to be thrown out. Most stores in Clifton Harbour lacked refrigeration and because of this, the margarine sat on shelves beside the flour. We were excited to find homemade yogurt in a small 'gourmet' shop that also carried olives, cheese and dried pasta. The yogurt was some of the best we had ever tasted and we would have purchased two week's worth if its shelf life had permitted.

In the middle of town, several small, colourfully painted kiosks, each with a large wooden shutter tied open to the ceiling by a string, stood together in an arc formation. Clifton village women sell fresh produce from these booths while older family relatives and friends, who are in charge of the children, sit nearby taking part in a hail of gossip and daily chit chat.

While purchasing fruit from each stand, I learned the fruit was shipped from the island of St. Vincent. The vendors told me that Union Island was too arid to grow crops. Tita, who ran the largest fruit and vegetable stand, mentioned the houses on the island were not fitted with plumbing, requiring each house to collect rain in barrels, although rain was not something they saw very often. She was surprised when I told her that I too grew up with a water collecting system, called a cistern, in my house. "What country are you from?" she asked in disbelief.

With her help, I learned to identify local oranges and lemons. The oranges look nothing like the flawless easy peel oranges of Florida and the warty skinned lemons are not yellow even when ripe, but they are the juiciest and most fragrant I have ever experienced. St. Lucia bananas have a citrus taste when ripe, but since they never turn yellow, my freezer held several overripe ones because I hadn't known when to eat them. Passion fruit was new to me, and I found squeezing the jelly-like substance into our morning fruit cocktail, along with some freshly grated, potent Caribbean ginger, flavoured the dish with a wonderful zing. Dark green vegetables were hard to find and one night I sautéed a bunch of dark leafy callaloo. The ladies advised me that I was lucky to have cooked it long enough, because eating under-cooked callaloo is apparently like swallowing razor blades.

Not far off our bow, a tiny island just large enough to support a thatched roof bar and space for sitting, sits anchored in coral with waves lapping around its miniature shoreline. White plastic chairs scattered in a small area of loose beach sand sat empty during the day, but come sunset, every seat was taken. We joined others maneuvering dinghies carefully around the coral in the shallow, crystal clear waters, to reach the conch filled steps of the islet. The builder of the island, Janti, was also the bartender, and he welcomed us dressed in a flowing green Caribbean caftan. He suggested we try his specialty rum punch mixed earlier in the day in five gallon plastic drums.

Some years before, Janti had had a vision to clean the town of Clifton of discarded conch shells. He loaded tons of them, one by one, into a small motorboat and hauled them out to a shallow portion of the reef where he stacked them high enough to form an island. After securing the perimeter with conch shells and concrete, he transported a huge amount of sand to fill it in. He christened this whimsical structure, Happy Island, and now the island is on the must-see list of everyone who wishes to enjoy a sundowner while visiting Clifton Harbour.

THE FOLLOWING MORNING, sailing under grey skies, we left Union Island and headed towards the nearby island, Petit St. Vincent. It was a gusty trip with easterly winds blowing twenty-five to thirty knots. Seas hit us firmly broadside splashing their white salty crests over our decks. We expected to find good shelter in the anchorage. There were several boats already there when we arrived. Most yachts were tucked up close to the island in shallow water where the nearby hills helped break the wind most efficiently. We anchored at the back of the pack, far enough outside the fleet that Mike laughed at my choice of location. But I was still feeling gun-shy from our earlier collision in Spain. I now looked upon all anchored boats as potential hazards.

It rained and blew all day like we had not seen since leaving England. The weather forecast had failed to predict the tropical wave system, and I wondered what had happened to that five month Caribbean forecast that was supposed to be so reliable. In any case, we made good use of it with a boat wash-down until the gusts increased to such velocity that it became dangerous to be standing on the foredeck. It was one of those days when you accomplish all sorts of small indoor jobs that have been set aside for so long.

Earlier, we had made dinner reservations at a small resort on the island, but by late afternoon we cancelled, feeling it would be unsafe to travel by dinghy and unwise to leave the boat unattended in such high winds. As the evening progressed, we were pleased with our decision as we watched the weather turn worse. Driving sheets of rain pelted the hull while substantial gusts tested the strength of the anchor.

The three of us were sitting on the settee enjoying a DVD of Arrested Development, an American sitcom and Christmas gift from David. Suddenly a heavy thud jolted *Baccalieu III*. We ran up the stairs.

Through the dark of the night, we saw the bow of a 13 metre (42 foot) yacht. The bow had struck us broadside and was careening down *Baccalieu's* hull while dragging its anchor. Sliding down our port side, the delinquent sailboat gouged out one of the heavy stainless fairleads from the teak of our cap rail, the same cap rail we had replaced just weeks before. The jolt that we had felt, was her slamming into *Baccalieu III's* bow pulpit distorting the pulpits fine lines. Continuing her travels, she rammed several stainless stanchions. Then the stainless steel gate contorted under the pressure. Although there were lights inside the offending boat, no one appeared to be onboard. The boat drifted out to sea, heading for a mid-channel reef.

We were located the furthest seaward from the fleet of anchored boats but I shone a spotlight on the runaway boat while Mike sent out a security call over the VHF radio to make known a boat was off its anchor. While sounding our fog horn, a number of boats joined in with their fog horns to intensify the warning signal. It was not long afterwards, we received a radio call from a boat anchored among the fleet near shore. It reported the phantom boat had earlier been located in front of him when it began to drag. It had momentarily caught his anchor chain but in defense, he had motored forward fearing his own anchor might be yanked from its hold on the bottom. Apparently several other boats fended off this same rogue vessel. The offending boat continued to drift freely crossing the bay. Before escaping from the anchorage, it sought us out like a heat seeking missile, and ran us down in the lonely and isolated waters we were in. We never learned if there had been any alarms sounded before we sounded ours. We hadn't heard any.

The operators of the chartered boat were, where else? At dinner in the very restaurant we had not gone to due to weather conditions. Upon hearing fog horns, the crewmembers of the chartered boat had looked out from the restaurant to discover their boat had gone adrift. The three men left the restaurant, jumped into their dinghy and raced through the pelting rain after their drifting yacht. In darkness, across choppy seas, without life jackets, the driver of the dinghy managed to maneuver near enough to the runaway boat that the other two were able to board her. They returned it to the anchorage.

When no one from the chartered boat came to see us the following morning, we lowered our dinghy from the davits and went to visit them. The chartered boat was named *Pouglett II*, a 42 foot (13 metre) Jeanneau. It was brand new and had just been put out for chartering. We sat in their cockpit with one of the crewmembers and took notes regarding the charter company's name and details of their insurance.

For the privilege of sailing in Caribbean waters, our insurance premium and deductible had doubled. It's not a wonder. The area is remote, quality workmanship is hard to source and too many inexperienced sailors, whose priority is to enjoy their short holidays rather than exercise good seamanship, sail these waters.

We returned to Clifton on Union Island so that David could catch a flight to Barbados and then on to Toronto. Mike and I returned to Petit St. Vincent where 'Phantom' boat attacked innocent Canadian family, and dropped anchor again. The following four days were fraught with more rain and I was beginning to wonder whether the ladies back in Clifton Harbour were pulling my leg regarding the lack of available water on the island.

In fact, a tropical wave of weather had been making its way

up from South America when it had stalled over the southern Grenadines.

That evening, stars peeked through the clouds for the first time in several nights. But what began as a lovely evening soon turned sour. Winds up to forty knots blustered through the anchorage. Large flat drops of rain hit the salon windows reproducing the tap of a thousand fingers. The anchor chain stretched and creaked as each link fulfilled its duty. The stainless frame, holding the canopy, shook so violently one of the battens began to shimmy towards the water. When I went into the cockpit to attend to the batten, rain drove into my cheeks with needle-like sharpness.

I laid out our foul weather gear and life vests in the chance we might need to attend to emergency work outdoors. Then we took shifts watching the anchor alarm on the chart plotter to confirm, and reconfirm, that our anchor was not dragging. We also tried to keep track of the neighbouring boats so we would know if *their* anchors were dragging. It was difficult however, to see very far through the onslaught of bad weather. When I stood on one of the seats in the salon to look out the window, I could barely detect the reflection of our own masthead anchor light. Around two in the morning the wind settled into the twenties and stayed there until morning when we were doused with brilliant sunshine.

As other boats entered the anchorage, we heard stories over the VHF radio of collisions, yachts dragging, and even boats that had been beached in other bays. It would have been chaos to have been located in the Tobago Cays or Clifton Harbour in such wind.

We had been at anchor a month without dockside water or electricity. The watermaker and generator allowed us to be self-sufficient. We needed diesel to keep things running, but our fuel tanks held ample fuel for the generator. I had been washing clothing by hand because we needed to be in calm waters to use the washing machine. But when conditions were right for the machine, I strung clothes lines from the mast to the bow and back, from side to side and from spreader to spreader, until the foredeck looked like the beginnings of a spider's web. If I pinned shirts to allow air to blow through the middle of them, and I turned the garments inside out after an hour, they would usually be dry in less than two hours. But there were many times I had to run up the stairs to save the laundry from an incoming squall, which is what happened that day. If not for the hefty, spring-loaded electrical clamps that I used for clothespins, our clothes would be circling the world.

An insurance surveyor from Grenada Island arrived at our boat to estimate the boat damages. His report was worse than we had suspected. He estimated they were going to require several days to repair. Besides having to order parts from Oyster Marine in England, we would need to sail the boat north to Antigua, over two hundred miles distant, in order to find professionals capable of handling the work. We decided to put off the repairs to coincide with our future plans to travel north. In the meantime, we would carry out some makeshift repairs to avoid further damage.

The island of Petit Martinique is less than a half kilometre from the island of Petit St. Vincent. However, the islands belong to two separate countries; Petit Martinique to Grenada and Petit St. Vincent to St. Vincent and the Grenadines. Customs officials don't exist on either island resulting in sailors skipping the required procedures for entering and exiting, while hoping neither country shows any interest.

Petit Martinique has few amenities. The island is small,

dusty, and tranquil. The population of seven hundred is mostly descended from slaves who once worked plantations of cotton, sugar*, and corn in the 17th century under French or British rule.†

Today, the men seek employment on bulk cargo ships or are local fishermen. There are still boat builders among them who have sustained a small fishing industry using locally built vessels. White cedar and pitch-pine continues to be used in the construction of the boats. Pitch or tar is pressed between the boards to prevent leakage. Many of the younger generation have opted instead to supply yachties visiting the Tobago Cays with locally caught fish, lobster and island baked bread. Their brightly painted, wooden cigarette-designed boats are often products of Petit Martinique boat builders.

THERE was hardly anyone to be seen the day we visited. There is no collection of streets to wander down, no cafés where locals or tourists congregate. Oddly, this sparsely populated island was the only place I had seen a chocolate cake mix since leaving home. The small grocery store even stocked Venezuelan beer, a brand we had not seen elsewhere.

A one lane concrete road threaded through a scattering of small weathered houses braced on a hillside. Goats, some tethered to stakes, and free roaming chickens, shared backyards with fluttering laundry in the warm and almost continuous breeze. We walked past a clapboard Roman Catholic primary school where long, thin timber boards showed signs of needing a new coat of paint. The walls of the classrooms had none of the brightly coloured posters or displays

---

* During the 16th and 17th centuries, sugar was a luxury in Europe. Up until the 1970s, sugar was thought to have medicinal properties.

† First colonized by the French, Petit St. Martinique changed ownership several times during the 1700s. In 1974, the island became a dependency of Grenada.

we expect to find in North American primary schools. But even way out here, on this tiny remote island, the influence of former British rule is still evident with school children wearing uniforms.

Across the road, two posts with warped steel basketball hoops stood embedded in cracked pavement. Not even a shred of string was left to suggest there had ever been a net. I wondered if the school possessed basketballs.

Directly behind the grocery store was a small, unkept cemetery with weather stained memorial stones. Weeds crawled out of the dry volcanic soil, clinging in scrawling patterns over the headstones. A fence surrounding the small plot was fixed with a lock and from outside the rusted links I could read the fading inscriptions on a few of the headstones: age 26; age 105.

Waves rolled onto a beach valued more for the work space it provided than its beauty; a sure sign there was little tourism on the island. The beach was instead a parking lot for boats that either sat waiting for repairs or as donators of parts. Fencing marked off someone's storage area for nothing that looked worth keeping.

We wandered into the island's only restaurant and sat at one of five small tables, each covered in home sewn green patterned table cloths. Hens pecked for grubs in the dry grasses surrounding the property. A rough-hewn shake roof offered shade while our eyes settled on waving palm trees along a shoreline in the distance. Palm Restaurant is family owned, and the cuisine reflected the tastes of delicious home cooking. We gorged on large plates of spicy seasoned fish, deep fried lambi and sides of salad, rice, peas and sweet yams.

WE returned to Clifton Harbour to collect the generator parts we had ordered and then moved to Chatham Bay, where we sat out several more days of continuous rain. It was the strangest feeling, when at night wind blew through the portholes fluttering the sheets over our legs as if someone were in the room attempting to get our attention.

Mike continued to get up regularly during twenty-five knot gusts to check the anchor and take note of those anchored around us.

On the morning of the tenth day of rain, droplets teemed down bouncing off the deck like miniature explosives. We decided to take a positive approach to the situation and wash down the deck with nature's gift of fresh water. The teak deck had been wet for so many days it appeared to be sprouting gardens of mysterious growth.

We pulled on our bathing suits and emerged in the downpour. Lightly scrubbing with mild deck soap across the teak's grain, we accomplished the job in an hour's time. And then the rain stopped! For ten days it had rained. Now where was the rinse water?

We never saw so much as a spit for days afterwards.

EARLY the next morning, I grabbed my exercise mat and MP3 player and headed to the aft deck. As I took up my first yoga position, an early morning breeze brushed across my skin. The hot tropical sun had not yet climbed over the hills, and with no boats located behind us, everything was perfect for exercising outdoors. My former yoga instructor might not approve of the amendments I was forced to make for my constantly moving world, but she would be insanely jealous of my work place. I had the most idyllic venue. With the saintly voice of Sarah Brightman singing in my ears, I was easily swept away to a world of calm relaxation.

MID-January, Jennifer arrived from Asia to spend two weeks with us aboard *Baccalieu III*. She was young, independent and had ample support from her Thai friends following the tsunami and probably didn't even feel the necessity to visit us. But to her credit, she made the trip. For Mike and me to have the opportunity to set eyes on her, to feel her presence, was a relief. She was uncommonly silent about what she had seen in the aftermath of the tsunami.

We had picked her up in St. Vincent an island known now for the movie 'Pirates of the Caribbean' but better known to yachties for the high incidence of theft in its harbours. We generally avoided islands with poor reputations and we stayed only long enough to visit the airport, do a small provisions shop in a grocery store armed with several security guards and then we moved to the neighbouring island of Bequia.

Although not far from St. Vincent, the town of Port Elizabeth, on Bequia Island, has an entirely different reputation; one of friendliness and welcome. The biggest threat on this island comes from the manchineel trees located along the beaches. The trees contain toxins that, when in contact with skin, cause painful blistering. The fruit is said to be fatal if eaten and the smoke from a burning manchineel is even known to cause blindness!

The people of Bequia share a history of seamen and boat builders. There are still ship builders among them crafting small vessels on the shore beneath the shade of palm trees. Bequians still have the right to kill four whales a year when the migration heads south to bear their young. There are not many who attempt hunting whales with hand thrown harpoons in small boats, but they proudly hold the privilege.

Bordering the frontage of the scattered town, a waterside concrete walkway is sometimes submerged during an incoming tide. A jumble of casual restaurants, bars, small inns, colourfully painted boutiques, and a coffee shop face the ocean front attracting cruisers to the bay.

Most produce arrives, as it does in the village of Clifton, by coastal freighter from the lush neighbouring island of

St. Vincent. The largest produce market in Bequia is located on the edge of town and is run by Rastafarians, a spiritual group who worship a late Ethiopian Emperor. Rastafarians often wear brightly coloured striped, crocheted tubular hats in colours of red, green and yellow. Wearers of these hats attempt to stuff long lengths of their intertwined hair under them, but ropes of the dreadlocks frequently escape, falling to their shoulders in twisted, frizzy tangles.

As soon as I entered the large covered market, several Rasta vendors converged on me, each cradling two or three pieces of fruit. Standing among the sweetness of ripened fruit and stale marijuana smoke, each vendor went into a spiel swearing that whatever they held in their hand was the juiciest I would ever taste. Whether pawpaw or limes, mangoes or sour sop, each challenged me to find a better price than what he offered. A price for two, a price for six; words flew at me in a jumble of sentences. Their assertive selling technique was overwhelming and exasperated, I yelled, "Stop!" "Stop pressuring me, or I won't buy a single item!" My plea made no difference. Piercing, high pressure garble suffocated my ability to think and I walked out empty handed.

The Rasta market was once the main source of produce in town, but last time we visited, much to the relief to anyone who needed fruit, independent greengrocers had established businesses selling out of stalls just down the street.

We returned to Mustique. After tying to a mooring buoy we took the dinghy to shore where someone stole our custom-made engine cover while we were away touring the island. And if that wasn't enough, while motoring back to the boat, the dinghy's outboard engine coughed and sputtered and we were forced to accept a tow from a high profile tender driven by a handsome young man from a 45 metre (150 foot) yacht.

You can imagine how impressed our twenty-two year old daughter was with our marine capabilities.

I rose early the last morning of our stay to find the boat on the mooring next to ours, lying against our life lines. The wind had died leaving the currents to turn and twist each boat in different directions. It appeared as if the moorings had been placed too close in proximity.

We had been the first boat to arrive on the mooring, which under the law of boat etiquette, would give us the freedom to stay while expecting the other to leave. But the French Madame aboard the neighbouring boat babbled away angrily while pointing to our boat as if we were at fault. We were planning to leave anyway and quite frankly, we were tired of the inadequacies of other sailors. We dropped the mooring line and left thankful we hadn't incurred anymore damage.

We moved on to Tobago Cay where the outboard motor continued to be unreliable in spite of Mike's good mechanical skills. That problem took us back to Union Island for repairs, and it was from there that Jennifer left, on her way back to Thailand. She sent an e-mail to acknowledge that she had arrived safely.

LEAVING THE GRENADINES

WE HAD SPENT two months exploring the Grenadines. The boat boys were beginning to call us by name and the taxi drivers were greeting Mike with a knuckle greeting. It was time to leave.

As we travelled north, islands were more developed. Behind us were deserted beaches, fishermen's bays stacked with mounds of conch shells, and goats that poked their curious heads into village internet cafés.

We were distant now from the pelicans in Chatham Bay that perched on white splattered rocks. We used to watch them lift their clumsy bodies into the air, and burdened with heavy bills, plunge into the water when they dove for fish.

The resident turtle in Chatham Bay and the schools of needle fish that glowed brilliantly blue in the shadow of our stern light were already just memories. And so was upbeat Caribbean music.

On some islands, music accompanies the locals almost everywhere they go. And they play it loud. Around Soufrière on the west coast of St. Lucia, it seems to be a Sunday thing locals do: ride into a peaceful anchorage on a giant catamaran full of sun seeking islanders, while the vibrations from the music blaring from the cat's speakers almost loosen the fillings in your teeth. We could hear the ear rupturing rhythms before we saw them, before they had even rounded the corner; a little rumba, a little calypso, hip hop and invariably the lyrics of Bob Marley's reggae.

Behind us was Mustique, the island that sits in contrast to all the others. An island developed by someone's fantasy of bringing famous people together leading to our afternoon lunch a table away from Mick Jagger. Later that night, he had joined us for dinner at the Cotton House Restaurant, well, he didn't exactly join us, but we were in the same room.

WE were sailing away from the Windward Islands, cruising past islands of lush green mountains that appeared to have given birth to multiple inland hills. Peak after peak of greenery fell vertically into deep, sharp ravines. I wondered how trees could grow so densely, up so high. They seemed to almost snag drifting clouds with their branches. This was the island of St. Vincent, an island of pointy lush tropical covered cone-like mountains. Where shorelines support fiords, inlets and bays, and small fishing villages tuck into gorges cupped by the giant hills. Higher in the hills, banana plantations, provide a living for farmers. Higher yet, marijuana plantations support the majority of cannabis users in the Caribbean.

We stopped in Martinique for a night. The forecast in the morning was for light winds around fifteen knots. Our next planned anchorage was eight to nine hours away. I had planned to serve a hot breakfast while underway. A breakfast of French toast and maple syrup would be a treat.

As we sailed up the coast in early morning light, the sun climbed up the backs of the Cabaret Mountains, poking light between cleavages of intertwining valleys. With the glow of a new day's light, dark foliage on the densely treed hillsides burst into palettes of shimmering lime greens. A school of dolphins, swimming off our beam, broke through the water in leaps and bounds. With white underbellies glistening in the sun, they duplicated our speed with ease.

It was a magnificent morning and we were pleased to be under full sail.

As we cleared the protection of the island, we were surprised to be hit by a thirty knot wind. It hit us like the backlash of a jet engine, punching full force into our main and Yankee sails. The boat heeled abruptly to port.

We immediately reefed both sails to balance the load of wind but while doing so, I mismanaged the Yankee sheet, causing it to tangle with itself at the bow.

The past two days of high winds had stirred up the sea and we were suddenly feeling the effects of 5 metre (15 foot) waves. The further we sailed from shore, the steeper the waves. Airy white plumes of foam smothered the foredeck and we concluded it was unsafe to go forward, even harnessed, to undo the mess I had created. The wind continued to increase. Soon it was blowing in the forties. The seas steepened. When the waves built to eye level, sunlight transformed the cresting waves into the most beautiful translucent, emerald green prisms.

Our sail plan was not appropriate for the conditions; high winds, too much heel, not enough boat speed. We needed to replace the Yankee with the staysail. The required maneuvers are relatively easy on an Oyster if you haven't allowed the sheets to tangle.

I insisted on cleaning up my own mess and I left the cockpit to go forward. Staying low to the deck I moved my tether along the jackline that would hold me fast to the boat if I should slip overboard. The toe rail was partially buried and my feet were often submerged under sizzling water. I inched myself forward in a crouch position, my right hand grasping and sliding along the boat's stainless handrail and my left hand along the lifelines. My wet, salty hands were too slippery to be of much help for gripping and the thought occurred to me that the wobbly stanchions and resulting loose lifelines, that we had not yet replaced since our last collision, might not do their job of keeping me onboard if I should fall against them.

While riding the heaving deck, I kept an eye out for waves that I knew would crash against the bow, run up the deck and saturate me. If I saw them in time, I turned my head away in an attempt to avoid the wet, stinging assault to my face.

I reached the foredeck.

Safety aboard a boat dictates that anyone maneuvering forward keep at least one handhold. But my harness tether, which was clipped to the jackline along the toe rail, was at the end of its length and prevented me from reaching either of the tangled sheets easily. I let go of both handholds, and inched my way towards the centre of the sloping foredeck on my hands and knees. I leaned with all my might into my harness in an attempt to gain an inch or two in the direction of the tangled lines. *Baccalieu III* speeded forward, her bow dipping into oncoming waves, splitting some mid-centre, and causing explosions of ocean to strike my foul weather gear with crisp, clear whacks of salty rain. Water poured off my head into my eyes.

The Yankee sheets hung from the foreguy in a twisted clump of knots. Straining towards the flailing sheets, I grabbed one and pulled. Miraculously, the knot came untangled.

With the end of the sheet in my hand, I inched my way back to the cockpit.

After pulling out the staysail, the boat performed with much less stress. We settled into the next six hours of hand steering through the heaviest weather we had yet experienced onboard *Baccalieu III*. Waves hit the hull just aft of the quarter, sending salt spray into the cockpit fully saturating us and coating our sunglasses with crystals. Unable to see, I recalled an accomplished sailor in Cowes, who had reminded me to let myself be guided by the feel of the wind on my face. I had become so comfortable with using wind instruments, I had forgotten the basics.

The boat felt well balanced and powerful. It was an exhilarating ride. I'll never forget that feeling, that first experience of reigning in the boat in high winds; setting her up with what she needed to perform. She was like a racehorse that needed a little TLC and some direction.

We spent the night in an anchorage off the coast of Dominica, then carried on the next morning to Guadeloupe. We were disappointed to leave Dominica without doing a recommended hiking trip, but the weather was right for us to move north and we had a deadline to be in Antigua, not only for repairs, but our plans included returning to Toronto for two weeks.

When we arrived in Guadalupe, it was the first time we had been tied to a dock in over two months. We spent two days absorbed in maintenance; the engine was due for an oil change, a few small repairs needed our attention and the deck was due for a serious cleaning—one of those 'get down on your knees and scrub' jobs. As well, we were at the point of taking our dirty underwear out of the laundry bag to wear it again, if I didn't get it washed soon.

Taking a break from all this work, we rented a car to tour the island. Our plan was to visit Carbet Falls, reportedly the tallest falls in the Caribbean. We were assured that if we followed the road signs, we would have no trouble finding it.

Cruising down the highway, following the directions of our rent-a-car map, we ticked off the exits until we caught sight of a sign announcing the way to the falls. With a quick turn off the highway in the direction of the arrow, we bounced down a road through the middle of a sugarcane field, trying not to bottom out the Renault in the washed out potholes. We came to a 'T' in the road. We took a guess and veered left, passed through a town, then more country road, only to find ourselves back at the very spot we had turned off the interstate highway. We attempted again to direct the car where the sign indicated. The single lane dirt road was further hampered by giant, encroaching shoots of sugarcane. Bisecting the field of tall grasses a second time, we chanced taking a different direction at the intersection, but we came once again to the same spot we had turned off the highway. I was wishing we could have sought directions from the hikers we had seen walking the road, but we speak little French. On the third attempt we passed them again. I smiled meekly and waved.

We headed down a road resembling more a cattle trail than a road. It dead-ended in front of a lone country house. A sign announced parking for the falls. A lady stepped from her house. We offered to pay for parking but she proclaimed, in broken English, that the parking was free as long as we purchased a drink or something to eat from her restaurant when we returned from our hike. Looking down at our sandaled feet, she shook her head disapprovingly, indicating our foot attire would not do. We followed her to a shack where she secured a pair of high rubber boots for me and a pair of rubber shoes for Mike. She wiped out the inside of my boots, then handed me a pair of men's dress socks.

I couldn't recall the guide book mentioning any of this. It had stated that it was a simple matter to locate the falls and once there, it was a thirty minute walk on a well laid-out trail. But our lady friend thrust two walking sticks into our hands and indicated she would see us in "deux heures!"

Walking through dense rainforest of bamboo and mahogany trees we trekked over a road embedded with stones and intertwining tree roots in our slipper-like soled foot wear. Mike announced he wished he had his sandals back.

We waded through mud and crossed bridges constructed of fallen limbs. The trail led to a rock face where a rope helped hikers avoid headlong plunges. We lowered ourselves to river level.

The falls we came to was probably the smallest in the Caribbean rather than the tallest. It was hardly worth taking a picture of. It had taken us so long to reach the falls that we had to forgo eating at the ladies restaurant in order that we could return the rental car on time. We tipped the shoe lady handsomely and sped back to town.

We had obviously trekked to the wrong falls. I hoped our navigation abilities proved better than our map reading skills.

THE following day, we left Guadeloupe to anchor off a secluded island in the Îles des Saintes. It was a reclusive island concealed from any sign of habitation.

Not long after settling in, we felt the boat jerk against the anchor. Then a distinct thud sounded beneath the keel followed by a rumble similar to that of a jet breaking the sound barrier.

The cause was an aftershock, an adjustment in the earth's plates resulting from the massive earthquake in Indonesia several weeks earlier. The jolt brought thoughts of Jennifer.

Following sunset, we sat in stillness with a thousand shimmering lights showing from across the bay on Guadeloupe. On the barren hill above us, a giant illuminated cross beckoned fisherman and seaman to a safe refuge.

ANTIGUA AND BARBUDA

*This place might not be burglar
proof but you are not bullet proof*

SIGN IN STOREFRONT IN ST. JOHN'S

IN THE YACHTING world, Antigua is known as one of the better places in the Caribbean for boat repairs. And we certainly needed some repairs. Our stanchions were bent, the bow pulpit crushed, the cap rail gouged, the gate contorted, and the heavy stainless fairlead torn from the teak capping.

It's no wonder Antigua has professional yacht facilities. During Antigua's annual Superyacht Cup some of the largest racing vessels in the world come to compete. Mike Slade's 30 metre (100 foot) *Leopard* and Peter Harrison's 35 metre (115 foot) *Sojana*, frequently moor here. Owners of mega racers often float second yachts to house crews preparing for Antigua Week which attracts over two hundred boats from around the world.

Other luxury yachts, such as the world's largest single masted cruising yacht, the 75 metre (247 foot) *Mirabella V*, are often docked here. The mainsail on *Mirabella V*, weighs 1.4 tons and her cruising spinnaker is almost the size of three tennis courts. For the pleasure of her guests, she stows a 9 metre (29 foot) Hinckley tender, four laser dinghies, two small high-performance inflatable boats, jet skis, kayaks and four windsurfers. She has the facilities to serve twelve guests, and these include a cinema theatre, sauna and gym. Below, in the drop-down stern, a Jacuzzi accommodates thirty. In 2012 she was dry-docked in Plymouth, England, for an extension to her hull and emerged in 2014 thirteen feet longer!

Sometimes the *Maltese Falcon*, a hundred and thirty million dollar Perini Navi is also in port. The Perini is fitted with three self standing masts, similar to a square rigger. Each of her masts rotate, allowing the 2,400 square metres (25,800 square feet) of sail to fold into the innovative rigging. With that, she can reach twenty knots of speed under sail.

Another Antigua attraction for super yachts is the Classic Yacht Regatta that attracts fifty to sixty restored wooden ketches, sloops and schooners annually. Tall rigged ships like *Tenacious*, will often run the course simply for entertainment.

The Boat International Concours d'Elégance is another competition that takes place in Antigua when classic yachts show like immaculately groomed, Thoroughbreds. Stainless fittings are polished to the standards of Royal silver while lines and sheets are laid out on teak decks, curled and twisted into perfected rope patterns. Coach roofs, pilot houses and coamings are so highly varnished, the wood glistens like transparent ice. With steady hands and unimaginable patience, the varnish is applied by Antiguans who have become known worldwide for their expertise. During the off season they are beckoned north to both the U.S. and the Mediterranean, to work on yachts that migrate there for the summer.

WITH the knowledge that Antigua attracts all these magnificent yachts, I expected to find an overdeveloped, touristy jungle. But nothing could be further from the truth. The flavour of English Harbour is pure naval history, with little sign of modern luxuries. A Naval officer's house circa 1855, officer's quarters built in 1810, a pitch and tar store from 1788—all these structures have been restored to some degree and are now used for customs, immigration, small businesses and hotels and restaurants. Even the sail loft, which handled our canvas needs, was once used to cut masts from huge logs of timber.

A small grocery store, sans air-conditioning, donates as much space to spirits as it does to groceries. A chandlery, several marine services, women selling Antigua T-shirts and numerous casual restaurants with chalk board menus and streetside patios, dot the roadside along uneven sidewalks. Restaurants in English Harbour serve very good food; there is even one that offers daily "crispy fire-roasted suckling pig".

ANTIGUANS who varnish yachts and are known by their nicknames, Country, Hambone, Skill and Acid, offer to wash hulls, scrape barnacles from the underside of boats and clean stainless. But like everything else in the Caribbean, an owner needs to know the going rate or suffer inflated costs.

Several laundry services, run by local women, pick up soiled laundry from visiting boats and return it with everything ironed, including underwear.

Roti Sue visits the docks daily, hauling behind her a refrigerated cooler filled with beef, chicken and shrimp roti. Custom orders she takes during the day, are made that very night and delivered the next day. Each roti is rolled in foil, allowing them to be easily frozen and reheated. They are well worth the price she charges.

Two large bays in Antigua, English Harbour and Falmouth Harbour are located on the south coast adjacent to one another. They were used by the British navy from 1725 until the late 1800s. From the sea, the entrance to English Harbour is difficult to locate. Its camouflage of protruding rocks and extending cliffs were crucial features when hiding a naval force. The harbour offers excellent protection from severe weather. It is well known as a hurricane hole, a place to secure yachts during storms. At the entrance, remnants of Fort Berkeley sit crumbled on a natural peninsula and Shirley Heights, an old guard post, is now a scenic lookout that rocks with music as the sun sets each Sunday when local bands play an assortment of party music and food is cooked over an open barbeque.

Captain Horatio Nelson arrived in 1784 to develop British naval facilities at English Harbour for warships whose purpose was to capture valuable sugar islands in the eastern Caribbean. The harbour was later the base for ships that enforced the very unpopular Navigation Act, a series of laws imposed to stop illegal trading between the English colonies in the Caribbean and traders from the United States.

Nelson's Dockyard in English Harbour is today the only remaining naval dockyard of that period in the world. Naval warships were repaired here, maintained, careened and loaded with supplies. Square riggers and brigantines threw their ropes ashore to wrap around bollards which are still anchored in the soil. During this time, Antigua became the gateway to the Caribbean, controlling sailing routes to rich island colonies. The facilities on the island allowed ships to remain in the Caribbean rather than having to return to the UK for their maintenance. The Dockyard is now almost fully restored and today provides similar services to visiting yachts. Nelson's Dockyard, is a UNESCO World Heritage Site and National Park.

IN 1694, two brothers of British background, by the name of Codrington came to Antigua to assess the island for its possible future in farming sugarcane. At the time, most of the island, like the majority of other Caribbean islands, was completely forested, but by the middle of the 18th century the land had been cleared of trees, and in their place stood more than a hundred and fifty cane processing windmills, each doing the work for a sugar plantation. The Codringtons had owned nine of these plantations and had also established a stock farm on Barbuda, a neighbouring island, for the purpose of supplying food and slaves to the plantations. For over three hundred years sugarcane remained the dominant crop in Antigua and today there are almost a hundred of these windmills remaining throughout the island, several incorporated into restaurants, bars and resorts.

Most Antiguans are of African heritage, descendants of slaves brought to the island to labour on the plantations.

When Britain abolished slavery throughout its empire in 1834, Antigua announced an immediate emancipation of slavery rather than choosing the optional four year apprenticeship period.* In 1981, upon gaining independence from the UK, then Prime Minister, V.C. Bird stated, "We have finally shaken the yoke of colonialism. You will never have to work on the land again." Bird's speech lead to today's standing joke among local Antiguans, that the people misheard the promise and thought he said they would never have to work again.

When farming sugarcane came to an end in the 1870s, the islanders struggled to earn a living. Today there are few who work the fertile lands of the island, with the consequence that fruits and vegetables are imported from the neighbouring island of Dominica. The country's prime source of income is tourism.

WE RETURNED TO Toronto and left *Baccalieu III* docked at the Catamaran Marina in Falmouth Harbour in the hands of a British Antiguan, and good friend, Mike Rose. Upon our return to the island, Mike, a retired Royal British Navy man,

---

* Following the Abolition of Slavery Act in 1833, the Emancipation Act (1834) stipulated that slaves would continue to work on plantations throughout the British Caribbean as 'apprentices' for a further six years. During this time, slaves were not paid, but were to be limited to working 7–10 hours a day. The Emancipation Act reassured plantation owners that their labour supply would not be affected.

invited us to spend an evening with members of the Royal Naval Tot Club of Antigua & Barbuda on board the three masted barque *Tenacious*.

In 2011, the Tot Club turned twenty years old. Its worldwide membership, which has reached over three hundred and fifty, supports Antiguan charities, improves local National Park hiking trails and aids individuals in need of assistance. Nightly tots while in Antigua, allows for meeting local expats as well as visiting yachtsmen.

One of the aims of the club is to carry on the naval tradition of daily toasts. The members get together at the end of each day to swig a 'half a gill' of Navy issue Pusser's Blue Label rum, or the equivalent, as was the custom in the Royal Navy up until 1970. One must be invited to become a member of the Tot Club and then partake in seven tots within a period of no more than fourteen days. The group gathers at precisely 1800, reflecting the customs of the Royal Navy. A pre-requisite to joining the club is an interest in Britain's Royal Navy and her exploits, as one must pass an oral examination of both Nelson's Battles and Royal Naval history.

At the daily gathering, a reading is given from the *Royal Navy Day by Day*, which catalogues significant navy happenings over the past eight hundred years. This is often followed by cheers and cat calls from those gathered, depending on the Navy's success or failure which occurred on the coinciding date. Following the reading, one of the original naval toasts is offered. Each day calls for a different toast. Wednesday's is "Ourselves, as no one else is liable to concern themselves with our welfare." Saturday's toast is "Sweethearts and Wives. May they never meet."

Following the daily toast, the standing toast of the Royal Navy lower deck is offered — "The Queen, God Bless Her" after which everyone downs the tot in one gulp.

Mike was a successful candidate who now has the privilege

of flying the Royal Naval Tot Club burgee from *Baccalieu III's* flag halyard. This is no small matter. The Tot Club, conceived by chairman and founder Mike Rose, successfully obtained permission from the British Admiralty to incorporate the Nelsonian pre-1801 White Ensign into its pennant.

JUST three boats down from where we were docked at the Catamaran Marina, Toronto friends were onboard their boat, *Entrada*. They had been in Antigua for several weeks, and they offered to take us on a drive through the countryside including a stop at the market in St. John's.

It was Saturday when we took the drive, a religious holiday for the Seventh Day Adventists when women and young girls dressed in an array of colourful Sunday-best dresses and wide brimmed hats walk the country road to their place of worship cradling black bibles. Men, on the other hand, while engaged in conversation, sat clustered with friends on verandahs; most holding a bottle of Red Stripe while leaning against posts or sitting on unpainted railings.

St. John's, the capital of Antigua, is a drab looking city with cracked sidewalks and ill stocked stores that look depressingly grey.

While approaching the market on foot, an evangelist, amplifying his voice through a megaphone, reprimanded the world for its sins while his comrade, standing on a wooden crate at the market entrance, targeted us as the focus of his preaching. Bent at the waist while his finger traced our steps towards the market entrance, he spoke as if the devil himself had come to visit and ranted that all should repent.

Inside the market were numerous wooden tables piled high with limes and lemons, miniature local pineapples the size of ketchup bottles, finger rolls, a sweet cousin to the banana, melons, passion fruits, dasheen, christophines and more. Outside, women sat stripping needles from cacti, which would be cooked for a vegetable. Vendors sold stalks of green bananas from the backs of pickup trucks. Others skillfully peeled sugarcane with giant cutlasses. The cane would be used in cooking or eaten as a sweet. Friendly, heavy-weight women sold jars of homemade mango and passion fruit jellies, unpasteurized honey and ginger sweet cakes prepared from recipes handed down from their great grandmothers.

Across the road, fish scales the size of quarters sailed through the air as gutters cleaned blue, tough skinned species known as old wife. An assortment of brilliant turquoise and orange reef fish, the sort that attracts scuba divers to a site, lay on ice with bulging eyes. In a separate building, men steadied large freshly killed carcasses with bare hands while lifting sharp cutlasses above their heads then plunging them through the remains, swinging down with accuracy between bones. A young apprentice, dressed in a long, white coat, cut large portions into more manageable sizes using a hand saw.

A DRIVE around the island showed areas of mahogany and cedar trees and lush hillside gardens coloured with the red and orange blooms of hibiscus trees. Old sugar plantations and mills are most often overgrown and barely visible. Subsistence farming is common among Antiguans and many own at least a small plot of land and a few farm animals like chickens. Hundreds of goats and cattle graze freely even though laws require cattle to be chained. Many that are seen roaming are often dragging their neck chains. Nighttime driving conditions can be dangerous.

The beauty of Antigua is appreciated best from the sea where hundreds of remote bays, most inaccessible by land, offer lovely anchorages. Often there are nearby reefs demolishing waves to create that ever-so-pleasant flat water needed for a steady night's sleep onboard a boat. Many a night we were lulled into sleep with the pleasant sound of pounding surf.

Just thirty miles north of Antigua lies her sister island, Barbuda. Barbuda's eastern shores lie along the Atlantic Ocean while to the west, lays the Caribbean Sea. Almost totally flat, the island appears featureless but for a spectacular beach with some of the silkiest sand I have ever sunk my toes into. Often we were the only persons standing on it. From Cedar Tree Point in the northwest to Palmetto Point in the south, forty-eight kilometres (thirty miles) of uninterrupted white silica graces the shores like a tablecloth of pale silk. The beach continues around the southernmost tip extending past Coco Point Lodge where dated but airy cottages attract those who seek privacy and can afford to pay for it.

Barbuda sits alone, out of the way of regular sailing routes. History documents at least one hundred and fifty-three ships lost on local surrounding reefs. For certain it should be approached with the sun well overhead in order to detect an anchoring spot free of coral heads.

Barbuda is one of the least populated islands in the Caribbean and has a genuine laid-back lifestyle. Barbudans do not live here to cater to tourists who require rum punches and mojitos; they live here because this is where they were born.

The population of fifteen hundred lives mostly in the village of Codrington, the island's capital and only town. When we first visited, there wasn't even a paved road on the island.

Barbuda wasn't always as quiet as it is today. The Codrington's, who owned several sugar mills throughout Antigua, leased the British owned island from 1677 to 1870. The island had been a source of food and a breeding nursery of slaves for the Codrington family who provided both food and slaves to their plantations and sugar mills in Antigua. At one time, the island supported five hundred slaves, three hundred head of cattle and thousands of sheep. Eighty acres supported fields of corn, yams and cotton.

During this time, slaves rebelled against living conditions, cruel punishment and separation of families, then again in 1834, when they learned that Britain had granted all slaves within her colonies freedom except for those on the island of Barbuda.

IN addition to the exclusive resort located at Coco Point, there was, until recently, another place on Barbuda that offered privacy to a small number of wealthy guests. The K Club was an unpretentious, cottage-like development offering a summer camp feel to its visitors. In the past it had been a winter holiday retreat for Lady Diana and her two sons, Prince William and Prince Harry. The K in K Club stands for the Italian fashion designer, Krizia Mariuccia Mandelli, who opened the simply constructed beach resort in 1990. But now the resort has been abandoned and left to decay.

Walking the beach, we walked past the resort's swimming pool, now an empty, dark mouldy pit. The place was deserted and our taxi driver, Lytton, a descendant of Codrington's slaves, said the Barbudans would like to have the land back. While throwing his hand in the air in a gesture of disgust, he added how the government of Antigua had leased it to the Italian designer with a ninety-nine year contract.

By chance, we had met up with South African sailing friends whom we had met in England several months earlier. We were touring the island together.

As we drove towards town, two salt ponds, formerly excavated for commercial export, lay like gouged wounds in the landscape. Islanders still visit the site to scrape salt for personal usage. Donkeys, once the primary means of travel during Codrington's time, had long ago gone feral and now grazed with their young alongside the road.

A small bungalow styled hospital employs one local doctor and a few nurses who are supported each month by a travelling physician from the United States. Not far from the hospital, children dressed in traditional school uniforms sat at desks near windows opened to the breezes. Each grade was housed in a separate building.

In the corner grocery store, basic food provisions sat on dusty shelves, while the shop keeper swabbed the floor trying to win a battle with sand that was tracked or blown through the opened door. Small wooden houses, some painted in the preferred local colours of white and turquoise, were fenced to keep wandering sheep from devouring scant gardens of beans and flowers. An unseasonable rainfall had recently filled the street's pot holes with inches of muddy water which now offered drinking holes for roving animals.

For lunch, Lytton took us to a house where the owners cooked home style meals in a small family kitchen. We were served large portions of stewed goat and fish over rice while we sat on their porch at plastic tables. To use the washroom, I walked past two bedrooms; each bare except for a double mattress lying on the floor. The living room was used as a take-out area.

FOLLOWING lunch, we headed toward the limestone caves situated at the highest part of the island. Barbuda is a mixture of coral and limestone and we could often identify shells and hardened brain coral under-foot. The area surrounding the cave is lush with tangles of low growing vegetation. Continuing past jagged boulders and balsam bushes, Lytton demonstrated how the leaves from the bushes could be used to heal wounds. We veered off onto a path that led towards the cave.

The cave is small and in fact not really a cave at all, but a vertical sided sink hole where a fossilized part of the upper tooth of a Pliocene shark, which lived two to four million years ago, was discovered in 1997.

We climbed up through the ascending cavern to reach

the cliff, only 30 metres (100 feet) above us. Stopping there, we overlooked Two Foot Bay, another spectacular beach on the northeast side of the island. Legend says that the beach earned its name when an escaping slave put his shoes on backwards to confuse his trackers.

It took us forty minutes to cross a wide shallow bay in a small open fishing craft, where a giant red ocean buoy, swept there from an unknown location during a recent hurricane, sat, orphaned in the bay. We considered how confusing it would have been to have come across the wandering buoy mid-ocean! A mangrove swamp surrounding the bay is a nesting site of the endangered frigate bird, a seabird that can neither walk nor swim due to its small feet. Barbuda's colony of frigates is the largest outside of the Galápagos Islands.

When we arrived at the mangroves, male frigates sat puffing their scarlet throats to balloon size in an attempt to attract females. It was mating season when the males tremble outstretched wings and produce a drumming sound by vibrating their beaks. Frigate birds have the most elaborate mating displays of all seabirds.

IT WAS APPROACHING the end of April, a time when boaters begin to leave the hurricane regions and migrate towards their summer homes. Some head to the Mediterranean, others go south of twelve degrees latitude, or like us, head north of Cape Hatteras, North Carolina, U.S.A.

Following the tour of the island, we bid our South African friends goodbye as they had chosen to summer their boat in Trinidad and we would be travelling in opposite directions.

That evening, we heard a dinghy approach *Baccalieu III*. It was our friends; they had purchased lobsters from the fishermen in Codrington and were delivering a gift of cooked lobster tails.

The following morning, with the sun announcing a new day, and our friends about to lift their anchor in departure, we manned our dinghy and delivered a dozen hot banana muffins to their cockpit.

Like so many others that we had met during our travels, we never knew if we would ever meet again. But we did. We saw them months later after arriving in South Africa.

NEVIS

*The higher monkey climb, the
more you see he backside*
EXPRESSION ON THE ISLAND NEVIS

IT WAS A Friday night when we anchored off the island of Nevis. Music from a small local band drifted across the water filling our cabin with simple religious tunes until around midnight, when it ceased. I know what time it was, because we lay there exposed to it hour after hour without choice. Not that the cessation of music indicated the rest of the night was going to be quiet. Far from it. The momentary silence was merely a cue that the pastor was about to fire up with some bible thumping accolades. A single monotonous drum beat accompanied a hallowed Martin Luther King voice that carried on until 4:30 in the morning. Then all lay quiet; the drummer's arm finally ceased banging out that monotonous one second beat, the pastor stopped yelling, even the moon took an exit.

LIKE a ruffled toupee, clouds snagged by Nevis' volcanic mountain peak appeared at first light. Then the whole sky began to streak with pink. As it did the following morning and the morning after that. That's why tourists come here. They can depend on seeing the sun most mornings. Not that any of them are out of bed to see it from the beginning, but each morning on cue, just like that preacher on Friday nights, the sun celebrates a new day with a splash of light from behind the mountain that sleeps nearby. While creating a conical silhouette, the sun pushes the mountain forward into the day when it becomes giant size, like you would expect a dormant volcano to be.

There are some things you can only witness from a boat.

IN ONE OF his three trips to the Caribbean, Christopher Columbus came upon two islands separated by a shallow channel. Some say he thought the clouds looked like snow falling over the lush green hillsides influencing him to name the one island, Las Nieves. Centuries later, a famous Canadian singer and song writer, Nelly Furtado, would love the island so much that she would name her daughter Nevis.

Who knows really if it was that exact adjoining piece of land that Columbus named St. Christopher? Mapping of islands was not that accurate in those days and there are several islands lying in the area. But it is fact that the island nearest to Nevis became known as St. Christopher, eventually nicked to a simpler form — Saint Kitts. The locals pronounce it 'Sinkits'.

The dividing shallow channel between the two islands is documented on charts as Narrow Channel but the islands are miles apart in the type of worlds they offer. St. Kitts is far more developed while a good amount of Nevis remains real-life Caribbean-charming, with little sign of mass tourism. Both islands are located off the regular cruising track; neither having marinas nor much in the way of protective bays that attract sailors.

Nevis is a one town island, with the main street of Charlestown boasting a mixture of boutiques and dusty old stores. Abandoned historical stone-walled buildings sit waiting for successful enterprises, while small coconut shingled houses look as if they could blow away with a sneeze.

Brightly painted cottages, some signifying the Victorian age with quaint gingerbread verandahs might offer bed and breakfast accommodations while more recent construction emphasizes Creole architecture. Early European influences such as louvered shutters and balusters and peaked roofs that were designed to help dissipate some of the Caribbean's persistent heat, are part of the historic town. Buildings sit on stone blocks allowing flood waters to flow beneath them. The blocks also allow the house to be moved easier when it's determined that it is sitting on someone else's land.

With only a few cars on the island, there is no need for the town to have a stop light. Locals from the countryside gather in the back of a pickup truck to travel to town.

Standing across from the Courthouse Square, we often saw a man standing on a corner whittling a stock of sugarcane in the hope of selling a piece to a passerby. By four o'clock in the afternoon the streets became a busy social network for uniformed students returning from school. It's a misconception that school uniforms are supplied by the government. In fact, many low income parents struggle to provide the required outfits for their children.

Several small groceries offer good provisioning, some catering to the yachtsman with disposable income while others remain loyal to their local customers offering the sale of pig's snouts and ham hocks. Produce, including pineapples and bananas, arrive on the Tuesday ferry and is sold by ladies at the harbourside market.

A chalk board leaning up against a hardware store announced the daily scripture reading and another one in front of the church presented a similar message including times of prayer. The day we were in town, two young school boys couldn't resist the available piece of chalk and mischievously made a few changes. There were more churches on this island than most others we had visited. In addition to the historic Anglican churches, today islanders attend Baptist, Seventh Day Adventist, Church of God, or Methodist services.

IN the 17th century, sugarcane was the main crop grown on most Caribbean islands. Eighty to ninety percent of the sugar consumed in Western Europe originated in the Caribbean. To keep costs down, thousands of African slaves were imported to the islands. Working sixteen hour days, they slashed the wooden-like cane stalks with machetes, schlepped the stalks* from the field to a mill, crushed the fibres to extract the juices and boiled the liquid to produce sugar.

The French colonies, Martinique, Guadeloupe and Saint-Domingue† [sic], also known as Santo Domingo, had some of the largest sugar plantations. Work was so grueling that plantations on Martinique required a thousand new slaves per year to replace those who died. In the late 1700s and early 1800s, Saint-Domingue produced forty percent of all the sugar consumed in Europe. In order to sustain a labour force, eight thousand slaves were imported annually.

France abolished slavery within its colonies in 1794.‡

Between the mid-1600s and 1700s, Nevis was the main landing port for slaves in the Leeward Islands. Sugarcane had been thickly planted from the shores of the Caribbean Sea right up to the base of the cloud topped mountains. Now the whole island seems to move in undulating patterns, swaying with stout cane stalks against a cerulean sky. The most famous estate, Montpelier, is where the wedding of Captain Horatio

---

* One stalk of sugarcane weighs approximately 1.3 kg (3 lbs.)

† Saint-Domingue was located on the western portion of the island Tortuga, which is today called Haiti.

‡ Slavery was abolished in the British West Indies in 1834, the French Antilles in 1848 and the Dutch Antilles in 1849

Nelson and a Nevisian, Fanny Nesbit, took place beneath the cool of a silk cotton tree. The last sugar plantation closed in 1930, leaving the remnants of lofty stone towered windmills to grace the countryside. Several planters' homes have since been developed into boutique hotels or plantation inns using the adjacent stone clad sugar mills for restaurants, artist studios or guest suites.

Up until a few years ago, Nevis was awash in poverty. Then Four Seasons Hotel and Resorts, a Canadian based company, constructed a luxury hotel on the island.

Nearby, a beach bar called Sunshine's offers a contrasting ambience to the hotel's five star luxury. At Sunshine's, country flags hang from the ceiling and old license plates decorate the bar. Sunk into the soft, beach sand floor, picnic tables provided tourists with a place to enjoy sundowners and bar food. A good stereo banged out an eclectic mix of reggae, rhythm and blues. A barbeque around the back cooked Sunshine's specialties of fish, chicken and ribs.

Sunshine, the entrepreneurial islander and owner of the bar, hails from St. Kitts. He had formerly been an employee of a local tour company catering to beach parties. He would be dropped off at Pinney's Beach with a grill and cooler of drinks to await the arrival of tourists.

It was during the time the Four Seasons was under construction and he was often visited by construction workers requesting that he barbeque them a lunch.

That's when he got the idea of setting up his own business. But after construction of the hotel was completed, management asked Sunshine to vacate the beach. In defiance, he constructed an open air thatched roof bar and continued to visit daily with his barbeque. Success did not come easy; he waited two years before he had any returning clientele.

Although his premises have been destroyed, in the

aftermath of eight hurricanes, and twice by fire, the dreadlocked Sunshine keeps putting up lightly constructed huts, each time with slightly improved conveniences. Now his establishment is brightly painted in a Caribbean pallet of tropical colours and has a real floor. The bar and grill is noted as one of the top ten bars in the Caribbean; one of those rustic drinking holes that sailors love to frequent.

Famous visitors such as Princess Di, Wayne Gretzky, Oprah, and Kevin Bacon have left their pictures to be hung on the walls.

When we returned to our dinghy, which we had tied to the town wharf, we found it piled onto other dinghies as if it had been involved in a mangled traffic accident. A small fishing boat had arrived and rammed into the small rubber boats on its way into the dock.

Back onboard *Baccalieu III*, I browsed through two local newspapers. The sports page in the *Leeward Times* reported the most recent developments in the present day soap operas, Days of Our Lives, As the World Turns and The Young and the Restless. The second paper, *St. Martin's Dock Talk* had a feature article entitled, "The Largest Slaughter of Marine Mammals on the Planet Has Begun on Canada's Atlantic Coast."

I considered taking down our ensign.

Leaving Nevis, we continued sailing north. We made a stop at St. Barts (St. Barths) sometimes called Saint Barthélemy. St. Barts is part of the French West Indies and just two hundred and fifty miles off the coast of Puerto Rico.

I woke early the following morning to the boisterous raucous of Laughing Gulls. "Ha ha haah haah." I walked to the foredeck and spread out my exercise mat. As early sunlight crept over the hills, the tiled roofs of St. Bart's appeared crimson in the distance. Above me, layers of clouds riding elevations of opposing wind currents crisscrossed without colliding. Lying on my back, I watched them stack one upon another, often up-curling like a mixture of boiling water. Low, wispy cirrus appeared to lengthen like threads pulled from a skein of wool. And Nimbus clouds, those grey-tinted combos that show best in the evening when beams of sunlight burn through like laser beams, blanketed small patches of the bluest of skies.

Nature's display of clouds rewarded those who got out there early, and could easily convert the most reluctant to experience the hours of early morning.

St. Bart's harbour once offered shelter to French buccaneers who sought refuge after plundering Spanish galleons. The pirates sold their newly acquired wealth here and took on provisions before setting off on another rampage of looting. In the early 1700s, the town of Gustavia was established a free port. Merchants sold all types of goods including cattle, which were sent there to avoid government procedures that were enforced on adjacent islands. The island has remained a free port ever since and now, while in the hands of the French, it has attracted French citizens to settle there.

We took the dinghy into town, a rundown sort of place where boutiques offer a variety of prestigious European fashions by the likes of Hublot, Cartier, Valentino, and Versace. The town is an oxymoron, kind of a rich man's 'down and dirty', where designer clothes are sold duty free in chic boutiques sitting in a town of broken streets and sidewalks.

The island is a must-stop for the elite, although at the time of our visit, most of the chic crowd had already flown back to Europe while their yachts were delivered without them back to the Mediterranean by professional crews. The harbour was full of smaller craft like ours waiting for the northern climes to warm up before venturing out of our comfy southern cocoons.

Wᴇ left the harbour at Gustavia and moved around the corner to a marine park, where we secured *Baccalieu III* to a mooring ball. The intimate bay, with adjacent parkland, is inaccessible by land. The following morning, when I stepped out on deck, the sea was creeping into the cove with undulating motion. Swells rode under our keel almost unnoticed, although the consequence was evident when water slid over the rock-strewn shoreline, rolling over one outcrop after the other, causing airy sea foam to ricochet up the craggy shore. Occasionally, waves broke on the far side of the rock jetty when I would witness explosions of water against a precipice, like bursts of shattering glass. A sea turtle, not far from the boat, surfaced for air in the rise and fall of the swell.

We wanted to go ashore, but with the surge as powerful as it was, landing a dinghy would be dangerous if not impossible. Instead, we took turns letting each other off in the water while the other stayed with the dinghy, waiting a safe distance from the rolling surf.

I lowered myself into the water and executed a simple breast stroke while heading towards shore and the breaking swell. I swam right into it. I felt the swell heave me skyward before swooshing me to shore. My knees scraped along gritty sand. I crawled, stumbling to the beach. Immediately I was concerned how I would break back through the force of water when I needed to return to the dinghy. It could very well be possible that I did not have the strength to catapult myself high enough over the surge and I would be repeatedly swept back to shore. Too late to worry about that now, I figured.

I found a set of wooden stairs to scale a steep embankment

and following a path, I trekked to the windward side of the island. I stood on the edge of a cliff watching waves bubble over the rocks below me. Swell after swell, rolled in filling jagged inlets while bellows of deep throaty sounds communicated the dangers of the shoreline. When a good force of wind met with my face, I came to appreciate even more, the protective anchorage we were in on the other side.

The path led me up yet another incline then descended on the far side of a hill. I found myself standing in a forest of cacti not much taller than me. Their prickly limbs reached towards a sky of tissue white clouds. Softened visually by the sun, the cactus needles took on the appearance of soft, silky threads. A swarm of white butterflies fluttered around me as if I had always been a part of their world. I stood there alone in the stillness wishing I could hold this sense of tranquility forever.

Shrubs without any particular beauty, some showing the scars of hurricanes, were like knights incognito. With sturdy waxed leaves, they offered protection for weaker, more beautiful species that grew beneath them. Single stemmed grasses sporting soft brown tassels waved gently in ocean breezes while guarding petite petals of wild tangerine marigold lookalikes. Huddled next to the earth, tiny white blooms, the size of my fingertips would honour any bride in her nosegay. Rose coloured morning glories wove creeping stems around tiny purple beauties, but the queen of flowers in this bouquet was an exquisite white bloom bursting with long slender petals like a cascade of exploding fireworks.

I wished I had had a camera. I stood there a long while etching the canvas into my memory. But then it was time to go; Mike was waiting. I trekked down to the beach. I could see him in the dinghy bobbing just beyond the surf. Ocean swells rolled into the shallows breaking into a wash after peaking. They collapsed in a crash of white.

I waded into the water.

Standing there I calculated it took about one second for the incoming surge to crest. In three more seconds it curled and shot down the slide. The first wave of water struck me in the shins. I teetered backwards, surprised at its power. I would need to make my way to the crest before any of it collapsed, then jump as high as I could to take the force as low on my body as possible. If I missed my timing, I would be picked up and thrown backwards towards the beach. I would land crumpled and maybe injured, but for certain I would be underwater.

I got on with it. I walked towards the breaking wave. I jumped; the surge seemed to lift me. I was through it; I just needed to make enough headway that I didn't become a part of the next swell.

I swam to the dinghy and climbed aboard. I told Mike how beautiful it was on shore, that it was worth every effort to visit it.

He lowered himself in the water, caught the first swell and rode it in.

THE MOON HAD just started to recycle, leaving a night as dark as any I had seen. We had just finished dinner in the cockpit when an interior light from another sailboat caught our attention. A boat that had not been there a few minutes before was now floating a few feet from our bow and it appeared as though no one was onboard. At least no one was in the cockpit.

The mooring we had tied to had placed us nearer to the rocks than we would have anchored. If this boat did not come to a stop on our hull, it was about to attempt passage through the narrow space between us and a shoreline of rocks. We picked up the red plastic fog horn we kept in the cockpit for emergencies and blew into it. We repeatedly sounded an alarm while spotlighting the approaching silhouette with our cordless hand held light.

Slowly, a body appeared in the companionway of the oncoming yacht. Whoever it was, appeared far too nonchalant for the emergency at hand, and we shouted the word, "Drifting!" The man onboard remained standing on his companionway steps for a few moments. While perhaps allowing his eyes to focus to the dark night, he heard our second warning, "Drifting!" Questioning our call, he called back, "Drifting?" His reply wasn't the excited tone one would expect in such a situation, it was more as if he were talking to us over a cup of tea. At any moment we expected to hear the scraping of an iron keel over a rock bottom when his boat would be thrown sideways into ours. I cupped my hands over my mouth forcing the word straight to its target and again shouted the word, "DRIFTING!"

It's not like we were kilometres from each other. I could have doused him with water had I been in possession of a good water pistol.

The boat had turned broadside and was inching its way closer, but instead of turning his motor on to prevent grounding, he slowly walked to the bow of his boat to inspect the situation. Bending over the bow, he searched for the mooring buoy that was there the last time he had looked. Surely, he would determine, in his sleepy, drugged state, something was not quite right.

We tried to jump start his adrenalin by flashing a million candle power spotlight on the rocks just ahead of him, but he casually turned and sauntered back to his cockpit, turned on the engine, pulled the throttle back, and just as nonchalantly as he had received the bad news, powered up the boat in reverse.

Wishing to avoid any possibility that he could not see our boat, we had by this time, thrown on all the outdoor lights we were equipped with: spreader lights, cockpit light, deck and stern lights. I think if we had been in possession of a hand grenade, as by now our thoughts were to be SWAT ready and 'take no hostages', we would have taken him out just as a precaution. Tactically, I think it would have been a good decision. Following what we had experienced in previous anchorages, I think our crime would have been forgiven.

As we stood in the cockpit, our boat lit up like the *Queen Mary*, we watched as he continued his backward journey in the direction of the mooring he had slipped loose from. As he floated past in reverse, he waved an appreciation and shouted thanks. The last we saw of him, he was travelling backwards towards the beach where he disappeared from our sight into darkness.

THIS anchorage was what we considered our last pleasure stop before heading north to Rhode Island U.S.A. Our next stop, St. Martin was only a jaunt of twenty-one nautical miles. Here we would prepare and provision for the passage north.

ARRIVING at St. Martin, (Saint Maarten), we dropped anchor and joined several other boats waiting for a lift bridge to open. It was the pass into Simpson Bay Lagoon, a large landlocked piece of water where captains of super yachts gather to take on duty free provisions. The bridge opens three times daily, however, if an owner is willing to part with $300 US, they will gladly open it anytime. It was obvious from the number of empty docks that the season was pretty much over and now sailboats outnumbered mega yachts. All were preparing for passages and watching for weather windows to proceed to their summer homes.

Simpson Bay's 12 square miles (19 square kilometres) of lagoon is also home to several live-aboards, many of which no longer have sails or even masts on their boats. Once a beautiful lagoon, miles of shallow water are now overwhelmed by the rusting, debris from hurricane-crippled yachts. Fishing vessels, disabled and deteriorating, continue to leak corrosive metals into the water while abandoned, damaged sailboats lay heeled at severe degrees creating a pathetic junk yard in a once spectacular setting.

The northern and larger part of St. Martin is French; the southern half, known as Sint Maarten is Dutch. This tolerable situation came about in 1648 when neither country could afford another battle. Consequently, the Treaty of Concordia (Partition Treaty) was signed. Based on the terms of this agreement, the peoples of St. Martin were to "live as friends and allies". Subsequently, each country established communities on either side of an imaginary midline boundary.

On the Dutch side, following the end of sugarcane farming, a tourist industry developed enhanced by the building of several casinos. The French side retains a more European flavour.

SIMPSON Bay had the best chandleries we had seen since leaving Palma Majorca and we shopped, stocking replacement parts and items to make small improvements while en route. We treated the deck with a mould reducer because the humidity and wet weather had nurtured a grey fungus in the teak again. I spent a few hours in the rigging doing maintenance while Mike dealt with mechanical issues. We were having problems with the main furling gear and the generator was mysteriously burning up impellers and shutting down.

All this had to be resolved before travelling north. As well, we needed to find a sail maker to reinforce the points where the sail attaches to the rigging. For this we needed to drop, fold, bag and deliver by dinghy, all three humungous pieces of sailcloth. After the work was completed, we wrestled with hoisting them in an opposing breeze that had chose to strengthen just as we were well into the chore. With sails billowing in the wind, we grappled with metres and metres of sailcloth until we succeeded in running them up in their proper places.

WE HAD RECENTLY noticed a marked change in the climate; cumulus clouds frequently bred stacks of grey storm clouds while mounting humidity increased the number of threatening wind squalls. The weather confirmed it was time to move on and we were both eager to get going. I possessed a nomadic spirit now, I think we both did. Moving from place to place had become a way of life. I wondered if I could ever accept a stationary lifestyle again.

As we awaited friends who were joining us from New York City, we watched weather patterns blow through creating adverse conditions for travelling north. It appeared that the timing of our friends arrival was going to be good. Light winds were expected and we decided to top up our nearly full diesel tanks one last time. We squeezed in another seventy-six litres (twenty gallons) of fuel in readiness for a predicted light air passage. Several hours after taking on fuel, we noticed a large stain on the deck, and discovered it was fuel seeping through the vents from the over filled tank. We cleaned it up as best we could, but watched frustrated the next day as it continued to seep from the tank.

HOMEWARD

*A bad day of sailing is a heckuva lot
better than the best day at work*

(At least some think this is true.)

THE PASSAGE TO Bermuda had been uneventful; too calm for even dolphin play. It had been a challenge for me to get through the passive night watches without wanting to nod off. I loaded up my MP3 player with lively music so my body kept rhythm to the beat rather than relaxing into the monotonous hum of boredom. Yes, I was groov'in in the cockpit, swaying the hips, dipping the shoulders, trying some new moves. I knew better than to move my feet during my secret dance parties because part of the cockpit is located over the master cabin and Mike would have wondered what the devil I was doing.

> Baby loves me yes, yes she does
> Oh, the girls out of sight, yeah

Don't you love how Neil Diamond sings the word *Alright* at the end of the verse? Aaaallright. His voice is so sexy. The hustle works well with this song; it's all upper body movement.

I also kept beat with the music by simply using a lot of goose necking. Another move I tried in the confined space was the twist, although it only seemed to be appropriate with certain tunes. The swim and the YMCA were good even though

I frequently banged my arms on the dodger. The Macarena kept me awake; I just omitted the ninety degree turns.

I suppose the chicken is another possibility but I like to think I have some standards.

ONE night I spotted a fishing vessel and after tracking it on the radar for an hour, I considered myself fortunate to have something to help focus my attention on. Mike nor our two guests got as lucky that night.

As the days passed, it slowly became less humid and nights became cooler, requiring that we dig out sweaters and long pants we had not seen since that fine summer we had spent in England almost a year ago.

The iron jenny worked in harmony with sail power for most of that trip, but we daren't complain as we knew the wind gods could have fun with us after our friends left us in Bermuda and we continued on the four day passage from there to Rhode Island.

The passage to Bermuda would have been surreal if you were trying to conquer ship-in-the-bottle folk art or were in need of a steady hand for needle point. Bearing a resemblance to the gentle movement of a gyroscope, the boat rolled ever so gently with heaving swells while the seas rippled beneath our keel like a rope bridge under foot. We simply became pieces of boat furniture moving in unison, and when I went topside, and looked out over the grand expanse of flat water, the sea was rising and falling like a massive air filled trampoline calmly bouncing with children's play. After dark, phosphorescence twinkled in our simple wake like floating stars fallen from the night sky.

Flying fish were our chief entertainment as they rushed in panic from our monster keel like shooting torpedoes of silver rain. Breaking the surface to enter an oxygen unfriendly world, they would glide great distances in order to save their lives.

Skimming inches above the water for the purpose of landing far from the predator, they would sometimes take a wrong turn and we would pick them off the deck in the morning, as hard as the bread I had made one day with expired yeast.

Our passage took us across the deepest part of the Atlantic Ocean the Puerto Rico Trench. The trench runs 500 miles (800 kilometres) long and reaches depths of up to 5.4 miles (8,690 metres) deep. Only one other area in the world's oceans is deeper, a long narrow trench located in the western Pacific Ocean east of the Mariana Islands. The Puerto Rico Trench is also known for being the area on Earth with the most negative gravity. Apparently scientists cannot explain this anomaly. Quite frankly, I was more interested whether my eyes were suddenly free of sagging eyelids, my tatas sitting higher on my chest or that flab around my abdomen back where it had started a few years back. Since no one remarked how fab I looked, I guess I need more than a little anti-gravity to make those things happen.

On the fifth day, we tied to a dock on cloud covered Bermuda. Eight hundred and seventy-five miles and we had seen only a dot of rain. But that night, while all snug at the dock, high winds and rain blew through the marina with a vengeance. It was as if nature had waited for us to arrive safely.

Bermuda sits mid-Atlantic, six hundred miles from any other land mass. The island was formed from volcanic rock which was then capped with limestone secreted from marine organisms.

Bermudian houses painted in a palette of pastel colours support whitewashed limestone roofs. The whitewash reflects the sunlight, helping to keep the houses cooler. With no freshwater rivers or streams, the island remains dependent on manmade wells and rainwater that is captured in large underground storage tanks. When the roofs accumulate dirt, they require power washing or brushing with a wire brush.

Norfolk pines stand tall alongside palm trees and whistling frogs sing piercing songs in the evening warmth. With little land for agriculture, Bermuda needs to import eighty percent of their food, spiking grocery prices to abnormally high amounts. This is one place sailors don't want to arrive needing to provision.

The island was settled by accident in the 1600s when a ship, sailing from Plymouth, England, bound for a new British colony called Jamestown, in the United States, sailed too far south. The ship ran aground on one of the many reefs surrounding the island. Several onboard survived, and ten months later they had skillfully constructed a seaworthy ship capable of sailing to Jamestown. After sailing to Jamestown and finding the British colony starving, the crew turned the ship back to Bermuda to acquire supplies. Many never returned to the mainland but stayed to establish a settlement.

In the mid-1800s, before refrigerator boxcars existed, Bermuda controlled ninety percent of the Easter lily market in the United States. Bermuda consists of only 34 square kilometres (21 square miles) and a quarter of that had been turned into a thriving lily garden creating the name, The Easter Isle or Easter Lily Island. One acre could provide forty thousand marketable bulbs. Along with potatoes and onions, Easter lilies were sent by steam ships capable of reaching New York within seventy hours.

The lily became a symbol of Easter when it was first introduced from Japan. The large trumpet shaped flowers symbolized purity, hope, innocence and peace in the Christian sense. But in the late 1900s, a virus decimated the Bermuda lily and it took nearly twenty-seven years for the lily to be reestablished. The decimation however, occurred long after an American had already taken a suitcase of hybrid lily bulbs back to the United States where a single farm might have a larger acreage than all of Bermuda.

The only export of lilies out of Bermuda today is a traditional gift arriving at the doorstep of Buckingham Palace each Easter. Today, the island enjoys the third highest per capita income in the world with the average cost of a house in 2000 exceeding $1,000,000 US. Several reinsurance companies have located on the island. The island's economy is primarily based on providing financial services for international business.

We stayed in Hamilton two days, then moved around to St. George's Harbour an hour and a half away, to check out with customs. I didn't want to leave so soon, but the weather, as always, dictated our travel plans. A low-pressure system had been hanging north of Bermuda causing gale force winds several miles out to sea. The plan was to sail towards the diminishing gale, timing our arrival to coincide with what we hoped to be, a dissipated storm. We couldn't wait too long before departing, due to predicted north winds forming in the upcoming days that would cause serious problems when we arrived at the Gulf Stream.

The 'Stream', as most sailors refer to it, is a powerful current originating in the Gulf of Mexico. Pushing warm water north, it travels parallel to the eastern United States coastline, eventually meeting with the North Atlantic Current. If a north wind blows against the Stream, the seas become steep and disorderly. The area is often unsettled due to cold fronts travelling from America, and violent rain squalls are common. From Bermuda to the far side of the Stream is three hundred and sixty miles. Should we leave Friday and take the chance the gale had moved on, or should we leave Saturday when the probability of it dissipating were better but we would be nearer to the day the winds turned north? Commanders' Weather Forecasters predicted the winds would be southwest moving to east on

Friday, swinging to southwest Saturday and northwest by Sunday. Northwest would not be good. We could expect twenty-five to thirty knot winds with forty to forty-five knot gusts accompanied by ten foot seas while in the Stream. It appeared as though we could make it across the Stream before the northwest winds arrived if we left early the following morning.

It was another game with Mother Nature, this one we really needed to win.

Before we sailed, our friends left us to return to their home in New York City. We bid adieu to their companionship and lively dialogue. We would miss them in the upcoming days.

THE following morning, we checked the weather again and we still felt it was a good time to leave.

St. George's Harbour passage is narrow and heavily travelled by cruise ships. As required, we called Bermuda Harbour Radio to request clearance. They asked for our float plan. We responded with the requested information: two persons aboard, destination Newport, Rhode Island, ETA—96 hours.

We finished a few last minute preparations and when ready, raised our anchor in a downpour. Shallow water creates short chop and we were immediately introduced to unpleasant motion while passing over the coral shelf just outside the harbour. The wind was coming from behind, blowing diesel fumes into the cockpit. I remarked that downwind sailing stunk in more ways than one.

We moved off the shelf into deeper water where we rolled like a sinner. My body would need to make a fast adjustment if I was to make this passage without puking.

We divided the shifts into day, evening and night watches. We each took five hours between 1000 to 2000, then four hour shifts between the hours of 2000 to 0400 and three hour shifts from 0400 to 1000 hours. We were still experimenting to see what worked best for us.

My first 2000 to 2400 shift was without the company of stars or moon. My eyes strained to see through a black pitch of night. The foredeck came into view, gently lit by the steaming light located halfway up the mast which indicated we were motor-sailing. I strained to see anything beyond the deck but thought I could detect whitecaps topping the waves. Morning would give us a better visual of the state of the seas.

I stood in the companionway clipped into my life vest, tethered to the cockpit. I cursed downwind sailing. My stomach was queasy but not yet bad enough to take a motion sickness tablet. I liked to wait until I thought I was going to toss my tarts then throw back a tablet and wait for it to transform me into a hardy sailor. Mike would relieve me at 2400 when I would lie down until my 0400 shift. Just before my watch ended, a rain squall passed through. I wasn't wearing rain pants and the bottom half of me got soaked. Clothes don't dry quickly on boats. You can be sure I remembered to put rain pants on before my next watch.

Around 0400 first light began to break. I could now see the 3 metre (10 foot) following seas responsible for slamming my stomach against my backbone. One after another the seas rolled up to our stern, rushing and hissing as if after us. I really hate downwind sailing and just for the record, I think I like it better in the dark. At least in the dark, the waves running up your Ying Yang don't look so threatening.

Trying to climb the companionway stairs with a cup of tea in one hand without falling, was pretty close to a circus act. And going to the bathroom was definitely life threatening, at least for me it was. The procedure turned death defying when having to pull down my drawers in a room raging with motion.

The wind had picked up to twenty-five knots but we were sailing cautiously with a staysail and reefed main. When daylight broke, I would put out more sail.

I added a jacket to the sweater I was wearing.

When the sky supplied enough light for me to see potential problems, I put out more mainsail. The wind was gusting to thirty knots giving us a steady eight knots of speed. Surfing down the back of a wave got me a ten. The sails appeared to be well balanced. I was off at 0600 and would rest until 1000.

I stayed in bed the whole four hours, not because I was so tired but because my next shift would span five hours. I wanted to be prepared.

Boy this was fun!

I took a motion sickness tablet before retiring because my queasy stomach hadn't improved and neither had the weather. With only two onboard, we both needed to be in peak form, always at the ready. Luckily Mike has a stomach like an iron bathtub.

While I was resting, one of those freakish large waves hit us broadside resonating in my cabin like we had been hit by a MACK truck. Smashing against the hull, the wave exploded over the boat. I could hear it rain down into the cockpit on top of Mike.

We had just completed our first twenty-four hours.

DURING my next watch the waves grew to 5 metres then to 6 (15 feet then to 20). The wind stayed around thirty knots. We tossed, turned and pitched. We were hoping to be across the Gulf Stream before the winds created steepened seas which would inevitably slow our progress. We were already experiencing the effects of the northwesterlies and we would not enter the Stream until later that night. We received an update from Commanders confirming we would meet northwest winds in the Stream and would experience some rough conditions getting there.

Yep, we could confirm that.

I TRIMMED the sails in hopes of squeezing out a few more miles on the rhumb line while keeping the present tack. It's frustrating to be forced off course when trying to beat the weather but that's the gist of sailing. Adding extra miles at a crucial time when you least need them is part of the challenge of arriving to your destination before getting pounced by bad weather.

The Gulf Stream can be seen by satellite. In effect, it is a submerged river in the sea. It has power to offer bonus speed to a boat travelling north or conversely, cause hectic seas with an opposing wind. All the world's oceans are mapped with fast flowing currents, camouflaged forces lying in depths actively running with enough energy to give a free ride or make life miserable. They are forces to be reckoned with, and to play to one's advantage when possible. In the early 1500s, Spanish ships rode the warm waters of the Florida Current from the Caribbean to what is known today as Cape Hatteras (US). Here, in shallower waters, where the Gulf Stream becomes evident, early Navigators utilized the five to six knot current to speed northward and then eastward towards Europe.

To emphasize the power of ocean currents, columnist Janice Posada noted in an article she wrote for *The Daily Harold* (Everett, WA) in 2001, that oceanographer/beachcomber Curtis Ebbesmeyer, forecasts that millions of Lego pieces spilled overboard from a container in the Atlantic in 2000 are expected to drift north into the Arctic Ocean and then through the Northeast Passage. In a few more years, they are expected to travel south toward the 49th state. Their expected arrival time on Alaskan beaches was 2012 and on Washington beaches in 2020.

Onboard *Baccalieu III*, our hourly log entries included sea temperature. The Stream carries warm water from the tropics to higher latitudes, and monitoring the temperature would help us determine when we entered and exited the Stream's current.

The water was presently a cool 22°C (70°F).

I GOT some deep sleep. When I reported for my watch, the same grey sky that had been with us since leaving Bermuda, was directly overhead. But just beyond, a belt of clear turquoise sky as bright and festive as one could hope for, and beyond that, a distinct long ridge of thick, heavy, blackened mass sitting ominously on the horizon. This was a cold front waiting to ambush us with high winds, rain and maybe even thunderstorms. Mike went forward to turn the dorade vents around in preparation for heavy seas breaking over the deck.

I had stocked several hearty, soups in the freezer which we depended on for meals. Conditions were rough; I needed to clip the galley belt around my waist to stay in place while heating them.

I got up for my 0300 to 0600 watch, pulled on my foul weather pants and jacket, then clipped on my life vest and tether. I had been in the same clothes for two days but I had learned how to conquer a dress change by not swapping out anything other than the underwear. And that I could do without even getting out of bed. I was born a bit of a gymnast.

The sea temperature read 24°C (76°F) and our speed over ground showed a four knot current indicating we were in the thick of the Stream. Our point of sail was so far off the rhumb line I decided to take in the staysail and try motoring in a direction that would get us across the Stream faster. Mike and I always discussed strategies before we changed watches.

In the process of taking in the staysail, the sheet ripped out of my hand just as it had done while leaving Martinique. Leaving the winch, it spun into the predicted clump of tangles on the foredeck. Hearing the flogging sail, Mike cut short his rest to standby while I went forward to untangle my mess.

I was surprised to get as much sleep as I did on my next off watch; I actually felt rested and ready to take on the next five hours. We referred to the lengthy off-time, as the BIG SLEEP.

Just before taking over, I refreshed myself with a rocking shower and it was worth every bruise I suffered.

We had now been in the mobile washing machine for forty-eight hours.

We were making eight knots over the water, but with opposing currents, only four over the ground. Only the four knots would really count towards getting anywhere. No matter what combination of sail plan we used, or even with the use of engine power, we couldn't manufacture more speed. The current ruled; it was as simple as that. A check on the sea temperature indicated 23.4°C (76°F) decreasing within the hour to 22.6°C (73°F). We were almost across the Stream, but crawling to get through the last few miles. Then the air temperature suddenly plunged, the water turned dark grey and the sea temperature dropped to 19.1°C (66°F). The drop in water temperature was what indicated we were on the other side of the Stream.

I prepared for much cooler night sailing by pulling on a pair of fleece pants and added a shirt under my foul weather gear. I grabbed a pair of light gloves.

As waves broke over the bow and ran up the foredeck, salt water seeped into the forward hatch through a worn gasket, dripping onto the spare bed. There are two things reckoned to be taboo inside a boat; one is sand, the other, salt water. And running out of wine of course.

The swells began to diminish and while riding in moderate comfort, Mike, who was forever conscious about engine maintenance, decided to check the oil in our reliable 114 HP Perkins. To do that, we turned the engine off, and floated freely until the oil check was completed. When we started the engine up, the autopilot would not engage. Mike pored through the pages of the autopilot manual in an attempt to determine the cause of its failing. The autopilot had been our third man, and many times we had given thanks for its reliability. We tried to reinitialize the autopilot's compass by following the instructions in the manual. We turned the steering wheel hard to port, then hard to starboard. We motored through a sequence of figure eights and three hundred and sixty degree circles while pressing all the appropriate buttons. Anyone witnessing our antics out there in the middle of the ocean would seriously have wondered if we suffered from temporary madness.

It was now sunset in a cloudy evening sky.

The guts of the autopilot are located under the aft deck in the bottom of the outside lazarette. The lazarette is similar to a basement in a house where numerous pieces of equipment are stored.

Mike went aft to unload the 'basement' and we had soon amassed a pile of dock lines, inflatable fenders, halyards, buckets, diesel cans, a foot pump, heavy duty electrical cord, bosun's chair, passerelle, knee board and metres and metres of endless spinnaker that lay coiled on the deck like a giant blue and yellow silk python.

While scrunched to half his size, Mike lifted the floor boards of the lazarette, and using a flashlight, inspected the workings of the autopilot. Finding nothing obviously wrong, we loaded everything back into the lazarette and went below into the salon to e-mail the company who had manufactured the equipment.

We then reevaluated our circumstances. We agreed that we should cut our watches into two hour parcels because it would now be necessary to hand steer the last two hundred and fifty miles.

There would be no more BIG SLEEPS.

SEA conditions that night were perfect for phosphorescence and I had never seen it as deep and thick as it was off our stern. Shooting out from the boat, where the propeller churned the sea into a whirlpool of eddies, a thick liquid path of fine cut crystal fell away to a dark, mysterious sea. A path so solid with sparkles you would have thought you could walk on it. I imagined that the next time I glanced over my shoulder perhaps a mermaid would be resting on the trail.

It was a no-show for the mermaid but it was definitely what legends were made of and a brilliant ending to the third day, the day we lost much of our freedom to move about because the watch person could not leave the wheel.

The next morning greeted us with blue skies. Dolphins romped nearby. The wind was light and the sea about as calm as you would ever see it. We received an e-mail from B&G, makers of the autohelm. They made suggestions as to how we might get the pilot back into service and once again we emptied the lazarette. We turned the engine down to an idle and floated, bobbing gently like a float at the end of a fishing line. Mike climbed back into the basement, checked and rechecked the set-up; the boat danced her figure eights and pirouettes again while we pressed all the required buttons.

Sadly, our efforts failed to re-engage the autohelm.*

Throughout the day we steered, slept, steered, slept, steered and slept, but we were thankful for the calm weather conditions because we knew our situation could have been much worse. When night approached, I dug out my ski gloves and pulled on warm knee socks and a toque. Before the night was out I had added another sweater and a pair of tights under my pants and foul weather gear. Heaven help me when I have to go to the bathroom, I thought, because it would take me ten

---

* Autohelm: the brushes in the electric drive motor were worn and needed replacing. We learned later we would need to replace them every 10,000 miles.

minutes to dig myself out. I even had to readjust my life vest because it was never meant to fit the Pillsbury doughboy.

We shortened our watches to an hour each because it was so cold. If there is one thing I hate more than downwind sailing, it's being cold.

At 0400, dog-tired we approached the shipping channel to Narragansett Bay just outside of Newport, Rhode Island. Dawn broke slowly; each half hour offering a little more light. But a lot of good it did us, because we were neck deep in fog with 4–5 metres (15 feet) visibility off the bow. I was on the wheel scanning our surroundings, as well as watching the outdoor radar screen.

In one hand I held a portable fog horn. Our yacht's automatic horn was already sounding every two minutes. Mike manned the indoor radar screen while tracking numerous vessels with the ARPA (Automatic Radar Plotting Aid). He would match what he saw on the radar screen with the Nobeltec Navigation chart then give me additional verbal guidance when necessary. We monitored ships on channel 16 and kept out of their way.

As if we didn't have enough to handle, a fish cage suddenly appeared a few metres off our beam which I hadn't spotted before we were nearly on top of it. I could have easily run straight into it. Now wouldn't this be a great time to get a rope tangled around the prop?

We collapsed the dodger to allow for a better view of the water in front of the boat. There were numerous crab pots and fish cages scattered about the area. As we approached shore, the fog thickened but we still had hope that heat from the rising sun would burn off the excess moisture before we entered the approach channel.

THE chart of Narragansett Bay is a cartographer's work of art. Covered in a mass of symbols indicating numerous restricted, regulated and precautionary areas, other labels warn of areas containing fish traps, underwater cables, dumping ground surveys and a section set aside for pilot boarding. A mess of ferry lanes, safety zones and submerged rocks, ledges, small reefs and shoals are fixed in their proper positions alerting inbound and outbound seamen to their whereabouts. Even a torpedo range and a few sunken, unexploded depth charges from 1947 are marked for their locations.

But a new discovery, not yet marked on the chart, is a fleet of British ships sunk in 1778. Discovered in 2005, the *Lord Sandwich* was identified among thirteen to twenty 18th century ships scuttled for the purpose of blockading the bay from an invading French fleet. The *Lord Sandwich*, a 106 foot (32 metre) 368 ton vessel, had previously been the ship Captain Cook had sailed on his 'voyage of discovery' in 1768 while accompanied by the naturalist Joseph Banks. The name of the ship at the time of Cook's voyage was the famed HMS *Endeavour*.

As we sailed nearer to shore the visibility did not improve; in fact, the fog became denser. We proceeded down the channel that separated the two headlands. I figured no one in their right mind would come out in these conditions, but then I recalled how fishing vessels work in all kinds of weather.

Mike entered a route into the Nobeltec chart for me to steer by. The GPS, (Global Positioning System) interfaced with the computer, displayed *Baccalieu III's* position on the computer's chart, and like playing a simulator, the icon moved with the boat as I steered the route that had been entered into the chart's system. It's in times like these that we appreciated having a repeater computer screen located outside at the helm.

Inside the bay, only metres from shore, we could see nothing. The exercise was unnerving; our well-being depended on a 30 cm (11 in.) square radar screen with a muddle of yellow squiggly lines.

We radioed Oldport Marine requesting someone come out and lead us to a mooring in Breton Cove. By 0:800 we were tied up.

Hand steering while motor-sailing for those last two hundred and fifty miles was the biggest piece of boredom I hope to ever experience. The day and night had been without wind, and there had been nothing to look at other than open water and the compass, which required much attention in order to keep a proper course. You need to be next to brain dead to do a job like that.

The day of our arrival was also our anniversary. If the day ever comes that we can look into our future, I would say, don't do it. Had I been told thirty-seven years ago while standing at the altar that my marriage would one day lead me to be on a boat on a cold day in June with my face dripping with mist, wet ski gloves and a toque, blinded by fog in the middle of a busy freighter channel, what do you think I would have done?

Since leaving England, twelve months previous, we had sailed 9,400 nautical miles. We had crossed the Atlantic in eighteen days, visited fourteen countries, eighteen islands, pulled into thirty-nine ports, and our biggest accomplishment—after collaborating in sixty-two anchorages—we were still married!

Don't take that achievement lightly.

5

Embracing the New Lifestyle

Antigua to Aruba

Aruba to the San Blas Islands

Transiting the Panama Canal

Panama City

Passage to the Galápagos Islands

The Galápagos Islands

I wish I could describe the feeling of being at sea, the anguish, frustration, and fear, the beauty that accompanies threatening spectacles, the spiritual communion with creatures in whose domain I sail. There is a magnificent intensity in life that comes when we are not in control but are only reacting, living, surviving.... At sea I am reminded of my insignificance—of all men's insignificance. It is a wonderful feeling to be so humbled.

Steve Callahan
Adrift

ANTIGUA TO ARUBA

WE CAME HOME to Toronto for the summer. During those few weeks, we made the decision to cross the Pacific Ocean and to sail as far south as New Zealand and Australia. We had no firm plans on how to get back, although there are choices. A boat can be shipped as deck cargo onboard an ocean going freighter or via a float-on/float-off specialty ship. Cruising boats use these facilities to span oceans with the resulting opportunity to use their own boats to vacation in international destinations. In our case, choosing the shipping alternative would bypass long passages, avoid possible confrontation with pirates as well as the adverse conditions of the Indian Ocean.

Although we never planned to sail around the world, I knew shipping was not high on my list; I simply did not want to miss anything.

IN NOVEMBER (2005), Mike sailed the boat from Newport to Antigua with a crew of friends. I joined the boat the day before Christmas and so did our son David who was on a two week school break. Together, we sailed to our favourite local anchorages and to Barbuda. We chartered a helicopter to fly over Montserrat a British overseas territory lying twenty-seven miles southwest of Antigua. Much of Montserrat had been buried in lava in 1997 when a volcano erupted forcing two thirds of the population to flee. Flying over the island, we saw that lava had filled in the lower valleys smothering several villages and drowning Plymouth, the capital, in 12 metres (39 feet), of liquid rock. If houses were not totally buried, smooth brown debris could be seen running like hardened rivers through doors and windows. If one were to walk through the town it would now be possible to stand on a roof or lean against the church's steeple.

AFTER David left us to return to school, Antiguan Mike Rose joined us for the four hundred and eighty-six mile passage to Bonaire. This was a significant passage. We were headed towards the Pacific Ocean, committing to an immense journey. We were cutting ties with a world where we could count on acquiring assistance. So many questions remained unanswered. How far would we get? How would we get back? Could we deal with mechanical breakdowns? What if we incurred medical problems? Would we have difficulty finding places to provision? What kind of weather would we run into? Storms? Giant waves? Catastrophic winds?

After making stops in Bonaire and Aruba, we were headed for the San Blas (San Bias) Islands located on the western Caribbean coast. There, we would join the Blue Water Rally, a fleet of twenty-five boats circumnavigating together with a plan to complete their global tour by 2007.

IF the passage to Bonaire was any indication, sailing south was going to be enjoyable. Twenty to twenty-five knots of wind carried us downwind providing us with three days of great sailing. Yes, it's true; I sailed downwind with not a single babbling complaint of sea sickness.

We landed at the most easterly of the Dutch islands known as the ABC Islands, Aruba, Bonaire and Curaçao.

Reaching Bonaire we tied up in a quiet marina, a short car ride from the town of Kralendijk. Song birds sang with the rising sun while small green parrots squawked and chased each other until the heat of the day forced them to seek shelter in the shade of trees. Across from the marina, cotton candy coloured flamingos stretched long elegant necks to search for shrimp in the brackish water of a shallow pond.

We arrived on a Saturday to find the town of Kralendijk closed for the weekend. It wasn't much busier during the week, but at least a good sized grocery store was available for me to shop for provisions—in Dutch! At home I was accustomed to reading nutritional labels as if missing one might be the cause of sudden death. Trying to understand Dutch labeling was like trying to decode an algorithm of tactical data. The *voedingswaarde* included the values of *verzadigde vet, natrium* and *suiker*. No wonder I purchased a package of 'smoked' fish that later, when prepared in pasta sauce, turned out to be salted fish that required soaking to eliminate the salt. We had such a thirst after eating, that if necessary, we would have been willing to lap water out of puddles!

MOST of Bonaire's coastline is designated a Marine Park, consequently anchoring is not allowed. Instead, there are one hundred moorings available for visiting boats to tie to. Jennifer and her boyfriend, Rok, joined us from Honduras, where they had been working as scuba instructors. They brought their scuba gear enabling us to enjoy several dives together. Bonaire's coastline is ringed with multiple reefs easily accessible from shore for scuba diving or snorkeling.

We rented a pickup truck to drive the picturesque coastal road and stop at some of these dive sites. Shore diving allows you to dive independently without being part of a group. It requires however, that you schlep your equipment over to the water's edge, maneuvering across stones and sharp objects while wearing rubber boots that offer about as much protection as a pair of moccasins. Fully suited up in neoprene dive suits, with BCs (buoyancy compensators) strapped around our torsos, goggles stuck to our foreheads and fifty pound (twenty-two kilogram) tanks cinched to our backs, we waded out waist deep to where we would be relieved of some of the weight once we became partially buoyant. And if that weren't enough, reaching some of the dive sites required descending stairs. I figured if I fell along the way I would simply become shore debris because getting to my feet would require about the same strength as it would to lift a house on my back.

BEFORE MOVING ON to Aruba, we added a few gallons of gasoline to the dinghy's tank and we were happy it was only the dinghy's tank that needed filling when we discovered the cost of fuel was $2 US a litre. Sailors recently arrived from Venezuela, only 80 kilometres (50 miles) away, boasted how they had filled their diesel tanks for nine cents a gallon.

SAILING to Aruba, a one hundred mile overnight trip, was hardly an inspiring journey for our new crewmembers. Seas were tossing and leaping from every direction while the boat rolled with the wind behind us.

It was 0130, while I was on watch in the cockpit, that we passed the northern tip of Curaçao, just a few miles off the coast of Venezuela. It was a dark, moonless night and all I could see were the flickering orange flames shooting from the stacks of a distant oil refinery. As the wind blew over our stern, it carried the pungent smell of sulfur mixed with burnt chemicals and I could hardly wait to out-distance the foul smelling pollution. I had been tracking cruise ships and freighters on the radar screen and also had each of their lights sighted visually. All except one. I was continuously putting the binoculars to the test searching for this one phantom vessel, but I only began to worry when the alarm from the radar sounded indicating it was nearing our boat. I scanned the surrounding area but still could not detect any lights from the direction in which the radar indicated a vessel was approaching.

The other crewmembers were off watch sleeping. I went below to silence the alarm.

We were making good speed and, according to the radar alarm, we were near enough to a vessel that we should be turning to avoid it. But which way was I to turn? This was no time for incompetence. We were on a collision path with something, something I couldn't see.

I quickly returned to the cockpit. On my climb out of the companionway, I momentarily caught site of a moving silhouette just off our stern. There it was. Then it vanished. I was certain I had seen some movement but staring into a black oblivion there was nothing to be seen.

It was a dark night. One of the darkest.

The alarm wasn't sounding a potential collision any longer but there was definitely something circling our boat. And it was big.

It was worrisome that they had chosen not to display navigation lights and had intentionally doused all interior lights.

I listened for the familiar dull throb of engines but I heard nothing other than our own hull swishing through the sea.

We didn't carry night vision binoculars but I brought our daylight ones to my eyes again and only then could I occasionally make out the silhouette of a small ship in total blackout mode quite near to us. It was obvious the vessel had some interest in our presence. It passed in and out of my vision as if slipping behind a black curtain and moved with unusual silence.

It seemed to me there was only one reason the occupants would not want to be detected and the reason could not be good.

Jennifer was sleeping in the cockpit; it was her idea of being on duty with me but she often suffered from seasickness and had taken a motion tablet, maybe more than one.

I woke her.

Suddenly, the two of us were standing in a fully lit cockpit. The phantom boat had blasted a high powered spotlight across our stern. It blinded us and then the light extinguished and we stood again in total darkness.

When the vessel moved towards our aft quarter, I caught sight of a machine gun mounted on its foredeck.

The radar alarm had woken Mike and Rok, and they ascended the stairs into the cockpit. I told them there was a ship circling us. We stared into the darkness. No one saw anything. We were so vulnerable.

Baccalieu III was still racing forward with a good wind filling her sails. But the four of us remained easy targets.

Then another blinding blast of light dazzled our eyes. I suggested no one move. I thought an innocent gesture might be misread as an attempt to reach for a weapon. We stood there in silence, defenseless, waiting for radio communication or some sign that we were about to be boarded.

Apparently satisfied with what they had seen—we were a family of four flying a Canadian ensign—the small ship pulled away, disappearing almost instantly, just as it had approached.

We learned later that armed forces from several countries often work in conjunction with the Columbian Navy to intercept drug smuggling in this area.

AROUND the same time, another Blue Water Rally yacht, *Fleur de Mer*, a Bowman 40 en route from the Los Roques archipelago in Venezuela, sailing towards Bonaire, ran onto a reef where the owner and crew watched her fracture beneath them while their liferaft ripped open on the biting coral. The crew managed to swim ashore.

ARUBA IS THE most westerly of the ABC islands, lying twelve miles north of the equator. It has the highest standard of living of any of the Caribbean islands, the result of a successful tourist industry.

We arrived around 0900, cleared customs and tied up Mediterranean style in the Renaissance Marina located right in the capital city, Orangestaad.

Jennifer and Rok left us to return to Utila, and Andy, a Toronto friend, joined us for the passage to the San Blas Islands and Panama Canal transit.

THE wind blew constantly during our stay. With it came rain followed by periods of even higher winds. Our mainsail had developed a tear along the foot and the stopover was the last opportunity to have it repaired before reaching Panama City. Finding several minutes free of high winds to take it down and then later run it back up the mast, was nearly impossible. But the job got done.

The weather delayed our departure for the San Blas Islands and while we remained in Orangestaad, we watched cruise ships unload thousands of passengers to shop and leave their money behind in the popular casinos there.

We were surprised to see *Gipsy Moth IV*, Sir Francis Chichester's boat, tied alongside just down the dock from us. We had seen her eighteen months ago in Greenwich, England, in a sort of carefree museum state, but hardly in any form to suggest she could float, let alone sail.

ARUBA TO THE SAN BLAS ISLANDS

A People Who Would Not Kneel
JAMES HOWE

WE CLEARED ARUBA customs and immigration, radioed the harbour master requesting permission for departure, then set course for the San Blas Islands, an archipelago of three hundred and fifty islands stretching along Panama's Caribbean coast.

The plan was to sail out to deep water, two thousand fathoms or more, to avoid as much as possible the standard mix of lashing waves and tumultuous seas that can be encountered in this area. Waves gain bulk and momentum while travelling unobstructed across the entire length of open Caribbean waters. They collide with the Venezuela/Columbian coastline where, bouncing back, they mix with coastal and offshore currents creating sea conditions called square waves. The passage is described in Jimmy Cornell's *World Cruising Routes* as one of the five most difficult in the world, and we can confirm the seas in this area reflect what is written about them. For three days we sailed through chaotic waters. Waves collided with the boat from every direction, tossing us around like we were part of a child's game of jacks. This was not just another downwind journey, this one showed aggressive behavior. In spite of all its nastiness, we made fair speed, averaging a hundred and eighty-three miles a day.

Sailing only sixty miles off the coast of Colombia we were suspicious of every boat spotted. Admittedly we were a little gun-shy from the night game played with the navy ship several days previous. The few vessels we spotted were more often seen during evening, as the light was fading, making us all the more suspicious. Columbia remains the world's main producer of cocaine and we were travelling a well-used highway where drug runners look to boats to transport cocaine by the tons. According to the United Nations office on Drugs and Crime, ninety percent of smuggled cocaine is transported by sea. As each load is worth millions of dollars, the transport boat is often scuttled after delivery and in some cases, the owners never heard of again.

THE first several hours following our departure from Aruba delivered light winds accompanied by rolling. We found it necessary to pole out the Yankee sail and assist our speed with engine power. Then the wind dropped even more. For a brief time, a few large, spotted dolphins played in our bow's wake. Towards evening, the wind freshened to twenty knots and we were soon reefing the mainsail and surfing down the backside of 5 to 6 metre (15 to 20 foot) seas. We were making nine knots of speed but the boat rolled through almost thirty degrees of heel from side to side.

I was on watch at 0130, sitting in the cockpit when a supersized wave, twice the size of the surrounding waves, met us broadside. In a sudden motion, the boat was lifted and heeled forty-five degrees. I grabbed the winch behind me to keep from flying across the cockpit. The seat on the far side became the floor under my feet. It takes a fair bit of power to throw a severe heel into a boat the size of *Baccalieu III*.

Mike, who was resting in the aft cabin, was thrown over the lee cloth, across the berth and against the locker. I hardly needed a reminder to keep fastened to a safety tether, but the experience confirmed we could never become complacent while travelling oceans.

We approached the San Blas Islands late on the fourth morning. A light haze camouflaged the islands until we came within a few miles of shore. The low lying islands appeared somehow insignificant to me. After what we had just sailed through, they offered no grand feeling of arrival. They were not the picture perfect tropical sight I had been expecting, but they were, as I learned later, quite perfect and a place of intrigue.

As soon as we were in the shadow of the islands, the waters calmed. The surroundings were peaceful and it was a relief to our weary bodies to stand on a steady plane again. It was almost like magic that after four days we finally stopped bouncing, pitching and being thrown around.

THIS is where we joined the Blue Water Rally. We had heard that transiting the Panama Canal with a group was more efficient in regards to time and paper work. There is an insurmountable amount of paper work, all documented in Spanish, to be put into the system before access to the canal is allowed. Every boat, no matter the size, falls under an identical registration procedure whether sailing yacht or ocean freighter. An agent can be hired to expedite the necessary red tape, but there were stories of freelance agents who did not produce the required results and even more stories of serious postponements and even damage to boats.

Delays for cruising boats transiting the canal, is due to more freighters that take up the entire space in the locks. It is the available space behind a small-sized freighter in a lock where a cruising boat is directed. Positioned behind the propeller of one of these ships, cruising boats can get knocked about by resulting turbulence. It is more difficult to control the yacht with shore lines when sitting in turbulent water which results in a higher incidence of damage to the yacht.

We looked forward to travelling with the Blue Water Rally, a group of like-minded sailors. Our plan was to leave the Rally when its schedule moved too quickly to allow us to explore the Pacific more fully. For the time being, our destination was New Zealand, 8,300 miles SW.

The meeting point with the fleet was tucked behind a tiny island named Sapibenega. Our computerized Nobeltec charts did not produce enough detail for the area but we carried paper charts and we studied them thoroughly.

We motored, winding between reefs and small islands, until we caught sight of the fleet anchored in the placid waters of a small, secluded bay surrounded by coconut palms. It seemed strange to come across a fleet of boats anchored in such a remote area.

THE COCONUT TREE-COVERED San Blas Islands are home to the Kuna (Cuna) indigenous Indian tribe who has reportedly inhabited the islands since 400 BC.

For two hundred years, the Kuna intermittently fought off the Spanish who attempted to seize the islands. This depleted their numbers considerably and forced the Kuna tribes to drift southward through the islands of the archipelago. Then Catholic missionaries arrived, followed by the Protestants, in a surge of competing priests and missionaries, each referring to the other as brothers of Satan. Each denomination vied for Godly leadership; each had their own agendas to save the Kunas.

But the Kunas wanted no part of it. They were comfortable with their traditions which embraced the use of medicine men, rituals, chiefs and hundreds of taboos. The one exception was a handful of Kunas who felt the need to learn writing and mathematics in order for their people not to be cheated by Spanish traders. But an education came at a price. It required those interested to learn about Christianity and to practice it, although the Kunas never proved to be easy recruits.

For years the tribe has been a mix of a few educated persons and those who continue to believe in traditional taboos and tribal cures. Many credit their nearly hairless bodies to not having used soap.

One of the smallest people in the world, slightly larger than pygmies, the Kunas have successfully fought to retain their traditions and govern themselves through elective tribal leaders. However, keeping possession of their land and retaining traditions remains a struggle.

The Kuna speak Dulegaya, 'people mouth'. They had no written word until missionaries living among them in 1949, established a Kuna alphabet and introduced vowels with pictures. Their language text book was the Bible.

Spanish is often used in written documents; consequently it is becoming more commonly spoken by those who go to school. Their history, however, continues to be handed down in song in the language of Dulegaya.

THE Kuna are a matriarchal society in which the line of inheritance passes down through the women. After marriage, the new husband must live in his mother-in-law's house. While working under the apprenticeship of his father-in-law, he will help to collect firewood, weave baskets, plant crops, construct huts, carve wooden instruments and gather thousands of coconuts a year from his allotted trees. We were cautioned not to take fallen coconuts because this would be a serious offense. Coconuts have been legal tender for centuries.

Women dress in hand-sewn traditional puffy sleeved

blouses appliquéd with molas* designed with abstract fish, birds, animals and musical instruments. Snug fitting skirts wrap around small waists accented with cummerbunds, all of which are a convulsion of designs and colours.

A red and black headscarf covers straight black cropped hair and a gold nose ring, far smaller than their ancestor's, is inserted in the nose. Beauty has always been determined by the shape of the nose and a single dark blue stripe, derived from jagua fruit, is painted down the length of the nose to enhance the feature. Small multi-coloured beads, known in Spanish as 'winnis' or 'chaquiras', often with an orange coloured dominance, are strung in long lengths around arms from elbow to wrist, suggesting the top part of an elegant evening glove.

The beads decorate slim legs like a pair of footless glass knee-high socks. According to their beliefs, winnis protect them from bad spirits which, in their world, hide almost everywhere. When a member is sick, coconut husks are smoked beneath the hammock of the ill person to keep evil spirits from encroaching on the weakened patient.

In need of hard currency, the women take every opportunity to sell their molas to tourists but it is the Kuna leaders who must decide to what extent they will bend traditions and to allow the sale, to make the most of a financial opportunity.

Accordingly, the women now produce inexpensive molas for tourists, thereby departing from their traditional, more intricately sewn styles and designs.

Hard currency is used to buy medicines, schoolbooks,

---

* Molas are constructed by first layering several pieces of various coloured fabric. The final piece is black where a geometric design is sketched. The fabrics are then cut to the appropriate layer to expose the desired colour when the edges are turned under and stitched with fine needles. The process is repeated with the second and third, fourth, fifth, leaving the last as a background. A collector's piece can take up to six months to complete.

It is thought the artwork stems from the early tradition of body painting which the women were in charge of when they wore a type of wrap around skirt leaving the upper body exposed.

tools, parts for boat engines and building materials. The dilemma they face is how to augment their incomes while retaining their culture. The Kuna we visited were friendly and allowed visitors to walk through some of their villages, with one condition: that any non-Kuna be off the islands by dark. Forty years ago, any white person remaining ashore faced a punishment of death.

We visited the village of Playón Chico where broad faced women, dressed in colourful apparel, stood outside their *nekas* (huts), encouraging us to purchase from their assortment of hand sewn molas they displayed on clotheslines.

Only women and children remain in the village during the day, leaving dozens of young barefoot children to sit with their mothers while observing the tall white people tramping through their village. Many played on sandy streets while pointing to simply made beaded necklaces and practicing the only English words they knew, "a dollar, a dollar." Reportedly, the population of Playón Chico, and surrounding area, is three thousand and of that, two thousand are children.

We walked through the village following the hard, packed sandy pathways that ran throughout the neighbourhood. Cane fencing surrounds each of the communes where thatched nekas are grouped around a focal hut owned by the grandmother and her husband.

Each neka consists of two rooms; one for sleeping, where hand crafted hammocks hang above bare dirt floors. A second room is for preparing and cooking meals. Nekas are not constructed with workable windows or doors because privacy among the Kuna is not an issue; a custom that missionaries had trouble accepting when living among them.

A church at the end of the main street stands in testament to the missionaries who brought Catholicism to the Kunas. A bakery hut offered small loaves of bread for ten cents apiece and these were a welcome addition to our meals onboard.

Beverage huts in the village sold Panamanian beer for the price of one dollar and Coca-Cola for fifty cents. Kunas suffer the negative effects of alcohol and many villages prohibit the sale of it. They allow binge drinking only during rituals of girl's puberty rites when it is required that a young girl be buried to her waist in sand for a period of four days. During the ritual, water is continuously poured over the girl's head in a ceremony of purification.

For these special occasions, cane juice combined with plantain is fermented to make the drink 'chichi'. Drinking continues for several days, sometimes for a period of two weeks.

On the outskirts of town, not far from the school that offers grades one to nine, teenagers were playing a refereed game of barefoot basketball on a sun-scorched concrete court. Basketball was introduced by the missionaries in the mid-1940s when a rim for the 'basket', was constructed of reeds and hung on the trunk of a palm tree. Elders felt that playing games was a waste of time until they became intrigued with the idea of competitions being played between the islands. Neighbouring islands had always quarreled among each other.

We stood beside the basketball court watching the fast paced game take place under a sizzling hot mid-afternoon sun while admiring the players' boundless energy and apparent ability to function without water. We found this common throughout our travels in the south. Few people in the most sun burnt areas of the world drink many liquids even when water is readily available.

A SIX foot Kuna male, delicately feminine and covered in skin as white as virgin silk, verified the Kuna acceptance of inbreeding which can result in albino children. That's one explanation offered for the high occurrence of albinism; one out of every hundredth Kuna is albino. A cleft lip is another birth defect that appears more frequently in the Kuna race. Scientists have not had the opportunity to study the reasons for these commonly occurring genetic traits. The Kuna people believe albinism occurs due to one of the parents gazing at the moon for long periods of time during pregnancy. It was helpful, they thought, to feed regular potions of charcoal to pregnant mothers to 'brown' the baby. In the past, when an albino child was born, the parents were required to put them to death. For that reason, no name was ever given to a baby or young child.

To stop the genocide, missionaries suggested that albinos were "at the very heart of God's creation" and God had sent his albino son to Earth to teach humans how to live. Now Moonchildren live a full life, but it took years to halt the killing of babies with cleft lip, even though a mainland doctor, who made occasional visits, could safely carry out the simple corrective operation on a kitchen table in a village neka.

Death has always been the answer to several Kuna dilemmas: only one baby in a set of healthy twins is allowed to live, and a baby with a crippling feature or anyone suffering from a mental disorder, was likely to meet an early end.

Today, Kunas believe albinos are highly intelligent and that some may even have supernatural powers capable of healing snake bites, healing with the touch of a hand, or the gift of foretelling the future. Because albino children cannot spend long hours in the sun engaged in physical activity, they have more time to dedicate to study. This has helped them become high achievers and eventually community leaders, medicine men, shamans or politicians.

Families that do not have girls often fill that void by raising a son as a daughter. Homosexuals and transvestites are readily accepted in Kuna society. Marriages often take place at the age of thirteen. While visiting the village, we witnessed a young girl cradling her recently born albino child.

Following the death of a village member, hours of chanting take place, encouraging good spirits to guide the deceased through jungles inhabited by crocodiles, wild cats and deadly snakes. The deceased is then taken to be buried in a cemetery located on a densely forested hillside, a resting place before travelling through the underworld where the spirit finds its way into heaven. Rolled, cocoon-like, into a hammock, the body is lowered into a shallow grave and then dirt is piled onto the body to resemble the fullness of a pregnancy, signifying rebirth into heaven. A deceased baby might be buried in the hut beneath the mother's hammock in hopes that the spirit of the child might reenter the mother during her next pregnancy.

Two men paddling a large dugout canoe took us on a journey up a narrow river snaking through twisted, exposed roots of dense growing mangrove trees. Large, leathery leaves formed a protective umbrella over us as their paddles swished silently through the brackish water. Our transport ended where the river curved and the river bank, worn raw by footprints, became a patch of reddish brown earth. The surrounding foliage was thick, offering shade and the coolness of a jungle. Two other canoes tied to a tree rested without occupants.

We trekked down a well-travelled path through a thicket of rainforest hanging with vines and stands of bamboo. Cuipo trees bulged with smooth, grey bark and kopoks, anchored into the earth by sprawling, ribbon-like trunks, stood towering like moss covered giants.

Kuna land has remained mostly untouched; hardwoods are not used in hut construction, and they do not keep cattle. Only small parcels of land are cleared to grow corn, sugarcane, coffee and medicinal herbs.

We walked past two well-kept concrete tombs, where revered tribal leaders lay buried.

It was midday; the jungle laid extraordinarily quiet, not a sound escaping from its interior. Then, from somewhere above, the screechy croak of a heavy beaked toucan broke the silence warning of our approach. Again and again it squawked its warning, crisp and piercing. Leaf cutter ants, carrying ten times their weight on their backs, marched in straight lines across the well-worn footpath.

As we began our climb up a steep hill to the cemetery following the trampled path of red earth, we were greeted by several inquisitive children playing in the forest. One with hair of creamed ginger, whose skin was as fair as cow's milk, was riddled with pink insect bites. His pale yellow eyes, squeezed into a watery squint, flickered with constant blinking.

I wonder now what a difference a simple pair of sunglasses might have meant to that albino child.

As we reached the top, the pregnant bellies of graves, some freshly dug, came into view. Each grave was shaded with a protective thatched roof.

Traditionally, women visit loved ones throughout the first three months following death, staying nearby to comfort the deceased, while the dead experience their rebirth into heaven. For the journey, which is long and dangerous, food is wrapped in banana leaves and placed in the ground with the deceased.

Mourners spend time sewing molas and lounging in hammocks near each gravesite. Drinks of chocolate and herbal teas are prepared over open fires as are soup pots of iguana, snails and lobster, coconut and mashed plantain.

Kuna women believe they risk losing their souls if they allow their picture to be taken. To avoid the threat they hide their faces from cameras. Their souls are apparently safe however, if they demand a dollar for each picture and you can be sure they watched us with the efficiency of an electronic eye while we were in camera range. The decision to allow picture-taking coincided with the discovery by the villagers, that picture postcards, depicting full facial profiles of Kuna women, were offered in the city for a dollar. The village women returned home with the suggestion they offer the same opportunity to visitors in their village. This has established another source of income for their community.

WE LEARNED THAT our canal transit date had been moved forward, shortening our time on the San Blas coast. We went off on our own to explore nearby islands. We visited two additional anchorages before heading towards the canal, one of which we found exceptionally beautiful, Cayo Chichime.

Reaching Cayo Chichime required studying a detailed paper nautical chart. Only then did we attempt to pick our way through shoals and reefs while watching the safe colours of bluish green waters merge and mix with darkened reefs. The entrance to the anchorage was announced with a sighting of foaming sea water sizzling over coral patches located just below the surface. Putting our faith in a guide book that was reported to hold tried and true information, we moved cautiously forward until we could distinguish the narrow channel between reef and island. We proceeded through and dropped anchor in a tropical paradise.

We were surrounded by three small islands. The smallest of the three, off our stern, was a mere islet large enough to bear three coconut palm trees leaning into the tradewinds. To port and starboard, the other two islands supported a few meager dwellings; huts of perpendicular cane tucked beneath the shade of thick and mature coconut palms. A steady breeze blew over our bow from across a sandy peninsula that stretched through a sea of tropical colours in the manner of a crooked finger. Out near the end of the meandering sand spit, an abandoned freighter sat solidly grounded, silted now with more sand that it had first swept onto. Listing to starboard with a sorry rusting hull, its pilot house lay crumbled in rotting lacy patterns of decay. Trees blown over in high winds from distant islands were beached on the sand trap. They lay piled up, locked together in tangles of deterioration at the head of the cove. A blue sky hung over it all; the sight was more than beautiful.

It wasn't long before we were visited by a young couple paddling a canoe, and with their welcome, came an offer to purchase more molas. When I first arrived in the San Blas Islands I had no intention of buying molas, I had no idea what to use them for. But between visiting Playón Chico and the island of El Porvenir where we would later connect with custom officials, I now have eight, including some fine looking pot holders and a small purse. The women at El Porvenir were very aggressive sellers. They swarmed our boat in two canoes of three and four women each while demanding our attention with calls of "Senora! Senora! Senora!" and holding their molas above their heads.

After I had purchased more molas from the woman in the canoe at Cayo Chichime, the young man with her, who spoke English well, invited us to tour their island. We motored to his beach and pulled our rubber dinghy onshore alongside his hand chiseled canoe. Earlier I had watched his six year old son maneuver the canoe with a rough-hewn paddle that was twice the size of the boy.

We walked the perimeter of their small island as we felt this was the proper response to his invitation. Scuffling along the sandy shore beneath swaying palm trees, we confirmed there was little on the island that would support a family; not even water. A few skinny dogs ran freely barking at our intrusion.

After completing the walk, we met up with the young man again. He showed us an awning he had made from a discarded sail and then his smokehouse where he laid fish to smoke over an open fire for two days of curing. The ground around their hut and clutch of shacks was as tidy as if it were a well swept linoleum floor. Every item they had collected appeared to have a purpose, like the plastic water containers hanging neatly at the end of one of the huts.

We purchased two coconuts which the young woman cracked and shelled by swinging a machete into stone hard hairy husks. Then we quenched our thirst with the translucent milk.

We stayed the night in the cove. The following day we headed for the port of Portobelo, where a Rally briefing regarding our transit Panama Canal schedule was to take place. Portobelo was only three hours from the entrance to the Canal and it would be our last scenic anchorage before leaving the Caribbean Sea.

CHRISTOPHER COLUMBUS, SIR Francis Drake and Henry Morgan were only a few of the explorers, privateers and pirates that had walked the streets of the small town of Portobelo during those early days of pilfering, exploitation and conquest. The deep, spacious bay surrounded by hills provided excellent protection from the elements, not only for today's cruising boats, but for ships that had once transported gold, plundered from the Incas in South America, to Spain. The town sits not far from the Isthmus of Panama, the natural land bridge connecting the North American continent, (Central America) and the South American continent. The isthmus, an 80 kilometre (49 mile) stretch of jungle, once lead slaves bearing gold and silver to waiting ships on the Atlantic side. Pillaged from conquered Aztec and Inca Empires, the spoils were first stored in warehouses in the town of Portobelo.

Portobelo became the main port of trade for slaves and for merchandise and at one time, the storage buildings were so full of silver ingots, they lay in the streets waiting for transport aboard Spanish galleons. Now the town has little purpose, and its historic buildings sit neglected and crumbling; even the wooden seats on the ornate iron benches are rotting, some already missing seats. But a sort of gaiety visits the town when *diablo rojos*, the 'red devils', pull into the town to pick up or drop off passengers. These privately owned buses compete for passengers by painting their vehicles with unique scenes of she-devils, flame-throwing superheroes and voluptuous women spilling out of undersized halter tops onto bus-sized engine hoods.

The bay is surrounded by four forts in various state of ruin, forts that were never pressed into battle but in later years conveniently provided stone for the breakwater during the construction of the Panama Canal. A small museum, presents the area's rich history through a documentary film available to tourists who arrive there in vans from Panama City. Genuine pirate's pistols and cannon balls sit on shelves in the museum, free of locks and glass cases.

At the far end of town, the famous statue of the Black Christ (Cristo Negro/El Nazareno)* hangs on the wall of the Roman Catholic Church, triggering an annual pilgrimage that ends with thousands of visitors coming together for a festival. Just outside the church, a covered awning offers shade to colourfully dressed Kuna women selling religious paraphernalia and hand sewn crafts. While we were viewing their merchandise, a serious faced Kuna lady was suddenly distracted from her selling. She turned away

---

* The Black Christ is a life-sized effigy of a black coloured Christ carrying a cross. The effigy resides next to the altar in Iglesia de San Felipe, a church constructed in 1814. It is believed the statue arrived in Portobelo from Spain around 1658. Religious followers believe the statue has magical powers and is why hundreds, arrive to pay homage by walking or by crawling on their knees to the site.

slightly to pull from her pocket a cell phone to read a text message! I gasped at her twenty-first century technology. In turn she flashed a broad, white toothed smile as if caught with something naughty, the first smile we had seen on the face of any Kuna woman.

TRANSITING THE PANAMA CANAL

A TRIUMPH OVER NATURE

*In effect, we need to raise ships up
over the American continent*

FREDERICK E. ALLEN
EDITOR *AMERICAN HERITAGE*

WITH OUR TRANSIT drawing near, we left Portobelo for the Port of Cristóbal, the northwest link between the Atlantic and Pacific Oceans located just outside the city of Colón. (Cristóbal Colón is Spanish for Christopher Columbus.)
Realizing that the Port of Cristóbal would be too contaminated to desalinate water, we motored slowly to give us time to run the watermaker before transiting the Canal. Our water tanks were low due to having shared our supply of water with others who had arrived in Portobelo with water tanks either close to empty or already drained. Not all boats in the fleet were equipped with water making abilities and others had broken down.
While approaching the Cristóbal breakwater, the radio came alive with communications broadcasting to ships from Port of Cristóbal Radio station, VHF 12. Soon a dozen or more international cargo freighters could be seen on the horizon. Freighters anchor here to wait for either transit dates or for cargo that is transported to the canal by supersized freighters too large to fit into the canal. Cargo is unloaded from these oversized freighters onto railway cars then delivered

to either Atlantic or Pacific ports where it is reloaded onto awaiting vessels.

After receiving permission from Cristóbal Radio, we proceeded through the breakwater to Limon Bay (Bahía Limón) where we dropped anchor in the Flats, a parking lot of dirty water where cruising yachts wait for their transit. The Flats is located at the gateway to the canal where huge cargo ships, fuel barges, cruise ships and pilot boats pour out of the locks in a steady stream of traffic. The size of these sea-going monsters seen at close range is spell-binding. At night, the canal's powerful lighting system converted darkness into perpetual daylight while ships lit up like small cities headed into the Caribbean Sea.

WHILE a few Rally boats found berths at docks in the Panama Canal Yacht Club, most others, including ourselves, were anchored just beyond. Many who were docked expected to find potable water to fill empty tanks but were dismayed to learn that both water and fuel docks were closed and not expected to reopen before our transit day. Those needing fuel were forced to transport jerry cans by taxi from a gas station somewhere within the city, then ferry them by dinghy to their boats where they filled their tanks five gallons at a time. Others hoped to solve engine, generator, transmission, watermaker, and sail breakdowns in the few days that were left before our transit. For some it was a scramble for last minute repairs, to find spare parts, to mend and replace worn mechanics. We were aware once we left Panama, little assistance was available. A breakdown before reaching Tahiti, over five thousand miles away, would result in delays, and most likely being left behind. Already, seven Rally boats had left the fleet.

While waiting for transit, we enjoyed delicious and inexpensive meals at the Panama Canal Yacht Club. Sadly, this club has since been demolished in order that the port's adjacent container terminal could be expanded. The Club had been the only area where boaters could prepare for a canal transit on the Atlantic end of the lock system. Much to the disappointment of those who tried to stop the Club's demolition, a back-hoe went at it in the middle of the night on a holiday weekend in 2009, while thirty to forty boats were still tied to the rickety docks. Although it had been rumored for several years that the Club was to come down, so secret was the demolition, that Club staff arrived the following morning to report to their jobs under the belief that it was business as usual.

The Panama Canal Yacht Club (PCYC) had been built in 1928, reportedly by those who had helped build the canal. Inside, pictures hanging on pale painted walls reflected the canal in various stages of build, while a few burgees circled the room adding gay colours to the otherwise worn decor of brownish Formica table tops teetering on chipped and cracked concrete floors. A non-descript, brown door at the entrance signaled not to expect much when you entered. For a barroom, it was a downtrodden looking place; no laughter filled the room nor was there a sharp looking bar-tender behind the counter. You can understand why it was a surprise to be treated to such good food when we sat elbow to elbow on long wooden benches at Formica tables in the very ordinary dining hall.

Above the bar, a large armless clock hung from the ceiling as if time had never meant much to those who entered and a well-worn notice board, nailed to a far wall, was full of notices from international hitch hikers looking for a berth to the Galápagos, Tahiti or to just about anywhere but where they were. The room may not have been pretty, but thousands had passed through that grungy looking door sharing stories of the sea, throwing back grog and grub while sitting at the highly polished bar, an outstanding piece of wood detailed with a thick varnished rope winding like a bow fender about a tugboat. From bow to stern, bending and curving for fifteen metres (fifty feet), the bar carried scars of hard core sailors who had taken up the challenges of the sea long before anyone could imagine that one day sailors might receive weather information delivered straight to their boat.

The PCYC had been an historic meeting place and watering hole that had stood open for eighty-one years, a pit stop for all sorts of characters, misfits maybe, but whose souls thrived on the sea. All of them had sailed from ocean to ocean, all had left familiar lives behind to enter the unknown. They were sailors so inquisitive about the world, so in love with the sea, that they would risk their lives just to be part of it and not even think of it as a risk; seamen who suffered long, perilous passages in wooden crafts but did not think of it as suffering. They left on journeys of discovery without the aid of electronics or weather forecasting but stood on rolling decks waving kerosene lanterns to warn approaching ships of their existence or made use of semaphore signals whether they had proper code flags or merely a logbook in one hand and a frying pan in another. Locking through the canal while tied alongside cargo ships, they went forth confidently with sextants in hand, parallel rules, dividers, paper charts, and yellow oil skins in preparation for rough times when taking water over the bow was as common as standing for days on end exposed to the elements while steering with a tiller.

Tough going seamen like the Smeetons onboard their ketch *Tzu Hang* and John Guzzwell who presented the canal authorities with the smallest transiting vessel they had ever seen. "Three tons?" — queried the canal official after examining Guzzwell's transit papers. "Why that's only $2.16!" But Guzzwell's boat was only 6 metres (20 feet) long.

They're the ones who had leaned their elbows on that bar. And I can only hope that the bar itself was salvaged.

During our visit a single bartender attempted to serve all who arrived and at a pace that guaranteed he not ever suffer from stress related ailments. A beer cost one dollar and could be paid, like everything else, in US dollars. Panama has no paper currency of its own.

The Panama Canal Yacht Club had been a unique asset to sailors. And now it's gone and apparently there is not even a dinghy dock left for tenders to tie onto.

Soon after we dropped anchor, a canal official boarded *Baccalieu III* to document details regarding the boat's condition. Cleats needed to be strong enough to handle the stress of warps while the locks filled. Four lines measuring at least 38 metres (125 feet) are requirements for transiting. If the boat's lines did not meet regulations, they could be rented for $12 US a day. Inspectors checked each boat's fuel levels as well as engines to determine their ability to maintain good speed.

The purpose of such an inspection was to avoid a canal shut down due to unnecessary problems. Time is money to waiting ships carrying multimillion dollar cargos. Penalties of several hundred dollars have been levied to vessels that break down during transit.

Allowing a group of cruising yachts to transit the canal is not a moneymaker or even a sustainable business for the canal. Ship's user fees can reach well over $150,000 US. For cruising yachts between 15 and 38 metres (50 and 125 feet), fees lie between $500 US and $2,400 US which includes immigration, emigration, inspection fees and cruising permits.

In addition, a deposit or buffer fee of $850 US is required which is later returned if the vessel does not experience breakdowns or cause delays while using the canal.

While waiting for our scheduled transit day to arrive, we ventured by taxi to the first lock to preview what awaited when our day came to passage the canal. We sped past rundown warehouses and tall, dreary concrete apartment buildings resembling bleak Soviet design. I thought the mouldy looking high rises were abandoned buildings until I noticed people idly standing at windows that appeared to have no glass. The apartment dwellers looked down on a hodge-podge of low strung electrical wires weaving in tangles over the gloom of the city. People plodded along in the hot sun on scorching concrete sidewalks, while cars sped by spewing exhaust fumes in their faces. There was not a tree in sight, not even a blade of grass. Litter sat where it had been thrown; tossing a beer can out a car window is the short answer to getting rid of it. It was to be one of the saddest looking communities we would see in our travels.

Security measures required those using the canal to be photographed and have fingerprint data on file. Tourists who wished to use the viewing platform at the Miraflores Observation Pavilion needed to pass through an inspection station fitted with a metal detector. It is here at the Miraflores lock that a webcam offers the opportunity for those around the world to watch live as vessels transit.

When we stepped onto the viewing platform at Miraflores lock, a freighter was already in the lock while another waited directly behind. Stacked with containers several stories high, the ship fit so snuggly into the 304 metre (1,000 foot) lock that its hull came within inches of the walls. Each lock measures 33 metres (110 feet) wide. When the locks were constructed, they were built to accommodate ships as large as the *Titanic*, although at the time, ninety-five percent of the ships in the world were less than 182 metres, (600 feet) long. Today, Panamaxes,[*] capable of carrying twenty-five hundred containers, are the largest ships to transit the canal.

---

[*] According to the Panama Canal Authority, Panamax ships cannot be longer than 294 metres (965 ft.), wider than 32 metres (106 ft.), and have a draft of not more than 12 metres (39.5 ft.). However, the canal is expanding. Certain locks will be extended by 133 metres (436 feet), widened by 23 metres (75.5 feet) and dredged 6 metres (19.5 feet) deeper. This will result in doubling the canals' capacity.

Mechanical mule trains located on each side of the canal run alongside the ships on tracks paying out and reeling in steel guide lines fore and aft to guide ships into place. Because of the tight fit, the largest ships are only allowed into locks during daylight hours. Engines of large ships are shut down often requiring four to twelve mechanical mules to pull the ship forward, while smaller ships move under their own power. Controlling the lines with the assistance of radio communication, the mules keep ships away from the walls of the lock, avoiding damage to both walls and ship.

Our fleet of twenty-five Rally boats had been divided into two groups with a plan to transit on two separate days. Nests, or rafts of twos and threes, had been formulated according to a plan which put a larger, heavier boat in the middle, with a smaller boat rafted along each side of it. We were to be one of the side boats that would handle the lines lowered from the top of each lock. After tying loops in the lines, the ends with loops are attached to a bollard at the top of the lock. The other end is then dropped to the yacht where it is secured around a cleat and is either taken in as the water fills the lock and the boat rises, or eased out as the water escapes from the lock and the boat lowers to the new level. It is the responsibility of the boats on each side of the raft to help keep the group of boats in the centre of the lock by using appropriate line tension. With the added tonnage of the combined raft, a knock against a lock wall can cause serious damage. When the lock is filled and the gates open, the centre yacht powers forward driving the raft into the next lock while local canal dock-line handlers walk forward with the lines still attached to the boat.

The canal authorities require that each boat have four line handlers, plus a skipper and an official canal pilot onboard. If needed, additional line handlers can be rented for $65 US a day. Because the Rally boats were to travel on two separate days, crews from yachts that were not transiting helped those who were in need of more hands. Although Andy was about to leave us to return to Toronto, he was available for the canal transit and our friend, Brian, from Victoria, B.C. had joined us in Colón. Each of them line-handled for other boats during the first day of transit while *Baccalieu III* waited for her transit time the following day. After the volunteers assisted other yachts on the first day of fleet transit, the group was ferried back by bus to the Atlantic end of the canal where the rest of the boats waited to leave the next day.

COLÓN is one of the most dangerous cities in the world, encompassing an unfortunate number of slums and desperate people.

When we first arrived in port, at the old Panama Canal Yacht Club, we were strictly advised not to step outside the gates which were secured with eight foot barbed wire fencing. There was no doubt, according to our advisor, that if we did, we would be mugged, as those inhabiting nearby apartment buildings kept an eye for those who wandered.

It was advisable, he said, to use only approved PCYC taxis, because even taxi drivers could be associated with criminals. It was one of these taxi drivers that told us the local vagrants referred to people who left on foot as 'customers'.

Criminal activity is so prevalent within the city that malls in Colón are guarded by police armed with submachine guns. During the volunteer line handler's return to the PCYC by bus, a traffic jam detained the vehicle, giving several young boys a chance to jump onto the coach's roof and terrorize the occupants by banging on the windows and doors demanding entry.

Earlier, one of the Blue Water Rally officials had met with even more of a horrific experience when a gang attempted to detain their rental car with a makeshift road block by suddenly surrounding the car with rubber tires.

TODAY's situation reflects the history of Panama, when Colón suddenly expanded with thousands of migrant labourers seeking available canal jobs. In the early stages of the French canal excavation in 1884, over nineteen thousand employees were at the canal worksite and most workers were black.

Twenty years later, a total of twenty-four thousand men, were working in the Canal Zone for wages of ten cents an hour, ten hours a day, six days a week. Unskilled workers dug ditches, swung axes against granite hard rock, hacked inch by inch through jungle growth with machetes, shoveled tons of dirt by hand, unloaded the contents of box cars on their backs, set dynamite sticks in predrilled holes and then ran for their lives after igniting them.

By the end of the project, thousands were out of jobs, and many were unable to return home. The city of Colón and its poor occupants were there to stay.

ON the day of our transit, a pilot was scheduled to board *Baccalieu III* at approximately four o'clock in the morning. We had been forewarned damage might occur when a 12 metre (40 foot) steel tugboat, delivering the pilot, would attempt to keep its bow pressed firmly against our beam. Sure enough, during the morning of the first transit, a boat in our fleet suffered damage to a toe rail and to one of its' stanchions when swells jostled the two vessels against each other. The tugs are designed to deliver pilots onto ships by essentially ramming their industrial sized, fender-protected bows into the waiting ship's hull and then holding them there under engine power while the pilot disembarks. Wake and surges can cause the rammed-together boats to jostle, knocking off stern barbeques and damaging life lines on cruising boats. Each boat had to endure this procedure three times when both pilots and ad-measurers were delivered on the hefty, bull-nosed tugboats in the same manner.

As well as using our own standard yacht fenders, we rented what some local brainstorming entrepreneur had invented—plastic wrapped used car tires, (probably stolen from some car attempting to leave the PCYC). After transiting, we discarded them at the Pacific end of the canal where they would be collected and offered again for rent to the next needy yacht.

Our canal pilot arrived sometime after four that morning and gave command to lift anchor and proceed towards the first lock. The pilot's job was not to take the wheel but to guide the boat with verbal instructions. It took several minutes to put aside my intuitive skills and follow commands of "forward", "neutral", and "reverse."

Thick concrete walls, made from part of the five million sacks of cement shipped to Panama from New York City during construction, run nearly a mile in length to guide ships into place as they approach a lock. Lock gates measuring six stories high, swing open like pairs of double doors extending into open air rooms. We felt like Tom Thumb standing in the hand of a giant.

Moving through canyon-like concrete walls, one could appreciate the enormous task undertaken when men had stood knee deep in concrete mix while spreading tons by hand, in excavations 18 metres (60 feet) below ground level. Suffering from extreme heat and stagnant, cement-dusted air, many were overcome with the conditions. Others died in landslides, cave-ins, dynamite accidents, and construction accidents. Cholera, dysentery, yellow fever, smallpox and malaria took countless others. Deaths numbered in the thousands.

Pairs of locks accommodating both north and south moving traffic were constructed side by side. While we sat in a southbound lock, a northbound ship, stacked with hundreds of containers, sat motionless in the lock adjacent to us, miniaturizing our boat. A chain lying in a groove along the concrete floor of each gate waits to be engaged in the event a ship approaches out of control.

The preplanned 'nests' organized by the Rally were never used. The experienced pilots recognized which boats they wanted to enlist as part of their rafts and immediately set about organizing their nest to their best interests. We were placed in the middle to be used as the steering boat while alongside, two 12 metre (40 foot) yachts were tied to starboard and port. We were to be the 'powerhouse' moving the raft forward, keeping it straight while entering and exiting the locks, thereby preventing the adjacent yachts from scraping the walls.

From the Atlantic side, a series of three locks named the Gatun Locks, lifts boats 26 metres (85 feet) to the level of Gatun Lake, a 50 kilometre (31 mile) long, manmade lake used to generate electricity and to supply water to the Gatun and Pedro Miguel locks. This tropical forest lake area is home to crocodiles, iguanas, monkeys, almost four hundred species of birds and numerous plant species. The area was once the Chagres River Valley,* and home to several Indian villages. Even the Panama Railroad, used to move dirt and construction materials during the build, lay beneath water now. When first introduced to the concept of the canal, Panamanian natives, living along the river, could not comprehend such a thing might be possible, and many who used the river for daily chores of bathing and laundry did not move much in advance of the flooding.

Water flows by gravity from both Gatun Lake and Miraflores Lake through giant tunnels controlled by steel gates built in the sides and floor of each lock.

Numerous culverts are distributed throughout a single

---

* The Chagres River is the only river in the world that empties into two oceans.

lock which delivers water so rapidly that a ship can be lifted in approximately fifteen minutes.

Arriving in Gatun Lake, we were informed we would need to wait two hours to allow a northbound ship to clear the channel and a southbound ship to proceed before us. Because ships cannot pass safely in the Gaillard Cut, the canal operates an alternate one-way system for larger ships. The Gaillard Cut, a 14 kilometre (9 mile) stretch, was such an immense undertaking during excavation, that it resembled an artificial valley.

WITH our raft still connected, we tied to a giant mooring ball and took the opportunity to have lunch. Prior to our transit, we had been informed that each boat was expected to provide lunch to their onboard pilot. This was not a surprise, but our Spanish speaking pilot took no chances and informed us that he expected something to eat.

The Pedro Miguel lock drops vessels nine metres (thirty-one feet) to the level of Miraflores Lake. One kilometre (one-half mile) further south, we entered a double lockage at Miraflores and dropped a further sixteen metres (fifty-four feet) to the level of the Pacific Ocean. The Pacific Ocean has a tidal range of 5 to 6 metres (18 to 20 feet) making this lock the tallest and the gates the largest; seven hundred and forty-five tons, each bolted and riveted with millions of pieces of steel originating from Pittsburgh, Pennsylvania.

Since the completion of the canal, improvements have been made, a second dam added and the Gaillard Cut widened and deepened to allow the largest ships to pass while travelling in opposite directions. The new expansion, due to open in 2016, will allow new Panamax-sized ships to have dimensions: 366 metres (1,200 feet) long and 49 metres (160 feet) wide.

During the remodeling of the canal, the canal continued

to work at capacity. In February 2011, there were four to five times the normal volume of ships waiting to transit due to the result of seasonal grain shipments. While eighty ships cued up to transit, an auction of booking slots took place. Two northbound Panamax ships jumped the queue: one, a container vessel winning the lead by offering a $41,600 US premium; the second, a dry bulk carrier willing to pay an additional $35,000 US. With the cost of a single container, travelling from China to the U.S. at $5,000 US, shipping rates are volatile and schedules tightly driven.

Bidding wars are more frequent now that canal construction can back up traffic.

Although fewer ships use the canal today than in the seventies due to the size of ships being larger, over thirteen thousand ships pass through the Panama Canal annually. In 2006, during our transit, the Canal authorities allowed, for the first time since 1999, an entire lock to be taken over by cruising boats.

IT TOOK US twelve hours to transit the canal. After releasing our rafted companions and letting off our pilot to board a tugboat, we passed beneath the Bridge of the Americas, the second-longest tied arch bridge in the world. We were in the Pacific! We toasted our arrival with a bottle of sparkly. This was the beginning of a great adventure. We had cast off the safety net, let go the ties of familiarity. We would sail vast areas of sea not frequented by ships. Set course towards some of the remotest islands in the world. Navigate through exotic named archipelagos. That it was the end of the comfort zone there was no doubt. We were about to begin a journey of unknowns. We were embarking on a worldly experience we were sure we would never forget and hoped we would never regret. This was a great moment; I felt we had just landed on another planet.

PANAMA CITY, PASSAGE TO THE GALÁPAGOS ISLANDS

Good luck is a residue of preparation
JACK YOUNGBLOOD

WE SPENT SEVERAL days docked at the newly constructed Flamenco Yacht Club and Marina just minutes from downtown Panama City. Panama City is one of the oldest continuously occupied European settlements in the Pacific coast of the Americas.

A taxi ride away, the original settlement Panamá Viejo founded in 1519, is located in the suburbs of Panama City. Panamá Viejo was the starting point for expeditions that conquered the Inca Empire in Peru (1532). It was also the centre of one of the most important trade routes on the American continent. Silver and gold were transported to Portobelo by mule trains then hauled across the isthmus to ships whose destinations were either Cuba or Spain.

Surviving years of slave rebellions, pirate attacks, fire and an earthquake, the city was destroyed in 1671 by Welsh privateer Henry Morgan. Only a scattering of walls and stone ruins exist. Two years after Morgan's attack, the city was relocated near the mouth of the river that eventually became the Panama Canal.

The relocated town, Casco Antiguo, (the Historic District of Panama), is a mix of narrow and wide streets lined with 17th century cathedrals, churches richly decorated with gold, wooden tenement buildings and French and Antillean townhouses built during the construction of the Panama Canal. The Old Quarter is made safe by the presence of numerous polícia on bicycles. The archaeological ruins at Panamá Viejo, combined with the Historic District of Panama, forms a UNESCO World Heritage Site.

OUR NEXT STOP was the Galápagos Islands, eight hundred and fifty miles away; seven days including a stopover in Las Perlas Islands. Provisioning in Panama was of major importance. The Galápagos Islands are not equipped with large supermarkets and Tahiti, the next opportunity to provision, would be nine weeks away.

During our travels, we often came across boats we had met before, and Canadian owned *Carpe Diem*, an Oyster 62, was one that shared a common route. Their first mate, Christina, was a lifesaver to me in Panama. Her fluency in the Spanish language enabled us to locate several useful places to provision, including a distribution market (Mercado de Abastos) where the two of us were likely the only English speaking persons on site. We inspected thousands of fresh fruits and vegetables stuffed into bags, baskets or crates, or strewn in colourful array over the ground and then hired a young man with a trolley to help collect our purchases. Produce was incredibly inexpensive here. Two dollars bought two dozen grapefruit or 100 oranges. A flat of tomatoes cost one dollar and pineapples went for twenty-five cents apiece. We were both provisioning for long voyages and when we were finished we thought we might need to hire two taxis to haul it all back to the marina, but somehow we managed to fit everything into one.

Each piece of produce needed to be washed then dried before stowing in the coolest, darkest areas of the boat, underneath the floor boards. We strung a hammock in the forward cabin to accommodate fruits that did not have a long shelf life and would need to be eaten early in the trip. A stalk of bananas was hung off the communications post on the stern. The refrigerator was so jammed that no one but me ventured to find anything in it. I knew where the items were because I had drawn a diagram.

As Tahiti is four times more expensive than Panama City, I stocked up with cans of tomatoes, vegetables, pasta sauce, UTH milk, pasta, cheese, and canned fish. There must be no place cheaper in the world to shop than Panama City. I marked the top of each can with its contents to make locating them underway easier. The same time, I listed all the stores brought on board so that I could determine what had been purchased. Having a wide variety of food allowed me to cook good meals which at times, were the best thing that happened in a day. The freezer was still filled with meats from Antigua. Thousands of miles later we would be eating poultry that I had purchased from Jolly Harbour. When we pulled away from the Flamenco Marina, *Baccalieu III* was a warehouse of food.

The downside of carrying so much frozen food is that it leaves no room for prepared foods, no stocking of make-ahead meals, no emergency prepared provisions for rough days or times when I didn't feel like cooking. I never froze large food items such as bread because it took up too much space. I would need to prepare two meals a day no matter what the conditions. Provisioning had been exhausting and I was happy to pull away from the dock heading towards the Las Perlas Archipélago (Isla de Puercos/Pearl Islands), located in the Gulf of Panama and only thirty-eight nautical miles south of the Panama Canal.

Each morning that we were anchored in the islands, flocks of pelicans flew by, one behind the other, like fighter pilots in formation, skimming just inches above the water. On the second morning a sloshing of water, and a mass bubbling and rippling suggested a disturbance of large fish frantically struggling to escape a mysterious predator. A local fisherman and his wife directed their boat towards the turbulence and were soon alongside *Baccalieu III* offering us fresh Bonita tuna for two dollars a fish.

Before leaving the Pearl Islands, we down-loaded a wind chart, the first of many that would assist us in our quest to find wind. Fifteen to twenty knot winds swept us away from the islands towards the Galápagos. The water was not that aqua tropical blue colour that I had imagined the Pacific Ocean to be, but instead, it was tinted with dark, brackish brown hues. Two days later when we changed the watermaker filters, we discovered the reason—the filters were green with algae.

A second surprise was that we needed to add long pants and sweaters to our attire even though we were approaching the equator. This was due to the cold water temperatures of the Humboldt Current, one of the major ocean currents of the world. The current transports frigid-like water from Antarctic, along South America's coast to the Pacific Ocean.

During my 0300 to 0600 watch, a ship appeared on the radar screen and appeared to be crossing our bow. By the time we reached its location, there should be no need to change our course. But I kept an eye on it both visually and on the radar screen.

Perspective of an object in the distance with no reference points can be misconstrued. Then there is the factor of distortion. These points always make it challenging to decipher targets that might become potential collisions. At night it's even more puzzling when dealing with the sight of one or more lights. That night, I misjudged my target and today, I feel the same sensation of wrong doing that I did then. I made a mistake and it could have been costly.

We were sailing downwind with the mainsail full out and prevented (lashed). The Yankee was poled to the opposite side and we were reveling in nine knots of speed. I had been looking at the ship's red port light through binoculars and knew which way it was headed. The lights confirmed it was headed in a direction that would have it cross our bow long before we approached its location. But it appeared to be moving slowly.

As time passed, we neared the ship and I could see that I was closing the gap rather quickly. It was highly unusual to come upon a ship that was stopped in the middle of the ocean. However, at this point I still did not know that it was not underway. There were only the ship's lights to inform me of its direction; mere dots in a dark environment. I went below to radio the ship but received no answer. When I climbed the companionway stairs to return to the cockpit, I was now looking at the ship's red and green lights. It had turned, and the lights indicated it was heading straight for us. I got Mike out of bed. The poled out Yankee and the lashed-down mainsail hindered me from changing directions easily. Tacking poles is a two-man job. I should have got Mike up earlier to help me tack.

We were charging ahead at nine knots, closing in quickly. There was no time to gybe the pole or even let off the preventer line. The ship turned, showing only its red port bow light. It must have been drifting and simply spun in the current. By this time I was far too close and I had to make a snap decision on which way to go around it. In the excitement, I lost faith in my knowledge of lights. I turned in the wrong direction, towards its bow rather than behind her stern. My decision was a double mistake because in making the incorrect tack, I back-winded the mainsail which fortunately was shackled to the preventer line keeping it from swinging out of control. We discovered later, the force of the load on the sheet bent one of the forward stainless stanchions on the foredeck. A lot of pressure is needed to bend one of those sturdy stanchions.

With the mainsail back winded, I had to tack again in order to get the wind on the current side. I was headed to cross her bow, now, by making a quick second tack, we sailed down the side of the freighter towards the stern. The Yankee was flapping noisily, folding into itself uncontrollably, then whacking open again and again, straining hard against its sheets as they cracked against the dodger's windshield. Interesting how noise intensifies a moment.

We were so close to the ship's stern as I rounded her that if I hadn't been so focused on trying to maneuver a boat with one of its sails on the wrong side, I probably would have been capable of reading the ship's name on the stern without the use of binoculars.

We were fortunate fish nets were not dragging astern or we would have most certainly been part of the catch. I don't even want to think about the possibilities *that* could have created for us. But luckily the ship wasn't a fishing vessel at all. What a drifting freighter was doing in the middle of the ocean is still a mystery. Perhaps it was a fish processing vessel.* Thank goodness we didn't collide.

In retrospect, I think the day had a hex on it from the start. Earlier in the day, Mike had attached the preventer line to the boom but failed to close the snap shackle. This left the boom hiked out over the water with little to prevent it from flying across the cockpit. Luckily, I had noticed it and secured the snap shackle or we might have broken the

---

* Fish processing vessels are designed to stay at sea for months. Catches are delivered to the vessel by a fleet of fish trawlers. Floating processing plants have the ability to cool, flash freeze and pack fish into cartons that are loaded onto pallets. A 115 m (377 ft.) processing vessel can process and freeze 3,000 tons of fish before returning to shore.

supporting gooseneck to the boom when I played chicken with the ship that night.

FOLLOWING my chance meeting with the ocean freighter, a sort of paranoia set in when having to read distant navigation lights. It's a wonder we made any headway because I nearly gave up tending the sails; I was instead glued to the binoculars, scanning the water for lurking vessels.

The following night, I watched arduously while a bright light, shinning in the distance, became brighter and brighter; a sign that we must be nearing it. When my eyes weren't peering through the binoculars, I was clambering up and down the companionway stairs to check the radar screen. But the light was nowhere on the screen. And why would this be? Because it was a brilliant planet rising from the horizon into a darkened night sky!

Mother Nature has a warped sense of humour.

There is no doubt I experienced my most anxious moments while night sailing in waters worked by fishing boats. You might think that I should add freighters to that list, but I swear I never had another problem with a freighter after my dance with that first one.

On the afternoon of our second day, the wind died; I mean it really died. We were forced to use the motor. The good thing about running the engine is that its constant hum helped to mask the insufferable whine of the autopilot in our aft cabin. The autopilot, sounding like a pair of sickly pigs, was annoying not only in its tone but in its unevenness of delivery. Screech,.... screeeeeeeeeech..... screech.

To avoid arriving in the Galápagos in darkness, we slowed our pace. Pulling back the throttle to not much more than an idle, we allowed *Baccalieu III* to drift with the two knot current.

When at sea for a few days, even the presence of a gull

is notable; something with a heartbeat other than the same two men I'd been looking at for days might catch more of my attention than normal. One begins to appreciate happenings never before given a second thought, and here I found myself studying the seagull's fishing maneuvers like I was some sort of ornithologist. The gull became a real thing of interest to me, sort of an untouchable pet or mascot. I admired it for its stamina and for the simple fact that it could fly. Why was it that men couldn't fly after strapping on one of those chicken-man suits? I tried to recall. I found myself pondering the dynamics of flying. Then I began wondering how far the bird could see, did it taste its food, did it ever get so tired of eating fish it wished it could steal a good French fry from a takeout box? Passing time without a whole lot of interest can do this to you.

The gull tailgated the boat for most of our journey to the Galápagos. During the day, it followed at a safe distance exploring the sea, drifting with wind currents, diving every now and again to pick off fish near the surface. At times I thought he had left us for good but each night it returned to fly round and round the boat like a windup toy, entertaining me with his transformations from feathered neon white, as he quivered around the steaming light, to glowing with soft reds and greens when his wings dipped through the reflections of our navigation bow lights.

One day I saw a large fish throwing its lumbering body into the air, twisting and somersaulting before falling back into the water. Time and time again he hurled himself aloft, in a frantic attempt to escape a predator. The outcome wasn't obvious, but the fight for survival continued right in front of my eyes for at least five minutes.

A few days later I saw the spew of a whale several metres off the bow and one night I smelled the breath of another. The ocean suddenly appeared to be teaming with life. One night the languorous bodies of dolphins slithering through the water disrupted a thickness of neon phosphorescence so dense, it appeared as if the dolphins were towing stocky luminescent snakes behind them. While they arched and dove through our darkened bow wake, luminescence dripped from their bodies like an entire constellation letting loose a trickling of stars.

At 0500 on the third morning, the first light shone on a calming sea and by afternoon the sea was a glassy reflection of the clear blue sky. The air temperature became increasingly warm and our skin glistened with perspiration. And the wind? What wind? We had sailed into the doldrums.*

On the same day, March 4th at 1945, we crossed the equator. I know this time to be accurate because we documented it in the log book. The GPS co-ordinates read 0°00'/ 88°75' W.

It was a momentous occasion because the equator is a landmark of the sea. In crossing it we were now officially headed towards exotic destinations. Places that we had only before read about in the South Pacific: French Polynesia, Tahiti and Bora Bora. No matter how you arrive at these places, they are distant and unfamiliar. We would meet people of exotic cultures, hear new languages and see customs we had never heard of before.

In the back of our minds was the fact we were travelling further and further from sources of assistance of any kind. And what we still hadn't discussed was how we would get back to where we had started. It's not as simple as turning your car around; winds and currents don't co-operate like roads. But the thought of returning never really stayed long in my mind. Those details would work themselves out. At the time I was swallowed by curiosity, intrigue, the excitement of travel and I

---

* The doldrums or equatorial calms, is an area of low-pressure around the equator where the prevailing winds are still.

could hardly wait to carry on. We were explorers, modern explorers with our own 'ship of discovery'. In arriving at the equator, we had signed a pact with the sea gods. We had crossed over. We celebrated with a steak dinner and toasted King Neptune with champagne, but to be honest, didn't offer him much. We were seventy-five miles from the Galápagos.

THE GALÁPAGOS ISLANDS

Of course in science there are things that are open to doubt and things need to be discussed. But among the things that science does know, evolution is about as certain as anything we know.
RICHARD DAWKINS

If evolution really works, how come mothers only have two hands?
MILTON BERLE

A RANGE OF giant volcanic mountains anchored across the ocean's floor breaks through the surface to form an archipelago called the Galápagos Islands. The islands, all small in size, are located 965 km (600 mi.) off the mainland coast of Ecuador.

The erupted mountains not only form the foundations for the islands, but where their peaks reach high enough, they trap vapour to provide a supply of rain and watery mists that make possible the survival of a host of curious creatures born only on the islands: penguins, fur seals, vines, thirteen species of finches and at least five hundred species of lichen. The islands were once known as Las Encantadas, the Enchanted Isles, for the magical way in which they can drift in and out of sight from behind a curtain of translucent moisture.

All this moisture and yet several islands in the archipelago are without any fresh water at all. This is a good thing because it allowed the islands to escape human interference for centuries. An accidental early discovery of one of the dry islands, documented in the late 1500s, discloses that the captain suggested to other seagoing vessels they bypass the bleak and barren islands. They were without fresh water, he reported.

When Charles Darwin arrived in 1835, to explore four of the islands during a five week stopover on the ship HMS *Beagle*, a ten-gun Royal Navy brigantine, the islands were still mostly untouched by humans.

By the 18th century, whaling ships were forced to sail further south while seeking whale blubber and baleen. Ships and hungry crewmembers spent more time at sea, and provisioning en route became challenging. In the Galápagos Islands, food was free for the taking and whalers found ample, live, easy-to-kill tortoise meat. The ensuing and frequent visits of the whalers to the archipelago brought an end to nature's purity on the islands.

Within thirty-three years, between the late 18th and early 19th centuries, an estimated seven hundred whaling ships plied the Pacific Ocean for whales. It is estimated that ships stopping at the islands might have harvested some two hundred thousand tortoises.*

Stored in the holds or on deck, without needing food or water, and with a shelf life up to one year, tortoise meat appeared to be the answer to having no refrigeration. Supply could not keep up with the demand and four species of tortoise were driven to extinction. Fortunately, before all tortoises became extinct, the inventory of whales lessened. This in turn, reduced the heavy traffic of ships stopping at the islands.

---

* To transport tortoises to awaiting ships, the reptiles were turned upside down, tied with empty cans and floated to ships where they were loaded onboard. Giant tortoises can weigh 300 kg (660 lb.) and a single tortoise could feed 300 crewmembers. Tortoise meat was kept fresh by placing the tortoises to be stored the longest, in salt water tanks and the others on their backs on deck.

THE volcanic islands support a specialized group of flora: lava cacti, prickly pear, salt brush, and other species that have adapted to the rugged conditions. Soil has slowly accumulated on several of the islands. These islands support forests of low growing scalesia trees, while other islands remain as harsh as any desert.

Darwin, a geologist, gathered information for his book, *The Origin of Species* and used his findings to develop his theory of Natural Selection. Darwin noted species on the islands were similar enough to be related but different enough to vary from one island to the next, as each species had adapted to their specific needs. Darwin collected finches, but it was in fact, his collection of mockingbirds from the islands of Floreana and San Cristóbal that became the most important species he had in his collection. He used the mockingbirds as a baseline of scientific facts. Darwin's original collection of mockingbirds still exists in the Museum of Natural History. Over one hundred and seventy-five years old, the bird's carcasses contribute to science when DNA, extracted from their feet, help scientists understand how to prevent the species' extinction.

Now, mostly due to introduced species, the mockingbird is extinct on Floreana and only two hundred exist on neighbouring islands. They are listed as one of the rarest birds in the world.

But the islands are more to scientists than a place where Darwin took away hundreds of endemic species followed by swarms of other scientists who carried away thousands more including hundreds of tortoises all in the name of science. The islands are also a study of Earth's spewing gases, hot spots, seeping lava fountains and shifting plates; studies in geology, biology and a continuous study of preservation of our precious Earth.

Situated on sliding oceanic plates, the islands continue

to move southeast towards South America, where one day, they will eventually disappear altogether beneath the South American continent. How unnerving is that? But not to worry, moving at 40 centimetres (16 inches) a year their final destiny will take millions of years to materialize.

In 1987 the government of Ecuador suggested restricting the annual number of visiting tourists to the Galápagos' to twenty-five thousand. Today, one hundred and eighty thousand tourists visit the islands each year. To protect the sensitive nature of the islands, the government restricts access of both walking tourists and visiting yachts. Only four anchorages in the entire archipelago are available for cruising yachts, each requiring permits, and those who wish to cruise the islands in their own boat must purchase a $2,000 US permit and as well, hire a guide at the cost of $150 US per day. Alternatively, small cruise ships are available with accompanying guides and naturalists, who offer seminars and take tourists to shore for walks.

Many species of flora, fauna, marine and land life are endemic to the islands and contamination can be catastrophic. Within a period of only five years, more than one hundred new plant species were accidently introduced to the islands which threatened the survival of endemic species. Fire ants, which can easily travel on airplanes and ocean vessels, can upset the balance of the insect population which in turn serves as a food source to birds.

For that reason, incoming airplanes and yachts are fumigated. Once pest control is completed yachts are presented with a "certificado de funigacion."

We dropped anchor in Puerto Ayora off the island of Santa Cruz. This is where we were fumigated. It was a simple procedure carried out by a technician who came aboard and squeezed pest control gel in several areas throughout the interior of the boat. The cost of this was conveniently added to our international arrival fees, anchoring fees, navigation light fees (whatever that is), access channel fees, port captain fees, and departure fees. We also paid a $100 US National Park fee which every visitor to the island is required to pay. The money raised from the Park fee goes to support the Charles Darwin Research Centre where endangered species of tortoises are hatched and cared for until they reach five years old. By then their shells have hardened and they are no longer threatened by the introduced population of rats. In 1959, when statistics were first gathered to determine the number of tortoises and their species, about two hundred old adults were found on Pinzón Island. For more than a century, all the hatchlings had apparently been killed by introduced rats.

THE Darwin Centre was also home to Lonesome George, a giant land tortoise. He had been the rarest species in the entire world, a sort of living international symbol of extinction, until he died in 2012. At one hundred years old, he was the last surviving Pinta Island purebred.

WE toured the islands aboard a government approved, modest one hundred passenger cruise ship the *Explorer II*. Each morning at 0630, a wakeup call signaled the beginning of a new adventure and by 0800 we would be embarking on one of the five, twelve man rubber dinghies available to take cruise ship passengers to shore.

As we disembarked from one of the dinghies at Santiago Island, gentle incoming waves wetted a series of natural volcanic steps where orange Sally Lightfoot crabs scrambled away on five pairs of legs for a quick getaway. We were glad that we had worn our hiking boots to walk the volcanic shores of hardened black folds, twisting and crinkling into shallow crevasses.

Always mindful of staying within the boundaries of white posts that marked the walking areas, we saw much of the wildlife at close range; male frigate birds pumping up their scarlet chests in courtship and young playful sea lions chasing swishing iguana's tails in the safety of small, saltwater pools.

We came upon a lava bridge spanning a volcanic crevasse where ocean waves lathered the shore like a frothy cappuccino. A few feet away, sea water squeezed under the stone bridge, swirling its way to the top of a deep lava hole. As soon as the sizzling foam reached the top, subsiding, it would flush back out to sea again. Someone had named the hole Darwin's Toilet.

Each morning after spending the first few hours hiking, we returned to the ship to listen to a naturalist speak in the ship's salon, followed by lunch at one o'clock. The afternoons were filled with more hiking, and occasionally snorkeling in the Humboldt's Antarctic sweep of near frigid waters. In the evening, a briefing detailing the island and the species that we would visit the following day would be accompanied with a slide show. Dinner was at eight o'clock and then we would fall into bed unless our friends insisted on a nightcap, which I could hardly stay awake for.

It was never planned that we meet up with other Blue Water Rally participants on the ship; in fact we had little opportunity to get to know other Rally members. Social time had been minimal since joining them in the San Blas Islands. We had booked *Explorer II* months in advance and luckily ten other BWR sailors had independently chosen the same cruise.

THE Galápagos archipelago spreads out over an area of 45,000 square kilometres (17,000 square miles) and straddles the equator. As it is customary while at sea to celebrate an equatorial crossing, the ship *Explorer II* organized a cocktail party including a toast, to celebrate the crossing. By chance, we met two travellers who had recently spent time in the rainforests of Ecuador near the equator. They were scientists who had taken part in an experiment regarding the phenomenon known as coriolis, a force that causes moving objects on the surface of the earth to appear to veer to the right in the northern hemisphere and to the left in the southern hemisphere. If the earth did not rotate, winds and currents would simply flow from high-pressure to low-pressure.

The scientists had filled a sink with water and set it 2 metres (6 feet) on either side of the equator which they had determined accurately by use of a GPS. They then floated a few small green leaves in the water. When the sink was located south of the equatorial line, the water swirled counterclockwise, when the basin was located on the north side of the line, the water swirled clockwise before draining out of the basin.

When the basin sat exactly on the equator, the leaves turned vertical before draining straight from the basin. According to our scientist friends, there is no conclusive explanation for this phenomenon.

BARTOLOMÉ Island has little soil and the few scraggly lava cacti flourishing in crevasses are proof that life can start anywhere. A small lava lizard, unconcerned with the scorching heat of the sun, scurried across the brown hued landscape of compact ash and gravel. We learned that the archipelago had not been born from the same type of lava. When Bartolomé erupted, the lack of available water created rock resembling the weight of light balsa wood enabling a person to hold good sized boulders above his shoulders with little effort.

Following a staircase to the top of a hill, we stood before an immense panorama of dry gravely hills, bare mountains and inverted peaks. It seemed that to be there was like standing on the moon.

In the afternoon, we rode the ship's dinghy to James Island. Our driver guided the bow to shore where travelling lava had rolled toward the sea solidifying into smooth black plateaus. The shallow plateaus now offer sea lions a resting place and we often had to walk around them as they lay nursing their young or simply absorbing heat from sun heated rocks.

Blue footed Boobies, sea birds similar in size to large seagulls, stood as if wearing pairs of oversized blue diving fins over disproportionately large webbed feet. Their ability to walk is hampered by their clumsy appendages, but they need only to visit land for the purpose of breeding. A set of eyes perched above large yellow beaks and spaced closely together give the bird a comical cross-eyed appearance. Consequently, the species has been christened with the Spanish term 'bobo', suggesting fool or clown. There is, however, nothing clownish about the way they dive from soaring heights, most often plunging inches from shoreline rocks.

On the island of Santa Cruz we travelled by taxi to the wet highlands, home of an inland turtle reserve. Branches of scalesia trees hung with soft stringy mosses looking as if a hundred old ladies' hairnets had come to land there in the wind. Tortoises on Santa Cruz are of the large, domed-back variety, obtaining food from low shrubs and grasses. When they need to rest, they drag their thick, bulky carriages into deep grasses beneath bushy low hanging limbs. Lugging a 300 kg (600 lb.) load over uneven terrain requires a good amount of energy. It was February, the tortoise breeding season, when beneath trees, cumbersome activity is taking place. The heavy old males, some in their hundredth year, too large to venture very far, wait for the females to trek up from the lowlands. After mating, the females return to the lower coastal regions to lay eggs in freshly dug pits softened with urine as they dig.

We met more than one tortoise strolling down a dirt road headed to wherever tough old dinosaurs go. Lumbering with their necks arched in lengthy stretches, their progress was slowed by stumpy feet and short stalky legs. Short legs maybe, but those squat leg mechanisms are capable of shoving aside boulders. Although tortoises are no speed demons, a tortoise might have travelled six kilometres by the end of the day, which is roughly equivalent to travelling one city block an hour.

FERNANDINA Island, one of the islands where Darwin collected mockingbirds, is the youngest island in the archipelago, and the only one with no foreign introduced species. The island had been home to thousands of tortoises. The tortoises have been hunted to extinction, however, Fernandina has remained pure, without the introduction of goats, rats, cats, feral pigs or introduced pests that might compromise the safety of natural wildlife, including that of the flightless cormorant.

We took one of our longest walks while on Fernandina, plodding over black lava fields rippling with hardened fissures where hundreds of small, scaly iguanas lay scattered on sun heated rocks near the shore. Propped on forelegs, with heads cocked to the sea air, these miniature dinosaurs looked ready for battle in their leathery, spiny armored skins. Flattish tails enable them to dive to depths of 30 metres (100 feet), earning them the distinction, the only marine iguana in the world. With an ability to remain submerged for up to an hour, the long tailed reptile had completely baffled the crew on Darwin's ship when someone attempted to drown one and it kept coming up alive! With salt caked faces frozen into continuous smirks and light coloured eyelids that stare with unsettling creepiness, these iguanas face you square on while carrying out a daily ritual of spitting sea salt through their nostrils. It is perhaps not something you would choose as a pet, but the males are notable because they master two penises. I know someone who remains baffled at why he would ever lose such a valuable commodity through evolution.

Nature can be cruel and we felt equally callous as we stepped around a young sea lion lying listlessly near the path. Sea lions are often taken by sharks. We observed that the nursing mother of this pup had not returned. Sadly, we recalled that we had to obey the rules of the Galápagos Islands and not to interfere with nature even when it seemed heartless to do nothing and leave the sea lion to contend with the forces of nature on its own.

Fernandina is also home to a small lava cactus which, by storing moisture in its leaves, survives throughout times of drought covered in a hardy outer skin as defense against the ocean's salty and abrasive air. Nearly all living entities throughout the archipelago require backup survival means because the islands experience cold currents and warm currents, seasons of ample rain, seasons parched by dry spells, tradewinds that cool and doldrums that suffocate. Every three to seven years, an El Niño, a warm band of ocean water, arrives killing the phytoplankton, which starves those that need to feed upon it and upsets the natural rhythm of those that are accustomed to swimming in cool waters. In one year El Niño depleted the marine iguana population, which could have numbered in the hundreds of thousands, by eighty-five percent. The weather is hardly ever idyllic for both the species that survive on land and those which depend on the sea. Tradewinds and currents are part of what creates these complexities. Equatorial currents, countercurrents, undercurrents, including the Peru Current System which includes the Humboldt Current, converge and surround the archipelago causing each group of islands to experience different water temperatures. The northern islands are surrounded by tropical water temperatures, the southern islands warm-temperate water and the more westerly located islands, such as Isabela Island, bath in much cooler water.

These currents and countercurrents carry rich nutrients that attract a wide variety of underwater sea life, from miniature-sized seahorses to giant-sized humpback whales. Where we swam, the water was so cold we had no problem understanding why penguins were content to be this far north. The cold temperature was challenging for us when we snorkeled near jagged shorelines, but worth it to view schools of juvenile black and white, gold striped Moorish idols swimming near protective underwater pinnacles. Then suddenly, we'd witness a scattering of fish darting frantically from penguins that shot past us at the speed of bullets. Curious sea lions joined us, turning their liquid bodies like twisted licorice to view us upside down and right side up, even sometimes playfully nibbling our snorkeling fins.

We swam over green sea turtles, young Galapagos reef sharks, star fish painted with nature's underused hue of blue and vast schools of fiery, ginger coloured Pacific Creole fish camouflaged beside auburn tinted, algae covered rocks.

To explore the depths more fully, we arranged for a water taxi to pick us up at seven one morning from *Baccalieu III*. Once on shore, a taxi took us on an hour's drive across the island, where we boarded a dive boat for a thirty minute ride to a dive site.

ON our first dive, cow-nosed rays glided beneath us. Nearby, large schools of whitetip sharks swam with effortless motion. Hefty moray eels with sharp serrated teeth set into large gaping mouths, peeked from protective caves ready to dart after small fish. Sea turtles, totally unconcerned with our presence, glided by, and large schools of fish, so dense, they resembled gigantic balls, milled about just metres from us.

With the islands surrounded by deep water, it is not unusual to find a large variety of sharks. Schools of hammerheads come in regularly for a cleaning in the Galápagos currents. With eyes and sensors located at the end of a flattened hammer-like head, the sharks have the ability to detect minute electrical currents as faint as the pulses emitted by the tiny hearts of skates and rays burled into the ocean's floor. Although solitary night hunters, the sharks sometimes school in the hundreds, and when we looked above us that day, against the sun's filtering light were the white underbellies and silhouetted long flat heads of a school of scalloped hammerheads.

Before embarking on each dive, the divemaster presented a dive plan to the divers. He would kneel on the floor of the small boat while we huddled around, viewing a chart that assisted in his briefing of the location: maximum depth, duration of the dive, hand signals to be used, and any obstacles we might encounter. Each of the dives were located only metres from small islands, where the seas swirled, bouncing off angular rock faces and overhangs, creating powerful underwater surges. We were to dive close to these walls and follow to the end of the island where currents and shore surge became more intense. Here in this intersection of ocean currents, large fish come in from the open ocean where reef fish congregate and rid the larger species of unwanted parasites. These locations are known as cleaning stations.

At times, currents were so strong it was difficult to make much headway even while kicking and pumping our legs with as much force as we could manage. It was necessary to grasp hold of rocks and boulders and to keep a low profile along the bottom, staying beneath the main body of rushing waters. If we allowed ourselves to be caught up in a surge, we'd be thrown against rocks or swept away from the wall into the middle of the channel where we would be grabbed by other currents. Water speeded past in forces that streamlined our bodies to flow with the current and we struggled to swim against it.

Early into our first dive, my regulator, the mouthpiece that reduces pressurized breathing gas to ambient pressure and delivers it to the diver, malfunctioned. I signaled to the divemaster that I had an equipment failure and I was returning to the surface. I swam back to the boat disappointed that I was about to miss the dive and perhaps even the whole day, but as I reached the dive boat, the dive assistants were hanging over the side communicating in Spanish while signaling for me to take off my equipment and hand it up to them. I pulled off my cumbersome inflatable vest and tank. Immediately they hauled it up over the side and onboard. When I climbed onto the boat I found them in an intense huddle around my gear. With wrenches in hand they appeared to be swapping out my regulator for a new one.

There was little verbal communication between us since they didn't speak English and I have little Spanish. I presumed by the look of what they were doing, they were installing a new regulator and planned to put me back into the water to join the others who must be waiting at the bottom. While they were completing the installation, I pulled on my fins, adjusted my mask and perched up on the rail. They quickly made the change-up and suddenly all three converged on me to refit my BC (buoyancy compensator) and tank, fasten my buckles, rejoin my Velcro straps and pump air into my BC jacket. There were hands all over me, snapping, pressing, securing. Miraculously, in no time I was suited up and ready to go. One of the assistants, recognizing this fury of attention might cause me to feel anxious, stepped directly in front of me. He grasped each of my arms firmly, peered through my mask to make eye contact and said, "Relax."

I smiled weakly in recognition of his message, and with no more time than to place the regulator into my mouth, certainly no time to check whether my new regulator was in working order, I heard someone start the countdown indicating I had three seconds to carry out a back roll or be pushed. I will never forget how his squeeze on my arms grounded me just seconds before I left the rail.

As I landed in the water, I felt like I had just had my tires changed during an Indy 500 pit stop.

The plan for our final dive on the second day went awry for me as well when I found myself separated from the group at 45 feet (14 metres).

On the day of my underwater solo adventure, our group consisted of four divers plus a divemaster. The plan was to drop to forty-five feet before proceeding to the tip of the island where we would watch for hammerhead sharks and manta rays, the largest type of ray in the world. After that, we would make our way across the channel towards a second island, stopping at three pinnacles along the way. The divemaster led the way, followed by two less experienced divers while Mike and I brought up the rear.

We were enjoying a leisurely Dive, peering into crevasses and rock formations, consumed in the discoveries of unique fish, eels, and all that the Galápagos waters have to offer. Without stopping to collect his divers, the divemaster left the wall to head towards the pinnacle located mid-channel. I didn't see him leave. I didn't see any of them leave the wall and by the time I noticed the divers swimming away from me, they were well ahead of me, their legs working hard pushing against the current. I began to swim in pursuit but within seconds, their fins disappeared, swallowed up by the murky water.

While watching that last fin fade from my sight, I felt a sort of emptiness in the pit of my stomach come over me. You don't have to be a master diver to know no one should dive alone. I knew that if I attempted to leave the wall with them so far ahead of me and I was unable to catch up, I might be lost in a murky space with no visual references. This would be far worse than where I was presently hovering. So I stayed along the wall and studied my situation. I checked my air gauge which indicated my tank was three-quarters full; I use very little air when I dive.

My depth gauge confirmed that I was at forty-five feet.

Just before the other divers went out of sight I had taken a compass reading noting the direction in which they were headed. I decided to set off for the first pinnacle trusting my bearing in an effort to locate the others. It didn't take long before I was out of sight of the wall but not yet in sight of the pinnacle. I was in a no visual zone, in an empty space of murky water where the currents were speckled so thickly with algae it was similar to fog. I was out of my comfort zone.

I proceeded on course and found the pinnacle but no divers.

I decided to surface, but before I did, I took time to gaze at my surroundings. I planned to never find myself in a similar predicament and although it may seem strange, I took a moment to enjoy the unique experience; a one on one with nature. How many recreational divers get a chance to do that?

The bubbles escaping from my regulator in rhythm with my breathing suddenly became notable to my ears, as if the sound had never accompanied me before.

It was spooky to be down there alone.

I held onto the pinnacle and watched a green sea turtle swim towards me. It must have found me interesting because quite unexpectedly he swam within one metre (three feet) of my face mask. With flippers gently moving, he stopped in the current to study me. For several seconds we remained eye to eye. Beak to beak.

OK, I'm outta here.

When I surfaced, I saw my diving buddies already on the surface, several metres distant from me. It was obvious they had cut their dive short. Nice to know they had missed me, I thought. But in counting heads, I calculated someone else was missing, and I soon discovered it was Mike.

While following the other divers towards the pinnacle, Mike had trouble dumping air from his BC and had accidentally surfaced. Knowing that I was not with the group he descended again hoping to reunite with the group and find me at the same time. But now the group was up and he was down.

The divemaster instructed the rest of us to return to the dive boat while he located Mike's bubbles and descended to escort him up.

As was customary, after we climbed onboard the dive boat, the boat assistants handed us a hot cup of tea. Believe me, that tea was very welcomed; the cold water had chilled me through.

When the divemaster returned with Mike, the divemaster suggested we all get back into the water to complete the dive.

You gotta be kidding! After warming up? Mercy! These guys were tough!

We saw numerous manta rays, magnificent, graceful creatures. With wing spans reaching two metres (seven feet) and more, they filter small organisms through their gills while gliding with wide, open mouths.

It was only later that I came to realize that the divemaster had never actually noticed me missing; it was only Mike he had missed and the reason he had directed the group to surface. I could still be down there conversing with that sea turtle for all he knew.

WHEN first arriving in the harbour of Santa Cruz, we were excited to see sea lions swimming among the boats while pelicans came so close we could count their feathers. But as time went on, those cute looking sea lions would catapult their slippery, quivering bodies into people's cockpits to lounge on their custom made cushions. One found our stern platform a comfy place to sunbathe. Fortunately, it was impeded from getting into the cockpit by lifelines, and was only able to leave his slimy, gooey trail on our stern scoop. We know of other boaters however, who had to forcibly shoo them out of their cockpits more than once, while keeping in mind, that the darlings are protected under Galápagos Law.

One day, one of those hefty pelicans, with a beak the size of commercial hedge clippers, roosted at the top of our mast on our delicate wind instrument, while another sat on the dinghy using it as a toilet. Their size is not to be underestimated nor is their toilet.

It was time to start thinking about moving on, but before leaving the Galápagos, the Blue Water Rally organized a dinner and briefing regarding the upcoming Pacific crossing. The briefing would take place at a five star hotel outside of Porta Ayora but the dinner venue was kept secret. Following the briefing, a bus shuttled us to our dinner destination and once we arrived, we stepped from the bus into the darkened night where no buildings were in sight. We were led to a rough-hewn underground staircase, overgrown with vegetation; hardly the entrance to a five star hotel, I thought. As I was about to place my sandaled foot on the first step, someone pressed a flashlight into my hand.

We proceeded to pick our way cautiously down a series of uneven steps which I soon learned was a collapse in the roof of a cavernous lava tunnel. I was wearing a long casual dress and thankfully flat shoes. My flashlight glowed weak with yellow hues. Not everyone was equipped with a flashlight, perhaps every fifth person, and those not covered by the weak refractions of light needed to shuffle their feet even more cautiously to feel their way.

At the base of the stairs, we found ourselves in a dimly lit passageway where rivers of lava once thundered towards the ocean.

Above us, muted lights threw mysterious shadows on a ceiling exposing a deep, blackened cathedral cave leading off in another direction. As we followed the irregular foot path, a bridge took us across a deep crevasse, where another tunnel, dark and unfriendly, disappeared underground.

After a further fifteen minutes of making our way around lava pinnacles, and what appeared to be prehistoric Earth, we climbed a steep wooden staircase to the surface to stand beneath a clear night sky riddled with crystal-like stars. Just outside the tunnel we were offered glasses of champagne. Then we walked through a field of grasses to the dining room.

It was the most exciting approach to dinner we have ever encountered, and keeping it a secret was all the more intriguing.

Before leaving the islands, we prepared for the long journey ahead by taking on a few locally grown vegetables and a small purchase of beef. It was a good thing I didn't buy more. Not only was the beef expensive, but it was to ruin my future stews. It was a sad cow that owned meat as tough as that.

As Puerto Ayora has little in the way of yachting facilities, diesel fuel was delivered by barge to Rally boats while they lay at anchor. An eighteen foot barge, equipped with 500 litres (110 Imp./132 US gallons) of fuel, used an electric pump to deliver the fuel through a hose that reached the deck. Then we filtered the fuel before it went into the tanks. When it was necessary to slow the fuel for filtering, the attendant needed to simply squeeze the hose with his hands. After we emptied the large tank, they refilled it with fuel from the two smaller tanks, first siphoning it by mouth.

We were one of the last in our group to leave the Galápagos Islands and had watched, over the last couple of days, as many had difficulty pulling up their anchors. We had been there for thirteen days, with winds and swell helping to bury them deeply. It was February, a busy time of year for the small harbour, as many boats arrive here before crossing the Pacific Ocean. Tour boats, dive boats, yachts and small coastal freighters that supply the island with everything from mattresses to food, gather in the small harbour. It is advisable to drop both stern and bow anchors to keep from swinging and also to make the most of the small space so that it can be shared. As new boats would arrive, they found it necessary to squeeze into small spaces. They would often unwittingly drop their anchors on top of anchors already in place. Then, when it was time to pull them up, sometimes more than one anchor was lifted, causing boats to drift into one another. At times it could be quite chaotic and water taxis were called to assist in lifting stern anchors and to unfoul lines.

Brian went aboard a water taxi to lift our stern anchor, which was no small job without the assistance of a winch. Once freed, we moved forward to winch in our bow anchor, located beneath the hull of another boat.

With petrels skittering across the water, pelicans scooping fish into their pouches and frigate birds soaring overhead, we motored out of the harbour to begin our passage across the Pacific Ocean.*

---

* During the 16th century, Portuguese explorer Ferdinand Magellan (Fernão de Magalhães) while in the employ of Spain, was the first European to cross the Pacific Ocean. Magellan had just navigated his ship between South America and Tierra del Fuego. He called this rough-water passage, Strait(s) of Magellan. When finally arriving in calm waters, he christened it, Mare pacífico—peaceful water.

6

Leaving the New World

CROSSING THE PACIFIC OCEAN

FRENCH POLYNESIA, MARQUESAS ISLANDS
Fatu Hiva, Nuka Hiva

TUAMOTU ATOLLS

A REEF TAKES ANOTHER

TAHITI, BORA BORA

COOK ISLANDS
Rarotonga; Niue, Tonga

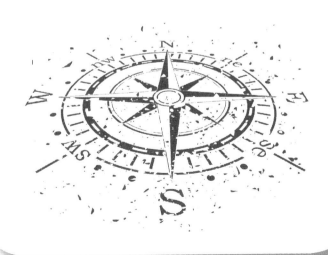

You could drop the entire dry landmass of our planet into the Pacific and still have room for another continent the size of Asia.

DAVID STANLEY
MOON HANDBOOKS *SOUTH PACIFIC*

CROSSING THE PACIFIC OCEAN

*To-morrow, and to-morrow,
and tomorrow
Creeps in this petty pace
from day to day*
WILLIAM SHAKESPEARE
MACBETH, ACT 5

As the last of the Galápagos Islands disappeared into the haze, my thoughts dwelled mostly on how well had I provisioned? Tahiti was a long way. My freezer was full and I had purchased new potatoes, onions, and some green tomatoes while in Puerto Ayora. There had been no large grocery store in the small town and it had been necessary to walk the streets visiting one store after the other, one to purchase eggs, another, potatoes, then to the butcher where I purchased some of that cow that appeared to have pulled a plough all its life. After gathering it all, it was necessary to make two trips with the dinghy to get it to the boat.

I figured I now had a sufficient amount of food, but my real concern was whether I could provide well balanced, enjoyable meals because even after crossing the Pacific, I would still need to prepare over a hundred meals before we reached Tahiti.

My second concern was having enough propane fuel for the stove.

The Pacific is the largest ocean in the world comprising sixty-four million square miles, larger than all the other oceans in the world put together. In fact, it's larger than all the earth's land surface combined. In 1520, Ferdinand Magellan took almost a year to cross it. By the time we had accomplished the feat, I felt we had sailed the whole sixty-four million square miles.

Thousands of small islands lay sprawled out in archipelagoes across miles and miles of the Pacific. Throughout these islands, diverse cultures, languages, religions and customs are to be found, brought to the islands by people while on their own 'voyages of discovery'. To arrive here, the early Polynesians sailed and paddled large, double outrigger canoes, capable of travelling over two hundred miles per day. If we sailed two hundred miles a day aboard *Baccalieu III*, we considered it a great accomplishment.

Polynesians were skilled navigators.* Using no instruments—no sextants, clocks, compass or charts, studying instead the habits of fish and birds, reading cloud formations, currents and ocean swells, noting the rising and setting of stars and measuring the angles with hands, Polynesians were capable of long distance voyages centuries before European explorers.

The rhumb line from the Galápagos Islands to the Marquesas Islands indicates a distance of three thousand and fifty miles, and for most people, including us, it is the longest, non-stop offshore passage they have sailed.

Southeast tradewinds are dominate throughout the tropics but so are the doldrums dominate near the equator.

---

* In 1976, Mau Piailug (1932–2010), a traditional way-finding navigator, guided *Hokule'a*, a 60 foot, double hulled sailing canoe, on a non-instrumental, historic voyage from Hawaii to Tahiti (2,500 mi). Piailug was a *palu*, a master navigator, one of the last experts in the ancient art of Pacific Ocean wayfaring.

We ordered weather updates from Commanders' Weather, a group of meteorologists whose job it is to keep yachts informed of where weather systems lie. They suggest routing that takes advantage of upcoming weather patterns including wind speeds and ocean currents. We often used them throughout our travels when making passages. They start with a synopsis like the one we received before starting across the Pacific Ocean:

> "La Nina" is affecting the temperatures in the eastern Pacific tropics. La Nina is normally a cold water pattern around the Galapagos and west to 140°-150°W along the equator. However, the past few weeks, the water temperatures S, SW, and W of the Galapagos are warming and this warmth is extending from 90°-15°W which is leading to much more convection, (squalls), than normal between the equator and 10°S along your route to the Marquises. On Satellite, the heaviest areas of convection now extend ...... The other weather feature that will generate wind along your route is the southeastern Pacific high currently centered near...... Showers and squalls head E and W in this region and will come from behind with surprising speed. Be sure to watch your back. Winds will be stronger and gustier in sunny areas and lighter and more stable under the cloud cover. Any winds (down draft) coming out of a thunderstorm will move towards you from the centre of the cloud so if the cloud moves to your N, you will get a N wind. If it moves to your S you will get a S wind etc. Usually thunderstorms will become more active at night time and early morning when the cloud top cools and the thunderstorm becomes more unstable.

If there was to be a large area of squall activity, the forecasters would route us around it. We would order a seven day forecast and in addition to this, we downloaded charts that indicated the direction of ocean currents and wind charts to do our own routing and weather predicting. As Navigator, Mike followed the weather closely.

Once underway, rather than heading straight west towards our destination, we routed five hundred and fifty miles southwest to skirt around a large area of squalls. We predicted it would take us about four days before we could straighten out and proceed due west to our target, the Marquesas Islands.

THE FOLLOWING IS my diary: (Mileage covering the twenty-four hour period is noted beside the day.)

DAY 1 — 115 nm

We have only 8 knots of wind but the current is providing enough lift to allow us to move along. A two knot current can offer a 300 mile boost during a passage of 3,000 miles. In addition to the 1,000 litres of fuel we carry in the main tank, we have two 5 gallon (19 litre) jerry cans onboard for emergency use. The fuel in the tank will take us approximately 1,000 miles, depending on sea conditions.

DAY 2 — 146 nm

Today was hot and sticky. Ocean swells continued to build throughout the day. With a diminishing wind, we needed to use the motor in conjunction with the sails. The seawater is clear and we have started to top up the water tanks with desalinated water. Tonight, the stars are spectacular and the moon is shining brightly into the cockpit.

DAY 3 — 150 nm

A truly Pacific Ocean sky hovered over the horizon today. White fluffy clouds appeared as if tinted with a smear of red rouge. It was the first time I have ever seen coloured clouds in the middle of the day. We are nearing an area of active convection and can expect squalls accompanied by rain. It's sweltering hot during the day and we sweat while doing nothing.

It's Sunday; I only know the day of the week because we are Rally radio net controllers today requiring us to document positions of other Rally boats including their wind conditions. Most boats, although scattered from 2° to 8° S, are reporting little wind in the areas they are sailing in.

WE are motoring south hoping to find some wind. We have already used 200 litres (53 US/43 imp. gal.) of fuel. Waves mixed with swells rock the boat making it difficult to sleep.

I often feel lethargic during the day and lay down on my off hours. There is no stable pattern to our sleeping. Flying fish and a dead squid we picked off the deck today, are the first signs of ocean life.

There have been no sightings of cruising boats or ship traffic, day or night.

DAY 4 — 170 nm

Today is cloudy with rain. What a treat to not have the sweltering sun searing us. If not for these breaks in the sky, we might resemble dehydrated cornstalks.

I made lousy bread today. I think I've discovered an environmentally friendly way of making bullets for handguns with flour.

Although there is very little wind, we turned the engine off to conserve fuel. We have used almost half the tank of fuel and we're less than 600 miles into the passage. Because there is so little wind, swells roll us around in relentless motion making the smallest chore difficult.

I'm tired of being tired and tired of not feeling well.

We saw a ship today. It crossed our path at close range. The sighting was almost an event.

DAY 5 — 144 nm

Today is cloudy with rain. I like it like this. Sometimes the sun can be our enemy. It's essential that we drink enough water but I hardly feel like drinking in my nauseous condition. I'm sure I will get my sea legs soon.

We flew the sails for nearly two hours before needing to use the motor. It's too early in the passage to be using so much fuel. We attempt to squeeze out some mileage with the sails in a wing on wing formation but the winds are very light. Quite frankly we're going nowhere.

We learned during BWR net radio time, that a boat named *Golden Eye* has lost the use of their watermaker. To make matters worse, the crew aboard *Golden Eye* left the Galápagos Islands without filling their tanks with local water. Apparently they are not carrying a supply of emergency water jugs either. *Golden Eye* has a crew of three onboard.

I just finished my 0300 shift. It's been a good one. We have been sailing four straight hours! This is like a miracle.

DAY 6 — 171 nm

Another cloudy day offering relief from the scorching sun.

We sighted our first sailboat today; one of the smaller boats in our fleet that had left one day earlier than us. It has now disappeared off our stern.

We've been sailing for twenty-four hours! Due to our good speed, the boat holds a much steadier course and has the ability to cut through the slop, relieving us of some of the stressful motion.

We were all up for longer periods of time today. Apparently, we have found our sea legs. I even did some hand washing, sewing and organizing. I put out the fishing line for the first time. We lost a good sized fish when it wiggled free from the lure but at least we retained the lure.

A BOAT named *Saoirse K* reported a squall swept their radar scanner from their mast today. Not long ago, they somehow lost their SSB radio antenna preventing them from transmitting but they can still hear radio messages. They also have the ability to send and receive e-mails. Using e-mail on boats requires dialing into a server, therefore it is not generally available 24/7 due to its high cost. *Saoirse K*, is a six year old Hunter Legend 12 m (40 ft.) built more for coastal sailing than for ocean crossings. Onboard, there is only the husband and wife. Marian is apparently not a confident sailor. She stands her night shifts while the engine runs in idle. To have taken on a circumnavigation feeling such uncertainty, makes her a hero in my mind. She is here helping her husband fulfill a dream. Can there be any love stronger than this one?

Onyva, a Hallberg Rassy 39 (12 m) owned and sailed by a British couple, lost its twizzle rig (two foresails) in a gust today. They managed to drag it back onboard but they have not yet determined whether they can salvage the rig.

HUTCH, onboard *Fenella*, recounted an exciting occurrence they experienced. He confided he had been below doing his "George" (as he refers to his personal bodily function), when he heard the whipping of helicopter blades. He shot out of the "loo" and up the stairs to see a helicopter hovering overhead. Taking into consideration that we are about as far from land as you can possibly be on Earth and therefore well beyond normal helicopter range, seeing a helicopter overhead is one of the strangest sightings one might see out here. And then to have people waving at you from the helicopter, might make you think you had become unglued. Earlier in the day, *Fenella* had passed a fishing vessel with several large outboard dinghies secured to its sides and a helicopter sitting on its heli-pad. Helicopters are used to aid ships in locating tuna. The helicopter pilot often follows dolphins that tend to congregate around schools of yellow fin tuna. Once tuna are spotted, the mother ship steams to the location where sea going dinghies are lowered to the water. The small sea boats surround the school of tuna with nets. Pulling the ends of the net together, they imprison the fish. Using automated hydraulic equipment, the mother ship hauls the full net onboard where they are processed and stored in freezer holds.

Day 7 — 172 nm
Another cloudy day. Hooray!
Speed — 8 knots with the Yankee and mainsail positioned on a port tack.

Fenella reported they had caught up with *Golden Eye*, (the boat that can no longer make water) and transferred a few jugs of water to them. They did this by coming alongside *Golden Eye*, then rigging up their spinnaker pole on the mast and loading the water jugs onto the end of the pole. The pole was then directed over the water in the direction of *Golden Eye*. This resulted in knocking off *Golden Eye's* GPS antenna. Sad to say, the antenna is crucial for navigation purposes.

In a second attempt to transfer the water, several fenders were tied together into a sort of raft and then loaded with the water jugs and towed. *Golden Eye* picked them up while standing on their bow. This was successful, however, this is only a temporary solution. We all have at least two weeks of sailing before arriving in the Marquesas Islands.

Baccalieu III is too far away to offer any assistance.

Due to a 3½ hour time difference between the Galápagos Islands and the Marquesas Islands, we periodically adjust our time clocks.

DAY 8—164 nm

Speed—6 knots under sail.

It's Saturday, March 25th; I documented the date because I wanted to feel a sense of time. Other than for making entries into the ship's log, there is no other reason to be aware of the date and I rarely pay attention to it. One day merges into another with each day appearing to be near identical to the last. Water, sky and horizon, that's our view of the world. In the days when sailors relied on hardtack, salted meat and green slimy drinking water to sustain them, suicides were contemplated and mutinies promoted in conditions like these. At least I can serve good meals.

This afternoon the wind lightened considerably, allowing large swells to rock the boat. The rolling motion spills wind from the sails causing the sails to snap with a severe jerking motion before flying open with an audible crack! They do this again and again. Not only is the noise irritating but the forceful snapping and cracking places added stress on the sails and related hardware.

WE had been trolling for several hours when we snagged what felt to be a good sized fish. While Mike struggled to reel in the line, the reel began to wiggle loose from the fishing pole. I grabbed a screw driver from the tool box while Brian slowed the boat. Just as the fish was reeled up to the stern, it bit through the line and escaped.

DAY 9—154 nm

This morning blue skies hold a host of cumulus clouds. This is typical for weather and skies near the equator. Some days the formations change constantly and I watch as they tear apart in high altitude winds.

The wind continues to blow from the SE over the aft quarter. Waves are larger today and are peaked with whitecaps. They knock the boat around even more than they did in the past few days. More boat speed would solve that problem.

Golden Eye reported they are rationing water to one and a half litres per day until they make landfall. I don't know if this amount is per person or for all three crewmembers. Emergency rationing requires liferafts to be fitted with one half litre of water per day per person for survival purposes. Crew aboard *Golden Eye* will need to use salt water for bathing but will have no fresh water for rinsing. This in itself can cause problems to the health of a person's skin.

They are presently 300 miles behind us and there are no other boats in their vicinity to offer assistance.

Today I got serious about fishing and fitted a steel trace on the fishing lure to prevent fish from biting through the line. Around 1600 we heard the reel spin out. Mike went aft and took hold of the pole. The drag on the line was more than either of us had ever felt before. Then the line went slack allowing Mike to bring the catch closer. But when the line tightened again he yelled, "Cut the line, cut the line!" Ignoring the fact his veins protruded like mole tracks up his arms, and he looked braced to pull in a team of sumo wrestlers, I responded, "What?" "This could be the best fish we ever catch."

"Cut the line," he yelled in heightened tones.

"Reel it in," I encouraged, "and don't lose the pole!"

"Cut the line!" he shouted curtly. Then suddenly, off to our starboard a 5 to 6 metre (15 to 20 foot) marlin broke the surface. In and out of the water it arced, thrusting itself in massive strides through the air. Yikes! Its size far outmatched our capabilities of handling such a creature. Comparing the sword it carried to the little gaff I held, it was easy to see who was going to be the victim here. "Why does it not bite through the line?" I yelled. "They all bite through the line."

"You put a steel trace on it! Cut the line! Cut the line!"

Day 10 — 154 nm
Wind — 12 to 15 knots.
We've been sailing on the same tack for five days now. We used a flying fish that we found on deck as bait but I think it fell off. How do you keep a dried up fish on a hook? I will try again tomorrow with something else. But I'm not willing to risk losing any more lures.
We learned today that *Onyva* lost her spinnaker and halyard in a squall yesterday. All of it got swept beneath the boat and wrapped around the propeller.

THE tuner on our SSB radio is not working properly. Consequently we are unable to transmit messages efficiently. The problem shows up intermittently. Mike and Brian took everything out of the lazarette to check the connections but they were unable to identify the problem. We will wait to get some information from the installer through e-mail.

Day 11 — 169 nm
Wind — 12 to 15 knots. Sails set wing on wing.
Part of the day was sunny and breezy, a perfect day to dry laundry. We washed our clothes on the stern using a bucket then hung them on two lines strung over the lazarette.
We learned that *Freewheel*, a Tayana 16.7 (55 ft.) lost her topping lift last night. With the sails and rigging in constant use, abrasions are difficult to avoid. The best anyone can do is to make daily checks and occasionally move the lines to prevent wear at the same point of contact.

TODAY we reached as far south as we need to go, Latitude 10°58' S. Turning west, we are now sailing downwind.
Since leaving the Galápagos Islands, we have travelled 1,500 nm. We are now at our halfway point; only another 1,500 to go before reaching the Marquesas Islands. For a celebration

dinner, I prepared ribs, sauerkraut and potatoes. To save propane, I cooked the entire meal in the breadmaker on the 'bake only' cycle—a new galley development of mine.

Everyone onboard is doing well. Now if we could only catch some fish. But other boats in the fleet have also mentioned they have had challenges landing fish. Many tell stories of how fish have either escaped from the hooks or have bitten through their lines. I think the fish are pretty big out here.

DAY 12—177 nm

We are sailing due west and tonight we sailed straight down a brilliant, golden trail of sparkle left on the water by the setting sun. The experience was magical.

The boat rocks with a slow, steady roll in the light winds. The movement doesn't bother my stomach anymore but by the time I get to land I expect to be waddling like a duck.

Due to having to keep the ports closed in the living quarters below, our cabins are hot and stagnant. It feels like living in a jungle. Without air flow, we sweat even while sleeping leaving our bed sheets dampened. Small fans provide us with some relief. On some boats in the fleet, crewmembers leave their stern hatches ajar. This is risky. *Fenella* reported that when a wave broke over their boat, it splashed through an open port dousing the person who was napping in the aft cabin. Their bed will be damp now until they have an opportunity to rinse their bedding and mattress with fresh water.

They also reported that over the past few days, they had an unusually bad odour drifting from their head. They dismantled the toilet; a nasty piece of work especially when squeezed into a small, rolling hot room. Lodged in the toilet, he found a rotting flying fish that had evidently glided through the porthole and ended up in the toilet! Then they lost their dinner when the boat took a roll and their meal of Thai fell to the floor.

We all get to enjoy this refined entertainment as it arrives daily over the SSB radio during BWR radio net time.

Day 13 — 137 nm

Our SSB radio still doesn't transmit messages. We can hear the communications between other boats, but we are unable to make contact. I went up the backstay in the bosun's chair today to inspect the connections. Cleaning the wires did nothing to improve our transmitting ability. We report our position via VHF radio to the yacht *Freewheel*, who is for now, approximately 15 nm west of us. They in turn, relay the information to the Rally net control. *Freewheel* checks in with us each evening to confirm that we are not experiencing any major difficulties.

We've changed our clocks three times during the crossing to get in line with landing in the Marquesas. The sun sets now around 1700.

Day 14 — 177 nm

We drifted through another day of 8 to 10 knots of wind speed. Every three hour period, we travelled about 15 nm. I think I can swim faster than this.

The Intertropical Convergence Zone (ITCZ) is an area near the equator where the northeast and southeast tradewinds meet. You would think with all that wind coming together we might get some. But instead we're in the doldrums. Those who study atmospheric science, conclude that when the tradewinds come together, they are forced up into the atmosphere as is warm air and evaporated seawater. This sets up a climatic theatre to produce typhoons, monsoons, cyclones and hurricanes. This is where they are born.

The ITCZ can cover thousands of miles and while in this zone, everything from thunderstorms, squalls to stagnant air can be experienced. All three can happen in a matter of minutes.

EVEN though there was barely more than a light breeze today, the temperature in the cockpit was pleasant because the sun was positioned behind the mainsail. At least the sail is good for something other than making that infernal snapping noise every few seconds when it collapses then snaps open again. Sitting in the cockpit was like trying to enjoy a summer afternoon in my backyard where the kid next door has a pop gun I'd like to make him eat.

800 nm to go before reaching our destination.

OUR two friends onboard *Tzigane*, a new Jenneau 54 (16.7 m), have experienced a multitude of problems on this passage. A few days following an autopilot breakdown, the valve on the engine room's fire extinguisher released, sending a spray of chemicals all over the mechanics. They have no idea what initiated the discharge of the cylinder. Following that catastrophe, their spinnaker halyard chafed at the masthead resulting in losing their spinnaker. Dragging loose in the water, the spinnaker halyard wrapped around the propeller. This forced John to free dive on the propeller and while working underwater, he injured his elbow.

Today they reported that having noted a sewage smell in their bilge, they discovered their 24 volt battery system was fried.

WE haven't trolled the past few days because I refuse to feed any more lures to those selfish fish. I had planned to wait until I found another dead flying fish on deck but then tonight I did something really stupid.

We were sitting in the cockpit having our twilight Happy Hour drink. The boys were drinking their precious allotment of a single beer, and me, my Gatorade. While sitting quietly and listening to some fool chatter about the stock market, all of a sudden, something hit me on the back of my head.

I had been hit by a flying fish! The thing bounced off my head and landed at my feet. While it was flopping violently about the cockpit floor, I thought, "Bait!" But then, as I watched it thrashing in death throes, wings stretched in one last effort to get back to the sea, I got weepy over the poor thing's struggle, and threw it back into the water!

Day 15 — 154 nm

We did more laundry today and hung it to dry on a line over the stern lazarette again. At the time, we were flying the spinnaker. From the bow, we mirrored a hot racing machine and from the stern, we resembled a laundry specializing in men's underwear. But the spinnaker went up flawlessly. That should be noted because our execution doesn't always go so smoothly. The sail didn't wrap around anything, just straight up and out, like we knew what we were doing. For that achievement, we were rewarded with a speed of a mere 6 knots!

Last night I had the banker's hours or P shift (preferred) as we call it around here; 2000 to 2400 followed by 0600 to 0900. Those are decent hours and I feel pretty rested the following day because they represent the nearest thing to normalcy. Not that I requested to have the same shift again but I was imagining what it would be like to have the same hours back to back. Just one more combination of normal hours and I might feel like a real person again. But no, the rotation moves on and I have the midnight to three tonight. We're all going to find ourselves in sleep disorder clinics when we get home.

Day 16 — 154 nm

We put the spinnaker up again this morning. We take it down each evening because it takes more attention to fly than a regular sail and if a problem arises, the problem is never a small one. We've certainly learned that to be true. Mike and I have lots of experience with spinnaker problems; we can't solve them—we invent them. Sometimes however, it's just bad luck. Take this afternoon for example.

Noticing a squall approaching, Brian and I went forward to drop the spinnaker while Mike manned the sheets in the cockpit. In our attempt to douse the sail, which should have been a simple maneuver, the spinnaker sock caught at the top of the mast, preventing it from collapsing the sail. So there we were, the squall announcing its arrival with a quick freshening breeze, the spinnaker still flying, and flying better than it had in days, the boat accelerating, and with the key piece of equipment that would take the wind out of the sail stuck at the top.

The squall was still a good distance away but if we didn't get the sail down we might soon find ourselves airborne. At the very least the sail could tear into shreds.

We were forced to drop the spinnaker halyard resulting in metres and metres of silky sail smothering the entire foredeck. Puffy mounds of slippery air-filled cloth buried the deck like a collapsed tricoloured parachute.

The stage was set: man versus wind. Competing to keep the sail onboard, we sat on it, lay on it, rolled on it, sprawled across it with outstretched arms while clawing it, grasping at pieces of what appeared to be alive and fighting for its freedom. This must be what wrestling with a greased pig is like. Tucking it within the folds of our arms, collecting it metre by metre, we stuffed it into its bag and tied it to the mast.

That night, the weather continued with sloppy windless conditions interspersed by rain squalls accompanied by gusts of wind. That's just what kind of day it was. Tomorrow, we'll probably have no wind at all and the most exciting part of my day will be the tasteless high fibre cereal I eat in the morning.

I was thinking today how nice it would be to have clean bed sheets, a luxury I will have to wait a long time before fulfilling my dream. But I also made a great discovery today. If I sleep with my head at the foot of the bed, I hear less of that insufferable, mind-altering whining from the autopilot. Not that I dare say anything derogatory about our dear autopilot; we love the thing, and I'm sure the whiny, screechy noise will hardly have any effect at all on my psychological well-being. Just because it sounds as if a tortured cat is clambering about in the lazarette scraping its claws across a window, doesn't mean it's a bad thing.

It was during my night shift while I was standing alone in the cockpit that I noticed sizable spots of green diffused light appearing beneath the surface of the water a few metres from the boat. I stared through the darkness, peering down into the black water unable to determine what it might be. The lights appeared similar to underwater lighting in a swimming pool. It was pretty eerie when the lights continued to follow us.

Day 17 — 149 nm

Today we rolled along with the same flogging sails, mastering our second worst afternoon of sailing yet. As we slopped around with 10 knots of wind, the sails continued to snap while waves rocked the boat like we were helpless creatures caught in a floating barrel.

Only by documenting distance-made-good can we ever measure that we have made any headway at all. It all comes down to watching numbers grow larger; the mileage and endless minutes and degrees of latitude. And the numbers aren't growing larger fast enough in this grand space we share with nothingness. Where is that leisurely, enjoyable trade wind sailing I have read about? Those steady tradewinds that fill the sails on a beam reach. Effortless sailing they say. "Catch the trades and it's a milk run."

I think we've been duped.

It was another dark night and what little moon there was, hid beneath a heavy cover of cloud. As I stood in the cockpit during my watch I could barely see the bow.

A couple of hours into my shift I witnessed a repeat performance of the underwater lighting show that had taken place the previous night. Perhaps the ghostly lights were angry spirits of crewmembers who had worked aboard tall ships; sailors who had lost their lives while climbing aloft on tarred ropes and lines to bend jigger and mizzen sails or stow billowing canvases during high winds. Or topmen who had scampered up ratlines under orders to reach vantage points during storms and were then knocked off their perches when they lost their handholds or were struck by bolts of lightning. Falling helplessly, they were engulfed by a chaotic sea. Dead now, I thought, their restless souls living in underwater chains of mountains twice as high as the Rocky Mountains or in canyons far greater than Arizona's Grand Canyon. That's what it's supposed to be like down there, the part we can't see, the black — the abyss.

Although it was as gentle a night as you could get, I snapped the tether to my life vest just in case something tried to take me. My mind continued to expand with explanations for the green lights. I recalled 17th century paintings I had viewed in museums depicting sailing ships engulfed in lengthy tentacles of sea serpents. Clasped securely to the boat, I confirmed that I wasn't going anywhere without a fight and if I had to, I would take the whole bloody boat with me. I wasn't going alone, you can be sure of that.

In the end, I discovered the lights were dolphins keeping pace with the hull, stirring up luminescence while creating magnificent looking pockets of lit underwater light. But in those previous hours, when unable to distinguish the dolphins from the water, when I couldn't see their fluent forms breaking surface just five metres distant from me, I was able to detect only the light of white sparkling luminescence following in their wake. I only sensed their presence tonight by the sound of their breath. It was dungeon dark out there.

It rained hard while I was on shift tonight. I don't know how so much water can fall from such gentle looking clouds. Around midnight, the little wind that we had died and then the autopilot ceased working. The instrument panel flashed 'error' indicating the autopilot could not find enough headway to operate. No surprise there, we were hardly moving.

I had to leave the helm to get Mike out of bed. Meanwhile, the sails flogged languidly, snapping on one side of the boom before moving across where they snapped again: the pattern of travel and snapping repeating over and over. The boom banged like a series of car crashes, sharing the same rhythm.

Aside from these little breaks that the autopilot occasionally takes, it has been reliable and relieves us of having to hand steer throughout hours and hours of monotonous near-windless conditions. It is far more accurate than any one of us can steer in light winds.

Shortly after resetting the autohelm, the wind not only increased but veered 180°. Now we were backwinded, the poled-out Yankee being on the wrong side of the boat. In spite of the rain, it was the best wind we had seen in hours, maybe even the entire trip. We floodlit the foredeck using the spreader lights. Mike went forward to begin the time-consuming job of tacking the pole and releading the lines while I manned the sheets in the cockpit. In such conditions, it took us about an hour to make the tack but it was worth the work because we began sailing at eight to nine knots.

We haven't had a flying fish land on deck since that evening I got wonked in the back of the head and threw that poor critter back into the sea where he will certainly be eaten by larger prey.

DAY 18 — 162 nm
Light winds. We motored through the windless holes.
Fuel tanks reading low.
We learned that *Freewheel* tore her jib while sailing in light winds today. The sails undergo a huge amount of stress while snapping in these light air conditions.

Each boat reports their latitudinal and longitudinal positions to Rally Net Control along with wind conditions. Stretches of 600 miles might lie between the boat in the lead and the boat at the rear. The weather can be as different as one boat reporting 5 knots of wind while others report a 40 knot blow. This can happen even within a fifteen mile radius.

At night, one little light at the top of the mast is all that represents our existence in our water-filled world. It appears like a single travelling star moving among the millions that sometimes light the sky. We can easily distinguish it from the others because it's the one that's swaying back and forth through a forty degree arc! It's the 'star' that has the ability to make me feel I might toss my cookies if I continue cranking my neck back to follow its back and forth motion. Our star, however, doesn't appear to be working tonight. It must be those cheap Chinese bulbs we purchased. I can guarantee not one of us is going to volunteer to go up there and change it. No midway thrill ride could compete with the motion you could feel up there.

We'll use the steaming light instead.

AROUND the time that darkness sets in, we normally extinguish the white cabin lights to avoid night blindness and disturbing those who are resting. We set all the instrument panels to night settings so they illuminate with colours that won't interfere with night vision. That's somewhat ironic because there's nothing to see out here. This is too far for domestic fishing boats to travel and the islands we are approaching have no commercial enterprises.

Other than a couple of red interior lights, and outdoor navigation lights, we move through the water hardly making a difference to the night. With my eyes needing to work less, sounds become amplified and I can hear the most silent whisper of water swishing past the hull. It's wonderful.

DAY 19—111 nm

We may feel as if we are a lone vessel in the Pacific, but we are part of an invisible community. The SSB and VHF radios are the tools that enable us to belong. Today, we learned that John, aboard *Tzigane,* has an infection in the elbow he injured while diving to untangle his halyard from the propeller. His whole forearm is swollen. A doctor in the fleet advised him to lance it. *Tzigane* is positioned about five days behind us.

We had a good sail today even though the day began with only an 11 knot breeze. By afternoon it had increased to 15 knots, allowing us to sail with less roll.

When listening to the Rally net on the SSB radio, we heard other crewmembers anticipating their arrival to the Marquesas in one or two days. Now that they are approaching their destination, they speak freely of their frustrations during the long windless days and lumpy seas. All are anxious to arrive, but those feeling the most stress, are the smaller boats a few hundred miles behind us who hear of our early approaches but know they still have several days to go.

EARLY this morning we arrived at the island of Fatu Hiva the most southerly of the Marquesas Islands.

We ate the last of the fresh fruit today. There must be a good galley manager onboard.

PASSAGE summary: We had been out of sight of land for nineteen days. We averaged one hundred and sixty miles a day over a distance of 3,050 nautical miles. Of that, we used the engine ninety-three hours, approximately five hundred and fifty-eight nautical miles.

An obliging current carried us an additional two hundred miles.

During our crossing, there had been few spectacular sunsets due to an almost constant cloud cover or mist on the horizon in the evening. These are common conditions found around the equator. As a result, many days we did not see the sun go down at all. But one evening Mike and I were standing facing west while the sun was setting over an unusually clear horizon. We remarked perhaps we would see our first green flash. The flash we witnessed that evening was magnificent!

Much to our surprise, we discovered at the end of the journey that the bottom portion of the hull, the part not covered with bottom paint, was plastered with gooseneck barnacles. Thimble-like in appearance, but as tough as concrete, they needed to be scraped off using a heavy-duty Brillo type pad and scraper. Mike spent hours in the water chipping them off with a putty knife.

FRENCH POLYNESIA

MARQUESAS ISLANDS: FATU HIVA, NUKA HIVA

*The first experience can
never be repeated*

R.L.STEVENSON
IN THE SOUTH SEAS
WRITTEN WHILE ON APPROACH TO NUKA HIVA

FROM THE MOMENT we arrived at the Marquesas Islands, they exuded a sense of mystery and intrigue. We had snuck up on the remotest of the islands in the dark. Or had it hid from us until it was ready for visitors? I wasn't sure. But I knew that we were just metres from it and yet could not detect the faintest of outlines. We really *had* landed on another planet, one that refused to recognize our arrival with a simple acknowledgement of its existence.

When Fatu Hiva was ready, it humbled us with its size and even stole from us the sound we made while entering its bay. It was one of several islands belonging to the Marquesas group known for cannibalism, sacrifice and rituals.

IT WAS THREE in the morning when we approached the island. It was one of those solid black nights when you see more on the radar screen than you can when standing outside. How dark does a night have to be that you can't see a gargantuan object in front of you?

Guided by the radar, we brought the boat within a quarter mile of shore to await early morning light that would illuminate the entrance into the bay.

When light began to flush darkness from the sky, a soft creaminess began to backlight the monstrous form of a mountain. I was surprised at its size.

Very slowly, light revealed colossal cliffs. Rugged ridged mountains took shape, bulking to unexpected proportions and dwarfing our boat as it floated in the shadows of the hulking rock face. The eroded ridge, harsh and jagged, fell towards the sea in folds of hardened lava as if some giant had dragged stiffened fingers deeply into the newly forming mountain, gouging out rippling vertical grooves. Black and barren, the folds fell straight into the sea.

With enough light, we proceeded into a bay surrounded by dramatic cliffs and tumbling hills where, so dampened were the sounds by the enclosing heights, our voices seemed swallowed by thickish air while the dulled hum of the motor dragged behind us. As if tiptoeing into the bay, we drove forward choosing an anchoring spot between dense, wooded hills, now a palette of sunlit greens, and windswept etched rock; their roughness softened by the rising sun to the colour of honey. This place was magical.

At the top of the bay, sitting adjacent to one another, twin protrusions stand erect commanding the bay and the mountains they sit atop. From the beginning, Polynesians had felt a connection with these peaks and named the bay Hana Vave, (Two Penis Bay). No wonder the islands were named, the Marquesas, 'Land of Men'.

In an attempt to bring some civilization to this savage island, or at the very least some Christian decency, Roman Catholic missionaries have since changed the name to what it is called today, Baie des Vierges (Bay of Virgins).

The Marquesas Islands (Îles Marquises) or *Henua Enata* were the first of the Polynesian islands to be settled by people arriving from Samoa, eighteen hundred miles away, in dugout canoes around 300 BC.* DNA analysis indicates that prior to landing in Samoa, their homelands had been located in southeast Asia. After arriving in the Marquesas, some set off in canoes again to discover several more islands within the Polynesian Triangle, including Hawaii, which was not discovered until AD 200, and Easter Island, discovered around AD 300.

POLYNESIANS were adventurous people. Often entire villages would set sail in double-hulled canoes, chiseled from tree trunks with stone tools. Tree trunks are tubular shape and so were the hulls, causing them to be extremely unstable vessels. For this reason, two smaller logs were attached to poles lashed perpendicular to the hull. When the canoe tipped to one side, the protruding outrigger saved the canoe from turning over. This would have been one of the century's greatest inventions.

THE Marquesas Islands with their rainforest covered valleys flowing with fresh, cool mountain streams, offered good sites to establish villages. In some areas, it was easy to land canoes along the coastline and then leave again to fish. Nesting seabirds and turtles were available for food. In its prime, the total population of Fatu Hiva has been estimated to have been eight thousand, even though it consists of only 85 square kilometres, (53 square miles). Today fewer than six hundred people live there.

Clothing was made from the branches of 'cloth trees' by

---

* The issue of human (fully-modern Homo sapiens) expansion into Oceania is an ongoing debate. Archaeologists commonly link the first human colonization of 'Near Oceania' (Solomon Islands archipelago, Island Melanesia, Bismarck Archipelago, New Guinea) to times of glacial low sea levels, as population movement would have been easier. This suggests the first people could have arrived in French Polynesia 45,000 years ago.

soaking, stretching and beating the inner fibres with mallets until it became a sort of white paper cloth called *tapa* (*tappa*). Entire valleys might resonate with the tapping of little mallets making the fibres, soft and malleable. The cloth was then decorated with intricate designs; the Polynesians are very artistic. Today, islanders still pound the fibres of the mulberry tree with wooden mallets to make tapas for wall hangings. They paint them with traditional geometric designs that were once used in the decorating of their bodies with the art of tattoo.

Before missionaries arrived, it was customary for bare breasted women to wear only skirts of leaves and grasses. Bone carved earplugs, inserted into earlobes, were regularly worn by both men and women. Both genders had intricate designs tapped into their flesh by a tattoo artist. When boys reached teenage years, they received their first tattoo during a ritual. By the time they were adults, their entire bodies, including their faces, could be completely embellished.

Tattoos were a way of announcing and documenting accomplishments, family positions, what island they had come from, and even what tribe they belonged to. The tattoos were a sort of diary for a people who had no written word.

Tattoo designs flowed in spirals and detailed geometric patterns including the trademarks of the Marquesas: geckos and centipedes. Herman Melville wrote in his book, *Typee*, that, when he arrived at the islands in 1841, a tattoo artist expressed frustration when he was not allowed to tattoo Melville's white face. To the artist, Melville represented a rare opportunity to allow him to express his art form on a pale faced canvas, yet Melville would have no part of it.

To work the tattoo into the skin, indentations were made with a single sharpened shark's tooth or tiny rakes of the same bone while tapping with a mallet to form a pattern. Dipping the tine repeatedly into vegetable juice and ashes the indentation was coloured while picking the skin. It was the repetitive tapping of the hammer, known as *tatau* that was later translated into the English word, 'tattoo'. The experience was extremely painful and might require the receiver to be forcibly held or tied down over long periods of time. Several sessions were needed to complete a full leg design and many would have sensitive areas included in their artistic body work such as eyelids and genitals. But it was believed that certain designs would give them power. A motif resembling the swells of a large ocean, if tattooed on the shoulder, gave the canoe paddlers exceptional strength to combat rough seas.

Tattoos in the Marquesas are still common, most of which are large detailed designs covering entire arms, legs or backs. Marquesan tattoos are beautifully designed, even the one I saw covering half a man's face.

The Marquesas Islands enjoyed isolation up to the late 1500s when the population included several individual tribes, each headed by a high chief. Commoners were not allowed to marry or even touch those of the higher ranks, and babies who were born from parents of two different classes were euthanized. From island to island and from tribe to tribe, worship was unique, but all Polynesians prayed to deities who had once been humans: ancestors, great warriors, former chiefs or distant navigators, all of whom had played a part in their history. Some prayed to as few as two gods; others to numerous spirits who were thought to hold special powers. Occasionally prayer would require a sacrifice of an animal, a turtle or, at times, a human.

Most Polynesians believed their gods came from where their ancestors had come, from the west, a paradise in a far off land. But for most, their world was small, often no further than where the horizon touches the sea. It was believed following death, the souls of chiefs and upper classes found refuge in this paradise while common people, if their souls travelled anywhere, went underground.

Cannibalism was common, but human sacrifices occurred only on special occasions and prisoners taken from other tribes, would often be the subjects of this ritual. It may have been at this time that the acceptance of transsexuals became common, stemming from the fact that only males could be sacrificed; females were thought to be impure. Raising a male child as a female was one way of protecting the child from becoming a 'chosen one'.

Monuments and *tikis* representing gods were part of every Polynesian settlement until missionaries arrived to introduce Christianity, when many of the stone deities were destroyed and much of the Polynesian culture disappeared with them. This was a confusing time for pagan Marquesans. According to missionaries, it was wrong to eat people, which they referred to as *kaikai enata*, but it was all right to eat Christ. ("he who eats my flesh and drinks my blood has eternal life," John 6:53–56.) Or was it to *pretend* to eat Christ? They weren't sure. When they accepted Christianity, the Marquesans adopted Jehova as their Tiki. They had believed that to eat their foes was a way to obtain the strength of the person they consumed. Now they were confronted with the idea of eating a sacred Tiki, and they found the idea repulsive.

AMONG the many challenges missionaries faced in Polynesia was a religious sect known as Arioi, whose members believed in free love. Sharing spouses wasn't unusual in Tahitian society and putting to death their own children was an acceptable custom. After all, overpopulation was what had driven many of the warring tribes to leave their homelands in the first place.

The society was class oriented but even in the upper classes, children were sometimes euthanized because to overpopulate the upper class meant a strain on the lower class to provide food for them. Despite these bizarre customs, the Arioi preached peace.

Mass Polynesian populations were weakened, and later decimated, when Europeans arrived infected with tuberculosis and other painful, disfiguring diseases such as leprosy. On Captain Cook's third voyage to the South Pacific, crewmembers aboard the HMS *Resolution* were infected with syphilis, gonorrhea, tuberculosis *and* influenza. Other ships brought diseases such as small pox and measles.

In the 16th century the French Polynesian islands flourished with one hundred thousand indigenous residents, but by the early 1900s, just two thousand indigenous people were thought to exist. Presently the population is estimated to be over eight thousand.

THE VERY WORDS 'French Polynesia' ring with exotic tones bearing expectations of romance and mystery. When Herman Melville needed an injection of well-being to his health and to his writing, he boarded a whaling ship, the *Dolly*. It eventually delivered him, while on a quest for whales, to the Marquesas Islands. Once there, he abandoned the ship to live among the natives, and five years later published two novels, *Typee* (lover of human flesh), followed by the sequel *Omoo*, both stories of his life while living "among the cannibals." Robert Louis Stevenson visited the islands in 1888. Overcome by their beauty, he decided to live out his days there. Gauguin, the French artist, left France in search of an escape to his personal life and sought a place where he could "live on fish and fruit for nothing without anxiety for the day or the morrow." Gauguin discovered the magic of the Marquesas only after swinging pick axes in Colón during the building of the Panama Canal. His vibrant symbolist paintings indicate that he eventually found the world he was looking for. He is buried on the island of Hiva Oa.

In 1936, Thor Heyerdahl, a young Norwegian wanted to "run away from bureaucracy, technology and twentieth century civilization," which he called a "hippie's dream" when he wrote his first book *Fatu-Hiva*, telling of his experiences while living on the island. He and his twenty year old wife arrived at Fatu Hiva with only one suit case. The case contained his wife's wedding gown, his wedding suit and a few ampules for collecting specimens.

FATU HIVA IS one of the most remote of all the Marquesas Islands and is located over one thousand nautical miles northeast of Tahiti. The only way to arrive there is by boat.

The village of Hanavave sits in a former crater on the west side of the island, surrounded by vertical cliffs and lush greenery. We dropped anchor just off the shore.

Hanavave is not an official port of entry to French Polynesia, but it is often the first island to be visited by boaters who have arrived after crossing the Pacific Ocean. The local gendarmerie generously allows boaters to rest here a couple of days before they move on to the island of Nuka Hiva, where passports and crew lists are documented in a more official manner.

I found recalling the names of the islands a challenge, they sounded so much alike. Fatu Hiva, Ua Huka, Namu Hiva, Hiva Oa! I would never be able to learn even the simplest Polynesian sentence, I thought. But who could blame me? The word 'no' is pronounced "aoe" and the word 'I', is "oao" and 'who' is "oai". The Polynesians once called their language "people language" because they thought white men were gods.

Prior to going to shore at Hanavave on Fatu Hiva Island, we spoke to a sailor who had landed there before us. He recounted how the local gendarme, after having checked his passport, asked if he had spare life jackets to donate. When the sailor could not supply him with jackets, he offered two bottles of rum instead because he thought the gendarme was suggesting a bribe. We too presumed he must have been demanding a bribe, but there was more to the story. When the gendarme made the same request of us, we admitted to not having extra life jackets onboard but offered instead, other gifts. Surprisingly, he turned them down. We learned later, by reading a posted notice from the French government, that all fishing boats under French jurisdiction were facing a deadline to be equipped with life jackets, baler and anchors. As an overseas territory of France, mainland rules apply even if the island is well over 16,000 km (10,000 mi.) from Paris, and located in the middle of the Pacific Ocean. How they were to obtain the equipment was the challenge the officer was attempting to meet. And who can blame him for accepting two free bottles of rum? Our offer of fishhooks and sandals apparently didn't hold the same attraction.

We had been advised not to offer alcohol to the islanders as it often resulted in inebriation and domestic abuse. Polynesians have never been able to drink alcohol responsibly. After its introduction by Europeans, islanders brewed it by fermenting oranges and other available fruits found on the island. In some villages, women and children were encouraged to take part in wild drinking orgies. Decades ago the most horrible slaughters took place while natives were drunk.

WE tied our dinghy to the village dock where we came upon a group of young men taking part in an ancient stone fishing tradition. Although modern amenities exist on the island — electricity and the occasional truck for example, the islanders practice many of their ancestors' traditions.

Wading into the water, two men held the ends of a fish net while others threw stones or made splashes in order to herd small fish into the net. After the fish had been driven towards them, the men handling the net waded towards each other to close it. Sometimes they take several small outriggers off shore where they form a circle. Armed with stones tied to ropes, they beat the water while others jump from the canoes to help drive the fish into the net. Flying fish can be caught at night with the help of torches to attract the silver coloured fish to the canoes. Often flying fish will land right in the canoes while others are caught, mid-air in nets.

FRENCH subsidies have supplied enough finances for the island to lay down a short piece of concrete road running through the village. The islanders live in small, pre-fabricated houses; it has been years since Polynesians lived in traditional thatched roofed dwellings. Heyerdahl remarked on that fact when he lived there in 1936.

High above the village, towering cliffs have, over time, let go of giant, eroded boulders that now sit in neatly trimmed front yards amid wild shrubbery and grassy lawns. In the front of one house, a wild hibiscus bush overflowed with large peach coloured blossoms. It was a surprise to discover such civility on an island so far from anywhere. Such caring for gardens would suggest, that not only did those who lived there enjoy leisure time, but made use of it with high standards of tidiness.

As we walked, colourful patterned curtains fluttered carelessly through open windows while a few chickens pecked at lawns for insects and well fed dogs lay tethered, content and silent. When a village woman spotted us passing her home, she immediately stepped out with an invitation to join her inside her two bedroom house to view carvings her husband had chiseled from rosewood. French and Tahitian are the official languages of the islands while most locals speak a mix of Marquesan among themselves. Brian's ability to speak some conversational French allowed us a degree of intelligent conversation.

The house was furnished with an electric stove and a small chest freezer and was immaculately clean. The lady of the house offered us a seat on the floor while she spread an assortment of wood carved tikis and bowls before us and then unrolled a fine piece of tapa cloth that she wished also to sell.

Because we had just arrived to the area and were new to the island's art form, we did not make any purchases, but the works were well done and of good quality. Marquesan art would be of the highest standard we would see in all the South Pacific. The people of the Marquesas have wonderful artistic abilities.

Before going ashore, we had packed our backpack with items for trade; swapping Marquesan goods for items not delivered on the coastal ferry is beneficial. Visitors to the island can be good suppliers of useful merchandise. After leaving the house, we walked back towards the harbour where a second woman suggested we sit on her porch to share a slice of island grown *pamplemousse*, a large sweet grapefruit. She peeled and sectioned the fruit into plump juicy sections. Sweet and tangy tasting, she knew we would be delighted to take some back to our boat and she enquired what we might have to trade. We offered the woman a pair of flip flop sandals in trade for some fruit. In return, the lady offered us six melon sized grapefruits plus a dozen limes!

Later, I was approached by two young women who enquired whether I had perfume to offer. I didn't, but I wished I had.

The following day, the three of us set off for a "pleasant one hour walk," as the guide book described the trek to Vaiee-Nui Falls. We followed the concrete road to the edge of the village where the road ended abruptly and turned into a dirt road gouged with tire ruts. Wild, shoulder height grasses and a tall mix of colourful tropical plants crowded the road. Coconut palms, a hundred feet tall, stood miniaturized by the surrounding colossal vine-clad cliffs, the walls of an extinct volcano. Our plan was to veer off the road once we found the path to the falls, but finding the way was not easy. There were no markings to direct us and neither the paths nor the dirt roads appeared to be well travelled. Following the road to the top of a steep hill, we realized we were nearing a ridge of rugged cliffs. This couldn't be right, we thought; we should be searching for the base, not the crest of the falls, and so we turned and backtracked. Near the bottom, we left the road to follow a second, overgrown path that eventually showed signs of being another unused road.

It began to rain as it often does there. Clouds get hung up on the mountain ridges and then rain douses everything with greenhouse precision. Then it ceases in a matter of a few minutes, as if it was a manually run sprinkler system.

As we continued, the track became wetter and soggier, and when the growth thickened to the extent it prevented us from walking around the puddles of mud, we waded through them. The path led to a shallow, bubbling mountain stream embedded with small, smooth rocks. We nearly got across it with dry feet.

Following the trail, we began to climb up and out of the valley. The road ascended to dryer ground where a small clearing of jungle supported a farmed plantation of coconut palms. Piles of unopened, decaying coconuts lay in heaps in the middle of the road. The span of clear, open road didn't last long and soon we became hemmed in by shoulder height weeds, thickets and red flowering hibiscus bushes so heavy with blossoms that we needed to bend at the waist to duck under them.

Assuming we were heading in the right direction, we left the road to continue beneath a dimly lit canopy of forest that continued with a gentle upward slope. The soft decay of the forest felt like a carpet beneath our feet.

We were far enough inland now to be part of the rainforest and to come upon an archeological site of early Samoan settlers. Eerie and haunting, several chiseled, stone structures indicated it had once been a flourishing community. Raised platforms and stone block foundations lay among the wild growth of tangled greenery. It was now nothing more than a shadowy, damp setting hidden in the forest. Except for being overrun with jungle growth, there were assemblies of stone here much the same as when the settlers had left them: tribal ceremonial complexes—*tohua*; breadfruit storage pits—*va ma*; and drumming platforms. These sites are so common in Marquesan forests that they easily support the theory that the local populations once numbered in the six figures. I knew if we took the time to explore, we would probably unearth carved stone images, sea shells once used as dinner plates or perhaps even a hair ornament carved from human bone.

Roots pushed through walls of stacked boulders and vines crept like tangles of snakes choking an ancient way of life. Clinging, suffocating moss smothered rock-hard surfaces hiding who knows what? I knew there had to be numerous skulls nearby. It was a practice for early Polynesians to set them out for nature to clean them, then stack them in giant, hollowed-out tree trunks or protective caves where they were guarded by wood and stone effigies. It was what was left of a culture that had prayed to stone gods, spoke in nasal tones and warred so passionately with their neighbours. But they left more behind. Well before Europeans knew much about relieving unwanted stress, the first Marquesans were massaging their bodies with smooth stones, smearing gardenia infused monoi oil on their skin and using pumice stone to remove calluses. Today monoi oil is used as a skin moisturizer and thought to strengthen hair, especially treated hair.

The walk past the site was chilling. We walked in silence, like walking through an old graveyard at night. This however, had been a site of pagan rituals and the stillness of the forest seemed deafening, to almost encourage our quiet. Even our footsteps were muted by the thickness of soft decaying matter.

Mysteriously, soft peach coloured hibiscus blossoms lay sprinkled every few metres along the rarely used trail. We never did determine the source of the blooms, but hibiscus wood was invaluable to the settlers. It was the best of all available woods for making fires when sticks were rubbed together, the bark was used for making excellent quality rope and the blossoms were made into medicines. At one time, there were reportedly hibiscus forests on the island. They are probably still there. The island remains wild and mostly uninhabited. Much of the land is impenetrable with steep forests, perpendicular cliffs, precipices and sheer descents.

The trail was approaching the same bubbling stream we had crossed earlier, when we spotted a pyramid of three stones stacked on top of a rock. Cairns, structures of stone piled one atop another, made by people who have navigated the same path for centuries, can still be found in the forest. They were guideposts then, and although I'm very sure this was not an ancient landmark, it directed us away from the lower path and up the hill. We had been told to keep a lookout for these markers. Glancing in that direction, we could see nothing suggesting there might be a trail, but following instructions, we began the steep incline even though we could barely see our feet as they shuffled over the fern covered forest floor scattered with sizable rocks. Each step needed to be carefully placed on the slippery, moss covered rocks which lay freshly dampened by rain. At times, I could barely lift my knee high enough to place my foot on the next stone.

Once we had climbed to some height, we traversed the hillside to arrive at a rocky ledge leading around a craggy rock face. The cliffside protruded into the pathway like a giant's smooth, extended belly. The narrow pathway, scattered with small boulders and vegetation, offered about a metre of width for our footing then dropped sharply into a gorge of rocks and foliage. After rounding the corner, we heard the dull roar of cascading water, confirming that we were going in the right direction and were nearing our destination.

Very soon, through the top of the trees, we caught sight of water gushing off the peak of the escarpment. We continued following the trail and descended to a small plateau where portions of cliff had fallen, then split into sizable boulders to form a natural basin that imprisoned the water before allowing it to escape through a narrow gap. From here the mountain run-off turned into a stream tumbling gently over stones and winding its way back through the forest. Stone cliffs loomed above us and if we craned our necks back, we could see the water shooting from the basalt cliffs hundreds of metres above us, and fall, plummeting over the shiny black rock face to land in the pool white and frothy. Rising from the falls, water vaporized into a beaded mist that floated in light clouds, wetting the surrounding area.

After spending time absorbing the experience and taking pictures, we began the trek back. I made the announcement that this would be the most difficult part of the whole trek. Stepping down is always more dangerous as one foot is already halfway to its mark before you know if it's going to meet with a good hold or not and the climber's centre of gravity is leaning away from, not towards, the topography of the land. Mike and I were wearing hiking boots, Brian, Birkenstock sandals! How he ever kept his footing in those things I will never know.

It was shortly after I had spoken about the challenges of hiking downhill, that I was preparing to ease myself off a one metre high boulder when my foot slipped from the top of it. In a fraction of a second I knew something bad was about to happen.

My centre of gravity fell forward causing me to land head first on the rock below. I struck the left side of my head when

I landed. The boys told me later how worried they had been when they saw me lying on the rock, but I had not lost consciousness and as soon as I received help getting my feet off the rock from above me, I was able to evaluate the damage.

I had several small abrasions, (some that I would not discover until the following day) but it was my right hand that caused me concern. It began to swell almost immediately. I needed to keep it braced against my chest as I continued to clamber to the bottom of the valley. It was hardly the ideal posture for establishing balance during the rest of the trek. Other than that, I had not incurred any serious damage and my hand gave me little pain. For such a fall I was extremely lucky.

We continued down the incline engulfed by a canopy of trees while careful to secure our footing while we retreated into the valley. I tried curtailing the swelling by stopping occasionally to lay the hand in the cool, mountain stream that flowed from the falls.

The total walk, including my extracurricular mishap, took three hours. We concluded that either there was a walk to another falls nearby or the author of that guidebook had never actually undertaken the hike described.

With regular icing over the next few days, my wrist responded well and what I had feared might be a crack, turned out to be simply a good bruising. In addition, I had a tender spot next to my temple, but no bump suggesting a hematoma. My ribs however, had taken a bashing and while sailing the three day passage to the Tuamotus, I became acutely conscious of how many muscles, tendons and ligaments attached to my rib cage needed to work to keep me balanced.

As for the boys, I think they were damaged as much as me. Days later, Mike would bring the topic up, recalling how he had no idea how they would have ever evacuated me out of the forest if I had been seriously injured. Several days would go by and he would remark again on the same thought.

From Fatu Hiva, it was an overnight trip to Nuka Hiva where we anchored in Taiohae Bay (Taioha'e), the caldera of a collapsed crater. The plan was to meet with members of the Blue Water Rally at an organized event in celebration of our Pacific crossings. The celebration included a dinner and a show of Polynesian dancers at the Keikahanui Pearl Lodge overlooking the bay. Just in time to join us and be greeted with flowered leis, Jennifer and Rok arrived after nearly twenty-four hours of airplane travel and numerous miles by vehicle over the island's hilly terrain. They would spend six weeks exploring the islands with us.

Nuka Hiva is the largest and most populated of the Marquesas Islands, consisting of 345 square kilometres (214 square miles), and home to a population of almost twenty-four hundred. Like all the Marquesan islands, it is volcanic in origin although this one was formed when one volcano stacked on top of another.

Upon our arrival, we too were welcomed with flowered leis, one of the similarities in Marquesan and Hawaiian traditions. Our dinner at the Inn included a traditional *Puaka*, (pig roast) when a pig is cooked whole in a wood and lava stone filled ground pit.

In the early 1800s, narrow-minded Puritan missionaries, who viewed anything delightful as sinful, abolished, along with flute playing, traditional Marquesan dancing. After Tahitian king Tu Tunuieaiteatua Pōmare II accepted Christianity, Marquesan dance and the worship of sacred stone gods was prohibited. It had taken over eleven years for the missionaries to get to this point, where a breakdown in Tahitian religion could be seen and where an opening for Christian beliefs might take hold.

It wasn't for a hundred years that the energetic Marquesan dance began to creep its way back into society, and then only in mild form. The new revival required that the entire body be covered in clothing, other than the face, hands and feet. For fifty years dance carried on like this, with expression strictly choreographed.

Traditionally, Polynesian dancing had been a way of retelling stories; passing information from generation to generation, welcoming visitors, praying to gods, challenging an enemy or seducing a lover; hips moved at a spirited pace while hands and arms symbolically spoke in graceful gestures of trees, birds and of the sea. Some dances were more intricately informative than others. Choreography revisited the chores of everyday life, the planting of crops and fishing.

While wearing traditional grass skirts, coconut shell bras, a garland of flowers around the neck and a hibiscus bloom behind an ear, (on the left side if one is spoken for, on the right, if one is available), women and young girls move their hips at incredible speeds to drum-beats capable of igniting latent savage juices even in the lily white new comer.

These hip gyrating dances, which are nothing like the slow, elegant movement of the Hawaiian dance, but more closely resemble the rapidity of paint cans mixing at your local paint store, is something to behold. Young women in hip-flicking movements corkscrew to the ground while long flowing black hair caresses bare shoulders above halter tops and grass skirts rest just below the navel. No wonder the first Europeans who landed here were in awe when they first encountered the island's bare breasted women, all wiggly and ready to share their love. And who could be surprised there was a mutiny on the ship *Bounty*[*] by crewmembers who didn't want to leave the island?

---

[*] In 1788, Captain William Bligh was on a mission to Tahiti to procure breadfruit (a carbohydrate-rich staple) in an experiment to transport a sustainable crop to other islands as a food source for slaves. It was the rainy season and the breadfruit was not ripe. Bligh was detained in Tahiti five months. While waiting, the crew of the *Bounty* came to enjoy the pleasures of the friendly Tahitians to the point, when it was time to depart they were reluctant to leave. In days following, the crew expressed displeasure over leaving and other grievances, by carrying out a mutiny. Bligh and 18 crewmembers were set adrift in a 7 metre (23 foot) open boat.

Polynesian dances portrayed by men include both seductive moves and macho displays of strength, emphasizing fierce, warlike abilities. Polynesian men are broad-shouldered muscular specimens bearing resemblance to the hulking physiques of Olympic weight lifters. During dances, they often balance on their toes while in a modest deep-knee bend when they knock their knees together in rapid motion. In this posture they turn in circles or navigate across a floor while the dancing warriors display threats of brute physical force. Dance musicians pound out wickedly powerful drumbeats from three decisively different drums, energizing the dancers in their choreography. Animal skins drawn across carved rosewood and more simply cut bamboo drums, pulsate with the same fervor as they did centuries ago while encouraging warriors into battle.

One cannot help but lose oneself in the rhythms of the drums which can go on repeatedly for several minutes and in earlier times, for hours. While wearing only loin cloths strapped about their waists, male dancers sweat profusely during this fast paced exercise while looking every bit the masculine warrior—strong, agile and threatening.

We hired a tour guide with a four wheel drive vehicle to tour the island. Several days of rain had washed out parts of the island's newly paved road due to the lack of culverts to divert the water.

We drove past dense areas of wild vanilla where the air was sweetened with its scent, past bushes in colourful arrays of bloom and towering forests of palm trees and pine trees that grew nearer the top. In the distance, waterfalls cascaded from heights so great that portions evaporated before ever having a chance to fall into the dark depths of the verdant valleys below. Volcanic outcrops, overlooking sweeping bays of black sand beaches, formed protruding, rugged cliffs.

As the jeep wound upwards, ascending toward the crest of

a spent volcano, switch back roads repeatedly twirled around cliff hanging turns. Shear drop offs falling to deep, shadowy canyons demanded our attention while we spun around corners. Guard rails? You must be kidding!

THE FIRST MARQUESANS preferred to settle in deep, hard-to-access valleys for reasons of protection and for access to both fresh water and the sea. They were a clean society, bathing often in rivers scrubbing their skin with leaves containing foam-producing powers and rubbing cleansing sand through their hair. It might be challenging to find ancient village sites on some islands, but on Nuka Hiva, there are hundreds, although most have been swallowed by jungle growth and now lie hidden. But it's not difficult to identify a *marae (ma'ae)*, an area of worship. They are located in proximity to ancient villages and nearly always have a banyan tree nearby which Polynesians transported from their homelands. They replanted the trees near villages, where the sites became sacred gathering locations for dances, celebrations, feasts, funerals, and sacrifices. Maraes were often used for signing treaties, celebrating the outcome of wars and worshiping gods. Once banyan trees are mature, long cascading roots fall vine-like from upper limbs of massive 30 metre (100 foot) trees, to take root in the ground where they thicken into stalks. By the time a banyan tree reaches maturity, its main trunk will hardly be visible beneath the stringy outer covering of hundreds of lanky roots. The trees are so remarkable, you cannot pass one without stopping to admire its greatness. Archaeologists have discovered skulls and leg bones tucked into the straggly root systems, not only on the island of Nuka Hiva but all across the Marquesas, wherever Polynesians had settled. Not far from these sites, villages developed in organized, rectangular layouts, defining the territory for housing, cooking areas and medicine huts.

One such site is Hikoku'a Tohua. Heavily treed with palms, thick pandanus and lush, succulent grasses that grow at a rate difficult to control, workers struggle to keep the hardy, fast spreading growth from smothering the treasured antiquities. Ancient, sculpted stone tikis projecting large, bulging eyes and thick, plump lips spread across broad faces, stand or squat while clasping hands across their bellies. A phallic fertility statue with an unrealistic swollen member stands at the entrance of the site.

Terraces, constructed of large blocks of stone, lent elevation to the worship site where a *tahu'a* (priest), gifted with high spiritual powers, oversaw important rituals. Various flat stone *paepae* (platforms), lay smoothed and leveled, ready for the circumcising of twelve year old boys. Others were designated for sacrifices. Body tattooing beds can still be found with rounded pocket-like indentations, formerly the containers which held colouring substances of charcoal and plant mixtures. Not far from the platforms, small cavernous pits, resembling deep wells, stood prepared for captured warriors. These subterranean prison cells were capable of holding three to four standing prisoners. When needed, a prisoner would be lifted to an adjacent single pit to await his part in a religious sacrifice. The prisoner would then be transported, accompanied by drumming and chanting, to a low, free standing stone structure. There, while kneeling, his head would be positioned into the stone skull-cradle to await a fatal blow. Following the ritual, parts of the prisoner would be cooked and eaten. Adjacent pits were used to dispose of the viscera. The remnants of this history are still to be found at hundreds of sites.

WE SPENT THREE days anchored in the rolling swell of Taiohae Bay outside the town of Taiohae on the island of Nuka Hiva.

The town was small, but modern, supporting a hospital, post office and bank, yet there was no fresh water available for the boats that had arrived with empty tanks, and we filled several jugs from our freshwater holding tanks for others. Then we too began to run short when several days of rain poured a muddy runoff into the bay, prohibiting us from using our watermaker.

There were three small grocery stores in town where I could purchase pasta, rice, flour and canned butter at very reasonable prices. France heavily subsidizes certain groceries while others, such as breakfast cereal, are very expensive. We were careful not to purchase large quantities of any one item because the island's supplies arrive by coastal freighter only every three weeks and mass purchasing could likely cause a shortage for the locals. But we needed flour to make bread and I was concerned about running out of it. I discovered, after baking with a bag of French flour, that it contains much lower gluten and nothing near to the strong characteristics of our great Saskatchewan hard wheat.

When our fresh water ran so low that we were scraping the bottom of the tank, we moved out of the bay and around the corner to what yachties call Daniel's Bay. We celebrated Mike's birthday here. Jennifer kindly reminded him that it would be the last in his fifties.

Daniel's Bay is known to be the best anchorage in the Marquesas because here, tropical treed shorelines surround the bay, with nearly three hundred and sixty degrees of protection. The bay was nick-named after a man who lived on an arm of the bay called Hakatea Cove (Anse Hakatea). For years, Daniel had been welcoming and helpful to those who arrived there by boat. He lived among an assortment of wild fruit trees: pamplemousse, lemon, lime, papaya and banana. Daniel offered their harvest to those who would most appreciate the gift of fresh fruit. For the past thirty years, cruisers have landed on his shores, but in fact, the land was not really his, but the government's. In 2002, the tranquility of this bay was overturned, and this is the origin of that trouble.

In previous years, when boaters arrived, they tied their dinghies to a small dock Daniel had constructed with scavenged materials, but when we arrived, the dock was no longer there. Previously, a showerhead had offered a chilly mountain water rinse to those who swam in the bay. Daniel had laid a pipeline leading from the river to the white sand beach where he had installed the showerhead and a tap to allow boaters to fill their water containers. For some, this would have been the find-of-the-century. Many cruisers face the challenge of finding fresh water when they cruise.

Neither the tap nor the shower was there any longer.

Daniel's Bay is located in a remote part of Nuka Hiva, which is why CBS's TV production of *Survivor* was so attracted to it. David Content, a cruising sailor, was in the bay on his boat in October 2002 and witnessed the destruction of Daniel's home. He subsequently wrote an article for *Sail Magazine*. "[I was] watching the yellow bulldozer on the beach scrape up portions of the foundation of Daniel's house. Only the white toilet and bathroom sink remained, standing exposed on their concrete base."

During this time, Content was asked to remove his boat from the bay, but he persisted and stayed.

> At six o'clock every morning men in white suits, boots, and masks, with tanks on their backs and nozzles in their hands, boated in to spray insecticide on the beach to suppress the white no-nos, a local type of no-see-ums.

DANIEL and his wife, Antoinette, confided to Content that they had not wanted to leave the little home they had built and surrounded with orchards of fruit trees, but there had been strong pressure to do so.

David's article goes on to describe how over at "Taioa Bay, (Taiohae Bay) the main village on Nuku Hiva, the 1,700 residents faced an onslaught of two hundred and fifty American and Australian *Survivor* staff."

> All locations [Contrôleur Bay, Anaho Bay, Aotupa Bay, and Daniel's Bay] were off limits to tourists, sailboats, and even the local population. Native fishermen were unhappily barred from adjacent waters. At the new pier, a "prop" crew of Australians was busy ten hours a day with power saws, lathes, sanders, stain, and paint, making crude paddles, torches, tikis, rafts, canoes, and similar Polynesian items for the production.
> ...then from Los Angeles came the 320 foot luxury cruise ship *Spirit of Oceanus* to provide refuge for the workers, video and sound crews, and production staff.

WHEN it all came to an end, about three months later, Daniel and his wife had been relocated to a prefabricated house while the other houses built for the production crews were to be donated to low income families. Apparently the government offered to rebuild Daniel and Antoinette's home but according to CBS, Daniel and Antoinette preferred their new home. CBS has assured the citizens of Nuku Hiva that the areas used by *Survivor IV* would be returned to their original condition.

Daniel was seventy-four years old at the time.

NEARLY four years had gone by since the 'Survivor occupation,' when we were headed towards the shores of Daniel's Bay by dinghy. A local man, looking perhaps in his seventies, suddenly appeared. He stood on the beach, and with hand signals, proceeded to guide us through the reef, safely to shore. The man was Daniel. Apparently he and his wife had returned to live on the beach after all.

Daniel indicated that we should pull our dinghy high up on the beach to protect it from an incoming tide. He lent a hand while we dragged it, with great effort, almost to the tree line. At the time, the tide was low and the breadth of the beach exceptionally deep. It was no small job to drag it up that far.

We announced that our plans were to hike to the Ahui Waterfall. We offered Daniel a gift of rope, something that he could use for trade or as a gift to a friend. Daniel's simply constructed hut was located only a few metres from the beach, part of the floor of a spectacular deep valley where rugged, jagged cliffs and thick, dark green jungle sweep upward, surrounding you like giant protective arms encircling your body. A river, fast paced and clear, tumbled over rocks towards the bay.

While walking towards his sparsely furnished shack, Daniel picked a pamplemousse and suggested we take it with us on the hike. I looked at the thing. It was the size of a large cantaloupe! I was not overly keen to lug it to wherever our jungle path would take us, but I placed it in my backpack as a sign of appreciation.

Inside the dimly lit hut, Antoinette greeted us from her semi-recumbent position on the floor. Daniel pulled out a log book that had been signed by arriving yachties since the early 1970s. We added *Baccalieu III* to the list.

Leaving Daniel's home, we followed the river through a valley hemmed by surrounding uninhabited hills. Our feet scuffed along the same dirt road early Marquesans would have used to travel through the deep, lush elongated valley. Two wild horses stood ankle deep in rushing mountain run-off. We climbed over rocks and waded through ankle deep mud to arrive at our first river forging. Laying hands on boulders, we steadied our footing while carefully shuffling over the rocky bed of shallow water. We found a path on the other side, although it was obscured by an overgrowth of vegetation and we found ourselves backtracking several times in an attempt to find our way. Uncertain of our direction, we never ventured far from the river and we forged it three times when this was the only viable way to pass through the dense jungle. Pushing our way through powerful, knee deep, rapids, we inched our way over slippery fragments of broken rocks while struggling to keep our balance. My ribs had not entirely healed from my fall on Fatu Hiva and I made every attempt to avoid stumbling.

We came upon an early Polynesian site where long, dangling roots hung like elongated fingers from a monolithic banyan tree. The trees always appeared in the forest like single, gargantuan structures — guardians of a past culture and keepers of secrets. Green mosses crept over a floor of decay concealing not only the foundations of an earlier settlement but hairy legged tarantulas and giant, poisonous centipedes that hid in the underbrush and rocks. The scent of the jungle lived here; the smell of bamboo and damp leaves.

Beneath the solid foliage of tree branches, where the sun could not offer its gift of heat and where moisture lay trapped in diminished light, the former settlement appeared dark and still, like a day just about to end. Blocks of stone, layered together without concrete, were vague examples of how an early civilization had somehow severed pieces of rock into cubic forms then stacked them forming foundations and platforms. Dampness hung in the air so intense that I understood why the mosquitos that arrived with early European explorers, thrived so heartily here. Elephantiasis, a tropical disease transmitted by mosquitos, was the bane of many nineteenth century Polynesians.

I suspect that early in our hike we must have missed a turn that would have kept us on a more travelled path. Cruisers spoke of trekking to a substantial falls but we were many times breaking in our own path, blindly seeking some kind of clue as to how to find our way.

We walked out of the jungle keeping our sights on the escarpment. Scampering over huge boulders we entered the riverbed again where the cool mountain runoff came hard against our shins.

At the base of the escarpment, a small sunny plateau, void of any vegetation higher than ankle deep grasses, appeared like an oasis. It was a magical kind of place although simply furnished with nature's charms: succulent undergrowth beneath a clear cobalt sky. Coming across such a sunny area was a surprise. We had suddenly left acres of dampness to come out into a small pocket of brilliant sunshine that doused us with heat and transmitted a sort of joy. The falls we had been seeking was nearby and while standing in the sunlight, the fall's misty air wet our clothing and dampened our hair. We stood there peeling and eating the delicious grapefruit that Daniel had given us and we were very grateful to have it. Its sweet, tart taste was perfectly refreshing.

Water pouring over the edge of the escarpment followed the vertical slashes in the basalt, but at the top, the gushing motion fell well behind protrusions of rock, making it impossible for us to see where it fell from. The falls was not a spectacular sight but the experience of reaching its location had been an interesting and memorable challenge.

We had worn bathing suits under our clothing in the hopes of refreshing ourselves in the pool at the base of the falls, but as we tossed the thick yellow skin from the pamplemousse into the water, slick, black hefty eels, some close to a metre long, broke through the surface like huge water snakes. The pamplemousse had been instrumental in attracting the wildlife that existed in the pool, just as Jennifer was about to wade in!

Surprisingly, throughout our hiking, we had experienced very few insect bites. Even in the jungles we did not have the need to wear repellant, although I always carried it with me. We had, however, been warned about the no nos on the beaches. I hadn't really paid heed to the warning as I figured the sign to slather on the repellant would be when I felt I was being bitten. However, the bite of the no nos, as I later learned, cannot necessarily be felt and it is not until the following day that one might feel the effects, when the bites swell and turn into a blemish of torment. The bites can be so intense that they send victims to hospitals, and in the upcoming hours I would come to understand why this was so.

I must have been attacked the day we dragged our dinghy up on Daniel's beach, because the back of my thighs and lower legs had broken into a red mass of holes. Back onboard *Baccalieu III*, the holes began to itch with an intense fiery sting that responded to nothing other than an application of ice. Even antihistamines did nothing to relieve the torment. But the worse was still to come. Two days later, the bites were excruciating and by then, even more bites had made an appearance.

During the passage to the Tuamotus, while I slept on my back to minimize rolling, the itch intensified to an almost unbearable degree. The warmth that I created while in contact with the bed sheets exaggerated the itch severely. I couldn't sleep, I couldn't rest, I couldn't find a position that didn't amplify the irritation. I would get out of bed, place ice cubes in a cloth, then return to my torture chamber. It was imperative not to scratch them, even though they screamed for attention. Scratching deepened the itching to a level that was supremely torturous. But often I would scratch them helplessly while sleeping, only to wake with the most insane irritation. I could easily dig a gaping hole into my skin with my short fingernails but even when bleeding, the discomfort continued and intensified. It was as if I had dabbed the wounds with acid. It was a torment that took five days to settle down.

We have since learned that Daniel has passed on and his granddaughter and husband are carrying on his tradition of welcoming yachties with similar generosity.

TUAMOTU ATOLLS

In 1947 a Norwegian explorer, Thor Heyerdahl, wished to prove that it would have been possible for people of South America to have settled Polynesia in pre-Columbian times. By constructing a raft using technologies of the time period and using balsa logs which would have been available to the early explorers, he set out on an expedition from Peru, across the Pacific Ocean, hoping to reach the Tuamotu Islands. The expedition of 4,300 miles took him 101 days. When he arrived in the Tuamotus, his raft ran up on a reef and smashed to smithereens. He had named his raft Kon-Tiki.

AFTER LEAVING DANIEL'S Bay, a good wind pushed us five hundred miles south to one of the atolls located within a chain of tiny islands named the Tuamotus* (Archipel des Tuamotu). These low lying islets lie strung like a broken necklace for 1,600 km (1,000 mi.) making them the largest group of atolls in the world. The atolls were formed millions of years ago when volcanic islands sank beneath the ocean leaving the coral reefs, which had once formed around them, lying only metres above the water. Through an accumulation of sand and debris, the atolls grew to a height of only two metres

---

* Visiting yachts can clear in and out of French Polynesia with the gendarmes (French Police) at the ports of entry in the Marquesas, Tuamotus, Gambiers, Australs etc. and complete all customs and immigration formalities in the one place. However, visiting the local gendarmes upon arrival on each island is appreciated.

(six feet) above sea level. Today, some of these atolls support whole villages, even though no fresh water is available other than what is collected from rainfall.

ON OUR APPROACH, the island of Kauehi did not seem to exist. It certainly couldn't be seen with the naked eye. Only when we were about five miles from shore, did some lanky palm trees appear through our binoculars. Poking skyward like a mirage of lost masts, the trees frequently vanished from view with the bounce of the sea.

The fact that these low lying islands were discovered at all by early explorers paddling in kayaks is almost miraculous. Later, their discovery by European seamen was another piece of luck. This part of the Pacific is not today, or was it ever, a part of the usual path of merchant ships or freighter ships or even explorers on quests to discover new lands or a route to the Far East. Only those who were blown off course, or swept here by storms, discovered the islands and then, caught in the grasp of strong currents, the ships struggled, often in vain, to avoid coming to grief on the extensive stretches of coral that run around the islands like sharpened teeth. Planted here as if islands of mercy and rescuers of seamen, the Tuamotus present hope to the crippled but can then unexpectedly sink them with their guarding reefs where waves break, hurling shattering spume.

Impossible to detect after dark and very difficult to approach even in daylight, several wrecks lay beneath us as we made our approach.

THE islands were first discovered by seamen from South China, Fiji and Somalia who were navigating by currents, reading the clustering of clouds and taking direction from the stars, all while fearing what might lie beyond the curvature of the earth. Often early Polynesians settled near reef passes that lead to calm, protected waters and to where fish and shallow water mollusks, could be sourced for food. Not until the early 1800s did Europeans discover the islands by literally running into them, and those that survived charted their existence.

The way to approach an atoll is to steer your boat towards a devouring reef while blocking out common sense warnings from your brain. Just as our instincts direct us not to drive towards a tornado, so do they instruct seamen not to approach exploding foam. But while pushing our minds to override our natural instincts, and while listening to the sound of crashing rollers ahead, we proceeded forward, waiting for a sign to confirm that there was a safe pass through the reef. In times like this, our charts were our soul mates; we relied on their accuracy and refused to think of the occasional times our electronic charts had directed our route *across* a land mass rather than around it. Sailing like this was a test for us, and for the accuracy of our charts.

It was not long before the distant plumes of white foam were now enhanced by thunderous roaring. Soon, the crashing of waves was not so distant anymore. Thousands of miles of free rolling ocean strikes the atoll's submerged coral collar, releasing exuberant energy into folds of fury. Beyond this beautiful evil, we still could not detect a passage, although the palm trees grew taller and the graceful movement of swaying branches signaled that we were nearing land.

Running before us as far as the eye could see, an elongated stretch of white water pounded against the reef with the force of the Titans. The spectacle awakened us to the approaching danger, but we had already locked down our minds and fully expected the narrow passage through the reef to suddenly appear. The charts indicated it was there.

Thousands of years ago, passes through the coral had been created when fresh water ran towards the sea from mountains that now lay beneath the ocean. Fresh water inhibits the growth of saltwater reef polyps, preventing the reef, in that location, from entirely closing. Not all atolls have navigable passes, but our charts indicated that Kauehi did.

Then we spotted a single, slim navigational post ahead.

Currents and wind conditions play an important role when navigating a pass like this. Ebbing or flooding tides can cause water to sweep through a constricted space at eight to nine knots. Entering the pass at slack tide is ideal but how good can one's timing be after travelling five hundred miles? When the wind blows against tidal currents, 'standing waves' can develop, and they are just what they sound like, waves that stand straight as if powered by some source of high voltage from beneath. In conditions such as this, yachts, lacking the necessary horse power to punch through, fall victim to the current and get swept aside to an unwelcoming shore.

The pass into Kauehi lagoon is a 200 metre (655 foot) wide channel allowing for 9 m (30 ft.) of water beneath a boat's keel; a constricted space for a large lagoon to spill its tidal overflow. Even at slack tide, the pass was actively engaged with fast flowing waters.

On the shore, sailboats laid cocked on their hulls, beached from having lost control from stuttering engines and lost steerage. Naked, abandoned and stripped of their valuables, these sailboats lay there now, swept to the side like papier-mâché toys. There is a reason these islands are known as the 'Dangerous Archipelagos'.

From the sight of madly churning seas, we suddenly entered a serene calm that could have tamed the devil. Perhaps it was the sudden stillness of it all, it was as if we had closed the door on the tornado we had been driving toward, shut out the danger and perhaps found utopia. Maybe this was even heaven.

The lagoon lay before us like a giant fish tank. White coral beaches framed a pond of turquoise glass where tropical fish found a refuge from a turbulent sea and large predators. At least that's what they say about these lagoons, that sharks go no further than the passes, although they are often abundant within the pass. Certain Tuamotu passes are recognized as some of the shark capitals of the world.

Inside the lagoon, coral heads lying just below the surface are not noted on charts but can be seen easily if the sun is high overhead. Luckily when we arrived, light was at its best which enabled a spotter, standing on the bow, to direct the helmsman.

Large, dark coral heads protruded from the bottom in water so clear, you would be tempted to drink it if it wasn't for the fact that it is salt water. Judging the depth is almost impossible, and to avoid them we would swerve while picking our way through the fields of coral like we were maneuvering a car around pylons.

Although placed in a natural setting that would entice even the most reluctant of travellers, Kauehi itself is a rather desolate looking island, created by sand washing from outer coral reefs and now covered in hearty palm trees—those pokey poles we had caught sight of from beyond the surf.

THE island of Kauehi supports approximately two hundred people, some of whom are involved in the drying of coconut. But a far more lucrative crop is cultivated on this island, the farming of baby mother of pearl oysters used in the culture of black pearls. Lagoons offer the ideal environment for growing baby oysters because here they are protected from strong currents while submerged in the rich nutrients of warm, calm waters. The Tuamotus are one of the few areas in the world where these conditions are reliable. During the nineteenth century, Polynesian divers dove to collect oysters and the oysters were nearly decimated. Today, black pearl farming is a major industry in the Tuamotus, employing thousands from surrounding islands.

AFTER anchoring, we took the dinghy to shore where we tied the painter to a post supporting a long, wide, concrete dock. We were only the second boat that year to visit Kauehi. We felt like real explorers.

A tall, concrete block Roman Catholic Church dominated the far end of the dock. Churches play an important role in the Christian life of communities and their sturdy concrete structures are also invaluable as cyclone shelters.

There were few people to be seen on the island that day, although there were several well-kept homes, some with colourfully patterned curtains decorating their windows. Low buildings housing an infirmary, town hall and one small grocery store selling tinned goods and ice cream, were the only other public buildings in the community. Unlike the Marquesas Islands, the Tuamotus are unable to support any species of fruit tree, making the islanders more dependent on the coastal supply ship. A few small runabouts lacking motors sat resting on land, along with various immobilized cars now stripped of their body parts to keep other cars running. But on an island that measures only 19 km long by 12 km wide (12 by 8 mi.) I can't see there being much need for an automobile.

SEVENTY MILES FROM Kauehi lies the second largest Tuamotu atoll, Fakarava. Even though only 60 km (37 mi.) long by 24 km (15 mi.) wide, there is an airstrip here, and a concrete wharf, customized with black iron light posts, paid for by the success of local black pearl farming. It's an odd luxury to see in the middle of nowhere. A school, an infirmary and a bakery are part of the community of six hundred. To take advantage of the daily baked croissants and baguettes, we had to be at the bakery by six-thirty in the morning.

Fakarava has two passes into the lagoon, one about 275 metres (300 yards) wide, the other, 180 metres (200 yards) wide. Here, schools of fish, romping dolphins and hundreds of sharks, tiger, grey reefs, and whitetips, frequently visit to feed on rich nutrients that sweep through with the currents. According to the *National Post*, this dive site is one of the most extreme scuba dives in the world. It was certainly one of our favourites. Requiring quick descents to about 100 feet to escape strong flowing currents, once down, it was possible to see graceful open-mouthed manta rays, humphead wrasses and whip-tailed stingrays. Five of the seven species of sea turtles in existence make their home in French Polynesia and it's common for divers to see the Green and Hawksbill turtle either in the passes or in the lagoons.

ANSE AMYOT, LOCATED outside Toau atoll, lies forty miles east of Fakarava. A coral bank preventing access to the inner lagoon helps create a small cove. The entrance to the cove is a narrow slot through a reef that allows for only a single boat to pass through at a time.

We sailed parallel to the shore following a line of frothing breakers until spotting two navigational posts marking the constricted opening. Range markers, erected inside the cove, provided a bearing to slip between the reefs and enter the cove. By keeping *Baccalieu III*'s bow aligned with the range markers, we found the route in.

The cove offers space large enough for two to three boats as long as all three don't mind a cozy existence. Entering the cove was similar to driving a car with failed brakes into a cul-de-sac after an ice storm.

We expected calm water similar to the previous lagoons we

had visited, but once through the passage, we were met by a wild swirling of jostling currents. It was not like Mike to suggest we explore such confined quarters. There is no doubt he was surprised at the conditions we found inside the cove. We all were.

We had experienced large ocean swells en route to Anse Amyot, and the swells were pouring from the far side, flooding the lagoon with more water than it could contain, then spilling over the reef into the little cove. The water couldn't flow out the entrance fast enough and instead, was forced into numerous circling currents and eddies replicating a vast whirlpool bath. The anchor would need to go down without incident and dig in immediately if we were to stay out of trouble.

After successfully engaging the anchor and dowsing the motor, the currents spun *Baccalieu III* around at a pace that changed our view from the cockpit every five minutes. There were two small houses on the northern islet and it seemed possible that our boat might be sitting inside one of the cabins before night was over.

No sooner did we get the anchor down than we saw a runabout skipping across the inner lagoon. It charged through a camouflaged, shallow opening in the reef, sped through a fish trap, then came alongside *Baccalieu III*. One of the three French speaking locals onboard suggested our boat would be better secured if we tied off to one of their buoys. They assured us the buoy would have no problem holding a thirty ton boat. But after the wind came up that night and they watched us swing in pirouettes just in front of their veranda, swishing past like an amusement park ride just metres from their house, they suggested we move a little further away to another buoy that they guaranteed was even stronger.

The owners, Valentine and Gaston Damiel, invited us to shore to walk their property.

Coconut palms were plentiful and provided building

material for both a sleeping house and a separate cooking cabin where Valentine baked bread in a coconut husk fired oven. Attached to the cooking hut was a verandah, cantilevered over the water; the one we swept by at close range the night before while twirling around with the current.

The buildings were located among a small community of relatives consisting of Valentine's nephew, who lived next door to the boathouse, and Gaston's parents, who occupied a small house nearer the lagoon.

A coating of white paint protected the tinned roofs and some of the buildings from salt air erosion while other buildings stood weathered. Valentine and Gaston's property was neat and organized. A sow snorted and scuffed around in a small pen, eating coconuts from cracked shells while piglets suckled at her underbelly. Hens with chicks roamed freely scratching for food in the short grasses. A single, crippled piglet stood in a small crate fattening on more cracked coconuts.

There were two friendly dogs running about which encouraged Jennifer to enquire of the Damiels if they ever ate dog meat. She had heard that some Polynesians did. Valentine replied that she did not, but her brother did.

Valentine and Gaston obtain their income from copra farming and fish they trap and sell to the Tahitian market. They also work in pearl farming. Valentine grafts oysters at a rate of two hundred per day, while Gaston operates a small assembly line of oyster sorting and preparation. That season they had 15,000 oysters that would need grafting.

A couple of shacks also stood on their property including a simply constructed chapel and a French telephone booth with a live telephone. That had to be the oddest place to find a public telephone! An extended family of nine lived on the island.

An outhouse had been erected over the water, but it was located several metres off shore and there was no dry means to access it. I learned that for the past fifteen years, the outhouse had been abandoned following new French government laws that had forbidden the use of the toilets. Imagine that, a law prohibiting outhouses in an area so remote! And it would have been used by no more than nine people! I didn't ask them what they do now, now that the toilet was gone. Perhaps the French government has forbidden them to defecate!

Valentine offered to prepare a meal for us for the following night. She asked Jennifer if she would like them to slaughter a pig for the dinner. Jennifer replied with a quick and decisive, "No", and immediately ordered the alternative: live fish from their traps and lobster from their shores. Later that night, Gaston walked three miles across the island to where he knew lobsters could be found not far from shore.

The following day was Sunday and Valentine invited us to attend a church service in the chapel that Gaston had built behind their house. Brian and I rode the dinghy in for the ten o'clock service.

Although the couple had been up early that morning decorating the veranda with palm fronds for our dinner, and already food preparations were underway, with yeast for the coconut bread bubbling in the bowl, Valentine and Gaston met us outside the chapel changed from their work clothes into their Sunday best. Before entering the chapel they both slipped off their shoes; Brian and I followed suit. The floor of the chapel had been laid with plain, white floor tile. Crosses hung on the white walls behind a cloth covered alter flanked by fake potted flowers. I was invited to take a seat on one of the white plastic chairs when Gaston handed me an English bible and a song sheet printed in French.

Oh Lordy, was I expected to sing?

Brian impressed the pants off them by bringing his own FRENCH bible! I was impressed too.

It had become obvious that Valentine was the matriarch of the island, the engine that made everything happen. So it was not surprising she was the one to conduct the service. She began her evangelical service in broken English and suggested we start with personal prayers. Gaston and Valentine prayed out loud in French dialect so the only words I recognized were several 'halleluiahs'. I hoped they would not overhear me pray for the buoy that we were tied to be of sufficient strength to hold our boat. I threw a couple of 'halleluiahs' into my prayer; I thought they would like that.

Gaston and Valentine were leading quite a lengthy prayer, so I had time to ask for a little less current in the anchorage, a little less wind while we swung on the buoy, and absolutely no surprises during the night. I guess I didn't say enough halleluiahs because that night the wind came up, and we were awake most of the night on watch. While anchored in such a small space, you can be sure that we watched intently for the slightest indication that the buoy might be drifting. Our boat didn't have far to go before it would be on shore.

Because Gaston had been up into the wee hours of the morning gathering crabs and lobsters for our dinner, he had trouble staying awake during the service. But in his defense, it was not an easy sermon to listen to. Valentine was no smooth orator. It was evident however, that Gaston's duty in this service was to lead us in song, and Valentine's was to reach over and give him a clout with the back of her hand to wake him each time she wanted to hear those pipes of his filled with song. Then he would stir, open his eyes, and sing, like a doll that needed shaking in order to work.

I had no idea what the words in the songs meant let alone what the tune was, but there were only the four of us and it would have been bad form not to take part, so I continued to mumble the words and depended on Gaston to stay awake and sing louder than me.

That afternoon, we received weather information indicating that our location would receive high winds that would blow directly into the cove. Small cove, high winds—bad combination. We reluctantly announced to the Damiels that we needed to leave immediately. We were all bitterly disappointed to miss dinner. Valentine really wanted us to stay, and suggested that we had nothing to worry about because God was with us and would protect us and we should really stay for dinner. But we felt it was wiser for us to move while we could do so safely.

After we paid them for the meal that we could not stay to eat, they hurriedly cooked up the lobsters and a blue coconut crab, tucked a squash under my arm, gave us a few low grade pearls, and wished us well.

It was a clear night when we sailed the one hundred miles to Rangiroa, one of the largest atolls in the world. The lagoon is so large, that you cannot see to the other side. The economy here remains the same as it has been for the past one thousand years; fish and coconut are collected for food and copra is dried. The only difference today is that the copra travels to Tahiti to be sold for cash rather than traded. Almost twenty-five hundred people live in Rangiroa.

We arrived in the morning and turned the boat towards Avatoru Pass where we were met with swirling water mixed with eddies and surface rip tides bouncing like little geysers. Giant rough toothed dolphins played whimsically in the current. With the current flowing out, and wind blowing into the lagoon, four foot standing waves riddled the pass. The same sizable swells that had poured into Anse Amyot the day before were now breaking over the southern edge of Rangiroa's lagoon, creating seven knots of current against us in the pass. Waves struck the boat from every direction, as if we were the enemy and they were the knights protecting their castle's moat. While the current rammed and cranked against the rudder, we could feel the effects of the tugging right through to the steering wheel.

We pushed through the half mile pass using full throttle, sometimes making only one knot of headway. One couldn't help but imagine the consequences if the motor should suddenly experience a hiccup.

DURING our stay in Rangiroa, we visited an oyster farm where we were shown the procedures necessary for the regulated development of pearls. There was far more work involved than I had imagined. The oyster used is the black-lipped *Pinctada maxima*. Technicians pry the oysters open to insert small marbles made from Mississippi Oyster shells. These seeds encourage pearl development. Two years later, the shells are pried open again so that a technician, using a fine instrument, can remove the pearl. A graft taken from an oyster that produced the most desirable colours in a pearl is inserted into other oysters.

Rangiroa offered the best prices for pearls that we visited.

THE Tiputa and Avatoru passes in Rangiroa offer some of the best diving in the world. Outside Avatoru Pass, where ocean depths fall to hundreds of feet, seas pound against coral covered sides of an ancient sunken volcano. Here, an assortment of wildlife gathers to devour rich nutrients. During shark mating season, hundreds of sharks congregate in the fast sweeping currents when they remain almost motionless, while oxygen rich waters flow through their gills.

Rangiroa has one of the highest concentrations of silvertip, black tip, and silky sharks in the world. Schools of hammerheads, lemon sharks and tiger sharks, will often congregate in and around the pass.

At the time of our visit, the local dive shop confirmed that we had arrived during mating season and reported they had seen large numbers in the pass the day before.

After suiting up in our dive skins, a dinghy driver drove us into the pass. Due to the strong currents, the small boat was incapable of holding its position and we needed to hurry to put on our equipment. In order to stay together, we simultaneously executed backroll entries off both sides of the boat.

The rest of the plan did not go well.

The plan was to drop immediately to the bottom at 24 m (80 ft.). Once down, we were to meet in one location where we would grasp hold of rocks or coral pieces to secure ourselves and watch the rituals of shark mating. But before we could all reach the bottom, the current swept some of us out of the pass like we were feathers in a windstorm. The current had enough power that it could easily rip the facemasks from our faces if we were to turn our heads sideways.

I had made it to the bottom and was one of the few that were not swept away with the current. And why was this? Because I was snagged on a rock!

When I reached the floor of the pass, the camera, which I had strapped to my wrist, caught a piece of coral and held me fast. Millions of litres of water were spilling out of the lagoon creating such current, that I was forced away from where the camera was snagged. I was held there, streaming just above the seabed, with the strap cutting painfully into my wrist. I must have looked like Supergirl!

I learned after surfacing that Jennifer, who had been swimming above me, had seen that I was in trouble, but was unable to offer assistance because she too was caught in the current and being swept out the pass.

To release the strap on my wrist, I needed to pull myself up-current towards the rock where it was snagged; no simple task against such current. Once I managed to push my hand through the oncoming current and catch hold of the rock to pull myself forward, I was able to slacken the strap and detach it. Then I surfaced to rejoin the others.

When we came up, we were at the far end of the pass where the dive boat was waiting for us. After we climbed aboard, the divemaster directed the driver to take us back to the mouth of the pass, this time to drop us further away to give more time to get down to our mark. This would not be a text book dive. Descending to eighty feet so soon after surfacing put us all into decompression mode because none of us had stopped on the way up to rid ourselves of excess nitrogen.

Like skydivers attempting to hit a target on a windy day, this time we managed to drift into the required area where we each quickly grabbed onto a piece of dead coral. The piece my fingers landed on was so small, that it didn't allow for the use of my whole hand but forced me instead, to hold myself in place using only a finger grip. I was not very secure but I was hesitant to seek a second handhold because if I missed, I would be swept out the pass again and might knock the others from their grips.

As we lay secured at the bottom of the pass, our knuckles whitening under the pressure of our tight grips on the coral, we looked across the channel towards the expected congregation of sharks.

We were a day late! The mating season had ended. The sharks had left.

A REEF TAKES ANOTHER

We had first seen *Gipsy Moth IV* during a visit to Greenwich, England in 2004 where she had sat forlornly in a dreary concrete dry dock for thirty-seven years. Abandoned in her drab tomb of concrete, it appeared as though she had been placed there for lack of anywhere else to put her. I doubt whether many visitors had given her a second glance; her dirty hull and peeling paint camouflaged any indication of her celebrity. Only those who knew the incredible story of Sir Francis Chichester, who had left Plymouth in 1966 to sail her single handedly in what was then, the fastest ever around-the-world voyage in a small yacht (53 feet/19 metres)—29,500 miles in 226 days—would ever have taken the time to glance her way.

Imagine our surprise when we saw her sitting just down the dock from us in the Renaissance Marina in Aruba eighteen months later. The wooden ketch had been restored to celebrate the fortieth anniversary of Chichester's epic voyage. The United Kingdom Sailing Association, UKSA, a registered charity and nonprofit organization, had purchased the yacht and then launched a campaign to save the ketch. When we met up with *Gipsy Moth IV* in Aruba, she was on her way to join the Blue Water Rally fleet in the San Blas Islands, just as we were. Weeks later, the BWR fleet rendezvoused in Rangiroa.

We had just returned from a day trip to a small island inside Rangiroa's lagoon. The anchorage at Motu Nao Nao had been too exposed to weather and we returned to where we had been anchored just hours before, just off the Rangiroa Hotel. Not long before, other Blue Water Rally boats had been anchored there but most had moved out of the lagoon and were now en route to Papeete, Tahiti, 235 nm away. Around 1600 we saw *Gipsy Moth IV* pull up anchor and leave the lagoon as she too, was headed for Papeete.

Our friends aboard *Carpe Diem*, who were sailing independent of the BWR, had arrived in Rangiroa and we invited them for cocktails at 1800. We were sailing similar routes and when we had the opportunity, we enjoyed sharing travel stories.

It's rare that we should receive a call through our satellite telephone. The phone was costly to use and we reserved it for emergency calls and e-mail. But at 1900 hours that evening, while sharing hors d'oeuvres and drinks with our friends, it rang. Mike answered and heard a young boy frantically announce, "This is *Gipsy Moth*, we're in trouble! We've hit a reef. We need help!" Mike immediately requested their coordinates. After noting them as 14°55' S, 147°49' W, the phone went dead. Mike called back but no one answered.

A boat named *Black Bird* had been in the anchorage all day. Mike radioed the yacht to find out which boats had left just prior to *Gipsy Moth IV*. When we learned the boats were *Onyva*, and *WhiteWings*, an Oyster 485, Mike radioed them relaying *Gipsy Moth IV's* coordinates with the message they had gone aground on a reef and were in need of assistance. Upon receiving the coordinates, both boats turned back towards the vicinity of the grounding and reported seeing a flare. At the time, neither *Gipsy Moth IV's* VHF nor SSB radios were in working order.

Glenn, the French speaking captain aboard *Onyva* proceeded to put out a mayday relay call on his VHF radio which was soon picked up by local authorities. Antonia, the skipper of *Gipsy Moth IV* called us again on the satellite phone to confirm their situation. Because their radios were not working, she didn't know until Mike informed her, that *Onyva* and *White Wings* had turned back to offer assistance and that a local rescue effort was in progress. Antonia confirmed the crew was in no immediate danger.

Gipsy Moth IV had run aground in the roaring surf of Rangiroa's reef. The nearest village, Avatoru, was several miles away. At the time of the grounding, the wild coastline was in complete darkness and could not be visually detected.

Once aground, *Gipsy Moth IV* continued to be driven over the coral platform by breaking surf until she was less than 90 metres (300 feet) from shore, but due to the blackness of the night and the fact there were no lights on shore, the crew and passengers had no idea that it was so near. Even if they had been aware of that fact, there would be no way of knowing whether they could reach the shore without the assistance of a rescue team. Waves continued to break over the reef, then slam broadside into their grounded boat.

When the local gendarmerie received news that a boat was on the reef, they manned two small fishing boats and travelled to the site. The challenge in reaching *Gipsy Moth IV* was made even more complex because there was only a small amount of moonlight to assist in the rescue. This placed the rescuers in jeopardy. The village rescuers radioed *Onyva* requesting they relay the instructions to *Gipsy Moth IV* that the crew was to disembark from the grounded yacht and walk across the reef. This would require the crew to step into the aftermath of foaming breakers while surf broke behind them in forceful rage but the rescue members believed this could be done. The rescue boat planned to meet them on the lagoon side.

And so it came about on this moonless night, with the surf crashing behind her, Linda, the *Yachting Monthly's* journalist aboard *Gipsy Moth IV* volunteered to test the possibility of walking to shore. She told us later how frightened she had been to push her way through knee deep water, blindly shuffling each foot along the uneven, partially submerged reef, while keeping her balance and not knowing if the next step would cause her to plunge off a ledge into a chaos of turbulent waters.

By 2100 hours the crew had safely made it to shore and were taken to the local police station where they were put up for the night.

The rescue that night had been carried out by a night-duty policeman, the mayor of the village and local fishermen, who had driven two small boats to the site through a current-riddled pass.

Antonia, the skipper, did not go ashore that night but stayed onboard alone. It must have been horrifying for her to hear the deafening roar of approaching surf; the creaking, the groaning and shuddering of loosening bulkheads as the hull gyrated against the stone-hard coral. Antonia's purpose in staying onboard was to protect the boat from local salvage. It is not uncommon that a vessel, which has run aground and then abandoned, be stripped of everything by morning.

It's not far from here that Thor Heyerdahl's *Kon-Tiki* raft smashed to pieces in similar surf in 1947.

WE STAYED IN Rangiroa two extra days to be available to *Gipsy Moth IV* in case additional shore assistance was needed, but the UKSA had mobilized support resources from Tahiti and were already working on launching her rescue from the reef. At 1800 in the evening of the second day following the tragedy, we left through a different pass than the one we had entered the lagoon. Here too, just outside the pass, two boats sat wrecked and abandoned on the beach.

EN route to Tahiti, we sailed parallel to the coast, staying well beyond the reef but near enough to get a glimpse of where *Gipsy Moth IV* still lay grounded. Forty minutes from the pass, we located her at the coordinates that had been frantically called to us two days before. She was lying on her starboard side at a seventy degree heel while waves bashed into her beam. A shelter had been erected on the beach for the skipper and mate, and it appeared that three or four people were attempting to remove items from the boat and carry them ashore. We later learned that salvage experts had been summoned from Tahiti to pull *Gipsy Moth IV* from the reef, and tow her to Tahiti where she would be hoisted aboard a ship that was heading to New Zealand. While in New Zealand, repairs were carried out before she was freighted to Australia in time for celebrations attended by Princess Anne (daughter of Queen Elizabeth II and Prince Philip of Edinburgh), the patron of the UKSA.

TAHITI, BORA BORA

Tahiti was the fulfillment of a sailor's dream, a dream as old as the legend of the Sirens. And that was also the beginning of the Tahitians' downfall.
David Howarth
Tahiti, A Paradise Lost

There is little in Tahiti, the largest of the Society Islands (Îles de la Société) that wants to devour you: no beasts of prey, no tormenting insects; even the scorpion exists without poison. It's no wonder the first Europeans who landed here fell in love with the island.

When Europeans arrived, (and exactly when that happened is unclear except to say it was in the first half of the 17th century), Tahitians lived mostly in the outlying Windward Islands. In the 1960s, France developed a nuclear testing site 1,200 miles south of Tahiti. The first nuclear test explosion contaminated countries as far away as Peru and New Zealand. In 1974, protests forced the French to explode bombs underground. The results and activities from these nuclear experiments drove islanders from their homes in the southern islands, to the city of Papeete, today's capital of French Polynesia, located on the island of Tahiti.

Our plan was for an early morning arrival in Tahiti, but conditions en route were ideal for passage making and we arrived in the dark. Fortunately, the pass through the reef is well marked. A set of leading lights guide boats into the outer bay, then into Papeete's interior basin where we dropped anchor while backing stern-to against a concrete wall, Mediterranean style.*

A NEWLY built wharf had been constructed along a park-like setting running adjacent to Boulevard Pomare at the base of the city, not far from a five lane highway. Who would have thought the first sounds of exotic Tahiti would be a speedway?

Whatever happened to that laid back, peace loving Polynesia and the exotic Tahiti we think of as the most serene island in the world? A get-away destination of blue skies, swaying palm trees and continuous soft, warm breezes where dark skinned people smile sincere welcomes beckoning you to their near perfect world. Where was this place spoken of by Captain Wallis aboard the HMS *Dolphin*, on May 29 1768, who wrote, "Tis impossible to describe the beautiful Prospects we beheld in this charming spot?"

It has been suggested that Tahitians lost their culture seventy-five years after the first European ship landed on the island. When the HMS *Dolphin* dropped anchor off Tahiti's shore in 1767, they were first intercepted by canoes of men throwing stones. It wasn't long before peace prevailed and crewmembers were able to trade buttons and beads for provisions and other favours.

Ships that followed were welcomed by canoes with hundreds of islanders including smiling, bare breasted women stretching arms and palms high in greeting. Canoes full of green breadfruit, stalks of yellow, ripe bananas and woven baskets filled with exotic fruits were delivered to the ships.

---

* At Tahiti as well as Moorea, located 22 nm west, visiting boats are required to register at the Yachtmaster's office (*Entrance Declaration*), regardless of whether they have already cleared into French Polynesia.

To the Tahitian, any need was a need to be catered to and they made no differentiation between the need for food and bodily needs. The Tahitians were a kind and generous people; they believed in giving to those who did not have. They had no reason to think anyone, white skinned or not, would be any different. This was a society, who had, according to David Howarth in his book *Tahiti, A Paradise Lost*, had "conceived a heaven but not yet a hell."

But it would not be long before they believed in both hell and sin. Thirty years later, the ship *Duff*, would arrive to deliver missionaries.

The same year the *Dolphin* discovered Tahiti, so did the French captain, Bougainville whose name is connected to the white flowered climbing shrub and who was, just a few years earlier, serving his leader, General Montcalm fighting for territory in Quebec, Canada.

Even though, in the following eighty years, the British were most influential in Tahiti, the country was never secured for Britain. Tahiti fell instead to the French.

Once the sextant had been invented in the mid-1700s, it enabled navigators to document positions and allowed others to follow in their wake. More ships visited the island and by 1840, Tahiti was irrevocably changed, and so was the bloodline of the people. What was left of Tahitian spirit, unselfish generosity, free love and innocent happiness, was all but lost. Even the dour missionaries after landing there were surprised to find such complacent people. These were not the savages they had imagined.

During the twentieth century, the island needed to increase its income and in 1960 an airport was constructed to encourage tourism. Where it once took six months to arrive at the island, it now takes only hours.

With the development of an airport, Papeete became the hub for surrounding islands, the place to source supplies, boat building, ship repairs and construction materials. A beer and soft drink enterprise was established. With progress, Tahitians lost their traditional way of life. The Polynesian hierarchy of ranked titles and chieftainship was replaced by a French class structure reflecting upper, middle and lower classes. Polynesians greet each other now by shaking hands and kissing each other on both cheeks.*

It seems fitting that Gauguin, who in 1897 painted what many consider to be his masterpiece, entitled the work— Where do we come from? What are we? Where are we going?

FROM the waterfront it was an easy stroll to the centre of downtown where we found a good French restaurant and an art gallery showing original Paul Gauguin paintings. In the evening, we'd return to enjoy chilled pilsners and full bodied lagers sitting around little tables in open windowed pubs while small bands rocked the bars with old favourites like *Surfin' USA* and *I'm a Believer*.

The waterfront had been rebuilt with money from a restructuring fund related to post nuclear testing. Besides a bandshell, a well-lit patio square offers locals a place to arrange their motorized restaurant-vans. Owners of the travelling restaurants arrive each evening to cook meals with supersized woks and portable barbeques. They put out an assortment of inexpensive plastic tables and aluminum chairs. The food trailers, known as *roulettes*, but more commonly referred to as 'roach coaches', offer everything from pizza, steak and French crepes to local Tahitian food, in an atmosphere of very casual dining. But in fact, French food

---

* With the loss of traditions came a ninety-eight percent literacy rate and a longer life expectancy.

dominates the island such as *canard à l'orange* and *poissons en sauce à la vanilla*. The island also has two fast food McDonald's restaurants.

PAPEETE was one of the meeting points for yachts sailing with the Blue Water Rally. A bus was organized to take the group on a sightseeing tour of the island. The entire coastal road measures only 117 km (71 mi.), but after four hours of sitting on the hard benches in an open-sided wooden motorbus known as *le truck*, that was as far as anyone would ever want to go.

From the mountaintops in the centre of the island, lush green-slopes cascade into gorges that rip through jungle growth, funneling rivers and streams towards the sea. Due to the lack of useable land, Tahitians do not live in concentrated villages but instead, are spread around the circumference of the island with homes backing onto breadfruit and coco forests set against the base of the mountain. A narrow coastal road follows the contour of the island, skirting the ocean where, in many areas, lapping waves lick the shoreline just metres from the road. There is little room for beaches except in the far southwest where the town of Teahupoo, (pronounced cho-po) lies. This is where the road ends.

Here, just off shore, in the wide span of open Pacific, high winds help to create waves of gigantic proportions. World renowned surfers take to the water in hopes Teahupoo, the heaviest wave in the world, will not disappoint them. Surfing has a long history here. Ma'ohi ancestors partook in the sports of javelin throwing, outrigger canoe racing and strongman stone lifting, but surfing was always the sport of kings. This is where the sport of surfing began. In early times it was called wave riding.

"Le truck" let us off at Point Venus, an extended width of black, sandy beach edging sprawling Matavai Bay. While the sun sets, stray dogs settle in for the night by digging shallow trenches that they nuzzle their bodies into to feel the warmth of the solar heated sands.

It was one of the broadest beaches I have ever stood on, and yet one of the least appreciated due to the colour of the sand. Although hundreds arrive daily at Tahiti's international airport, many head straight for Bora Bora where the island is strewn with white sandy beaches and busy resorts. Bora Bora is a forty-five minute flight from Tahiti.

Just off the beach, fishermen, paddling *pirogues* returned from their workday while teams of athletic rowers practiced competitive sculling drills. It was here at Point Venus, in 1769, Captain Cook accompanied by an eminent astronomer (Charles Green) and eight other scientists, came ashore from his ship the HMS *Endeavour* to track the transit of Venus and to apply astronomy. This was Cook's first voyage around the world. It was during a period when the Royal Society of London for the Improvement of Natural Knowledge (Royal Society), a prestigious club of scholars, was devoted to seeking a way to determine longitude so that a ship's navigator could define his position accurately while at sea. The procedure for determining latitude had already been established. The sextant had been invented but making calculations using the moon and certain stars was complicated and many captains were unable to use the instrument accurately. Captain Wallis, aboard the *Dolphin*, was an exception. His documentation of Tahiti's location just months earlier, allowed Cook to find the island.

Establishing longitude involves, time. No timepiece had been invented that was capable of keeping accurate time, especially a device that could withstand the trials of a ship's pounding motion.

The observatory at Greenwich, England, had been founded ninety-three years earlier, when scientists from around the world worked to find a solution to determine a ship's accurate position. Most believed the solution would be found in either an accurate timepiece that would not lose or gain time while being carried aboard ships, or in mapping the universe with all its stars and moons.

Cook had been sent to Tahiti because Edmond Halley, an English astronomer whose name we are familiar with because of the comet named after him, predicted before he died, that the planet Venus would pass directly between the sun and the earth in that year and by taking sightings at strategically determined places around the globe, one could determine the distance between the earth and the sun. While scientists stood on Point Venus, other astronomers and scientists were scattered around the world in seventy other locations recording the exact same scientific sighting. With these combined calculations, it was possible to calculate the distance of Earth from the sun and thereby establish a basis for astronomy and navigation.

We could not find a plaque to commemorate Cook's landing, however, erected in a shady part of the Point was a large sculpture in the shape of a ship's bow commemorating the arrival of the London Missionary Society,* in 1797. The sculpture represented the British vessel *Duff* that had brought missionaries to the island from England. They came here for the purpose of saving the souls of the Tahitian savage. Seventeen evangelists including five wives and three children were let off to experience a new life here on Matavai Bay where, through the generosity of the islanders, they were allowed to set up their first home. However, it was years before any Tahitian adopted Christianity.

---

* The London Missionary Society, a non-denominational society, was formed in England in 1795, by evangelical Anglicans and Nonconformists.

During the years in which Christianity attempted to take hold, objects associated with ancient gods were destroyed while new religions, Protestant and Catholic, slowly became powerful organizations. Today Tahiti has very few tikis or religious sites or even evidence of ancient culture.

Following our island tour, we sauntered back to the boat to discover *Baccalieu III* was not lying on her anchor stern-to the wharf as we had left her, but instead, was neatly tied broadside to the dock. While gone, our anchor had dragged.

Rally members had taken charge of her rescue by lifting the anchor and securing her alongside the dock. We realized, having arrived late and tired the night before, we had not set the anchor properly. We were lucky *Baccalieu III* had not hit any other boats, and doubly lucky to have had caring people who took the time to secure her.

Two basic needs requiring replenishing onboard *Baccalieu III* were diesel fuel and propane gas. We were efficient with generating our own electric power and making water. We never ran out of fuel or propane although this required some planning and constant watching of gauges. In Spain, we had to refill our propane bottles with camping gas and in Tonga they were filled with butane. In another location, we had to swap the propane regulator for one that fit a local filling system. Now that I was using my trusty breadmaker as a little oven, I was using far less propane. To avoid depleting our batteries, I often timed using the breadmaker when the generator was recharging the batteries.

While in Papeete, Mike and Rok attempted to find a filling station to refill an empty propane tank. Climbing into the dinghy and placing the tank on the floor, they proceeded across the harbour to where they believed the station was located. Papeete is home to a small naval fleet consisting of a few surveillance frigates and patrol vessels. While travelling across the bay, a French naval ship, maneuvering within the basin, directed a message to them through a loud hailer. However, neither Mike nor Rok understand much of the French language. Unable to interpret the words, they continued racing towards their destination, curious about the navy's contact but unconcerned. The second time they heard French blasting through the hailer they thought it sounded a bit more urgent. They finally recognized that the navy was uneasy watching a dinghy travelling at high speed while carrying a possibly explosive propane tank towards their naval base. Wisely they turned back, and approached the propane station from another direction.

Papeete offered wonderful places to provision. In the Municipal Market (Marché de Pape'ete), tables were overflowing with colourful arrays of fresh vegetables and juicy ripened fruits. An assortment of whole fish and freshly carved meats lay displayed on hunks of ice in butcher's showcases. Upstairs, vendors displayed carved tikis, wooden bowls, T-shirts, straw hats and locally made jewelry. On Saturday mornings, from four to eight, farmers joined regular market vendors and brought fresh basil, thyme, lettuce, tomatoes, wild chestnuts the size of a person's fist, presses to extract juice from stalks of sugarcane, freshly baked breads, pastries, cooked and seasoned chicken, pulled pork, sausages scented with garlic and bottled home cure remedies. We returned to the boat fully loaded.

At a Carrefour hypermarket, located just outside the city, we left with a check-out tape that was a metre and a half long, proof that it had been a long time since we had seen such choices. 'Buy it when you can', was my motto because I never knew when I might see the product again. Besides, we were headed for several more remote South Pacific islands.

When we returned to the boat by taxi, the driver warned us not to leave our merchandise unattended on the dock while loading it onto the boat because the local 'bad boys' would quickly scoop it up if we gave them a moment's opportunity. Just a few nights before, our friend Christoph Rassy aboard *Bamsen*, an 18.9 metre (62 foot) Hallberg Rassy, was sleeping when he discovered two men had boarded his boat and were inside collecting items from his salon. Christoph, a great big German fellow with a voice the sound of a base drum, had no trouble scaring them off. But later that same night, after he had returned to bed, he heard footsteps again. He looked out to see the same young men standing on his deck, surveying other possible opportunities for theft. It was for this reason that in certain locations, we lifted our passerelle at night securing it into place like an opened drawbridge, which deterred unwanted visitors.

Shortly after this incident the city supplied the Rally yachts with twenty-four hour security.

BEFORE leaving Port Papeete (Port Autonome de Papeete), it was necessary to radio airport control requesting permission to use the channel. Sailing masts could interfere with low flying aircraft.

It was evident that the Chenal de Faa was a common practice area for serious canoe and kayak paddlers. Spotting our boat entering the channel, two men, paddling single man *va'a*, (Tahitian outrigger canoes) fell in behind *Baccalieu III*, and in an attempt to catch up, positioned their boats in our wake. Plunging their paddles into the water with continuous rapid strokes, they manipulated their blades in precise movements. Heads down, faces taught with determination, they forged ahead, never once letting up. Lifting and pulling again and again, their hands directed the shafts of their paddles alongside their small crafts. With short paddling rhythms they moved faster and faster, making real but small gains. Several minutes went by. Nearer and nearer they came until they were right alongside us! We never for a moment had throttled back on engine power.

They stayed with us, stroking the water with the necessary speed and frequency to stay positioned just off our beam, every now and again requesting that we relay the numbers displayed on our analogue speed instrument. From the moment they had taken up the challenge to overtake us and then stay alongside, we had been motoring a steady six knots!

These were no doubt serious racers, members of Tahiti's Outrigger Canoe Club, who take part in world class races so refined that they use security cameras on their start lines to judge false starts when well over five hundred va'a leave the start in unison. Our paddling companions were practicing for both the Te Aito, a twenty-one-year old competition that is now recognized worldwide, and the Super Aito race, staged between Tahiti and the island of Moorea, a distance of twenty-two miles.

When we reached the point where we needed to turn away, we threw them each an ice cold Coca Cola. They were so profusely thankful you would have thought we had presented them with the prestigious Super Aito trophy.

Moorea, Huahine and Raiatea, three small islands in the Society grouping, are relatively near to one another. We stopped at all three.

We anchored first in Cook's Bay, a large natural harbour in Moorea (Mo'orea) with the clearest most sparkling water imaginable. Green covered mountains fall away into valleys running deep into a dark interior of jungle. Moorea is a dreamer's fantasy island, an island you can escape to and discover the same ambience that enveloped it a hundred years ago, apart from the topless Polynesian women and half naked men. It is thought that this island is the backdrop for James Michener's *Bali Hai*.

Never, had I heard roosters crow so relentlessly at midday and even I, the most avid animal lover, could have easily wrung their necks. It sounded as if we were anchored in the middle of a hen's brothel! We learned that cock fighting was a popular island sport and I can confirm there are roosters on Moorea that carry some serious clout. There was one that I saw that I would have no problem using as a watchdog.

Europeans have come here to express art on canvas and with clay. There is lovely pottery to be purchased on Moorea, sculpted by those who landed here searching for freedom, a place where they would not be judged or require a timetable.

Many who have come here from foreign countries married local women. Marriage to Polynesian women allows foreigners to own land and open businesses on the island. They might never have the need to return to crowded cities other than to make use of art galleries to sell their work. Even here you need money to survive.

The island is lush, serene, perhaps even mystical in its unhurried manner. Bora Bora is often described as the most beautiful island in French Polynesia, but my vote goes to Moorea, which is far more beautiful and far more tranquil.

With no central town, its houses and shops lie strung along a narrow, coastal road squeezed between the mountains and the shore. Palm trees gracing the shoreline stand ringed with aluminum trunk bands protecting the trees from coconut-devouring rats and crabs. Small wooden boxes, resembling mailboxes, stand erect in front of each bamboo house, not for mail, but to receive the delivery of fresh bread—and not just once, but two times daily.

One morning, while driving around the island, we stopped

to pick up a loaf of bread at a roadside bakery and restaurant. The bakery was a popular breakfast spot where locals sat on stools at counters eating, not traditional Polynesian foods of pork in curry and coconut sauces, but huge plates of hamburgers and deep fried chicken. In many South Pacific islands, large physiques are thought to be attractive, unless they are young, competitive Polynesian dancers.

Our drive around the island took us through endless acres of wild forests, past small banana, pineapple and vanilla plantations to Belvedere Lookout which presents the two deep bays of the island, Cook and Opunohu, both guarded by twin jagged mountain pinnacles locally known as Shark's Teeth. The island is fertile supporting a wide variety of fruits and vegetables and aptly is home to a small juice factory selling fruit brandies and twenty-five proof coconut, and ginger liquors. Tahitian Drink, an alcoholic beverage sold in cartons throughout Polynesia combines the flavours of pineapple, oranges and passion fruit which is then spiced with island vanilla.

Each Polynesian island celebrates a legend accounting for its existence. Moorea is said to have been formed from the second dorsal fin of a fish, and the name, Moorea, meaning 'yellow lizard', was chosen by a high priest who once dreamt of a yellow lizard. Huahine, one hundred miles from Moorea, received its name from its mountainous outline viewed from the sea. In the eyes of early Polynesian natives, the island resembled a reclining woman. *Hine* means woman and *hua* translates to phallus.

Huahine, pronounced *wah-ee-nee* by visitors and *who-ahee-nay* by locals, was first settled around AD 850. Although only 74 square kilometres (45 square. miles), the island is home to more than ninety maraes, some now restored. The island remains one of the most important Polynesian locations for archeological ruins.

A channel between reef and shore allowed for anchoring in calm, aquamarine and emerald water where stingrays skimmed over the ocean's floor beneath our hull. With pulsating wing-like bodies, they stroked across the colourless sand in graceful flight like gentle, opaque waves.

Huahine is one of the least developed of the French Society islands. Wild in nature, manicured shoulders along the roads display a sense of island pride. Sitting on seats in the back of a pickup truck, our tour guide Poco introduced the island and stopped at one of several vanilla farms. The vanilla plant had its origins in Mexico where only a species of Mexican bee has capabilities of pollinating the flower. In order that the plant receives pollinating anywhere outside of Mexico, each blossom must be pollinated by hand. It was a twelve-year-old slave on Réunion Island, an island in the Indian Ocean, who discovered in the early 1800s how to hand-pollinate the blooms allowing for global cultivation of the plant. The high cost of pure natural vanilla is due to the necessity to use a small narrow stick to open the flap of each vanilla bloom then transfer the pollen from the anther of one plant to the stigma of the other with the use of the thumb.

Poco drove us to visit four hundred year old fish traps, a set-up made of simple stone constructed channels winding with labyrinth confusion where fish are unable to find their escape. The centre of the labyrinths are shaded by thatched roofs where still today, villagers sit while fishing.

As we climbed higher in the mountains in Poco's truck, driving deeper into the forested crater, small herds of well-fed wild horses grazed alongside the smoothly paved road. In the distance, waterfalls plunged from thousand foot high ledges surrounded by densely treed escarpments. The higher we climbed the more religious sites we came upon although most now are obscured by fast growing, smothering vines. Wild vanilla plants and forests including hundreds of introduced and endemic species blanketed the hillsides.

Down in the valley, robust blue-eyed eels, thrive in a mountain stream beneath a bridge. Islanders believe the eels are sacred and wade into the stream to fondle their slimy, squirming, dark brown bodies while feeding them canned mackerel that has been blessed by the local priest. The first eel in their mythological creation story once left a pool in north Tahiti to crawl across a vast mountain range to arrive in Huahine. Here, according to the myth, the eel courted a beautiful maiden from whom the present day inhabitants have descended.

THE town of Fare, with its tree lined boulevard and its main street running along the quay, is an attractive, working man's town where the pace is slow and the local policeman doubles as the mailman.

A well-stocked grocery, and a small clothing and hardware store with dirt or gravel floors, border the main street. A bakery sells long loaves of French bread and take-away sandwiches filled with mixtures of beans and French fries. An outdoor fresh fruit and vegetable market along the waterfront is a popular place for locals to gather and gossip on Fridays, when farmers come in from their small garden plots to sell produce and eggs from the back of their trucks. From here, loads of crated fruits and vegetables leave on coastal ships to be ferried to other islands.

THE ISLAND OF Raiatea, (Ra'iātea) is the second largest of French Polynesia. When we arrived at Uturoa's small town dock to take on fuel, the docks were bustling with visitors. Boasting only a small harbour, Uturoa holds great importance to the surrounding islands. People arrive to catch ferries to outlying islands and small container ships let their cargo off here. Coastal freighters then reload with provisions to be delivered to the more remote islands.

The main street of Uturoa is lined with numerous Chinese-owned stores. The Chinese population so monopolizes the retail trade within the islands that when Tahitians speak of going shopping, they say they are going to *La Chine*.

We hiked Tapioi Hill, a steep incline leading through pastureland with grazing horses and ferocious looking bulls standing guard over their herds. At the top, a grand view of islands and islets, hugging reefs and twisting sandbars, strewn among an ocean's palate of aqua and turquoise blues.

It was one of the best views of the reef system we would see while visiting French Polynesian.

Moreover, the stop-off in Raiatea was significant because fuel was available duty free. We happened to have had a customs officer in Tahiti who was well-informed and served us with the necessary papers to obtain it with. Later, we heard from several of our friends that many of them could not obtain the fuel duty free because they had not possessed the correct documents.

From Raiatea, you can see Bora Bora's dormant volcanic peaks drifting like magical islands on the horizon. There is only one pass to navigate in the approach to Bora Bora, where sapphire coloured waters are famous for their tropical hues. From a distance, the island is quite beautiful, but up close, we found it to be overrun with busy resorts, although the multitude of stilted *bures* built over the water does make a pretty picture.

The letter B does not exist in the Polynesian language and Bora Bora was originally known to Polynesians as Pora Pora. The name, meaning the first born, was misheard by the first foreign visitors who thought they heard Bora Bora and essentially rechristened it as such.

The island has been successfully marketed as a honeymooner's paradise, where young newlyweds fill numerous thatched bungalow-style hotels scattered around the island and pay hundreds of dollars a night for the experience. But everything in Bora Bora is outrageously expensive: 1,900 CFP ($17 US) for thirty-five minutes at an internet café, 1,430 CFP ($13 US) for a four pack of Danone yogurt and 3,300 CFP ($30 US) for one beer and a cheese and tomato sandwich! T-shirt shops sell low quality shirts for 3,000 CFP ($27 US). Numerous black pearl shops, where you can personally select each pearl and then have them set into earrings, pendants or strung into necklaces are scattered along the dusty, pot holed main street.

We walked into a classy, high-end jewelry store to learn more about how to choose quality pearls. We were their only customers and we were invited to take a seat at a highly polished French provincial desk located in front of two brightly lit display cases. The smooth, scarlet coloured carpet made me feel a bit like royalty although at this point in our travels, I looked far from regal. A tall, slim man, dressed in Gucci-casual, brought out a selection of pearls, each lying in its own little compartmentalized drawer. Selecting each rounded pearl with a pair of dainty pearl-tweezers, he placed them before us one by one on a plush velvet tray. We felt severely under-dressed in our well-worn shorts and sandals while in the presence of this pearl specialist, and I hoped he would not notice that one of Mike's sandals was coming detached from the sole.

Since the top half of the sandal had split from the sole a few days before, Mike had been walking around with it flapping as if it was a talking shoe while it often scooped up sand.

Following our session on pearl quality, we stood to leave

and the sole of Mike's shoe caught the chair causing it to flick a sizable amount of sand, like an oversized peppershaker, not only over the pristine carpet, but also to the desktop where the pearls lay. We stood there, peering down at the elegant European style desk where the pearls were resting on red velvet, but were now sprinkled with grains of sand. I thought the sand added a sort of arty-elegant-casual look but I'm not sure the proprietors would have agreed. After much apologizing, we turned to slink out of the store, Mike swinging his right leg forward rather stiffly to avoid leaving anymore sand behind.

We heard that diving in Bora Bora's popular lagoon might mean seeing more divers than fish. This natural habitat of manta rays and the friendly Napoleon Wrasse, one of the largest coral reef fish in the world (with males weighing in excess of 400 pounds), has been seriously compromised due to the lack of fishing regulations and the construction of over-the-water resort bures.

We were lucky enough to meet the owner of a dive shop who was planning to make a dive in deeper waters and invited us to join him. We would need to use Nitrox, a mixture of air containing higher concentrations of oxygen allowing a diver to stay down for longer periods of time. Using larger tanks with Nitrox, we would be capable of staying at 27 m (90 ft.) for a total dive time of fifty-five minutes. Legally, divers are required to hold a certification in Nitrox but the owner relaxed his policy. We did not hold the necessary certification, an impediment that was overcome due to our dive history, and the fact that we were diving with Jennifer and Rok who were not only qualified Nitrox divers but certified diving instructors.

It was the end of the rainy season and cold southerly winds had roughened the seas, creating difficult conditions for a diver when on the surface. Heavy seas could impede the dive boat from locating us among windblown waves and the owner took a high-powered spotlight into the water to signal our location when we surfaced. Boarding during rough seas always puts a diver in danger of being crushed by the overhang of the stern when it plunges into troughs. In rough conditions, divers float just off the stern while timing the heave of the transom, and then attempt to board a semi-submerged ladder without getting clunked by it.

WE were getting a bit jaded. It was harder and harder to find dive sites that satisfied our curiosity or offered unique experiences. In fact, during our diving careers, we had already dived three of the seven underwater areas officially known as 'wonders of the underwater world'.[*] But the water off Bora Bora was a balmy 30°C (86°F) and hard to resist.

Large schools of barracuda, reef sharks, manta eagle rays and the largest sea turtle we had ever seen, perhaps measuring a metre wide, swam unconcerned not far from us. A school of stocky, robust and curious lemon sharks, with a far greater tendency to approach divers than some species, came in for a closer look. It was our first experience swimming with lemon sharks and knowing they were analyzing the electrical currents created from our beating hearts was unnerving. They continued to circle, scanning us with disturbing intensity. Their tail fins sweep almost motionlessly in docile manner but the penetrating stare from white, unblinking eyes was unsettling. I knew one thing for sure, because I had witnessed this

---

[*] According to *Conservation, Education, Awareness and Marine research* (CEDAM), the Seven Wonders of the Underwater World include the Barrier Reef in Belize, Galápagos Islands, Reef (and Wrecks, Chuuk-Truuk Lagoon) off Papua New Guinea (listed by *National Post* as one of the most extreme dives in the world), Great Barrier Reef, Australia, Deep Sea Vents, Ecuador, Northern Red Sea, Africa, and Lake Baikal, Russia.

We had dived the first three sites, and we would dive the Great Barrier Reef before completing our circumnavigation.

with other shark species. If a shark needs to move quickly while targeting a potential meal, it can instantly propel itself with shocking speed, and then abruptly stop while tearing its prey apart, gulping whole pieces of bulky flesh so rapidly it can be a frightening experience to witness even if you are not the victim. A diver has little defense against sharks other than turning away to present the steel air tank on his back as a barricade, or backing into a substantial piece of coral if available and tapping the shark on the snout if they should get that close. I could never imagine myself stretching my hand towards a jaw full of teeth, but those are the two pitiful defense options for a diver when threatened.

Following the dive, I was sitting in the dive shop when I came upon an article in a magazine detailing habits of sharks. The magazine mentioned sharks were attracted to bright colours. I began to reflect on my twenty-year old black dive suit with four-inch florescent pink stripes running down each side. Suddenly I pictured myself looking like a giant fishing lure. Even my fins were florescent pink!

WE stayed in Bora Bora one week, moving to various anchorages in the lagoon. One night, while anchored not far from a shore reef, we experienced some of the worst weather ever to hit us while at anchor.

Three full squalls shot through, one after the other, carrying forty knot winds while rain drove past in sheets. In no time, three-foot waves developed within the lagoon.

High winds turned boats every-which direction, spinning them in circles around their anchors, a movement that threatens to pull them loose. Soon spreader lights illuminated most boat decks across the bay. One after another small concentrations of light shone down from masts in focused vectors. Single shadowed figures walked towards the bow where, they stopped to check the well-being of their anchors. Over and over again this occurred throughout the night, lights flipping on across the bay at irregular intervals.

All night we monitored our anchor location on the chart plotter and kept a lookout through the ports for potential problems. The boats we really had to worry about were those that showed no on-deck activity at all.

FOLLOWING Jennifer and Rok's departure from *Baccalieu III*, Mike and I spent our remaining time in Bora Bora tied to a mooring ball outside a restaurant named the Bora Bora Yacht Club. The mooring was free if we ate at their restaurant, which served expensive, but excellent, food. One day, Norwegian friends sailing a boat named *Blackbird* sailed into the bay with a crippled motor. At the time, there were no vacant mooring buoys and they put down their anchor not far from us. Two days later, when a mooring buoy became available they asked if we would tow them with our twenty-five horse powered dinghy to the buoy.

After knotting the towline into a bridle, we commenced towing their 14.6 m (48 ft.) Bavaria to the buoy. Our friends were not aware that our dinghy had experienced endless problems including complete motor failures. At the time of enlisting the tow, the dinghy was having problems with its gear shift including the steering cable, and it would always turn towards the right. But we were keen to help so we said nothing regarding our disabled circumstances and took up the challenge to move them.

The dinghy had a jockey seat running down the middle, which we straddled as though we were riding a Sea Doo. We steered with a steering wheel and changed gears with a lever located on the console. Lacking a power start, the motor needed cranking with a cord. Under the current conditions, we now had to sit on one of the side pontoons rather than on the seat, pull on a rope that we had attached to the motor in order to help steer it, while keeping a hand forward, near the steering wheel, to regulate the throttle. I could barely reach both at the same time and then I could hardly see where I was going if I managed the required athletic stretch. It put me in a position whereby my head had no other choice but to be tilted towards the floor. When we needed to shift gears, it was necessary to stand, leaning over the engine to push the gearshift on the motor. This meant we often cut our fingers since it had never been meant to be used manually. We had many times entertained the locals with sudden bursts of engine power when we yanked on the pull cord unable to determine whether the gear shift was in neutral or locked into gear. Once we had run up on a shore reef and another time, we ran straight into a concrete wall. The local kids had given us a standing ovation during the last maneuver.

While in town one day on Bora Bora, we walked to a Yamaha dealer on the outskirts hoping someone there could look at our dinghy. The two mechanics agreed. As they walked towards their pickup truck, I assumed that I would sit in the front cab with them and I followed on their heels. But while the mechanic took hold of his door handle with one hand, he made a firm gesture towards the back of the truck with the other. I looked at him questioningly. Me? In the back?

Throughout our travels, there had been many times we had seen locals transported in the rear of pickup trucks, balancing on the side panels, or even standing. Catching sight of this, I would often cluck my tongue over how dangerous it was for people to travel back there. But receiving my directions of where I was to ride, I thought perhaps I could sit on the floor and brace myself against the cab wall. But the bottom was covered in a rainbow coloured oil slick. So, while positioning our butts on the edge of the box, we white knuckled it back into town and I can attest to the fact that Bora

Bora's roads were among the worst we had seen on any island and the worst my derrière would ever experience.

In the end, the mechanics didn't have access to parts for our model of engine and could do nothing to solve our problems.

So there we were towing *Blackbird* and crew, who were unaware of our mechanical disorders, when they threw us that towing line. Our first challenge was to get the sailboat moving from a dead stop which was like trying to drag a donkey off its haunches. We gunned the engine forward, but of course we swung right. We hailed a passing dinghy, equipped with an even smaller motor than we possessed, to push against our bow so we could keep driving in a straight line. For some reason the dinghy tugboat failed to do the job and we flagged down a second dinghy that didn't do any better. What was wrong with these people I wondered?

We were not being efficient and all this was taking place just to get *Black Bird* near enough to her buried anchor so that the crew could raise it. Stubbornly, *Blackbird* slowly moved forward until she was over the spot where her anchor was located. But having arrived there under such duress, *Blackbird's* crew announced they would prefer hoisting their sail and attempting to sail to the mooring ball, rather than depending on our assistance.

The next day, one of them, looking quite somber, told me in all seriousness they were going to give me lessons on how to drive a dinghy!

We waited for a good weather forecast before setting out on the next leg of our journey towards Rarotonga in the Cook Islands. Before leaving, I went up the mast to replace the anchor light that had just been replaced by Jennifer a few days prior. Both David and Jennifer have been enlisted for the job because they can reach the light, which sits on the very top of the mast, while sitting in the bosun's chair, whereas I cannot reach it without standing on collapsible mast steps, raising me out of the bosun's seat.

Up until now, I had not been able to muster enough courage to complete the maneuver even though I had been up the mast on numerous occasions, carrying out small repair jobs. This time I was determined to meet the challenge and reach the equipment fastened at the top.

Once up as high as the bosun's chair would take me, I folded down the collapsible mast steps. Positioning my feet on the steps, on either side of the mast, I folded like an accordion; my knees nearly touching my chest. Without wearing a harness that would prevent an accidental fall, I took the weight on my feet and pulled myself up out of the chair. My heart hammered against my ribs. My waist was now even with the top of the masthead. From this position the masthead was too low for me to wrap my arms around, but I was able to press my elbows into it and install the light.

The mast stands seventy-five feet above the water and a light breeze, flowing through the anchorage, was causing the boat to sway. From such a vantage point I'll admit I had a tremendous view of the anchorage. I could see for miles unobstructed. But I was elbow-hugging the mast so tightly I wasn't sure if I still owned a set of arms and the swaying mast wasn't doing much for my equilibrium either. I looked down at the deck, to what appeared to be miniature-sized winches and ant-sized cleats. I communicated that the light bulb was in place.

Mike yelled up, "We should test it. I'm going to turn on the anchor light," and he went below to switch it on. The anchor light was working. All's good, I thought, I can get down. But the light has more than one function and Mike again shouted that he was now going to turn on the navigation lights. He disappeared below again.

Just turn the damn thing on, I thought, I don't need to know WHAT you're turning on, I can see it, my nose is pressed up against the bloody light!

Weeks later, I purchased a climbing harness that would prevent an accidental fall from the top of the mast.

COOK ISLANDS (RAROTONGA), NIUE, TONGA

Culture is multi-layered, like an onion—a system that can be peeled, layer by layer, in order to reveal the content

GEERT HOFSTEDE

WE WANTED TO arrive in Tonga fourteen hundred miles away, in three weeks' time in order to take part in a Blue Water Rally function. We contemplated making a stop in Rarotonga in the Cook Islands while en route. However, to visit Rarotonga, we would need to sail further south than was necessary to reach Tonga. There were no guarantees that once we arrived in Rarotonga that docking space would even be available in the small harbour or that a north wind would not have turned the harbour into a formidable wave pool.

There are no bays or inlets along the coast, only the small northerly exposed harbour at Avarua (Avatiu Harbour) which supports a few local fishing boats and the occasional coastal freighter. We might spend several additional days sailing to find, upon arrival, there was either no room for docking or conditions in the harbour were too rough to stay.

When we left Bora Bora the forecast called for north winds which made bypassing Rarotonga the sensible decision. But for the first two days of travel, we sailed a compromised course allowing us the option to divert to Rarotonga.

On the third day, a new forecast indicated winds would

swing east making it likely that conditions in the harbour would be good. Whether room was available would remain a question until we got there. We turned south and headed for Rarotonga the largest of the Cook Islands. Due to light winds, we motor-sailed most of the five hundred and twenty-five miles. But the night sky was a wondrous sight. Full of stars, it appeared to stretch beyond the horizon. It was as if we could see the outline of the earth's sphere curving with roundness. The clearest of the stars, those almost touching the horizon, often forced me to reach for the binoculars so that I could rule out that they were in fact stars and not navigation lights from a distant boat. But no ships ever came into view. We were alone in a vast ocean.

THE MORNING OF our arrival, the sun rose much the same way it went down the evening before, like cylinders of orange light puncturing through the clouds. Thirty miles out, I spotted Rarotonga on the radar screen. Drawing nearer exposed an island covered in mountain peaks. Resembling a feathery light, green meringue pie topping, the island was incredibly beautiful. When the sunrise added its colour of ginger, I thought the extra miles to reach it was worth the reward just to witness its' sighting.

The land mass of the Cook Islands including all fifteen surrounding islands and atolls, totals only 384 square kilometres, (150 square miles). But they're spread over an area of almost two million square kilometres (700,000 square miles). They're not only remote to the rest of the world but they are remote to each other.

Rarotonga has 32 kilometres (20 miles) of coastline. It was the first of the Cook Islands to be settled. Most Rarotongans live in houses scattered along the coastal road. The island is hit frequently by hurricanes and the traditional thatched cottages have been replaced by wood and tin roofing even though the *kikau* huts, constructed of palm-like pandanus trees, had been much cooler to live in and less expensive to build.

Rarotonga is a protectorate of New Zealand and citizens can move freely from mainland to island without technically leaving their country. The island is a popular holiday destination with New Zealanders because it does not require them to travel far for an exotic experience and they can use New Zealand currency on the island. On the other hand, Cook Islanders often emigrate to New Zealand and there are now more Cook Islanders living in New Zealand than reside in the Cook Islands.

Avarua, the main town on the island is a tidy place. Apparently it hasn't changed much in years. Stores shut down at noon on Saturdays and the town falls quiet on weekends. Even some of the restaurants close.

The islanders speak flawless English to the tourists and Māori (Maohi), one of eleven dialects of the Cook Islands, to each other.

A white sand beach runs around the island and is one of the most beautiful we have seen in our travels. The coast remains free of large hotels and over-the-water bungalows that consume shorelines on some of the other more touristy islands.

On the lee side of the island the water is so clear that from shore, you can watch graceful sting rays skim over the bottom with giant undulating wings. The north side is the windward side where giant rollers curl with plunging, transparent blue-green water. You can watch while tons of water lands on the reef then bursts into white spewing fountains of sea foam.

The interior of the island is rugged, hilly terrain except for small portions of flat, fertile soil. An abundance of star fruit, noni and pawpaw trees grow here and they say there are so many avocados and papayas, that they feed them to the pigs.

We arrived in June, the end of a long rainy season. It rained often during our stay. It was the beginning of the South Pacific winter and daytime temperatures fell to the low 20°'s C (70°'s F). At night it went even lower and we needed to add a blanket to our bedding.

We dropped our anchor then backed into a space not much wider than *Baccalieu III*. Space was tight and we felt fortunate there was room. The wharf can accommodate only six or seven boats. Our neighbour to portside was another cruising yacht but to starboard, a large, fishing vessel shared our confined space. Because the surge in the harbour can become rough, we put out several stern lines leaving plenty of room between us and the concrete wall. Not needing to attach either power cable or water hoses, because no power or fresh water was available, we could put a lengthy distance between us and the shore. The rusty ocean-going fishing vessel tied off to our starboard was a much bigger concern if the boats should start bouncing. The harbour is open to ocean surges.

Getting off and on our boat was always an adventure. Using our dinghy as a raft, we pulled ourselves towards shore using the shore lines as cables. Arriving at the concrete wall, Mike would step up on one of the pontoons of the dinghy, hoist himself up onto a hanging tractor tire, then reach a hand down to me. When we returned from a shore excursion we perched on top of the tire waiting for the surge to carry the dinghy to its highest point, which at low tide was not very high, and at the right moment drop into the dinghy hoping it would not move away until our feet hit the floor. I don't know how we didn't end up in the water with the number of times we had to carry out that maneuver, sometimes in the rain and encumbered with groceries. Trying to stay clean was another challenge as the shore lines often sank into the water then dripped with dirty water as we ferried beneath them. After a few days, the lines became even more of a threat when they thickened with brown gunk from the contaminated harbour water. We were always faced with the challenge of avoiding marks on our clothing from the black rubber tire we needed to use as a step to reach land. Gravel from the wharf accumulated on the floor of the dinghy when it stuck to our shoes and we had to be careful not to carry it onboard.

Shortly after arriving, the health inspector boarded *Baccalieu III* to request a payment of twenty dollars for a required health certificate. No one ever inspected the boat and I never understood whether it meant that we were healthy or the boat had passed an inspection. The following day, after we were already in possession of the certificate, an official came onboard to fumigate the interior using an aerosol can and to take notes regarding the origin of our food supplies. We were still carrying meat from Antigua, Panama, and the Galápagos and vegetables from various islands we had visited. I was anxious that he might confiscate our meat; we still had thousands of miles to go before arriving to a place where we could replace it. But the official seemed satisfied to document the origin of our provisions. I would have gladly given him what we had left of the chewy Galápagos beef that was taking up more space than it deserved.

The harbour on Rarotonga is located fifteen minutes from the town and every day during our walk, we were welcomed with salutations of "Kia Orana", May you live on. Most inhabitants in the Cook Islands are full blooded Polynesians.

A restored missionary house, not far from one of the island's twelve churches,* sold local art and locally farmed

---

* Churches in Rarotonga represent faiths of Mormon, Roman Catholic, Seventh-day Adventist, Pentecostal, Holy Spirit Revival, Cook Islands Christian Church and Baháʼí Faith.

Rarotonga pearls. Souvenir shops stocked a few woven coconut frond baskets but the elaborately decorated pandamus baskets *kete ngahengahe* that Cook Islanders were once famous for are no longer made. The art form has been lost.

A good selection of restaurants offered inexpensive meals and one day our British friends joked that you could rent a car in Rarotonga for the same price we paid for a Pina Colada in Bora Bora.

The Saturday morning market, located just around the corner from the harbour, was a lively place for both tourists and locals to shop for vegetables, fruits, jewelry, tie dye sarongs, freshly caught fish and bottled homemade medicinal concoctions. As early as nine in the morning, people were lining up for the chocolate sauced vanilla ice cream served on crispy, hot waffles. By eleven o'clock, barbeques were smoking with steaks, sausages, chicken and beef satays. Musicians in the band shell, strummed out traditional tunes on guitars and small ukuleles which added a festive ambience to the day. You could even get a tattoo at the market at a little outdoor kiosk; choose the design from a picture covered wall, sit in a folding chair, grin and bear the rest. I watched a young local woman have one needled into her back.

AFTER acquiring a Cook Island driver's license and practicing a little left hand driving in the parking lot, we toured the island.

The coastal road provided great vistas of a constantly changing ocean even though many of the prime ocean front properties were occupied by small cemetery plots and tombs. Ownership of land is hereditary (laws prohibit buying and selling) and a family might possess several plots throughout the islands. Traditionally, each family cares for their loved one's graves until there is no one living that remembers the occupant. Then the top of the vault is removed and the land ploughed under making room for the next person. Because women are well respected on the island, (domestic violence is severely punished) mothers are either buried in the front yard just metres from the front door of the house or incorporated into the back patio.

I should imagine there are many men in *our* society who would like to see their mother-in-laws buried in their back yard patios.

One day while walking near the water's edge, we met a young Rarotonga woman who confided how, after being away for several years in New Zealand, she had recently returned home for her father's funeral. Upon arrival, her mother had requested she "measure up her father." The young woman confessed she had lived in New Zealand so long, that she had forgotten the island lacked funeral homes and a friend or family member needed to measure the deceased. Once the measurements have been taken, the mourner visits the hardware store to obtain a coffin in small, medium or large sizes. Then the family proceeds to carry out the burial independently.

WE joined sailing friends for a hike across the middle of the island and headed towards the base of a volcanic mountain where we began climbing to a protruding rock face named Te Rua Manga. It is the island's most dramatic peak rising needle-like and barren above surrounding lush forested mountains. The trek to the needle was two hours of steep climbing with only exposed intertwined tree roots as our source of secure footing. Our feet needed to be placed cautiously on each root and after arriving at the peak, I realized I had seen nothing more than my feet and the roots they had stepped on. Once at the top, a constricted path led across a narrow ridge so thick with vegetation we barely noticed that a severe drop was only inches away. But when we rested on the rocky incline at the base of the needle, we had such a grand view, we felt like we were sitting on top of the island.

It had rained during our trek up and while descending the other side we found the trail to be steep, slippery, badly eroded and far more challenging. We needed to step down in massive strides, sometimes resulting in dragging our bottoms over steep portions of mud.

Level after level we slid through mixed foliage including a rainforest so dense, we were forced to push bushes aside to make our way through. Continuing to zigzag across the same shallow stream that we had crossed several times, we arrived at the bottom of a densely forested valley covered with gigantic ferns. I thought we must have arrived in Jurassic Park!

By the time we reached level ground, some of us appeared to have been mud wrestling. A waterfall caught one of our friends attention and they headed straight for a rinse-off. The rest of us stood reading a nearby notice board stating no swimming was allowed in the island's water supply!

MUSIC PLAYS A large part in the life of a Cook Islander. The islands are known to have some of the best dancers in Polynesia. Both male and female dancers wear grass skirts made from bleached fibres of the hibiscus tree sewn over bark cloth or cotton. Decorative halter tops and intricately designed headdresses, incorporating flowers and ornaments, are worn by the women. Men wear a circular headdress of green leaves. During a performance, women plant their feet flat on the ground and, while keeping their shoulders motionless, rapidly gyrate the hips. Any faster and they would probably be airborne.

The dance of warriors requires rapid knocking of the knees while spending most of the dance on the balls of their feet; similar to the dances in French Polynesia. The jerky, fierce choreography is carried out in unison with several dancers on the floor at the same time. To witness such entertainment is spell binding. Pounding drums and ukuleles provides the music for seductive dances while women flick their hips even faster than the Tahitians. Children begin to dance as soon as they can walk.

JUST about everyone on Rarotonga attends church and when our fumigator had come aboard armed with an aerosol can, he invited us to attend a church service at the Cook Islands Christian Church, originally established by the London Missionary Society and just a fifteen minute walk from our boat.

The colonial styled church was constructed from crude coral blocks but the interior could have been a church located anywhere in the western world. It had been newly renovated due to recent cyclone damage; five cyclones had hit Rarotonga in little over a month the year before our visit. The cemetery surrounding the church reflected the history of the early founders of the church and early heads of state. Notable was the resting place for the first prime minister of the island, Albert Henry (1968), who was knighted by Queen Elizabeth but who had his title revoked when it was found he was misusing funds.

WE were welcomed at the front door by two parishioners. After being invited to sit wherever we chose, we climbed a set of concrete stairs to a surrounding wooden balcony where we would have a clear view of the service.

The Cook Islanders are robust people who cannot hide the fact they love to eat. On Sundays, while leaving behind their regular weekday flip flop sandals to don real shoes, the ladies dress in loose fitting floral dresses and intricately woven patterned straw hats, known as Rito hats. The hats are a plaited art form unique to the Cook Islands made in the northern islands of the archipelago. They can cost $150 NZ (100 US) and upwards.

Most of the men, who sit separate from the women in dark suits and ties, are the size of defensive backs in the National Football League.

The church was packed.

The Bible was translated into the Māori language in the 1880s. The hymns, specially written for the Cook Islanders, require singing in male and female roles. The parishioners were the most enthusiastic singers you will find in any church. The men follow the female voices adding an echo effect followed by reuniting in other verses in what is known as polyphonic choral music. These songs are sung by memory. The first two rows of pews were reserved for ministers in training who were also belting out the hymns. There was no choir, there was no need for one.

The service was presented in a Māori dialect after a welcome was offered to guests in English. Following the service, guests were invited to gather in the Sunday school room to learn more of the history of the church and to share a lunch of tea, sandwiches, homemade cakes, doughnuts, corned beef and vegetables — all made by the big Mamas, the church ladies in their flowered decorated hats.

WHILE travelling to the islands, we had used up a good portion of our fuel. Our hiking friends also needed their tanks topped up. Mike arranged for a truck to deliver diesel fuel to the harbour. The truck was to deliver the quantity of fuel that would supply everyone according to their calculated needs.

When the truck pulled into the parking lot behind our boat, Mike ferried himself to shore in the dinghy, took the nozzle from the driver then ferried back stretching the hose out across the gap to our boat. I slipped the nozzle into our tank access and started to refuel. However, a poor fitting on the nozzle allowed diesel fuel to escape down the handle like water from a leaky faucet; all over my hands, all over the deck. Not only was this operation seriously environmentally unfriendly but we were paying for the spillage! The fuel truck came to us after refueling the other two boats and as they took more fuel than they had anticipated, the truck ran out of diesel before our tanks were full. The next day, Mike had to take jerry cans to shore, fill them, carry them back, load them into the dinghy and pour the fuel through a funnel into our tanks.

We stayed in Rarotonga for seven days. Being content in such a small place for that length of time is a credit to the people who live there. We celebrated our 37th wedding anniversary while there and had our friends for dinner. It was the same group of friends with whom we had taken the five mile hike, but also who had taken more fuel than they had calculated resulting in us being short. Several days following our dinner party, they confessed that while on their way to our boat the night of our celebration, someone suggested, good humouredly, they not bring up the topic of fuel. They were a fun bunch and we have great memoires of the times that we spent with them.

We left with a good weather forecast and pointed the boat towards our next destination, Niue, originally named Savage Island by Captain Cook in 1774. Cook had experienced an unfriendly welcome when the islanders had boldly charged them with spears while wearing smeared, blood red colouring on their faces. Today, the islanders claim their ancestors were adamant to keeping white-man diseases from decimating their population. They still hold a grudge against the famous navigator for saddling them with such an unfriendly image as Savage Island.

During the first twenty-four hours, we sailed with light headwinds and waited for them to swing east or southeast as had been predicted. The wind finally did swing to the east but it also swung to the west and all day the two of us were plagued with variable light winds that required putting up and taking down the reaching pole several times to keep moving under sail power.

By 1800 it was dark. Clouds covered the sky shutting us off from even starlight until two in the morning when the moon rose illuminating thin cloud covering and brightened the sky like a light bulb through a paper lampshade. If I had just come on watch, I would have thought dawn was breaking.

Our wing-on-wing configuration stood well throughout the night allowing us to squeeze six knots of speed out of the sails. Typically, while at slow speeds and with the wind behind us, we were at the mercy of large swells and too much movement to get any real sleep. I jammed myself against the lee cloth while packing pillows around my body like I was a piece of hand blown glass packaged for travel. After a few erratic rests like this I would get tired enough that I would begin to nod off, but we were working three hour shifts and if I got to sleep at all, it would not be long before I was woken for my watch. Groggy as I might be, I never had a problem staying awake for my watch which suggests simply laying down can do a fair job of recharging my batteries.

Morning brought the same overcast grey sky and dull grey water resembling more the North Atlantic than the South Pacific but the wind, although light, stayed with us fueling the sails for the entire five hundred and seventy miles to Niue.

Niue, pronounced *new-ay*, means coconut tree and all 425 square kilometres (264 square miles) of it boasts to be the most unspoiled island in the Pacific. It could well be true as it's a mere dot in the middle of nowhere. Tonga, its nearest neighbour, is two hundred and forty miles away. While this minute country would not even get a mention in the most detailed of guide books, several Niueans left their island for the first time to fight in the First World War (New Zealand (Maori) Pioneer Battalion) when, among other life experiences, they had to adjust to wearing shoes for the first time. Their home-based commander apparently asked their superiors to kindly take pity on them and not send them anywhere cold.

Niue sits high above the sea like a fruit cake turned out of a springform pan; one of the largest uplifted coral islands in the world with 60 metre (200 foot) high coastal cliffs and, similar to our own Newfoundland, is nicknamed, the Rock (of Polynesia). Although Niue is associated with New Zealand, it is the world's smallest self-governing state, having a population of fourteen hundred. Over the years, cyclones have wiped out the fruit trees and coconut plantations that were once main exports of the tiny island. In its struggle to recover, it is attempting to be the first pesticide free, entirely organic country in the world.

It was the limestone crevices and chasms that took us to this remote place and we looked forward to exploring with hikes and diving in the crystal clear waters. With no rivers or beaches, visibility is always excellent.

When we reached Niue we were the only boat there and we contacted Niue Radio requesting permission to pick up one of their moorings. There are no natural or manmade harbours anywhere around the Niue coastline but instead, twenty moorings have been set offshore to encourage cruisers to make the island part of their passage to Tonga. Anchoring is near impossible with depths ranging in the 30 metre (100 foot) range. The island's coastline raises almost perpendicular from the sea presenting cliffs that tower like giant, steep walls. With no islets or sizable reefs to offer protection, visiting boats are at the mercy of the weather.

We thought it had been difficult getting to shore in Rarotonga, but this place won first prize. With no accessible shoreline, even coconuts could not have washed ashore. Landing a dinghy there was impossible without the help of modern technology. Even landing with the help of modern equipment it was near impossible the day we arrived.

The reef near the shore, had been blasted to provide a channel wide enough for a coastal ship to deliver necessary supplies. We approached the wharf through this same opening with our dinghy.

There was no sign of civilization when we approached the shore other than the isolated concrete wharf, the only indication that anyone lived there at all and there was no way of catching sight of what might be on top of the island.

The morning we arrived, a powerful surge was rolling to shore fueled by a fifteen to twenty knot northwest wind. While steering the dinghy through the swells we noted the entire length of shore was unfriendly for landing. We watched as surge tumbled over the shallow rock-hard reef and we soon understood why a self-serve crane stood on top of the wharf.

Cement steps set into the quay, facilitated climbing the 3 metre (10 foot) high wharf if you could get out of your rocking dinghy without falling overboard. The stairs also presented a danger when the dinghy rose with an incoming surge and grounded hard on the bottom step with an outgoing surge. Under such conditions, the motor and prop were in danger of being crushed.

A line from the crane hung over the water to be grabbed in facilitating pulling the arm of the crane towards us. Mike attempted to keep the dinghy near the steps while I grabbed hold of the rope. I figured if I could manage snatching the line while keeping my balance on the heaving dinghy, I could be a candidate for a job with the Cirque du Soleil.

The industrial size hook from the crane was too large to fit into our bridle ring but luckily we had a spare piece of rope in the dinghy that we rigged to take the hook. When we were set up, I took a timely step onto the slippery steps while Mike stayed onboard the dinghy keeping the lines from tangling. Once on the wharf, I engaged the hydraulic lift, Mike hooked it up then stepped out on an incoming surge. The lift did the rest of the work and the dinghy came to rest on the wharf. Then we stood there, looking down at swirling foam as it heaved in and out of the steps and wondered how we were ever going to accomplish the feat in reverse.

A road, cut through the cliff to the top of the escarpment provided access from the concrete wharf. It was noontime on a Saturday when we hiked up the steep road to the town of Alofi where we hoped to find the customs office. We learned that the two stores, and anyone associated with diving tours or even renting cars, were about to close for the weekend. There was nothing left for us to do but walk around a one storey government building and peek into the windows out of curiosity.

We found a kiosk where we bought an ice cream just before it closed then we headed back to the wharf. We couldn't have been on shore more than an hour.

We put the dinghy back into the water and were back on the boat when, by afternoon, the wind came up to a steady twenty knots. *Baccalieu III* was lying at the end of a stretched-out mooring line, a mere 200 metres (655 feet) from the reef.

The quality of mooring equipment is always questionable and even more of a concern in strong winds; we took turns on watch throughout the night.

Why was it we often experienced plenty of wind when we

were at anchor but not enough when we were trying to get somewhere?

By morning, the boat was hobby horsing on the mooring and the latest forecast announced we could expect sea conditions to get even rougher.

The Niue Yacht Club has no facilities, only a member with a VHF radio and a good set of binoculars; sort of a virtual yacht club. We never met the man behind the binoculars but from wherever he was located, he saw *Baccalieu III* dancing around her mooring like she was a wild horse trying to escape. He contacted us by radio to issue the warning that when the wind swings west, as was predicted, large swells could make life pretty difficult on the moorings. Yes, we confirmed he was correct.

He suggested we had three choices; chance it on the mooring, which he wouldn't recommend, sail around the island to the lee shore and hove-to, or leave.

Tonga was our next destination and when we tuned into the SSB radio to hear reports from friends who were already en route to Tonga, we learned they were pounding through heavy seas and bucking twenty knot headwinds. *Tzigane* reported covering a mere thirty-seven miles in one day.

When we checked our mooring lines, we discovered our warps were already showing signs of chafe. We made the decision to move to the lee side of the island where, although there is nothing other than more rugged coastline, the island would shield us from the weather.

It took us three hours to motor to the other side and when darkness fell, the Rock was in total darkness; not a single glimmer from a window or street lamp, not a light beam from a car, not a lighthouse or navigational marker, not a hint of civilization, just one big massive rock of an island which we could hardly see accept on the radar screen.

With the stars and moon covered in cloud, our whole world was one big black ball of nothing.

Water around the island remained too deep for anchoring but the shoreline cliffs would offer protection if we could stay within their wind shadow.

We had no previous experience with heaving-to for any great amount of time and we could only recall short stints when we had back-winded the foresail on one tack and the mainsail on the other then locked the rudder to the opposite side of the foresail. This stalls the boat so it cannot set sail but at the same time, allows it to drift. Nothing to it really, the challenge was to watch where the current took us.

We set the boat to drift a mile off shore.

We hoped we had made the right decision to move around to the leeside and not just set sail for Tonga. It seemed like an odd place to be, so close to surge breaking on shore while not trying to move away from it. Not often had we made an effort to stay close to danger.

We were back on shifts again, this time watching the electronic chart for our drifting pattern and the radar screen for distance off shore. That night it was all about watching instruments. Without water tumbling from a bow wake or wind rippling through the sails, the night was exceptionally quiet; other than the light roar of breaking surf on distant dark cliffs, *Baccalieu III* floated in silence.

It was a lonely experience on watch and a strange one too; we were without the regular focus of trimming the sails to make as many miles as possible. It was imperative, however, to watch the instruments for an indication of how far we travelled and in what direction.

When carried by the current to a position that was out of protection of the cliffs, we motored back into the shadow towards the sound of the surf. I correlated it to approaching danger with my eyes closed. I didn't like that exercise even though the instruments offered what we needed to know and far more accurately than the eye is capable of doing.

We needed to direct the boat back towards the surf three times that night.

When morning came, we returned to the mooring ground. When we arrived, we found the high winds had fueled the surge to the point, where the boat danced even more violently on the mooring and was in threat of breaking loose. There was no guarantee that waiting a fourth day would prove to be any better and we decided to head for Tonga. But first, yes it's true — we had to clear out with customs and immigration and that meant going ashore again.

This time Mike let me off at the end of the wharf away from those concrete stairs that were so dangerous for the dinghy's motor. I would just have to throw myself up on the wharf. Mike remained offshore in the dinghy to await my return. While I was in town for the last time, I thought the least I would like to accomplish was to buy a T-shirt, proof at least that I had been there. But the store was still closed and apart from checking in and checking out and eating an ice cream that first day we had arrived, that was our total experience on the island of Niue. We had however, completed a circumnavigation of the island! I bet there aren't many who could claim they had done that!

We dropped the mooring line around 1330 and headed for Tonga, the group of islands Captain Cook named the Friendly Archipelago. Abel Tasman had previously sighted the islands in the mid-1600s. For the record, the Tongan islands were far from friendly even when Cook visited. He had just gotten lucky. Not only did the Tongans massacre visitors but they ate them, and they partook in eating of their own kind when starvation was an issue and when they warred among themselves, which was pretty much continuously.

We changed our watch hours to five hours a piece. Mike took 2000 to 0100 and I took 0100 to 0600. Both shifts suited our personal wake patterns. I really love the mornings, not as early as one in the morning, but the opportunity to watch a new day break while at sea can be one of life's most beautiful moments. Under the present sea conditions these longer watch hours worked better for us. It gave us time to intermingle required duties with some rest hours.

On the second day, having made good time, we arrived in the Tonga islands around 0130. We had travelled most of the way with twenty knot winds, although for a time, they had fallen as low as ten. Up and down, up and down, that had been our tradewind experience from the start.

Finding the island of Vava'u among Tonga's many surrounding islands was too complicated for nighttime navigation so we pulled into Vai'utukakau Bay for the remainder of the night. The moon had still not risen. Dropping anchor on a dark night, so close to shore, was always an unnerving experience for me. The bay was small and we could only judge our distance from shore by the yellow sketchy marks on the radar screen. I had trouble putting my faith in a simple bunch of uneven lines.

It wasn't until morning when we saw we were miniaturized by colossal, overhanging cliffs. It was if we had shrunk, and the rest of the world had grown by immense proportions. It's breathtaking to wake up in the morning to see such unexpected topography.

By 0800 we were motoring down a seven mile channel winding in and around forty densely forested, small, but dramatic rocky islands on our way to Port of Refuge, a large harbour just off the city of Neiafu.

Tonga consists of one hundred and seventy islands

scattered over an area about the size of Japan but only forty-five of the islands are inhabited. There are three groups of islands, each separated by sixty miles of sea. It was near one of these groups, the Ha'apai group, where the mutiny on the HMS *Bounty* had taken place, where Bligh and his crew of eighteen began their open boat voyage to Timor in Southeast Asia via Fiji.

We were required to dock at an industrial wharf in order to clear customs. I scampered up massive rubber tires to tie off our shore lines. Three officials representing customs, immigration, health and quarantine came on board at the same time. Each were dressed differently: one in a black suit, one in a traditional black mourning skirt and the other in trousers.

Together, the officers sat in our cockpit while each offered numerous forms that required Captain Mike to fill out with similar information. The poorer the country, the more forms it seemed, to be filled out. As they waited for the task to be completed, they were not shy in requesting a beverage. Perhaps this was an opportunity for them to be treated with what is rarely available in their own country. We opened the cockpit cooler to offer them a choice; two chose colas and the other, a beer and then one asked if we had any cookies. I offered them a generous plate of fruit bread that I had recently baked. They were quite taken by the taste of the bread and asked if I had made it. They remarked that they had never had sweet bread like this before and they were especially pleased it had been homemade. They consumed everything on the plate.

I'm not sure what part of the procedure had to deal with health; we were asked no questions regarding it but it came with the highest cost of all four of the port fees requiring payment equivalent to $100 US. Upon leaving we would be required to pay an additional $40 US outward clearance fee.

We were required to list each kind of produce that we

carried onboard, but we were not asked to dispose of any. Other boats, however, that had arrived earlier, were required to dispose of their produce. It must have been that fruit bread!

After paying port fees and clearing customs, we proceeded into the harbour where we picked up a mooring, completed our regular arrival tasks and drove to shore in the dinghy.

THE KINGDOM OF Tonga was the first site to be settled permanently by Polynesians around 500 BC when they arrived in canoes large enough to accommodate up to a hundred people. By the 18th century, Tongan canoes carried up to one hundred and fifty men on expeditions in attempts to conquer islands outside their archipelago. They raided parts of Fiji and established settlements there. Fiji lies five hundred miles southwest of Tonga.

THE Tongan archipelago remains a Polynesian Monarchy and the only South Pacific nation never to be brought under a foreign rule. Tongans for the most part, have retained their Polynesian culture, except for what missionaries found to be unfit and forbade. Of all the South Pacific islands including the Cook Islands, Tahiti and Fiji, the nation of Tonga is one of the poorest.

With few immigrating to the island throughout the centuries, the population of 108,000 has maintained a relatively pure gene pool. Recognizing the potential for research, a small Australian biotechnology company has established a data base within the country for collecting Tonganese DNA. Here, they search for disease causing genes such as various forms of cancer and stomach ulcers. Already, they have identified genes in people suffering from diabetes, and obesities. In turn, Tonga receives royalties from any drugs or other commercial applications which might result from the research. Here's hoping the people of Tonga will reap the benefits from the possibilities this new source of wealth presents. Tonga's Royals do not have a good history of sharing the country's wealth.

KING Tāufa'a āhau Tupou IV, the first Tongan King to obtain a university degree, was, until recently, the head of a system of hereditary chiefs holding similar titles from England called nobles. Tonganese cling to the belief that a small man cannot make big decisions and King Tāufa'a āhau Tupou IV weighed nearly four hundred pounds. Since we left Tonga, he died and is succeeded by his brother King Tupou V, who has stated that he is committed to economic development and democratic reform.

The Tongan Royal family surrounds themselves with thirty-three nobles and their families. Everyone else is a commoner. It is not possible for a commoner to obtain noble status through marriage as it remains a hereditary privilege, but a commoner can become a cabinet minister in the government. The Royal family rules absolute and has a hand in every decision made in Tonga. Many of the large businesses; banking, brewing, telecommunications, insurance, electric producing utilities, and phone company are owned by the Royal family.

One might get the impression from this list of assets that Tonga is a first world country but the proceeds from these companies have not benefited the citizens and the Royals have been involved in sketchy businesses that have proven costly for the nation.

Money earned through exports mainly pumpkins, vanilla beans and coconuts, is not always accounted for. When the misuse was reported in local newspapers, the King amended the constitution to make these voices illegal. Owners and journalists of privately owned newspapers, *Times of Tonga* and *Matangi Tonga*, often face harassment and even jail when articles reflect opposition. Radio and television are controlled by the government resulting in ninety-eight percent of the population to be ignorant of world events.

But times are changing and over 8,000 people are now communicating with others online.

A STRICT constitution surrounding Tongan Christian beliefs demands certain conservatism especially on Sundays which are held sacred. Planes don't fly, ships don't sail and taxis only take people to church; even swimming is not allowed. It is unlawful to trade, hold sport events or work on Sundays. Even a hitch hiker who would not have a problem hitching a ride any other day of the week would not be offered a ride if it were evident that he were on his way to the beach.

One day, a young sailing friend was jogging through town while not wearing a shirt when a local man shouted to him; "You're going to get arrested!" Tonga is a country of strict moral behaviour where both men and women still wear *valas*, a wraparound skirt, ankle length on women and below the knee on men. It is not permissible for women to show bare arms to the shoulder or for the opposite sex to hold hands or to kiss in public. But Tonga's customs are full of paradoxes. It's common to see girls and women holding hands while walking down a street. Married men often have affairs and men who take part in alternate gender roles, *fakaleitis* (lady like), are openly accepted. Lesbians, according to culture, don't exist. Serious crimes are an uncommon occurrence, but under normal daily circumstances, anything left unattended, even if left on a towel at a beach, or a drink at a table in a bar could well disappear. This is because the Tonganese hold to a tradition of sharing—"What's yours is mine, what's mine is yours." This is the *anga fakatonga*, the traditional Tonga way.

Even if they possess only meagre belongings, they will offer others what they have. Sharing is what's important.

We landed our dinghy at a waterfront bar named The Mermaid. The Vava'u Yacht Club uses the Mermaid as a club house. I don't know how active the members in the club are with their own boats but I know they enjoy racing miniature remote control Laser yachts.

The Mermaid housed a three stool bar and several small tables where we could choose between a local cloudy beer and a New Zealand import. The bar was open to the weather and we sat reading the quotes on soiled T-shirts hanging from the ceiling. The toilets were located in an outhouse behind the bar backing against a red clay hillside that appeared as if a good rain could bring the whole thing crashing down and take the bar with it. Following a clay path we were behind a mechanical shop littered with junk and every used part that had ever landed there in the past fifty years. At night, there was nothing to light the pathway and had we been in any one of a million other places in the world, we would have surly been mugged.

A long set of concrete steps, that must have been eye-ball-leveled during construction, lead to a road where, in daylight, we followed along the top of the hill into town.

The town of Neiafu is a pretty bleak looking place reflecting poverty experienced by the nation's citizens. Bungalow type buildings, some painted, some not, stood along cracked concrete sidewalks falling away in large chunky pieces. It was a poor man's town where people showed little pride in keeping it clean. Cans and plastic garbage, anything the free roaming pigs wouldn't eat, found a home in piles between the buildings. Scatterings of orange peels from wild sour oranges sat on sidewalks where the peeler had last sat eating the snack.

The peels would remain there until eaten by either pigs or severely underfed dogs. Mahatma Gandhi once said "The greatness of a nation and its moral progress can be judged by the way its animals are treated." This country owned some of the saddest domestic animals we were to see.

On the main street, a small shop displayed some very nice handmade baskets, but the store was never open no matter how many times we passed it. Further on, a small duty free liquor store and two grocery stores sat opened for business. Canned corned beef is very popular with Tongans and they will eat it straight from the can. It was the first time I had seen 'ship's biscuits', hard, plain crackers, once used as a staple onboard early European ships. The dry good stores sold basic staples and everything that Australia, New Zealand and the United States wanted to dump from their stockpiles like the Butler University 2011 NCAA Division I Basketball Champion T-shirts. The shirts were official and of highest quality, the thing is, Butler hadn't won the 2011 NCAA Division I Basketball Championship that year—Connecticut did.

Law prohibits even men to be shirtless in public, as our young friend had been warned of during his jogging spree. When locals swim, they are usually fully clothed.

Black coloured clothing might be worn for months after a relative or friend passes and since families are large, and relatives numerous, the colour is seen frequently. Sometimes only a simple black armband is worn to suggest mourning. When a royal subject dies, Tongans are requested to wear black for months and all sports and entertainment venues are cancelled. The passing of King Tupou IV initiated one hundred days of mourning.

Nearly all Tongans are Christian. Children attend religious affiliated schools with each school identified by the colour of their valas.

When students were finished school for the day, the streets were brightened with the cheerful colours of their valas; green for Latter-day Saints (Mormons), blue for Free Wesleyan, burgundy for Catholic and orange for the Church of Tonga. The girls often walked down the street four or five abreast while chatting gaily; each with their long black shiny hair tied snuggly back into tight French braids. From behind, they looked like clones. The boys wore ties with crisp white shirts and it wasn't unusual to see a shirt tail that had escaped and now poked from a traditional waist band of coconut fibres.

At the local market, dismal looking women, some with a single child, sat on the sidewalk twisting twine around stems of wild, sour oranges onto plant fronds for a carry-away item. Several vendors sold the same small variety of vegetables and fruit, but like so many other locations we visited in the south, green produce was scarce.

Inside the market, coarsely woven baskets, large roughly made tapas cloth, poorly executed carvings and shell jewelry including pieces carved of polished equine bones, sat on shelves in small kiosks. Quite frankly, the Tonganese do not display a great deal of artful talent.

When I visited the market a second time, I went prepared to offer an idea to a bone and shell carver. I thought if he possessed an inkling of talent he could quite possibly make napkin rings that he could sell to tourists who arrived on cruise ships. I had brought a pewter one from the boat that had been a gift and I held it up for him to examine. He took the napkin ring, examined it closely and then coupled it in the palm of his hand. While still holding it, he let his hand fall to his side. I thought this an unusual movement. I stood talking with him for some time while his hand with the napkin ring remained out of sight. It was apparent he did not want to return it to me and it crossed my mind that he was probably thinking in Tongan terms, "What is yours is mine." I may have trouble getting it back, I thought.

When we completed our chat I held out my hand. He reluctantly set the ring into my palm. I left him with eight cloth napkins that he could use to help display his new creations once he made them. He thanked me and when I purchased two shark's teeth and sailboat pendants from him he gave me a third shark's tooth as a gift.

I had also brought a wine basket from the boat. It had been purchased while on another island. I showed it to the woman next to him, who was a basket weaver of sorts. So many of the handmade items they offered for sale were not only crude attempts but repetitive pieces. I left her with two bottles of wine to display in her wine baskets in the chance that she chose to make them. I should not be given credit for leaving the wine. It smelled like a wet basement and tasted like paint-thinner mixed with grapes. If the woman ever decided to sample it, there's no fear she will ever want more. Following in Tongan tradition, she reciprocated by offering me a papaya. I was definitely the winner in that exchange.

AFTER residing there a couple of days we discovered two or three small restaurants hidden behind some uninviting looking doors that served nothing more than mediocre food. But behind one of the doors was—Tonga Bobs!

The night we visited Tonga Bobs, crewmembers from *Black Bird*, one of the Rally boats, were saying their goodbyes; they were departing from the fleet the following morning to fly home to Norway and would not be returning. The two young men and their father were well liked. They knew every bar from Gibraltar to Tonga and knew how to make the best use of them.

That evening, the bar collected a three pa'anga ($1 US) cover charge at the door. It was that night that I discovered where the foul smell was coming from inside my hand bag. Tongan paper money is so old and grimy with greasy dirt and filth that my wallet was emitting the reek of a lapsed oil well.

The bar scene in Neiafu exists only for tourists and the few tourists that arrive at the town come mostly to charter sailboats from the locally established Moorings Charter Boat company. In time, they all find their way to Tonga Bobs. Tongans are restricted from taking part in the bar scene by their own personal traditions and church values. But that is not to say some are not curious.

The bar consisted of a thirty foot room where a three man band sat squeezed into a corner playing an assortment of pop and western music; they were pretty good. Two sides of the room were open to an outdoor balcony which provided handrails for a few young local men a place to lean against while still keeping their distance. They did not participate in drinking nor did they speak to anyone or even to each other and, while there, showed no sign of enjoying the music; no tapping of feet or any other sign that the rhythms were affecting their souls. They simply observed.

When we left later that evening, their mothers were waiting for them outside.

The sailing tourists sat at the three small tables and a couple of bar stools that rested on a dirt floor. A small space on the loose, sandy floor was reserved for dancing. A lightly bearded foreigner, who looked like a drifter, someone seeking escape from a more modern world, stood grooving with one of the fakaleitis. All of us were dressed casually in shorts and T-shirts except for the two fakaleitis, the he-she girls. They wore smart looking clingy black dresses, one with an inlay of black netting stretching across a delicate looking bare back. Well groomed and attractive, they could have easily fit into any heterosexual Toronto bar scene without drawing unnecessary attention.

The fakaleitis were quite striking, presenting perfectly coiffured shiny, black hair and high sculpted cheek bones that gave them an air of sophistication. Black hose pulled over a set of great legs were anchored into smart looking shoes. They were not garish in any way but quietly displayed laid-back dancing talents with their partners. There was no question about who in that room appeared to be most feminine. And it wasn't me.

PROPANE IS NOT available in Tonga but butane worked well with our system and we hired a cab to take us to the refilling station. I sat in the back with two of the driver's children while the third child, straddled the console between Mike and the driver. The boys were ages seven, eight and nine; a small family compared to the regular eight to eleven that is more common in Tongan families. But the driver was an educated man, and noted that it would be difficult for him to provide for several children.

We took an immediate liking to him, and you can be sure it was not due to the cleanliness of his vehicle. An old discarded banana peel lay on the floor under the seat in front of me. The seats were soiled and grungy; the windows, dirty. It was obvious that cleanliness in his taxi van was not a high priority. But look at the rest of the town! Anyways I was thankful we had a windshield; there were vehicles driving around without them. I also had a bench to sit on and these are not things to be taken for granted in Tonga. Seat belts? Get real. Not even the remnants.

Safety in Tonga is not a priority. The uneven broken sidewalks just lie there waiting for a foot to stumble and break a leg and if a driver doesn't drive his car down the middle of a bridge, he could quite possibly become part of a riverbed because they lack any form of guard rail. Open gutters, no railings, no reflectors—land travel can be dangerous. Don't consider me brave because I sailed across oceans, consider me brave because I got off the boat in places like Tonga.

We asked our driver if he would tour us around the island. He was delighted to get the work and we made arrangements for him to meet us at nine o'clock the following morning. In truth, we wondered if we might still be waiting for him by ten o'clock in the evening or even into the next day because we suspected that time and promises wouldn't mean much to him. "It will happen when it happens" is the way of the Tongans. But we were surprised when he turned the corner into the parking lot right on the dot of nine. Seeing us already standing there, he asked if he were late. He confirmed that this was unusual behaviour that he be on time to arrive anywhere. He confided that his son had enquired why he was in such a rush to leave the house that morning. In reply, he had informed his son that he was going to pick up some *palangis* (foreigners) and the two most important things about dealing with palangis, were being on time and telling the truth.

In Tongan society, telling the truth is not as important as being polite. Responding with the answer one is hoping to hear is the right thing to do and is even expected. Whether the answer has any merit to it is insignificant. Conversing is not about truth nor is it about promises, in fact, there is no such word for 'promise' in the Tongan language. Getting along with others is all about maintaining relationships, not about certainty. In order to maintain a rapport with others, it's helpful to be of a generous nature and Tongans are very generous. When someone needs help, others pitch in as best they can; someone needs a cooking pot, they give them their cooking pot with the expectation of never seeing the pot again. Someone asks for food, they share their food even if they don't have enough to feed their own family. Even when celebrating a birthday; when the party has cost the host all they could afford and gifts have been presented to the birthday person in celebration, most likely it will be the guests that take the presents home.

SIALE, or Charlie as we called him, was not only an educated man, but apparently a dual thinker capable of processing both Tongan culture and the culture of the western world. He had what Tongans call the ability to operate in two different contexts, *anga fakatonga*, the 'Tonga way' and *anga fakapalangi*, the 'western way'. When Tongans live within their culture, no matter how minute or grand a plan is, they are never fixed and the plan is rarely carried out. The fact that Charlie came on the day that we had arranged, and arrived during the pre-planned time, would have been highly unusual in his society. Having used the word, "truth", when explaining to his son how to communicate with foreigners indicated an intellectual awareness of the differences of our cultures. He knew the meaning of truth.

While driving us around, Charlie recounted how his son David had snuck into the van that morning to join his father while he toured us around the island. I noticed that David, who sat in the back with me again, had the same smeared dirt on his legs that he had the day before, and he didn't hesitate to wipe his nose on his arm either. The missionaries still had some work to do here and as far as I was concerned, they could start by teaching both men and women not to spit on the sidewalks. The nose wiping lesson could wait but daily personal hygiene might be an idea to explore.

Charlie, who was well groomed, was a school teacher at the Latter-day Saints school and would be retiring in two years with forty years of service. According to local estimates, in 1999, school teachers made roughly $2,000 US per year. Teaching is considered a well-paid profession. Due to his service with the school, his children would be eligible to attend university at half the price of regular fees and he hoped that one day, at least two of his sons would attend a Mormon university in Hawaii. In doing so, they would gain a toehold for migration. (Tongans do not have automatic migration rights). As Charlie approached retirement, he was experimenting with other occupations that might provide an income for his family. He was trying his luck at raising pigs, working as a disc jockey and driving taxi, and with that, gave us a thorough tour of the island with a detailed running commentary.

VAVA'U IS FERTILE and flourishes with breadfruit, orange, lime, papaya, mango and lemon trees, all free for those who wish to harvest them. But to use the land for the growing of crops, squash pumpkin, yams, cassava and taro root, all high yield staples, the soil needs to be cleared of brush and stones by hand. And that is one monumental task.

Most families live in shacks constructed of tree roots and thatched palm fronds. Those lucky enough to have someone located in another country sending them money might build colonial wood houses with corrugated tin roofs. Pigs, some so skinny their ribs protrude, roamed freely in front yards sometimes wandering onto roads. Most islanders are not wealthy enough to own cattle, but occasionally, an undernourished cow could be seen standing in suffering circumstances; tethered among scrub brush within a perimeter of a minute portion of pastureland. It is most likely that tethered cattle would rarely be moved from their small grazing space or even offered water.

Wandering dogs competed with the pigs for food and survived only if they could scavenge enough to eat and have the presence to stay off the road. Reportedly, there are thousands of stray dogs in Tonga, many running in packs; hundreds suffering from skin related diseases and starvation.

It was not until 2010, that the government of Tonga signed the Universal Declaration of Animal Welfare acknowledging that "animals can feel pain and have the ability to suffer, that the welfare needs of animals must be respected and cruelty towards animals must end."

The main roads on the island were paved, and the most refined buildings we saw were well kept, white painted churches. Once off the main road, we drove down dirt side roads where we came upon family crypts decorated with plastic flowers and hand sewn quilts. Gifts are an important part of the Tongan funeral, when an entire ten days are set aside for the event. The house where the deceased lived is used for the funeral and is decorated with white silks, flowers, lacy drapes and red ribbons. During the first five days, food is prepared for crowds of up to two hundred people. Tongans traditionally sit on mats while eating with their fingers although utensils are becoming more common. At funerals, foods such as *topai* and *lu* are eaten; both dishes require various cuts of meat or fish to be mixed with onions and coconut milk then wrapped in leaves of the taro plant and baked in an earthen oven, an open fire or a wood stove. Doughboys, flour and water dropped into boiling water then served with syrup of sugar and coconut milk is a favourite funeral food because its low cost.

The deceased is kept cool with the use of ice and on the fifth day the body is buried wrapped in silk and soft tapa cloth, in a tomb where their ancestors are also buried. As they did not live life alone, Tongans believe they should not dwell alone in death. Traditionally, the men of the family dig the grave and while taking the sand out, lay the bones of the previously buried relative neatly aside. It is important they not be mixed.

In the days that follow, close relatives, while demonstrating their grief, cut their hair which is in turn woven into mats with strips of pandanus leaves to form belts worn by men in mourning. Full length mats, *ta'ovola*, are also worn over regular clothing tied with rope constructed of coconut fibres and human hair of a deceased ancestor. It was common to see men wearing these mats while going about their daily chores and school boys wearing the belts over their school uniforms while in the town of Neiafu. Woven mats are handed down from generation to generation and are the "crown jewels" of Tonga at the Royal Palace.

We came to a two lane bridge that Charlie reported had been designated not strong enough to hold two cars at one time. I wondered what scientific study they had used to determine that it was structurally safe to support even one car. As we waited for an oncoming car to clear the bridge, we watched a woman, standing ankle deep in a riverbed, swish strips of hibiscus bark back and forth in the salt water. After a good saturating, she laid them flat, leaving them for the tide to wash and bleach them white. They would later be woven into the top part of a grass skirt that women wear over calf length dresses for special occasions. Bodices are often sewn from used western clothing using treadle sewing machines.

Not long after we spotted an elderly lady weaving a grass skirt while sitting on her porch. I asked Charlie if we could stop to observe her weaving.

The woman was sitting in a white plastic chair beside a pile of bleached hibiscus bark. Her pink, floral dress flowed over her knees and fell, pooling around her calloused, dry feet that were fitted into well-worn flip flop sandals. She was twisting thin pieces of light bark into a weave to construct the waistband of a soon-to-be completed grass skirt.

As we approached, a skinny white dog growled with a sense of protective duty but retreated with a yelp, when a stone she threw, struck him in his side. The weaver was proud to display her work and was pleased we had stopped to take an interest in her project. With the help of Charlie's interpretation skills she informed us it would take about two days for her to complete the skirt.

The main source of family income on the island comes from the handiwork of women's weaving. By custom, women have greater prestige than men and a man's sister will outrank him even if he is older. Customarily, it was taboo for an adult male and sister to be in the same room together. However, the recent introduction of television to city dwellers is slowly changing the taboo.

WHEN our tour was over and Charlie returned us to the town of Neiafu, we presented him with a picture book of Canada, three small toys for his sons, and, in appreciation for his excellent tour, we paid him more than he had requested. In doing so, we were aware that we had crossed a cultural line that might cause him to be embarrassed. But Charlie was good at rationalizing and said that he too had enjoyed being with us and felt that we had become friends. So now in the Tongan tradition, it was proper for us to share our wealth with him.

IT WAS ALMOST time to leave Tonga, to embark on the passage to Fiji. In preparation for the upcoming passage, two days had been arranged for BWR boats to refuel with duty free diesel. Once we had taken on duty free fuel we would be required to check out with customs immediately and leave the country. As one of the larger boats in the fleet, we let others fill their tanks on the first day because it would take them longer to make the passage. Following their departure, there were only four boats left in the harbour to take on fuel. When it was our turn, we were instructed to dock *Baccalieu III* alongside the commercial concrete wharf first in order that the others could raft to her for fueling.

As I guided the boat into the wharf, the wind pushed her against one of the large, black rubber fenders. As a result, it left a harsh black and pink abrasion mark on the hull. The pink colour was the remnants of the red hulled ferry that crushed up against the tire once a week and was just turning the corner behind us and would demand the very space I had just maneuvered into. I pulled away to stand off while the ferry docked and unloaded a slew of passengers that had spent the last thirty-six hours sleeping on the open decks of the ship. After docking, families carrying numerous packages, boxes, crates and children, walked the gang plank to shore.

After pulling *Baccalieu III* back into the wharf and tying up, we learned that the fuel truck had left to make room for the passengers to disembark, and we were to move the boat forward to tie alongside a shipping yard where 12 metre (40 foot) ocean containers stood ready for shipping. After tying up the third time, we learned that the fuel truck couldn't get through the gate because the shipyard workers had gone for lunch. We waited there an hour for the gates to be unlocked. When the fuel truck gained entry, the driver informed us that we were tied up in front of a container loaded with explosive materials and he could not safely unload fuel in this location. We would have to move, he said. As much of a nuisance this was, we were happy to oblige.

We untied our lines from shore and shimmied the entire raft of boats forward several metres to the far end of the wharf where it turned out, there was not sufficient room for the fuel truck to get near enough to unload the fuel to our tanks. With that conundrum, the diesel hose needed to be dragged from the fuel truck and walked down a row between several shipping containers. Then, with three men hoisting the hose onto their shoulders, they carried it across our boat to each of the rafted vessels on the other side of us. Black rubber hose softens while sitting in the sun and it can stain a deck wherever it touches. The hoses are often embedded with gravel and debris; as you can well imagine, the last place it had touched down had not been pretty. Even with our conscientious efforts we were left with several hard-to-remove black marks. Moreover, when we started to fill the tank in the starboard boat, the high powered nozzle overwhelmed the small diesel pipe and fuel gushed onto both their deck and ours. And, when we filled our own tanks, we too had the same problem and the diesel again ran onto our deck.

By the time we had completed refueling, we figured the money we had saved was not worth our time or the effort. It had taken a good part of the day to top up with a mere 300 litres (67 Imperial gallons/80 US gallons).

We had checked out with customs and immigration earlier that morning and were obligated to leave within a few hours of refueling. However, the weather forecast predicted nasty weather for our upcoming passage. Wind predictions were for forty knots with 4 to 5 metre (15 foot) accompanying seas. Rain would be part of the package. We and three other boats decided to wait until the following day when we would update the forecast, but *Tzigane* left the wharf to head for Fiji. We would later hear reports of problems they had suffered.

The following morning, the weather forecast had not improved and it looked as though it would take approximately three days for the wind to settle. By law, we needed to leave Tonga, we had already overstayed by several hours. Either we leave immediately or we would be forced to go through more of those endless, drawn-out expensive check-out procedures. Unless—we went into hiding.

We opted for the latter and decided to find a remote anchorage where we could hang out incognito until receiving a good weather forecast. We suspected the BWR-VHF radio channel was being monitored by local authorities so the three boats agreed to communicate on a different channel while we each used a newly derived name to identify our boats. *Freewheel's* contact name became 'Expensive Lady', *Fenella* called herself, 'Lucy in the Sky', *Onyva* responded to 'On Your Bike' and *Baccalieu III* became 'Stink'n Like Diesel'. As the day went on and we sought to find an appropriate anchorage, our names got even more ridiculous.

THE paper charts we used in the Tongan islands were mapped by British naval commanders in 1895 and 1898 while assisted by the surveying ship *Penguin*. The fact that the charts are still in use today indicates how accurately the coastlines had been recorded over a hundred years ago. The charts, however, did not show submerged shoals, reefs or rocks lying around the hundreds of small islets. Our electronic chart did not supply these details either. In fact, the electronic chart was so muddled that it looked like someone had spilled a green spinach smoothie all over the computer screen.

EACH small island sits on a wide rocky pedestal carved out by centuries of water erosion resulting in today's appearance resembling giant mushroom caps sitting on thick wide stems. Often deep water runs right up to the mushroom look-a-likes but frequently the islands are connected by rocky shoals running just below the surface. With the same overcast conditions that had plagued the area for the past several days, the shoals were difficult to detect by the naked eye. But we all agreed that a secluded anchorage was what we needed to protect us from high winds as well as curious authorities and we went on motoring in and around the islands like a car driving through the suburbs looking for an address. We marked our twisting path with an electronic trail marker which would be useful when needing to backtrack through the passage. If we managed to miss the reefs once we might as well mark the route in order that we might miss them the second time and with less worry. Our electronic trail markings were sort of a Hansel and Gretel breadcrumb trail.

The anchorage we choose was open from the north and did not protect us from the winds that were presently blowing, but the wind was predicted to swing southwest during the night and increase in strength. When this happened we would be sitting in more comfortable conditions. At least that was the plan.

When we lowered the anchor on the windlass, we couldn't get the anchor to bite. Using the windlass again, we hoisted it back onto the roller. We lowered it a second time. Still we were not successful and when we hoisted it a second time, the fuse overheated resulting in an inoperative windlass. That condemned us to motoring in circles for thirty minutes while waiting for the fuse to cool. Around and around we drove in the pouring rain while the depth sounder warned us of shallow bottoms running out from shore. Staying clear of four anchored boats and an old rickety dock with submerged pilings, we continued to circle. You can be sure we learned from that experience to let the anchor free-drop to eliminate overheating the fuses.

It was four in the afternoon by the time we got dug in and soon afterwards the wind picked up and the rain fell a little harder.

The anchor light at the top of the mast, (the one I had changed just a few weeks ago), had gone out again requiring us to hang a portable one looping it temporarily over the preventer line on the boom. We were not expecting more boats to arrive during dark hours but if one of the boats already in the anchorage broke loose from its holding and had to relocate, our anchor light would mark our whereabouts.

As the evening progressed so did the wind strength but it never swung southwest as predicted nor did our anchorage ever become that protective refuge we had hoped for. All night the wind blew from the north pushing us towards shore. *Baccalieu III* lay at the end of her stretched out chain while the galvanized links creaked in uneven intervals over the stainless roller. Mike pulled on his foul weather gear to go forward to check the snubber but after analyzing the overall conditions, we thought it unsafe, and decided it best to wait for the wind to subside before anyone walked to the foredeck. The wind never let up, and that night was the worst night we ever spent at anchor. We thought of our friends who were already at sea and learned later that one boat had experienced a knock down.

Again, we took turns on anchor watch. I took the second watch.

To save energy and to keep a dark interior that would enable us to see into the darkness, the cabin lights were kept off. The chart plotter set to monitor the position of the anchor was on night mode and barely added light to the cabin. The plotter would be the most accurate reference if our anchor shifted and if that occurred, we would have to act quickly; turn the motor on and try to reestablish holding in another location. God forbid we should have to do more circling.

Besides watching for our own anchor drag we wanted to keep an eye on surrounding anchored boats.

Not that we were paranoid or anything.

OUR life jackets lay next to our foul weather gear on the settee. In reality, we probably wouldn't have time to put on all the pieces. It was a small bay, and if we dragged, it wouldn't take much time for us to meet with a reef or shoreline.

High winds blew waves into the restricted bay. When the wind climbed into the thirties it howled through the rigging imitating the spooky sound effects of a horror movie. Whooo. Added to the eeriness, were the creaking and grating of the galvanized links rubbing over the anchor roller. The wind jiggled halyards inside the aluminum mast as if they were a confined set of chains. Every now and again, when a gust of sizable strength pushed *Baccalieu III* even further back on her anchor line, I could feel a quiver run through her hull. Rain fell in continuous forceful taps on the windows.

The anchorage experienced such waves that it caused *Baccalieu III*'s bow to pitch forward allowing for slackened anchor chain, then immediately following, she would be thrown backwards. The anchor, the chain and the windlass, took the whole load of the resulting whip causing a severe snap while it handled the burden. Inside the darkened salon, I kept an eye on the yellow plotter line that represented the boat's swing. The line was moving back and forth over the radar's black background with a slow pendulum-like motion. Soft light glowed from the computer as it stood ready to show the exit route we had plotted earlier. Red lighting illuminated the floor below the steps.

The wind continued to howl.

I often stood on the seat at the navigation table to look out the window while checking the position of our neighbours. Rain obscured my ability to see and all I could detect was the soft illumination from our own portable anchor light throwing flickering shadows against the lifelines. At times, our friend's white masthead lights appeared to be suspended like low slung stars in the rain. I knew the pattern in which they should appear; if there were changes in it, it would be cause for alarm. Sometimes someone else's problem ends up being yours too. Who knew that better than us?

I was glad when the sky turned light grey with morning light. Around three that afternoon, the wind started to turn southwest. We watched the anchor pivot and nicely reset itself. Thank goodness for that. However, the wind still had a few degrees to turn before the total prediction was realized. We were not yet in a position to relax.

That day, the wind settled into the mid-twenties and the rain let up. But not for long; it returned time and again to blast by in torrential downpours while sluicing by the windows in horizontal sheets.

Then suddenly our anchorage became popular. Boats that had found comfort in other anchorages the previous night, began to get pounded when the wind changed direction. That brought them into our location. Five sailboats and a power boat arrived and much to our relief, they anchored a good distance from us.

The second night was not nearly as bad as the first but Mike spent much of his sleep time monitoring the gusts that plagued the bay again that night. It was as if an angry wind goddess wished to blow threatening squalls at us through a straw. One moment the boat would be sitting at rest and the next, we would feel her snap back with a jerk in a violent gust. It was far more stressful for the anchor and deck hardware to undergo such irregular, heavy yanking than a steady thirty or forty knot wind.

It wasn't until the third evening that the weather began to settle and the following morning we lifted our anchor to begin the passage to Fiji.

It was winter in Tonga and sufficient light, allowing for good visibility, didn't arrive until nearly seven in the morning. The shortest day had passed a few days prior and thankfully they were about to get longer. I got up in the dark, put some bread ingredients in the breadmaker, filled a container with freshly chopped fruit then prepared a few chicken breasts to be cooked underway.

At the first sign of light, we began to wind our way back through the islands feeling our way with the use of the depth sounder while watching the numbers diminish 9, 8, 7, 2 — blank. We were definitely on edge but Mike had accidentally erased the computer's 'bread crumb' trail we had plotted on the way in. With the existing low, flat morning light, we found it nearly impossible to detect the reefs by eye, but with one of us standing on the bow on watch, we cautiously moved through the fields of coral and managed to stay out of trouble. Then we made our way out to sea where swells, stirred up from the previous high winds, greeted us with the rolling force of an assaulting sea.

Not far from here lies the Tonga Trench, a valley within the ocean's contour where in places, it reaches almost 10,882 metres (35,702 feet) deep; one of the deepest portions of the Pacific Ocean floor. Most of the islands in Tongan waters are raised coral atolls; except for two, which are part of exposed peaks of a sub-oceanic volcanic mountain range extending all the way from New Zealand to Samoa and Hawaii. One volcano still remains active today and upon leaving the islands, friends who left several days after us, reported so much pumice in the water, that it sandpapered the gelcoat right off the bow of their boat.

It was one of those passages that required us to lean against the walls in order to make our way around the interior of the boat. But we made no complaints; we knew it had been far worse in previous days and the sun was shining for the first time in two weeks.

The tradewinds were light requiring the use of engine power to push through heavy rolling swells. This presented us with some very uncomfortable conditions.

The passage to Fiji was four hundred and twenty miles. We decided to do whatever was needed in order to arrive in daylight. Fiji's coastal waters are a mass of islands, shoals and reefs and daylight would be our best friend when attempting to navigate them. While moving through the heavy swells, we used engine power to back up the sails.

On the second day, the wind swung round behind us causing nasty corkscrewing that boats succumb to in rolling seas. We poled out the Yankee in an attempt to capture the light winds and give some balance to the uncomfortable motion, but the wind fluctuated between nine and twenty knots the entire day and we were forced to adjust the sails and maneuver the cumbersome pole several times. We arrived at Nanuku Passage, an area of islets, sand banks and reefs, around midnight. That was a tense time! We never saw the navigation light on Wailagilala Island which would have given us comfort and confirmation of our location. Light rain may have obliterated it or it may not have been functional which we found to be common in many of the areas in and around Fiji. Perhaps it no longer even existed. That was common too, that navigation marks were missing.

The night was black as soot and while some islands showed on the radar screen, others were not high enough to be picked up by radar. Navigating kept Mike busy using a combination of radar plotter, electronic charts and paper charts to confirm and reconfirm our positions.

With a turn through the passage we picked up a steady twenty knot breeze allowing for some full out sailing. Boy that felt good! We had babysat those sails for so long, squeezing out whatever we could from next to nothing, that the arrival of a good wind was almost an occasion for celebration.

You're never entirely alone at sea when you have an SSB radio and planet Earth co-operates with some good propagation. Mike, and Hutch aboard sailing yacht *Fenella*, organized a Royal Naval Tot over the SSB radio and called three other Tot members, who were located several miles away on other boats, to join in. *Valhalla*, a Hallberg Rassy 10.5 (35 ft.) was sailing from the island of Raiatea and heading for Fiji, nine hundred miles away. She had been held up in Raiatea for three weeks with mechanical problems waiting for an oil cooler body to arrive from Sweden. Now, en route to Fiji, *Valhalla's* new autopilot-computer had failed forcing the owners to hand steer. No one deserved a stiff drink more than they did and at 1800 that evening, they joined us for a tot of rum. The Monday night toast was appropriately—"Our ships at sea."

As I climbed out of the companionway at dawn for my last watch before reaching land, I spotted the grey mountainous coastline of Fiji. We used the binoculars to search for a concrete tower that marked a shoal running half a mile out from the northern tip of Vanua Levu and kept a wide berth as we rounded it. Savusavu is located at the mouth of a river which we couldn't locate even with the use of binoculars. We did see what appeared to be a supply ship docked stern-to at a small river pier in that very location. As we approached, we discovered the bow of the ship was in fact tied off to the river buoy which had the effect of hiding the entrance. While rounding the ship's bow, a workman in a run-about waved a warm greeting to us. This was just the beginning of our experience with the friendly people of Fiji.

7

Heading South

Fiji, the Cannibal Isles: Musket Cove

Passage to New Zealand

New Zealand

Fiji—Second Time Around
Yasawa Islands

Leaving Musket Cove

*There are no foreign lands. It is
the traveler only who is foreign*

ROBERT LOUIS STEVENSON

FIJI, THE CANNIBAL ISLES: MUSKET COVE

WE LIKED IT IN FIJI; THEY CALLED OUR BOAT A 'YACHT'

Fiji consists of over three hundred islands as well as hundreds of scattered islets. The archipelago spreads across a vast 320,000 square kilometres (200,000 square miles) of mostly placid, turquoise sea. The 180th meridian, (International Dateline) doglegs around the islands allowing all Fijians to experience the same day at the same time. Over one hundred of the islands are permanently inhabited. The main island, Viti Levu (Big Fiji) is the largest. The second in size is Vanua Levu (Big Land). These two make up eighty-five percent of the country's total land area.

Dutch explorer Abel Tasman was the first European to visit Fiji, in the mid-1600s, while searching for the southern continent. Captain James Cook along with young William Bligh acting as Sailing Master, aboard the *Resolution* followed years later in 1776. Natives called their land Viti but Tongans to the north, where Captain Cook visited first, knew the land as Fisi. Cook mistakenly interpreted the word as Fiji.

Thirteen years later, the mutiny of the *Bounty* took place in Tongan waters. By then Bligh was captain of his own ship until he and his eighteen crewmembers were forcibly removed and set to sea in a row boat. After rowing over four hundred miles and reaching Fiji, he continued down Fiji's coastline, never ceasing to chart the shoreline. No matter how desperate Bligh and his crew were for food and water, they never stopped along Fiji's shores because a crewmember had already been killed near Tonga and they had no weapons to defend themselves. It was a wise decision not to stop because Fiji was a place of unsettled, vicious, tribal warfare where cannibalism was common. Even as far away as Tonga, Fijians were known as ferocious fighters.

By 1871, two thousand Europeans had arrived interested in using the land to grow sugar and cotton. During the time in which the American Civil War blocked most cotton exports from the southern United States, more labour was needed to work larger plantations. Native Fijians were not interested in regular sustained labour, forcing the owners of cotton plantations to look elsewhere. The British, who had been instrumental in ending slavery a few years earlier, attempted to set standards for recruitment. The new rules stated that Melanesian labourers, (people from the New Hebrides (Vanuatu), Solomon Islands, Papua New Guinea and Fiji) were to be recruited for a maximum of three years, paid three pounds per year and given necessary clothing. In spite of the plan to involve only voluntary workers, many Melanesians were deceived and tricked into boarding ships, where they were then imprisoned. This was known as *blackbirding*. Melanesians suffered greatly, not only while en route to Fiji, but under substandard living conditions. One medical officer in 1875 listed a mortality rate of five hundred and forty labourers out of every one thousand. Following the end of their three year working period, labourers were to be returned to their villages, but most captains simply dropped them off at the first island they sighted. Unable to reach their homes, many stayed and married native Fijians, and despite adopting Fijian customs and language, they today remain a distinct society and have mostly settled around the city of Suva, the largest city in Fiji and the capital.

A few years later, indentured labourers were transported from Calcutta and Madras to work sugar plantations. The contract between employer and worker was written in duplicate on a sheet of paper, then separated by cutting a jagged edge resembling 'teeth', in order that the two pieces could be later joined together for confirmation of their authenticity. From this practice, the word 'indentured' was born.[*]

Once contracts expired, many indentured immigrants stayed on the islands. Almost forty percent of today's population originates from India.

When early missionaries arrived to the islands, they standardized several dialects into what is today the Fijian language. The country has three official languages: Fijian, English and Hindustani.

We moored our boat at the Copra Shed Marina just outside the Savusavu Yacht Club located on the south coast of Vanua Levu island, the more remote of the two larger islands. This is where we cleared immigration. The late 19th century shed, which is now known as the Savusavu Yacht Club, was one of the first copra mills in Fiji. Historical pictures decorate the walls of the building's interior which houses three rooms for short-stay rentals, a small restaurant and an open air bar.

While the harbour was once used to load sandalwood and copra, today only copra is exported in large quantities. The harbour is a protected refuge where sailboats can seek shelter. With the view of smoky blue mountains in conjunction with the light mist that rises in delicate softness, each morning was like a piece of calming art when we awoke.

---

[*] The practice of matching pieces of paper together arose c. 1300. There is evidence of its use for military purposes.

There are fewer tourists in Savusavu than in some parts of Fiji and the town bustles with islanders. Numerous native women wait regularly at a bus shelter to catch a bus that will transport them back to their villages in the countryside. Encumbered with gigantic colourful bags and twine-wrapped packages, they stand dressed in long, printed missionary dresses, transforming the bleak bus shelter with an array of gleeful colours.

The heavily travelled main street is a mish mash of small cafés, restaurants and a general store selling large bales of imported clothing covered in opaque white wrapping. Scattered about the town are restaurants run by Chinese and the local Indian population, offering traditionally seasoned food but also hamburgers and pizzas to please young back-packers. Food shacks, where food is served from opened windows, do a good business in chicken and vegetable curry rotis coloured brightly with yellow turmeric.

A good sized, but grim looking super-market was full of items that I didn't recognize and those I did were too expensive to buy. Large sacks of rice, too large for even the lower shelves, flopped over onto the floor. Breads, pickles and condiments filled aisle after aisle. Smaller, independent shops sold metres and metres of brightly coloured fabric, traditional saris, carved wooden bowls and handicrafts of finely made tapas cloth. Colourfully decorated masks that have nothing to do with Fijian culture seemed to be popular among ill-informed tourists.

In the middle of town, a busy open marketplace housed several vendors who sold farm fresh vegetables and bundles of kava root resembling rotting brown flower bouquets. Because Fijian custom dictates visitors present a gift of kava to each village chief when visiting their islands, we purchased the dry roots to carry with us on the boat in preparation for touring the outlying islands.

Kava *Piper methysticum*, is used to make a popular drink prepared by pounding the dried roots into powder form with a mortar. When ready to use, the powder is wrapped in cloth and the bundle is tied and dragged through a wooden bowl filled with water until the water turns brown.

The custom of kava drinking is ingrained throughout the islands of the South Pacific. Alcohol was not available until the Europeans arrived, although Indonesians brewed palm wine and the practice of chewing betel with lime arrived with the influx of Asians. Traditionally, the kava root was chewed into a mash then spit into a bowl of warm water. After allowing it to ferment, the fibres were strained resulting in a concoction that was still not alcoholic, but a salivary ferment that was drunk in the honour of divine ancestors.

Today, kava or *yaqona* is sometimes referred to as the peace drug. Drinkers of kava never become rowdy as might happen with the over consumption of alcohol but instead, become relaxed and unproductive. Fiji exports kava to pharmaceutical companies in the U.S. to be used in the production of antidepressants and muscle relaxants.

In well-run Fijian villages, the custom of kava drinking is presented to young people as a drink of respect only to be used as a sacramental ritual at births, marriages, deaths, and the installations of new chiefs or welcoming special visitors. But in modern times it has become far more common to drink kava for pleasure. Drinking in moderation has become a current day challenge. A local saying states, "Yaqona is a good friend, but a bad master."

THE Blue Water Rally organization had arranged a fleet reunion dinner where we had the opportunity to experience the local custom of greeting. This included taking part in a welcoming kava ceremony at a nearby hotel. Two guitarists sat crossed legged on the floor of the stage. A third man, in charge of welcoming, sat on a woven mat in front of a traditional, four legged wooden carved kava bowl. One at a time, we were offered a seat on the mat. The kava server dipped a coconut shell into the ceremonial bowl and presented it to us in welcome. I was first to be offered the cup of kava. I was instructed to clap my hands once and take the coconut cup in both hands then down the contents in one gulp. I responded with *"bula"* and tried not to suggest disapproval while handing back the empty cup. Then, as instructed, I clapped my hands three more times. The muddy looking drink immediately numbed my lips and throat and I wondered how the musicians could sit drinking it all night and be capable of moving their lips in song.

When Fiji was known to the outside world as the Cannibal Isles, the coconut shell we drank from that night would traditionally have been a skull cap from a defeated enemy. Not only the men from warring tribes were eaten, but local women from opposing tribes who might be caught while fishing alone. However, boiling people in a cauldron is nothing more than a cartoonist's fanciful depiction. The most common way to prepare human flesh was to wrap it in leaves and cook it in an earthen oven. One chief who lived on the island of Viti Levu is said to have eaten eight hundred and seventy-two people. He recorded his achievement by putting a stone in a pile for every person that he consumed. Eating their enemies was thought to be a way of inflicting the ultimate revenge but it has been noted that the islands of Fiji had few other options in supplying meat to their people. The only endemic mammal found in the Fijian islands other than whales, dolphins and porpoises, are monkey-faced bats *Mirimiri acrodonta*.

Sailors, who had shipwrecked near the islands and managed to escape, reported to their statesmen that Fijians were fierce warriors and should be avoided at all costs. Vivid reports of their experiences kept future explorers away until the 19th century when whalers, sandalwood* and sea cucumber† traders began arriving to the islands.

Around 1870, Fijians accepted Christianity and the custom of eating people came to an end. In spite of their barbaric culinary traditions, the Fijians were hospitable to any strangers that they did not wish to eat, and centuries later, when we explored the islands, we found the Fijians to be some of the friendliest people we had yet encountered. "Bula", the wish of good health, was the greeting bestowed on us many times throughout a day by those who passed. Even those on their way to work in taxi longboats would wave and shout greetings in the early morning light.

Traditional Fijians live in villages along rivers as unified family members, similar in style to living in a commune. The society resembles the family system of the North American Iroquois Indian. Each man believes he has descended from a common ancestor. A body of advisory elders, the most respected members of the village, supports the chief who occupies his position through hereditary progression. Each family lives in separate huts; one hut may be the home for two or three generations. Food is cultivated in gardens and fish is harvested from the sea. Staples like sugar, flour, and rice, gas for motors, bus fare and school books need to be purchased, requiring that the community earn an income. Those who hold jobs outside the village are expected to share their earnings while others may not generate any income at all but share crops from their fields. It is always expected that one pays another back with whatever they might possess. Wealth

---

* Sandalwood has been burned for its incense for centuries. India grew sandalwood but China did not. It was and is today, used to manufacture inlaid boxes, fans and ornaments, perfumes, cosmetics and for medicinal purposes.

† Sea cucumbers are marine animals resembling giant slugs. After gutting, cooking and drying, the product is called *bêche-de-mer*. In China and Southeast Asia, it is considered a delicacy and is used as an aphrodisiac.

is determined by the ability to help others, not by how much can be accumulated. It is therefore an honour, in the eyes of the natives, to have others dependent upon them.

The custom of sharing does, however, hinder advancement in business and the majority of the remaining population, Indo Fijians, who were once indentured from Bengal and Bihar, now own and operate most of the businesses. Indo Fijians are forbidden through local law to own land or hold political office even though they have lived in the country for over a hundred years and contribute greatly to the economy. The Indo Fijians have made Fiji one of the most industrious countries of the South Pacific islands.

Native Fijians still practice the ancestral customs of kava drinking, the wearing of the whale tooth, fire walking, turtle calling, and the making of tapa cloth and pottery. They are people who wish to maintain privacy and many do not welcome foreign visitors into their lives. But an opportunity, arranged through the BWR, allowed us to visit Naweni, a remote Fijian village on the island of Vanua Levu. The village offered a tour entitled, "Visit the Red Prawns."

Fiji is home to several species of prawns, but red prawns, *vra buta* (cooked prawns), are a rare species of shrimp appearing pink in colour while in their natural habitat. They are found in only two locations in Fiji.

For centuries, the prawns have been revered by local natives as the spirit of Urubuta and the prawns probably still exist today due to the superstitions surrounding them, promising shipwreck or even death to anyone who attempted to remove them. One location where the prawns can be found is not far from the Naweni village situated along the coast 32 km (20 mi.) from Savusavu.

Six of us climbed into a rickety old van. The driver took us over a washboard road towards the village, an hour's ride through a heavily treed countryside. A few well fed beef cattle browsed lazily in the corner of a former copra plantation and sheep, scrawny and gaunt looking from recent sheerings, had been let loose to forage in a blackened slash and burn field. Small, spindly tree branches, planted a metre a part, provide support for fencing while greening the countryside with lush, newly sprouted leaves. Numerous bus stops throughout the countryside were occupied by waiting passengers who raised their hands in friendly greetings in our passing.

The tide was out along the coast, baring young, sprouting mangrove trees that poked through muddy tidal flats for several miles. Our driver turned down a side road where the bush was denser and the holes in the road outnumbered the flat stretches, and I wondered how many more bumps the van could take before the sides fell off and we all sat exposed on the chassis.

When the road came to an end, the driver stopped at the edge of a paddock, just metres from a house. A plain cotton curtain fluttered from a top-hinged window propped open with a stick. Most homes in the commune stood on stilts or concrete blocks protecting them from flood waters. It reminded me that early Fijians used to build houses using their enemies as supporting posts. It was hard to believe the friendly Fijians that we had met had descended from ancestors capable of such cruelty.

Wild flowering shrubs, coconut and banana palms grew sporadically among the modest, unpainted houses where freshly washed laundry hung on lines between slanting bamboo poles. Electricity lines reached to only one building in the commune and I recalled that two thirds of the rural population in Fiji lives without electricity.

It was a weekday that we arrived at the village and little sign of life was evident. A skinny dog sniffed around in the open grassy field, a solitary chicken strutted, searching for grubs and a man, bare chested with a sulu wrapped around his waist, stood looking back at us from inside his house as if surprised to see anyone, or at least anyone peering from the elevated window of a bus.

We learned that the elders had only recently voted to open their village to tourists, and our group was only the second to visit the site.

THE driver instructed us to stay in the vehicle until we were formally announced by way of a letter-of-introduction which he had in his possession. We knew it was considered rude according to Fijian custom to wear hats and sunglasses, and we removed them while we waited.

More important matters than meeting us had taken the chief away but one of the elders, a solid, stocky man whom we came to know as Joe, approached the van. Joe was wearing an oversized T-shirt embossed with a large number 29 and the words Miami Dolphins. It hung over a sulu that reached just above his athletic runners. After reading the letter of introduction, he invited us to follow him across the communal village-green, which occasionally served as a rugby field, and was surrounded by several unpainted wooden dwellings.

When paspalum, a local wild grass, once the main construction material used in traditional Fijian bures, became scarce, wood was substituted. Thatched roofs had been replaced with iron corrugated roofing, which were now rippled with rust from the salty ocean air.

Each bure was built either in single room style or with two rooms. Few held furniture although it was common that hand-woven cane mats were spread across the middle of rough-hewn plank floors. Occasionally, we saw one that might be furnished with a simple table, but chairs were not customarily used. It was routine to sit cross-legged on the floor even at mealtime when food is set on a cloth that is unfolded onto floor mats. Preparation and the cooking of yams, sweet potatoes, rice, bread, fish and green leafy vegetables is carried out in separate sheds from the main house, enabling the house to remain cool. Washing up takes place outdoors in plastic dishpans where cool, running water is available. Villagers share outdoor privies.

We were led to a small communal hall where village elders often met for discussions and assembled to drink yaqona. Joe asked that we remove our shoes and then invited us to sit on a bamboo mat spread in the centre of the floor. A teacher and a small number of preschool children were already present but the children quickly scurried to a corner when we arrived, some to snuggle to the teacher's side after sitting. While Joe went over his plan for guiding us to the site of the red prawns, the children sat quietly and were barely noticeable.

The rafters in the room were decorated with orange paper pumpkin cutouts and the letters of the alphabet, running in series from right to left, were tacked just beneath them. A few wooden stacking blocks sat neatly piled in a corner and a small chalk board sat on an easel. The floor was covered with random pieces of oil-cloth stamped in multiple designs. A few of our visiting men friends were unable to sit crossed legged in customary Fijian fashion and needed to sit in the traditional female style, with legs off to one side. In Fijian society it is rude to sit with one's feet pointing towards another person.

Confirming that his tribe had always held the red prawns sacred, Joe told us that outsiders had rarely seen them. No one had taken pictures of them and it was only after a lengthy discussion with his elders that he had been given permission to take a group of tourists to the site. Joe's objective was to better the lives of his people by earning money through tourism. Smiling, he recounted how several years ago the village had applied to the Fijian government for funds to purchase an outboard motor. His people were still waiting for a reply. Years earlier, Joe had left the village hoping to earn an income by joining a Japanese longline fishing vessel. When he found the pay not equal to the long, hard hours of dangerous labour, he returned to his village.

A LONG, wooden walking bridge, leading away from the village, spanned a tidal river that wound through the nearby mangrove swamp. The ageing, weathered bridge was missing some foot boards and we needed to watch where we placed our feet. When the bridge ended, a raised boardwalk seemed to continue endlessly and we were informed that it led the way across the swamp towards the village's secondary school. We were directed onto two planks that descended into the swamp. The ground was becoming wetter from an incoming tide and we needed to move quickly to reach our destination and still have time to return before it flooded entirely.

We followed a narrow, winding channel through thick tangles of mangrove roots clawing through soggy muck like thousands of knobby, arthritic fingers. Overhead, leafy, intertwining branches blocked the sun's heat, creating damp, earthy smells. Thick vegetation, some with saw-toothed blades of foliage, grabbed our outerwear and lacerated our skin.

Wading through shallow puddles, we followed the channel in and out of the bush until we arrived at the edge of a shore. Briskly we navigated the coconut strewn beach knowing that upon returning, the beach would be partially flooded or not there at all.

In the distance, a village woman wearing a wrap-around sulu now clinging to her ankles from wading on the sandbar, bent to collect crustaceans. Joe told us earnestly that he ate fish three times a day and was by now good and tired of it.

After rounding a corner, we saw a small limestone islet. To reach the red prawns we needed to cross a channel now rushing with the incoming tide. We had little time to complete the trip before we might all be stranded on the island for the night.

Once on the other side, we climbed a makeshift ladder leading up a steep, eroded dirt embankment. Joe went first, pounding rungs into place with his fist and drawing our attention to others that were missing.

A short walk through thick foliage and we came to a shallow gorge; the sacred site of the red prawns. We stepped down over the embankment to where the mouth of a low, rugged cave jutted out over a shallow pool of still water. With barely enough room for all of us to stand, I climbed back to the top to photograph the prawn sighting, which Joe had given me permission to do. I was not there long when I felt something crawling over my feet. Looking down, I discovered my feet swarming with red ants. Knocking them off just made room for the next swarm and it was challenging to stand still long enough to take the pictures.

Traditionally, it is believed that the prawns can be coaxed into leaving the cave by a sacred song. But two pale, red prawns were already outside the cave and crawling across the floor of brackish water. Joe boasted that he and the chief were the only two members of the tribe who were capable of calling the prawns. Then Joe raised his head, as if singing to the wind and chanted a solemn melody, *"Keitou oqo na marama ni vuna, Keitou mai sara Urubuta......."* When no other prawns came into view, Joe announced that if we were to get back to the village we would need to leave immediately.

By the time we returned to backtrack through the swamp, the path had already flooded calf deep. Nonetheless we easily navigated it, and arrived back in the village in good time.

We were surprised to learn that while away, the women in the village had prepared lunch for us. We were ushered into the community hall and were again invited to take a seat on the mats on the floor. A second man from the village joined the group to begin lunch with a short, opening ceremony. Then cheerful, smiling women placed plates of fried and steamed cakes stuffed with an assortment of savory fillings on the mat. The women had not spoken and in fact had sat behind the men after serving jugs of freshly squeezed lemonade. During lunch, when only the men ate, they displayed as much curiosity about our homes and cultures as we did about theirs. This was an unusual show of interest that we had not experienced from native people on other islands.

Following lunch, the preschoolers sang songs accompanied by their teacher and then a grandmother, the only elderly person we were to see that day, invited us to join the children and have our pictures taken with them. The older children were fascinated by their likenesses on the digital display, but the younger ones appeared confused and uncertain. Perhaps they didn't understand that they were viewing copies of themselves; mirrors are not part of native Fijian society.

A welcoming ceremony followed the lunch, when *salusalus*, traditional leis of rope-like greenery entwined with orange and red flowers, were draped over the shoulders of the visiting men. Then necklaces of waxy red, green and yellow leaves were placed around me and the one other visiting woman. To complete the welcoming ceremony, and to make us friends of the community, white powder was applied with puffs onto our cheeks and foreheads. The women thought we looked quite amusing and smiled at the ghost-like faces they had created.

Upon leaving the community hall we were surprised to be joined by even more women who had gathered outside. They welcomed us and stood cheerfully holding their children's hands while we took pictures.

We suspected the agency that had sold us the tour would keep a good portion of the fee, passing little of it on to the villagers, so to express our gratitude we took up a small collection to leave with them. Then, following our return to our boats, we gathered several useful items that we could send back to them including ropes, fish hooks and a few pairs of sandals. One BWR couple who had not come prepared with such gifts, but who had on board a first mate who applied blue makeup daily to her eyes, packed among the T-shirts, nails and hammers, a miniature compact taken from her makeup supply. French eye shadow called, *Plaisir de la Riviera*, (Riviera Delight).

I bet *that* gift kept our Fijian friends guessing what its purpose was!

We left Savusavu and headed for Musket Cove on Malolo Lailai island, 150 nm southwest, another official stopover for BWR participants. The island is part of the Mananuca archipelago, an assemblage of thousands of islands, some only minute pieces of land covered in rocky pinnacles greened sparsely by spindly, but hearty growth. Tucked away in the creases and short fjords of some of these smaller islands are the most sublime miniature beaches. Isolated and hidden from easy access to the average tourist, most islands remain untouched by humans, while others offer small bays, inlets and lagoons for adventurous boaters to anchor in. Most reefs, however, frequently go unmarked by any type of official navigational aid. Occasionally, casual markers such as branches are lightly anchored to the seabed to identify dangers. We found them confusing and we often couldn't determine the actual location of the reef that it was intended to mark. Was it to the right or to the left of the marker? To make matters worse, the symbols couldn't be trusted because they frequently get blown away or swept by currents from the spot they were meant to mark. We couldn't rely on the accuracy of any of them and when our charts didn't correspond with what we saw, it was always a time of concern. One pilot book described navigating around the banks of coral as 'rock hopping' and proposed steering towards a reef's breaking surge before proceeding to the next one while discovering a passage as you went. Our fear was that we would get into the middle of a maze and not be able to find a safe way out. We often used the chart plotter's track marker to visualize how to return the same way we went in. But with the number of times we needed to make turns, the lines on the chart plotter resembled a plate of twisted spaghetti making it difficult for us to decipher our own laid-down safe route out.

It was one of the most intense experiences of eye-ball navigation we would undertake.

THE Mamanucas are set in such a blissful and pure Pacific ambience that they attract numerous visitors from New Zealand and Australia seeking peaceful holidays. Blanketed in greenery amid the crystal turquoise waters surrounding them, the islands are a vacationer's dream—remote, idyllic and sun blessed. Sandbars appear to rise mysteriously from the ocean with a receding tide and then magically fall from sight again when the sea level rises.

MUSKET Cove is located inside a barrier reef and is one of the safest and most sheltered bays in the Mamanuca Islands. But surrounding the Cove, are several small reefs lying disguised like unexploded land mines. Due to the challenges of navigating the area, few sailors would attempt approaching Musket Cove in the dark, but if they did, and depended on the present day navigational leading lights, they would run straight into the end of Malolo Lailai. The leading lights, meant to keep mariners safe, were in fact never installed in proper alignment.

The charts indicated there were far more reefs in the area

than what we could see, but there was an unmarked channel in the mess of half-submerged coral that would keep us out of harm's way. We continued to comb the area searching for it. Several minutes passed as we second guessed our own decisions and attempted to decipher the graduated blue shades of various sea depths by sight. Mangled, windblown sticks, leaning at assorted angles, appeared to be markers but meant nothing meaningful to us. Some were topped with bundles of upright branches abruptly clipped like harshly trimmed haircuts. They worried us. What were they trying to signal to us? We couldn't imagine. Not having this local knowledge created added stress to our approach. We learned later that the anchored branches had nothing to do with navigation but were taboo markers erected by natives to indicate reserved fishing areas.

We motored around in a few tight circles to allow time for discussion of what we didn't have firm answers to, then we picked our way around the last headland and arrived safely just outside Musket Cove*. Moorings were available for waiting for high tide before entering the Cove. Even at high tide we only had inches to spare beneath our keel as we motored down the channel towards the docks.

Docks? When had we last tied to a dock?

SEVERAL Blue Water Rally members had arrived before us. Their schedule would allow them to stay in the Cove three weeks before moving to the next destination; a much-welcomed break in the push to conquer the world by sea in fourteen months. There were several husband and wife teams among the fleet that manned their own boats, and a chill-out in the sun was just what they needed.

---

* It was necessary to clear customs and immigration again when arriving to Musket Cove. A government official travelled from Lautoka to process the necessary paper work.

Our plans were to return to Toronto for six weeks. It was a timely departure. Mike had silenced his talking sandals with an application of glue and mine were being held together by duct tape. Our plans, for when we returned, were to spend more time exploring the South Pacific. We would need to say goodbye to our Blue Water Rally friends and we did so by hosting a farewell coffee party aboard *Baccalieu III*. Thirty-five BWR sailors joined us to sit and stand wherever they could find room, while Mike and I continuously refilled the resort's coffee carafes and served platters of homemade sweets aboard *Baccalieu III*.

Musket Cove is a haven for sailors who travel the tropical waters of the South Pacific. You will find yachtsman here from all over the world and I have heard it said by other sailors who have completed circumnavigations, that the Cove is a unique and special place. We highly agree.

It might surprise you that sailors are not welcomed everywhere they drop anchor. Some resorts, and even marinas, identify us as cheap and I confess that our needs are minimal. When we arrive at gas pumps to fill our measly five-gallon dinghy tanks and ask to use their facilities to dispose of our garbage and used oil, we seem nothing more than a costly nuisance. And because we do much of our own boat maintenance and do not use huge amounts of expensive water or electricity, few marinas make much money from us other than from dockage fees. Sailboats are of the RV's of the sea.

As well, there are many resorts that prefer their bathing beaches uncluttered rather than used as a parking lot for an array of sun bleached, peeling sailboat dinghies. There are those who don't even want us to grace their seascapes with our anchored boats. An open door policy for dinner reservations is not to be taken for granted. Some resorts might allow the yachtsman to dine with them but they may not allow us to arrive in our dinghies. But in all fairness, sailors tend to be a casual lot often without 'resort wear' and we can appear unkempt at times. Maybe even a little mangy.

But at Musket Cove, a classy resort of private villas and beach houses, owner Dick Smith, a self-made adventurer and great Australian entrepreneur, offered the amenities of his entire resort to all transient sailors; restaurant, swimming pool, beach, and even the resort's toys were available to us. Dick knew the needs of a sailor and provided his blue water visitors with their own island named Ratu Nemani or, more affectionately, Dick's Island.

The island has picnic tables, wood burning barbeques and a thatch covered outdoor bar known as the Three Dollar Bar. Any drink, no matter what the ingredient, cost three Australian dollars. Every evening, when sailors get together for a sundowner and cookout, inquisitive resort guests join the underdressed lot for some down-to-earth sea-faring talk and casual drink.

Each night the resort supplies dinnerware, napkins and condiments and on Sunday nights, 'mate's night-off', the bar offers reasonably priced pre-cooked baked potatoes, pasta and green salads to accompany whatever meat the sailors are flaming over the barbeques that night. And it was all just steps away from the bow of our boats.

Raise a glass to Dick Smith who once was a sailorman. Dick has since passed and will be surely missed.

FOLLOWING a six week home leave in Toronto, we returned to Musket Cove fully expecting to move the boat out of its storage hole and explore the outlying islands. However, upon our return, we learned that Musket Cove's annual sailing regatta was approaching, and it is an event not to be missed. This regatta is said to require more stamina in drinking skills than in sailing skills and it had all the makings of a week of good fun. The regatta is so popular that it attracts sailing friends from around the world year after year. One weathered looking couple had recently made their tenth passage from New Zealand to attend the regatta and later in the week, when one of the activities was a wet T-shirt contest, that old babe was right out there in the middle of it.

So it was that this 28th Musket Cove Regatta delayed our departure to the outlying islands.

It was one of the best decisions we ever made.

OPENING night: words of welcome, beating of the Lali (drums) and lighting of the torches. *Free* cocktails and nibbles and *free* salads for those barbequing their own dinners. Dick was generous.

Traditional Fijian dancing and a presentation of choral music by the island's local choir started the evening. Following the choir, each nationality represented at the Cove was required to sing their national anthem. That was fine for the Americans, Aussies and Kiwis who made up the bulk of the participants, but Canadians? There were only three of us!

The exercise might have gone well if any of us had been good singers. Our friend Ken B, a single-handed sailor and retired doctor from Milton, Ontario, took the lead with the worst out-of-tune rendition of *O'Canada* that you never want to hear. As a backup team, Mike and I were of no help whatsoever. And since we were singing with the assistance of a microphone, no one in the audience failed to hear a single off-key note.

The second day of the regatta was called 'Pirate's Day', when a boat race to Beachcomber Island was the order of the day. The rules of the race: get there any way you can.

An American couple, the owners of *Sundance*, a 55 foot (17 metre) motor-sailer, invited us to participate along with eight other pirate friends.

The entourage of boats left the Cove within minutes of each other encouraging, while en route, playful pirate attacks when some would hurl red tomatoes and water balloons at competing boats. In defense, we threw copious amounts of biodegradable toilet tissue torn from the roll and plunged into water for better density and mobility. But during battle, this top grade one ply was strong enough that it was picked up and hurled back at us! Among the other serious pirate boats was a converted fishing trawler armed with a very effective fire hose and pump. On occasion, when their gush of water did not meet their targets, they transferred the rig to a dinghy, which offered more maneuverability and allowed them to successfully drench their victims with showers of seawater. We could have really used that hose at the end of the day when *Sundance* was a scarred mess of red tomato puree and toilet paper bombs.

Beachcomber Island, located in a marine sanctuary, appears the size of an atom within a vast area of turquoise sea. A few palm trees extend from the sandy knoll, and white sand beaches encompass the island that takes a mere five minutes to circumnavigate on foot. As small as the island is, it claims to be the party capital of the Pacific, attracting young, bikini-clad women and a fine array of young male specimens.

So what were *we* doing there? Reliving our youth I guess, or wishing it had ever been so good.

When we arrived, it was obvious the young and beautiful were expecting us because an enthusiastic group dressed in pirate attire immediately dropped lassoes around our shoulders. We were 'dragged', by friendly pirates, up the beach to the inoculation station where we were ordered to down a shot of whisky and walk red hot coals (painted stones with smoldering dry ice), in order to complete 'immigration requirements'. A few drinking games and a tug of war, (which caused the rope to break), were followed by a tasty lunch and then we headed back to the Cove in our toilet paper splattered boat.

The following day, Mike and I entered the Hobie Cat Challenge. Never having sailed a catamaran until practicing the day before, we did well to win our first two matches and remained in the competition until losing out in the semifinals.

A large sand bank, located a mile off shore, becomes an island of lily-white sand when the tide is low but disappears for hours when the sea level rises. The area has the reputation of having the longest sunlight hours in the entire Pacific and on the fourth day of Regatta Week, during low tide, two large awnings were set up on the sandbank to offer a respite from the scorching Mamanuca sun. A beer and sausage and burger lunch was followed by games that had been formulated to be embarrassingly fun.

On the fifth day, christened, 'A Day of Sports & Absurdity', we played a best ball golf tournament with our Canadian buddy, Ken B. who kept his life simple by wearing clean white T-shirts every day that sported one simple logo: 'KEN B'. I asked Ken about his future plans and he replied that he just wanted to keep sailing; "When I can no longer hike my drawers down for a leak, I'm just walking off the back of my boat."

The cost to golf on any day was $20 FJ ($11 US), which included surprisingly decent rental clubs, golf balls and a push cart.

The nine-hole course ran along the shores of the ocean but was as dry as a parched throat in a desert. Not only does this part of Fiji receive more annual sunshine than any other, but the area is deprived of regular rainfalls, a fact that was evident when we repeatedly snapped the golf T's in half while attempting to poke them into the ground.

After completion of our game, two local men, sitting at a plastic table on the scruffy patio outside the rental kiosk, invited us to join them. We learned they were both cooks from one of the adjacent resorts. Their work schedules required them to work twenty-eight straight days followed by a four day break. With nothing to do and nowhere to go, they often spent their off-days relaxing with a few beers.

Many of the Musket Cove employees live in a compound on site, while others travel from a nearby village by communal water taxis supplied by the resort. Employees are encouraged to have spouses join them for employment at the Cove where they share on-site accommodations for couples. Many workers had even met their spouses at the resort and those who had children, had grandparents taking care of them in the village.

Throughout Dick Smith's lifetime at the Cove, he had been deeply involved in the welfare of the people of Malolo Lailai, including the education of their children. Among his humanitarian accomplishments, he had assisted in building schools and providing scholarships and funding for several projects which raised the standard of living for the people in the Malolo community.

THE second to last day of the regatta we joined another American couple and their friends aboard their Hallberg Rassy 42 (13 m) for a proper yacht race around Malolo Island. But the wind died during the race and when *Velocity* began to move backwards while in the grips of local tidal currents, we unanimously decided that it would be far more fun to be sitting at the Three Dollar Bar than perching out there like gulls on a lost raft.

The final day was 'Dress Your Boat Day', a competition for best-dressed boat when we dressed *Baccalieu III* in her forty colourful code flags, fore to aft and top to bottom. With yacht club burgees flying proudly from the starboard spreader, we hoisted the sizeable blue, red and white BWR flag off a halyard in the foretriangle and an assortment of larger rally flags in other spaces over the bow. All a fluttering mass of colour, each simple flag commanded a memory: a rally, an ocean crossing or a reminder of home.

On the stern, facing the dock, we hung one of my dresses (I had two) with a sign noting: 'Best Dress'.

THE closing ceremonies were celebrated with a pig-on-a-spit buffet where men were required to wear the traditional Bula shirt and wrap-around Sulu. Entertainment followed the dinner when the feverish beat of drums pounded out a Malay-Polynesian medley and were accompanied by a Samoan Fire dancer tossing fire batons into the air, catching and twirling them around and through his legs. The resort's employees, dressed in traditional costumes, put on a display of historic dance styles. The men represented the period before missionary influence with reenactments of war dances with pulse-quickening drums, naked chests, charcoal smeared faces and guttural war cries.

The women, however, did dances from the post-missionary period, when ankle-length dresses of blue and white frangipani prints were encouraged. Songs, strongly influenced by Christian hymns, allowed for simple hand and arm movements followed by a bit of swaying from a sitting position.

Native couples demonstrated how their ancestors were not allowed to dance facing each other but were required to dance standing side by side. A boring two-step-side-step accompanied by rhythmic clapping kept the art of dancing within the boundaries of the newly accepted religious beliefs. It wasn't until a few days later that we witnessed Fiji's present day dance style during the evening celebrations of Independence Day. That night, drums beat rhythms into frantic tempos while feet twisted, drilling divots into the fine, white beach sand and hips corkscrewed seductively downward with movements the missionaries would have fainted over.

The celebrations were a great ending to our visit to the

Cove and to our participation in the regatta. It was the longest we had ever stayed in one place—four weeks! But it was time now to say good-bye to this sailor's paradise. After attaching one of our yacht club burgees to the ceiling of the Three Dollar Bar, joining a host of others representing the visits of sailors from around the world, we untied the lines and pulled away on a high tide to venture into the Yasawa Islands, part of the Mamanuca Group.

THE YASAWA ISLANDS are a chain of twenty mountainous, volcanic islands scattered among countless other sister islets, some so near to each other that the volcanic ridges that connect them can be seen above the water at low tide. All together the islands stretch eighty-five miles into the idyllic blue waters of the South Pacific Ocean. Due to their close proximity to the international airport and Port Denarau, the islands are a haven for back-packers and are serviced by the *Yasawa Flyer*, a catamaran that whisks the backpackers out to resorts run by local fishing and farming families. It has only been since 1987 that the Yasawa Islands have been allowed to benefit from tourism. Up until that time, the Fijian government prevented land-based tourism and those who travelled to the islands on cruise ships, were required to stay onboard their ships.

Now there are resorts including low cost stop-overs providing dormitory facilities, communal meals, outdoor plumbing, and drinkable rainwater. Limited electricity demands the resorts keep in touch by radio and their indoor light disappears with the setting sun. The remote, intimate islands offer sparsely populated beaches and everywhere, the sparkle of the night sky persuades you that there are no worries in the world. It's a place where just being there can be a euphoric experience.

SAILING north we kept well away from neighbouring islands

where stunted trees and gangly shrubs poked out from rocky shorelines. The boat rolled with the swells and the smell of lamb shanks stewing in the breadmaker below was not as enticing to me as it might have been in steadier conditions. Wind stirred the seas into small waves and when one hit the side of the boat splashing over the foredeck, Mike grumbled about the salt residue it would leave on our recently washed boat.

That's what happens when you become a landlubber, your priorities become muddled.

We arrived in Nanuya Lailai Bay commonly known as Blue Lagoon. We planned to spend several days in the area but a tropical convergence zone moved towards us, bringing days and days of cloud cover, wind and rain. After a few inclement days at anchor we left the lagoon and returned to Musket Cove where we rendezvoused with Andy, a Toronto friend who was joining us for the passage to New Zealand.

Mid-October to mid-November is the ideal time to make the 1,200 nm passage between Fiji and New Zealand. Tropical storms commence near Fiji at the end of November. It was now mid-October and we knew to expect variable wind conditions while en route but between Fiji and New Zealand, 'variable' refers to high winds and headwinds. Talk at the Three Dollar Bar confirmed that few boats ever complete the seven to eight day passage without getting hit by something nasty.

Except for our little side trip through the Yasawa Islands, Mike and I had been at dock for a long period of time and we both felt a tweak of anxiety as we got ready to sail the open ocean again. There is no doubt we had gotten soft. We stayed focused preparing for the passage by checking the navigation systems, watermaker, deck hardware and rigging and generally preparing *Baccalieu III* to meet the challenges of the sea again.

PASSAGE TO NEW ZEALAND

Sunshine almost always makes me high
John Denver

In order to clear Fijian customs, it was necessary to sail 16 nm south to the city of Lautoka. Lautoka was not just the base for customs, it was also the location of a sugar mill that spewed grimy black residue into the lovely blue sky. Anyone who has taken their boat there, curses the day they saw the place and warns others of the sticky mess that lands on boat decks after only a few hours at anchor. It was a place to avoid if at all possible. As luck would have it, three other boats, also wanting to avoid Lautoka, had placed a request for a customs official to meet them in Port Denarau about the same distance as Lautoka but without the attendant pollution. This was not a government-approved arrangement, but Fijian customs officers seemed open to an opportunity to pad their wallets when one arose.

As we prepared to pull away from the dock at Musket Cove we untied the stern lines from shore and pulled them onto the boat as we motored forward. We had dropped the anchor a few metres from a reef and we allowed it to pull the boat forward. Then we proceeded to engage the windlass to haul it up. A fifteen-knot wind was blowing over the stern, pushing us towards the reef. Only a delicate maneuvering would keep the boat from sliding sidewise and grounding. Carrying out the procedure with good speed was important, but wouldn't you know it? We ran into problems.

A neighbouring boat had arrived in the Cove a few days after our arrival and had dropped his anchor on top of ours. The two buried anchors now lay in a tangle on the bottom of the anchorage. It quickly became evident that our windlass was unable to lift both anchors and with *Baccalieu III's* bow imprisoned, the wind caught her beam and pushed her towards the reef.

There's nothing like a boat in trouble to muster up a crowd, and we were highly entertaining to those looking on from shore that morning. But Richard, whose anchor we were tangled with, jumped into his dinghy and with his fifteen horsepower motor, combined with our own efforts, we managed to get *Baccalieu III* straightened out stern-to-wind. I backed her down between the two boats at dock where we had just left forty-five minutes earlier. During my reverse maneuver however, I discovered that the bow thruster switch, that Mike had rewired a few days before, had been installed in reverse. Suddenly I had to respond to the boat turning the opposite direction when using it. Try getting that sorted in your head while carrying out a reverse maneuver during an emergency! Then the thruster over-heated and cut out entirely.

It was a fun time all around for the spectators waiting to see if something really nasty would come of it all. But I'm afraid they were disappointed. Once we were tied up again, a free diver, one of those we had been entertaining from shore with our reef evasion tactics dove on the anchors, separated them and we were still able to catch the high tide we needed to leave the Cove.

THIRTY knot winds accompanied us to Port Denarau but our ride was fairly comfortable because we were sailing inside the barrier reef which knocks down the waves. I had noticed at Musket Cove that Dick Smith had a few wrecked boats lying around his property, some of which he had rescued from surrounding reefs. A little hiccup in our engine, I thought, and we too could be on display in Dick Smith's backyard.

Just outside Port Denarau we attempted to call the marina to announce our arrival only to discover that our VHF radio was faulty. Our cockpit handset had given us trouble before and now we had an outside handset that wouldn't send messages and an inside set that would not receive. With one of us transmitting from the radio at the navigation station and the other listening for the reply from the cockpit, we managed to communicate with shore.

We never determined the cause of the problem but later, while waiting for a good weather forecast to depart for New Zealand, we used the faulty radio as an excuse to overstay our allotted time after checking out with customs.

We knew that a single forecast could not carry us all the way to New Zealand and it was important to leave on the edge of a good one. The radio malfunction bought us an extra day which allowed us to travel to a nearby anchorage and hold up until we were satisfied the weather was as good as it was going to get. But when we left for New Zealand we did not have a functioning radio.

Before departing Port Denarau, we had several indications of what might lie in wait for us. A power boat down the dock had fortified his windows with plywood, and a recently departed boat was on a return route back to the marina due to a ruptured fuel tank caused by excessively active sea conditions.

The day before we left, a 20 metre (65 foot) yacht radioed in a mishap. On their first day out, while sailing under reefed mainsail and jib, the skipper reported that sailing had been steady but the seas had been hectic. Then suddenly his yacht had surfed down a wave into an enormous trough, but instead of climbing up and out, as one would expect, his boat appeared to come to an abrupt halt as if running into a wall. He recalled a loud moaning followed by a shudder that ran throughout the entire boat. The oncoming wave, broke onboard with strong impact causing a canvas dodger to tear from its stainless frame leaving the sturdy supports bent out of shape. The two crewmembers who were in the cockpit, were swept into a corner by the dump of water but because they wore harnesses that were attached to pad eyes, they remained onboard. Losing the dodger meant they would spend the following four miserably cold days with little to protect them against the elements while standing their watches.

COMMANDERS' Weather Forecasters sent us an updated weather report. In summary, the report stated: "Looks reasonable for most of the trip." This was the best report we had seen in days. We decided to leave.

The passage was going to take six days, however, after rolling out of bed at 0600, we immediately got into that antsy state that we often experienced before long passages. We stood while eating our yogurts and then started with last minute checks while sipping our hot morning drinks. We walked the deck checking and rechecking rigging, cowl vents, lines, hardware, jacklines and the position of cars on tracks. The jacklines were used to hook our harnesses to, when it was necessary for someone to go forward to carry out work on deck in rough seas. Below, we confirmed that all items were either attached to something or at least secured behind cupboard doors. I prepared lunch then tried to do a quick fix on an overhead flap on the helmsmen's bimini that I knew would be an annoyance when it tapped continuously against the canvas.

I didn't feel relaxed enough to do the job properly and, anxious to get going, I simply cut it off.

We pulled up the anchor and were off.

As we approached the pass a few miles offshore, moderate sized waves rolled over the barrier reef and the 4 metre (13 foot) swells that met us outside the passage seemed acceptable. It was the first time in days we had seen a blue sky, and even the wind seemed to be cooperating by blowing a reasonable fifteen to twenty knots. Mike went aft to take down our Canadian ensign, as we often did on long passages, and accidentally dropped it into the sea. I presumed this was an innocent accident and not a warning from either Neptune or Poseidon.

This presumption would soon prove to be wrong.

We sailed through wide streams of floating pumice, the debris spit out by a recently erupted underwater volcano, most likely in Tonga. Breaking waves washed lava stones, the size of quarters, on board where they came to rest in little piles alongside the cap rail. The gravel jammed the speed impeller and to clean it, can be a harrowing experience. The impeller is located below the waterline therefore, when the transducer is pulled out of its thru-hull tube, seawater gushes into the boat like a geyser and if the tube is not immediately plugged, the incoming water can sink the boat.

The boat had ten other thru-hulls. Months before, we had fastened lanyards attached to tapered wooden plugs, near each thru-hull to be used if a valve broke or a hose detached. We also carried spongy Nerf balls to take the place of a transducer or a wooden plug that couldn't be pushed back into place.

As the day went on, the swells increased in size and occasionally, a six metre (twenty-foot) wall of water would hit the bow and rain down on us in the cockpit. No one but me had lunch that day and I thought how interesting it was that the gal who couldn't make a Lake Ontario crossing without having to lie down was now the only one eating a sandwich.

However, by late afternoon I wasn't feeling so chipper and by 1800 hours I spent my off watch lying on the settee feeling even more nauseous. I didn't think I was capable of lifting myself off the sofa to retrieve a motion sick tablet, but I managed to get to one and gulp it down. The box read chewable but my stomach said chuckable and I ran for the toilet.

If ever I can report a great strength, this is where it lies, in the retching department. I could probably win an award for the strongest retch. Less dramatic perhaps than toads that heave their entire stomachs, but in the Homo sapiens category, my heave is dramatic. I croaked so hard I injured my throat and I forced myself to get off the settee again to retrieve an ice cube from the freezer to soothe it. I have never known Mike to be seasick, but that evening I was sharing the toilet with him.

This would teach us to spend so much time as landlubbers.

At some time I took a second tablet. Then my mouth turned dry and I felt as if I had been shot with an overdose of Novocain. I lay there wondering how I would ever manage to get off the couch to take my watch, but when the time came, I stood my shift and spent the worst night I have ever experienced on a watch.

The waves were large enough to frequently explode on contact and they continued to douse the cockpit. The magnificent luminescence that sometimes accompanied us on night journeys meant nothing to me that night and music from my MP3 player was an annoyance that I couldn't stand listening to. I recalled an article about seasickness being a manageable mental condition, and I wanted to choke the author or at least vomit on him.

Suddenly an unusually large wave collided with the stern, throwing me off my seat to the other side of the cockpit. That put a momentary stop to my whining and instead, I felt thankful I was still onboard.

I turned the deck lights on expecting to see the dinghy dangling from its davits, but everything was where it was supposed to be, and I quickly returned to feeling like a piece of road kill. By this time the two motion sickness pills I had taken had passed into the "Let's sleep" phase, and I forced myself to stand for the rest of my watch. I figured only cattle could fall asleep while on their feet.*

On the second day weather conditions allowed us to make seven knots of speed with only fifteen-knot winds. Nature is full of surprises.

The third morning I was standing at the stove, hoping to catch the kettle before it went into its whistle frenzy and woke everyone up. I'm just the right height to look through the port over the stove and I could see the sun rising while standing there. The light accentuated the somber grey of the water reminding me that we were sailing into the tail end of New Zealand's winter season. The new moon was still hanging up there silver-glazing the waves with a cold sterling look. But the wind and seas had diminished and I was feeling a whole lot better.

It sure had the makings of a great day.

Commanders' weather update indicated that we were heading towards some nasty headwinds and I made muffins while I could still stand vertically in the galley. Ahead of us was a smooth pennant of dirty grey cloud stretching from one end of the horizon to the other; it was the cold front with the headwinds that we were about to meet.

By noon the headwinds had arrived. We turned the boat

---

* Horses, cows, elephants, zebras and flamingos have knees that lock into place to allow for sleeping while standing.

fifteen degrees off course to lessen the effect but within the hour we were bucking twenty-five knot winds under motor. The slate coloured waves had increased in size and the space between them had shortened. Short is not good. The ride was going to get rougher over the upcoming hours.

And so it began. The waves built. Then the wind churned the tops into whitecaps and blew them off like pieces of snow. The 1600 RPM's, which under good conditions would give us six knots of speed, was only giving us four. The bow ploughed through the waves, splitting them and throwing sizzling seawater into the air. What didn't land back in the ocean rolled up the deck and came to a stop on the dodger's plastic windshield. I would watch the attack from behind the safety of the transparent windshield and even though protected from most of its assault, I'd flinch when it exploded with a thud on contact just centimetres in front of me. Water still reached me on the occasions when it rolled off the canvas and poured down into the cockpit in what seemed to be bucket-like quantities.

The deck scuppers gurgled and slurped with more water than they could handle and when I looked aft, we were leaving stripes of foam in our wake. Andy was bedded down in the forward bunkroom until he went airborne a few times, then he moved to where he would find the least amount of motion, and lay on the settee in the salon.

The sun showed itself several times poking out from clusters of cumulous clouds. I love it when the sun shines on a bad day; it seems to make everything so much better.

By afternoon we broke into 26° latitude. Only ten more degrees to go, I thought jubilantly, until I remembered ten degrees equaled six hundred miles.

By 1700 hours the wind strength was in the mid-thirties and the seas had grown with the wind. By 2000 hours we knew we were in for some rip roaring weather.

There were no showers for the crew that day, no clean,

squeaky hair, not even a change of clothes. Without getting out of bed, I could reach my clean underwear and while scrunched into a ball, wrench my legs into the openings. I'm pretty talented in some fields.

All day, we were either on watch, braced against the cockpit pedestal, or lying down. It was just that kind of ride. At least I could look forward to standing the "preferred shift" or "banking hours", as they came to be known; on duty 2100 to midnight, and then off until 0600. But as weather and sea conditions worsened, we doubled up on watches so there would always be two minding the boat. Consequently, my three evening watch hours turned into five! After standing three hours alone, I stayed up to stand two more with Andy. Andy said I was squeezed; that I had taken one for the team. In any case I used my sorry state of affairs as an excuse to grab some of the Cadbury Raisin and Nut chocolate bar that he had brought. Andy had brought about ten and by the end of the trip we had munched through almost all of them. I love chocolate and I have occasionally envisioned living on nothing more than chocolate. But it wasn't as great as I had imagined.

The temperature was not bitter cold but after being exposed to dampness and cool air for several hours on watch, we began to feel like thawing Popsicles. Even fleece shirts and pants under our foul weather gear didn't prevent us from feeling chilled. Water-proof gloves, boots and toques were accents to our ensembles and I was a long way from looking anything like that Anne Klein brochure that arrived at the boat when Andy brought our mail from home. Published by Holt Renfrew, it was one of those designer black and grey pamphlets that I have to look at four or five times to see whether the model is wearing anything different from one page to the next. Black pants, black sweater, black belt, black handbag, and black stilettos it seemed to repeat over and over on the following pages in only slightly different combinations. It was an odd piece of advertising to have at a time like this. The only thing I could relate to was the greyness of it all.

There were many times I would have loved to sip a cup of hot tea, but preparing it would mean going down to the galley and then later bracing myself in front of a toilet, taking off my jacket, pulling down the foul weather pants, pulling down the fleece, pulling down, pulling down. Remaining cold and dehydrated seemed the better option.

By nightfall the wind climbed into the forties. It was too dark to see the state of the sea except where the steaming light shone on the water near the hull but it appeared to be chaotic.

And then the boat started to pound. Pounding is when hardware works loose and subsequently might cause failures. We tried minimizing the pounding with a course change but didn't achieve much. The only thing we could do was to keep the sails balanced and ride it out.

Because of our course change, the estimated time of arrival kept moving away.

The autopilot was doing a marvelous job but no one wanted to mention it in case we hexed our good fortune. We rotated watches throughout the night, with each of us putting in long hours while the off person took the biggest risk of all when maneuvering through the constantly moving space below. Sleep wasn't an option for anyone that night.

While standing watch together, Mike and Andy caught sight of another boat approaching from the portside. The vessel was showing an irregular pattern of navigation lights and the boys couldn't determine whether it was under engine power or sail. Mike made contact by VHF radio and learned the ketch was using its spreader lights to fully illuminate the boat in order that we would not miss seeing him. But the bright lights camouflaged the navigation lights so the direction the boat was travelling couldn't be determined. Apparently he couldn't understand our heading either, because we were showing both a masthead light and a steaming light which should not be shown together. But our bow navigation light had burned out and we too, were doing our best for identification purposes. Anyway, not only did our two boats see each other and determine that we were on converging paths, we ultimately realized that we knew each other from Tahiti!

This marked the fourth time, that a potential collision with another boat had taken place during a night passage. It's astounding to me that there are sailors who choose not to keep twenty-four hour watches. One couple who we met (and sailed hundreds of miles with) not only did not keep watch, but they extinguished all navigational lights during night passages. They justified their decision by stating they didn't want pirates to see them.

I wondered how they'd feel about running into them.

During the fifth sunrise, the sun crept above the horizon in overwhelming proportions. Huge and fiery it dominated the early morning sky. Then it disappeared behind a series of broken clouds from which its rays burnt through like beams from a series of searchlights. 'God rays' is what some people call them.

That was the good part of the day.

When the wind strength diminished to thirty knots, we went back on single watches of two hours each. To stand three hours in the cold was too uncomfortable. The cold front we had seen in the distance, passed through during Andy's watch belting him with forty-five knot winds. Within forty-five minutes we were on the backside of the front where we expected the wind to let up. But it didn't. There was nothing we could do but brace ourselves against a wall when pulling off our foul weather gear and then lie down before we were knocked down.

We were halfway to our destination.

THAT night was hardly a time one would expect anything magical to happen, but while alone in the cockpit, I witnessed a phenomenal piece of nature. All around me, the wind and waves pounded in unfriendly fashion when suddenly, a minute illuminated speck, no larger than the head of a dressmaker's pin, appeared on the cockpit table. Bluish-green in colour, it glowed like a highly energized firefly. From where it came I had no idea. But it dazzled like a rare solitaire diamond. As bright as any LED light I had ever seen. Whatever could it be, I wondered? Where had it come from? Was it hot?

The night was coal black, clear and unclouded. I glanced towards the constellations. On nights like this I had seen satellites whirling in orbit across the sky and had several times, recognized Saturn by its unusual golden hue. Jupiter's large, brilliant glow accompanied me on many a night and several times I had mistaken the silver hued Venus for the navigation lights of another vessel when the planet rose from the horizon. I had seen more meteoroids falling into the earth's atmosphere than I could count. Could this tiny piece of jewel sitting on my cockpit table be a piece from some galaxy? Was it burning the table?

I directed my flashlight over it. There appeared to be nothing there. But when I extinguished my light it glowed bright again, like a modern day Tinker Bell.[*]

That little piece of nothing that joined me that night was spellbinding and even magical. I could have easily been convinced that it had come from Never Never Land, "Second star to the right and straight on 'til morning."

But even I, who would have loved to have had my own Tinker Bell during that dark, rough night, concluded the glowing dot must be a piece of bioluminescence that had been

---

[*] Tinker Bell was an animated fairy made popular by Walt Disney Productions after bringing to life JM Barrie's fictional story entitled *Peter Pan*, or *The Boy Who Wouldn't Grow Up*.

swept aboard by a wave. Whatever it was, I can only confirm that it was both captivating and mystical.

Then my Tinker Bell's light went out and I was, quite honestly, sad. I felt I had lost a companion.

During the night, the wind diminished and by the morning of the sixth day, it was necessary to use the motor. The barometer had increased by 14 millibars (MB) since leaving Musket Cove and was now reading 1030 MB indicating we were passing through the middle of a high-pressure system. You've got about as much chance of getting wind from a high-pressure system as you do getting a bank loan for a facelift.

By now, we needed to pay attention to our fuel consumption. Our fuel tank gauge read only 250 litres (66 US/54 Imp gallons) remained in the tank. We had another forty litres of emergency fuel in portable tanks lashed down in the lazarette. It takes a lot of fuel to punch through waves the size of what we were handling.

We were burning, on average, six to eight litres per hour and had approximately a hundred and fifty miles left before completing the passage. We determined that we had ample fuel as long as the wind remained soft and we weren't forced to buck more headwinds. In the back of our minds however, was the fact that lurking just west of our destination of Opua, there was another low-pressure system with thirty-five knot headwinds spinning off the top. It would pass over Opua and advance towards us if we were still out to sea. Headwinds would mean burning more fuel, perhaps more fuel than we had onboard. Ideally, we wanted to be in and tied up before another headwind hit us.

We barely got a glimpse of the northern most point of New Zealand before night fell. The country appeared like a mirage on a bleak and cloudy horizon before the night sky consumed it and all we could see were the orange squiggles left on the radar screen. But we knew it was out there and we were thankful we were so near to landing.

We arrived in Port Opua around midnight, just hours ahead of the low-pressure system. It was too late to receive clearance from customs so we were required to tie up to the floating quarantine dock located just offshore. The dock was there to help eliminate any agriculture contamination brought to port by arriving international boats. We were happy just to go to bed and have at least part of a good night's sleep in a stationary bed.

Opua's custom officials are highly organized for receiving international boats. They encourage boaties (we were known as boaties here, yachties in Fiji), to fax all the necessary information required to enter the country before arriving. They also prefer that recreational vessels check-in with one of the coastal marine radio stations at least four hours prior to arrival and encourage the use of one of the local radio freelancers who stand by on various stations to assist approaching boats with advice. In turn, these stations will contact the necessary authorities and arrange for them to meet new arrivals at the Custom's Clearance Wharf.

When quarantine officials arrived at nine the following morning, they headed straight for our freezer. They removed all the frozen meats and prepared foods that we had not eaten on passage; prepared lasagna, chicken cannelloni, beef stew, chili, and soups, even my stuffed breads because they contained either cheese or corned beef. All of it went straight into green garbage bags where it would stay until it received a sterilizing steam treatment and eventually a burial. Believe me that was sad.

I had already dumped all the dairy products and honey overboard and had been forewarned, before leaving Musket Cove, about emptying the vacuum cleaner bag and cleaning the soles of our shoes. I had done all that before leaving Fiji. Agriculture is a major industry in New Zealand and it's the only island in the southern hemisphere without fruit flies. Their beef cattle and sheep are all grass fed and one case of Foot and Mouth disease would knock out the country's prime industry. Consequently they are meticulous in inspecting visiting boats that might carry contaminants.

We were required to enter New Zealand waters with the bottom of our boat free of growth. We had been forewarned that it would be inspected upon arrival.

While we had been back in Toronto the boat had sat for six weeks in a nice warm, still-water basin at Musket Cove, raising very healthy, green furry microbes on the lower hull. But in preparation for our New Zealand arrival, Mike had spent hours scrubbing it clean.

Prior to entering the thirty mile New Zealand perimeter, I had cleaned out the vegetable storage areas below the floor boards and had tossed over potatoes, onions and garlic, including any dirt that may have been carried aboard with them. Our bilges were cleaner than the cupboards in my house. But when the officer checked the lockers he found two onions that had slid to the back and jokingly accused me of trying to hide them.

I laughed weakly, wondering what two-stow away onions were going to cost us. I'm lucky we didn't get fined.

The officer didn't stop there. He opened our pantry and searched through the canned goods identifying items produced in Ecuador, especially milk or milk products including mayonnaise. According to the quarantine officer, it's possible to transmit Foot and Mouth disease in products that originate in South America.

These went into the garbage bags as well.

It was exciting to be back in civilization again, where people drove cars, even if they did drive on the left side of the road. When we drove a few miles outside Opua to find a grocery store, the place looked pretty much like home. I had a feeling of being back, although I had never been there before.

It had been a long time since we had brought the boat into a first world country.

We stayed four days in Opua before setting out again for an overnight trip to Gulf Harbour, just outside of Auckland. It was October and our plans were to take the boat out of the water for the cyclone season and return to Toronto.

We were half way around the world.

NEW ZEALAND

A LAND OF PALM TREES AND PINE TREES,
GLACIERS AND RAINFORESTS

POLYNESIA IS DEFINED by a triangle that includes Hawaii, Easter Island and New Zealand. New Zealand is located at the southern tip of the triangle and was as far south as we had planned to venture.

The first colony to settle New Zealand, arrived there approximately eight hundred years ago. Modern-day indigenous Māoris, named the land *Aotearoa*, or 'Land of the Long White Cloud'. Native Hawaiians, Samoans, the peoples of Easter Island and the Māori of New Zealand, share the same ancestry, and in early times, spoke dialects stemming from the same language.

Directing their canoes southward, early seamen analyzed ocean currents by the tugs on their steering helms. Water filled gourds, fermented breadfruit and tubers pounded and bound with leaves, provided food.

Some of the islands they found were the islands now known as New Zealand. Imagine! Within a giant ocean, they found a group of islands no larger than 435,000 square kilometres (270,000 square miles)! It took until 1642 for far larger sailing ships to find these same islands.*

In the late 1700s, Europeans began arriving in greater numbers, for whaling and to collect timber. The British crown signed

---

* Abel Tasman, a Dutch explorer, was the first known European to discover New Zealand. He named it Staten Landt (Land of the States-General). Tasman's fleet consisted of a 120 ton warship named *Heemskerck*, and *Zeehaen*, a 200 ton fluyt.

the first treaty with several Māori chiefs in 1840. The treaty recognized land ownership by the Māori and offered them British subject status. At the same time, a British governor was appointed to the country. The treaty was written in both English and Māori languages which resulted in it having different meanings. The British believed the treaty gave them sovereignty over New Zealand while the Māori chiefs interpreted it completely differently. Since as far back as 1860, the Māori have demanded compensations for the loss of their land.

In the early 1830s, the sandalwood trade on the islands north of New Zealand, was in a slump. The whaling industry, however, was still strong and the sea cucumber, turtle shell and coconut oil trades were doing well. And so was the trade of smoked Māori tattoo heads known as *mokomokai*, the skulls of chiefs that had been removed after death by admiring warriors. Traditionally, the skin covered heads were smoked for preservation, and then displayed during special ceremonies. Rival clans also collected the heads of enemy chiefs in order to mock their defeated enemies. The heads were never intended as collector's items for white men, but the mokomokai became a highly sought item of trade.

When Māori chiefs discovered that firearms could be secured by trading mokomokai, they realized their value. Firearms could be used to defeat neighbouring clans. The demand for heads increased resulting in more raids between villages for the sole purpose of head hunting. In time, all villages needed firearms to protect their settlements. The heads became so popular with foreign collectors that chiefs demanded their slaves be tattooed and then killed for the purpose of trading mokomokai. Eventually the British passed a law to discourage the trade.

Many of the collected heads are now located in the backrooms of museums and scattered around the world in private collections. As well as demanding compensation for the loss of their land, the Māori want the smoked heads returned.

Those who have visited New Zealand sometimes refer to it as 'The Godzone' because of its immense natural beauty and the countless ways it can be enjoyed. Sailors recognize it as a safe haven outside the tropical cyclone zone. For us, it was a long way from home. We wondered how we would ever get back. Sailing south is one thing, sailing north is quite another. It's similar to enjoying a toboggan ride down a great hill then looking up to realize that it's going to require some hard work to get back to where you started from.

New Zealand's temperate climate is warm enough that most homes don't need furnaces. This is certainly true on the North Island where patrons of restaurants and bars spill onto the streets even during the winter months. The South Island also enjoys subtropical temperatures although inland it can be much cooler. The sun, however, can be blistering hot and even on a cloudy day you can find yourself sunburnt.

Unlike North America, where we sometimes bathe in warm south winds, here a south wind results in an Antarctic cool off. Many things are reversed in this part of the world. High-pressure systems rotate counterclockwise while low-pressure systems rotate clockwise. Ocean currents also rotate counterclockwise. On this side of the equator, fall is spring and spring is fall. And that's not all. Hot and cold water taps are located in reverse positions on basins. And restaurant waiters do not expect to be tipped!

New Zealanders generally take themselves far less seriously than people north of the equator. Easygoing, they often display a sense of humour. Even some of the place-names made me smile, like Cape Foul Wind and Rotten Row St. Many place names, however, remain native Māori such as Whangarei, pronounced fung-gar-i and Whangaparapara.

Frequently, phrases used in everyday situations are spoken in slang. Breakfast is brekkie and sandwich is sani, prezzie means a gift, and tinny is the word for a can of beer. Restaurant take-outs are take-a-ways and the beer store is called the bottle shop. There were times I had no idea what people were saying to me so if it was in the form of a question, I thought it safest to answer with a "No." It took three visits to the grocery store before I understood that the checkout girl was asking me if I had a 'One' card, something to do with saving money at the store.

The New Zealand accent, compounded by native jargon made deciphering the lingo even more difficult. The word 'yes' sounded more like yeepa. And sometimes it was the mix of words that gave me trouble. "This arvo I'm going tramping, Bobs not coming with me, he's a bit of a piker." (This afternoon I'm going hiking, Bobs not coming with me, he's a bit of a slacker).

I thought they spoke English in New Zealand!

According to New Zealand slang, if you're a hard worker you're a hard yacker. If you're lazy, you might be a dole bludger or maybe a ratbag. And if you should suggest to a New Zealander that their lingo sounds similar to that of Australia's, such as the everyday greeting of 'gidday', you will have delivered a grand insult. According to the Kiwis, Australia has stolen many things from them.

The British influence in New Zealand is obvious with place names like Nelson, Dunedin, Wellington and Canterbury Bight as well as numerous words Kiwis use in everyday language like petrol and rubbish. Driving is done on the left side of the road and once you conquer that, very soon you are faced with a roundabout, something that is seen only occasionally in Canada.

Navigating a New Zealand roundabout is like swimming into a chaotic whirlpool of swirling water. Streams of cars, racing at high speeds from several directions, rush in to converge in the same small circle. Sometimes I would drive round and round until I got the gist of how to get off.

I didn't see vanity plates while in New Zealand but what they have is even better. Written across the back windows of some motor vehicles were humorous sayings like, "Sex is not the answer, sex is the question. Yes, is the answer!"

New Zealanders walk everywhere. They walk to work, walk to shop, walk to restaurants and they dress casually, as if just coming from the garden. I fit in quite well there. The whole country appears to think casual except for the ruthless food inspector who swept through my galley like a pneumatic vacuum cleaner sucking up hazardous waste. In the airport in Nelson, there weren't even security measures prior to boarding a domestic flight. New Zealanders are trusting people and shop keepers sometimes allowed us to take the merchandise and pay later. And we were transient foreigners! No one trusts a transient sailor.

The country is the home of the All Blacks rugby team and the Black Caps cricket team. While touring the South Island by car, we often found ourselves eating at the only available restaurant in town, the local bar. Televisions were most often turned to rugby matches and everyone would be lined up sitting facing the tube while eating. No one ever seemed to speak in those bars unless it was about the game. But I learned a lot about rugby at those eating stops. Not only is it a rough, tough, fast paced game of push and shove, but the players wear no protective gear! The only exception is the guy in the middle of the scrimmage who wears a skullcap to keep from getting his ears torn off!

WE were half way around the world and articles in the *New Zealand Sunday Star Times* read as if it was right out of Toronto's *Globe and Mail*. Is the food we serve our children in school cafeterias healthy? Is our economy sagging? Should stores continue to supply plastic bags to customers? Should parents be allowed to smack their children? Too many people are being mauled by pit bulls and drunk driving is causing too many deaths. Treaty settlements and immigration concerns were discussed. The general population is having fewer children and residents are getting older. More marriages are breaking up. The cost of housing is going up.

I really felt like I belonged there.

The government had already eliminated the one-cent coin and the GST (goods and service tax), which was twelve and a half percent, was included in the price of everything you bought including food. I liked that—no surprises. I'm not very good at math.

The health care system is a combination of private and public care. I liked that too.

And I liked the food. Experiencing New Zealand culture, has to include sampling their 'greasies'. Hordes of restaurants advertise battered fish and deep-fried chips and they even compete to become known as New Zealand's 'Best Fish and Chip Shop'. Judged on the freshness of their fish and the colour and fat content of their chips, restaurants strive to serve the best in the land. But only those serving chips with an eleven percent or less fat content can ever hope of winning the award. To the New Zealander, this is serious gastronomy and in 2010 the whole country celebrated '150 Years of Fish and Chips'! But no matter what the colour or fat content of the chips, New Zealanders eat seven million servings of chips a week!

New Zealanders are also big on flavours. Chili and lime or herb flavoured rotisserie chickens sit in warming ovens in grocery stores, and as the largest consumer per capita of potato chips, the snack food comes in a wide assortment of flavours: chili and sour cream, tomato and red pepper salsa, lime and cracked pepper, Parma ham and sun dried tomato, blue cheese and caramelized onion, prosciutto and brie, feta and garlic cream cheese with peppercorn, dijonnaise, cheese and onion, sour cream and chilies, Greek tzatziki, lamb with mint and plain chicken. Why would anyone want their potato chips to taste like a farm animal?

It's not unusual for a hamburger to arrive at your table topped with sliced pickled beets or for a fish sandwich to be garnished with strands of spaghetti. The national dessert is Pavlova, a big crusty meringue topped with whip cream and fresh fruit.

New Zealand also makes good beer. One of my favourites was Mac's Gold—All Malt Lager which comes in a brown bottle with a rippled neck to offer the drinker a good handgrip. On the back of the bottle the label reads, "You hold what many believe to be ONE OF THE UGLIEST beer bottles in the world," then the label goes on to offer some history of the founder and ends with "To this day a beer from Mac's looks like a cross between a marital aid and a hand grenade."

That's what I like about New Zealanders: they're not afraid to make you laugh and they don't give a hoot if they offend you.

THE North and South Islands are quite different. The South Island, dominated by the scenic Southern Alps, displays the most dramatic mountain scenery of the two islands. From soaring waterfalls to snow-white glaciers, the South Island is a sanctuary for outdoorsmen. In fact, Queenstown is known as the adventure capital of New Zealand.

The North Island however, is where most of New Zealand's population resides. The climate is slightly warmer, and geothermal heat spurts through the earth's crust from numerous geysers in an area known as Rotorua. But in other parts of the island, sprawling dairy and sheep farms follow the contour of rolling pastureland over the most serene looking hills. Further north, vineyards produce New Zealand's finest Cabernet Sauvignon and Merlot wines.

CITIZENS in the south think the people in the north are crazy, aggressive drivers and they are, or at least they appear to be when they approach those dizzying roundabouts at such high speeds. Meanwhile, the people in the north think the Southerners are country bumpkins.

One thing both islands have in common is sheep, lots of sheep.* In total, at least forty million of them.

The country's agricultural industries are paramount to the island's economy and New Zealand invests millions of dollars to guard against invasive pests. A hound dog on duty at the airport received a reward for sniffing the scent of an apple that had been in my carry-on a week prior to my landing on the island. With the country being the only major South Pacific Island void of fruit flies, 7,500 fruit fly traps are set and maintained each year to ensure that it stays that way. Various strains of fruit flies can cause damage to horticultural crops. Presently, New Zealand can export its produce certified 'fruit fly free' while all produce entering the country must be treated before being admitted. At least one sample piece of produce from every import received is checked for larvae infestation. This explains the brutal attack on my galley stores.

---

* NZ exports approximately 100,000 metric tons (110,000 tons) of lamb and 118 metric tons (130 tons) of clean wool annually. Wool is used in the manufacturing of clothing, upholstery, carpets, mattress fillings, tennis ball covers and pool table baize. It is combined with moss to make hanging basket liners. Naturally water-repellent, wool is used in the manufacturing of pads to soak up commercial oil spills. (The pads are reusable.) A manufacturer in the UK makes handmade, ecofriendly, wool coffins. Wool batts used in home insulation, have no glues or chemicals and are naturally fire-resistant. Wool-insulated boxes keep items cool (or warm). Lanolin is obtained from wool and is used in lip balms and other beauty products, and is the precursor to the production of vitamin D3. Scientists are experimenting with wool proteins to create new wound dressings, bone graft implants, and medical sutures. Researchers are combining wool with seaweed to make stronger, longer lasting bricks for building construction.

We docked our boat in Gulf Harbour, a large marina about fifty minutes from the city of Auckland. During our stay we drove to the city several times to order more navigational charts, pick up parts for the boat and shop in some well stocked chandleries. Eighty thousand privately owned boats are berthed in Auckland and if you can't find the part that you need for your boat, you can at least find an operation that will order it and have it there within a few days.

We stayed a few nights in a hotel located across from the Sky Tower in downtown Auckland. The Sky Tower is a tall, free-standing telecommunications structure similar in shape to Toronto's CN Tower. It's fitted with a glass elevator, a revolving restaurant, an observation tower and a ride. The ride is a jumping experience with a controlled descent called the Sky Jump. We often saw people dangling from ropes from the observation deck just before they slid down guidelines screaming.

Back in our hotel room we saw a TV documentary on the Sky Jump and after watching I decided that I wanted to try it. I had, after all, conquered my fear of changing the light at the top of the mast without wearing a safety harness, how hard could this be? I had just had another birthday and this would be the perfect gift. So one day I walked across the road to the Tower and signed up. Someone handed me a Sky Jump suit that I was told to put on, then a harness was snapped onto the suit's hardware and I was led to an elevator that took me up to the observation deck where the jumping platform was located, outside of the tower. I was taken into a glass room where I was left alone to fret while watching someone disappear from sight after stepping onto the platform. Then I was called forward.

Following a second check of my harness I was led outside onto a plank that jutted far enough from the tower that I wouldn't hit the side of the building in my fall. The hardware on my suit was checked again and then I was taken to the end of the plank where the tips of my shoes jutted out into space. I think part of a good ride is the anxiety you feel just before you take off. Standing high above every skyscraper in Auckland seemed to do the trick.

After the attendants attached two cables to my harness, I was instructed to jump at the count of three.

"Jump?" I asked, surprised. "I didn't think I had to jump! The TV intro didn't show anyone jumping, only a controlled descent."

"All patrons are required to jump, and after free falling 12 metres (40 feet), cables control the rest of the fall," he replied. He didn't mention that I would reach speeds of 85 kph (53 mph) during the free fall!

In hindsight, I should have realized the exercise required a jump. The experience *was* called 'Sky Jump'.

I heard someone start the countdown and I knew that if I didn't go on the count of three, I never would. I had seen T-shirts in the gift shop printed with the word 'chicken' for people who couldn't go through with it. Somehow, I commanded my knees to push me off the platform. I cannot tell you how difficult that was.

The whole experience, as far as I'm concerned, was about conquering fear and forcing myself to do something that my brain suggested I not do. It was the hardest thing I have ever done in my life. Talk about an adrenalin rush!

AUCKLAND HAS A population of 1.3 million people including the largest Polynesian population in the world. The Auckland Museum, which sits on top of an inactive volcano, houses the largest collection of Māori and Polynesian artifacts in the world, including a full size 25.5 metre (85 foot) meeting house with almost every inch of interior wall intricately carved and painted. This outstanding structure represents a genuine meeting house whereby wall detail, including carvings, would relay tribal genealogy and legends.

After returning to Gulf Harbour and making arrangements for *Baccalieu III* to undergo several small refit projects, we flew to Queenstown on the South Island where we rented a car.

Queenstown has everything: helicopter rides, skydiving, bungee jumping, hot air ballooning, zipline rides through the forest's canopy and even a canyon swing ride whereby the rider is launched from a cliff to hurtle towards rocky cliff faces. The Skyline Gondola took us to the top of Bob's Peak where we rode three-wheeled luge carts back down the hill, skidding around bends and accelerating through tunnels. We were by far the oldest people on the carts, but as one of the guide books stated, "It is everyone's objective to get high one way or another while in Queenstown."

Yet even with all these tourist attractions, the place still had a homey, small town feel to it. Queenstown is mostly filled with young people sporting backpacks and hiking boots. In fact, more stores in town sell outdoor wear and hiking equipment than fashion wear.

In the countryside near Glenorchy a few miles outside of Queenstown, open meadows, snowcapped mountain peaks, and rushing rivers lay spread out before us in breathtaking beauty. A hike with a Māori guide introduced us to ancient Māori village life including hut construction and the wild herbs used in traditional medicines.

Within minutes we transitioned from ancient Māori customs to modern day technology when we stepped aboard a jet boat, a New Zealand invention designed to navigate shallow rivers while allowing farmers to check stock in the high country. After speeding across Lake Wakatipu, we headed up the glacier-fed Dart River, which meanders snakelike at the base of the Southern Alps. In some areas the depth of the river was no more than 10 cm, (3.9 in.), deep.

WE continued our trip by car coming to the small town of Te Anau, 172 km, (107 mi.), south of Queenstown. The town sits on the edge of Fiordland National Park and is the last place to fill your tank with petrol before embarking on the road to Milford Sound. Te Anau has a population of three thousand but it can swell to ten thousand during summer months when hikers arrive to tramp through the mountainous virgin forests teaming with rushing rivers and spectacular waterfalls.

When rabbits were introduced to New Zealand in the 1830s, for both food and sport, their prolific breeding habits caused plagues of them to devastate vegetation resulting in erosion from wind and rain. The government introduced stoats, a small, short-legged weasel they hoped would control the rabbit population. Stoats, however, are nocturnal and have done nothing to halt the abundance of rabbits. Instead, they have helped to devastate native birds that nest in tree cavities and lay their eggs near the ground. Stoats have been a key factor in the loss of flightless birds. The introduction of possums, rats and cats have had similarly devastating effects on native populations.

Stoats bear litters of ten and the females of the litter are often impregnated before they even leave the nest. Today they are captured in spring-loaded traps that line hundreds of miles of the country's walking trails and can be found tucked among plants like the Silver Fern, New Zealand's national emblem. When I confessed to a New Zealander that I had no idea what a stoat looked like, he reported that they were the things we would see lying squashed on the roads. And sure enough, the highways were littered with dead stoats, a confirmation of how seriously New Zealanders were taking up the cause to eliminate them. It appeared to be a citizen's duty not to let a single one survive a crossing. With two flightless birds, the New Zealand Goose and the Crested Penguin, now extinct, and the national bird, the Kiwi on the endangered list, New Zealanders are now united in the fight to revive their native wildlife.

To protect the natural habitat from rodents, the government has called upon every citizen to do his or her part to eliminate unwanted critters including rabbits, and there is no shame in the approach to rabbit hunting. Nearing Easter, the local paper ran a picture of several rabbits in a field with the caption — "Easter Hunt — 16,201 rabbits, up from 2,000 last year."

All the Easter bunnies in the picture were lying flat out dead!

Hunting and gathering is still very much a part of a New Zealander's psyche, and the millions of acres of available forest supports enough sport for anyone wanting to set a trap or tote a rifle whether hunting for the night-foraging possum or the docile, unsuspecting deer. Possum fur is proudly sold in souvenir shops sewn into hats, mitts, purses and small knick-knacks such as key chains. Venison steaks are a feature in many restaurants although they are often sourced from venison farms found throughout the South Island.

New Zealand sailing friends told us how they had started their small venison farm simply by constructing a paddock on a piece of their farm's property where wild, rambling deer could enter to graze but not escape. When another New Zealand couple whom we had met in Fiji, invited us to their New Zealand home for a typical dinner of local grub, we dined on scallops they had dredged earlier that day from the bay and lamb chops and venison sausages that had been locally butchered.

The scenery between Te Anau and Milford Sound is unforgettable. Snow-capped mountains, vertical gorges, valleys rippling with cinnamon-tinged grasses and steep hills winding with switch back roads running between walls of severed rock create scenery so vast and beautiful that it's impossible to capture it with a camera.

The Homer Tunnel, a government make-work project introduced during the Depression (1925–39), slices through the Main Divide at the head of Hollyford Valley among breath-taking scenery 945 metres (3,100 feet) above sea level. The tunnel's construction began with five men hacking away at the Darren Mountain Range with hand tools and a wheelbarrow. It took five years of brutal chopping and pummeling until light was seen at the other end and then fifteen more to turn it into the longest, single lane, gravel surface tunnel in the world.

Today, the unfinished, rough granite walls allow for a narrow, two-lane road, just wide enough to permit two cars to pass at close proximity. In peak tourist season, traffic lights and a radar detection system powered by diesel generators, control single lanes of traffic carrying three hundred thousand cars that make the journey to Milford Sound each year. Due to possible avalanches throughout the winter months, sitting at the portals waiting for light changes is not safe, and cars proceed simultaneously from both ends of the tunnel. Low intensity lights were installed in 2004.

While waiting for the light to signal that we could enter the tunnel, we were visited by one of New Zealand's endemic species of parrots, the olive green kea. Not only extremely sociable but highly destructive, these birds were not shy in their attempt to tear the rubber window seals off our car with their hooked beaks. Keas peck and tear things apart mostly for entertainment, and returning to your car to find two keas dragging one of your windshield wipers across the ground is apparently not an unusual experience; nor is finding one prying the chrome strips from your doors!

At one time, it was thought unlikely that a two-pound bird could kill a sheep. It has been proven, however, that keas landing on the hindquarters of these animals, dig into the fleece until they find the fatty areas around the kidneys.

A specially designed kea gun was developed in the 1950s and '60s when a bounty encouraged the elimination of more than 150,000 keas. Since the mid-'80s, the kea has been under the full protection of the government, but it is necessary in some areas to post notices where keas are particularly threatening to campers.

PRIOR to the construction of the tunnel, access to Milford Sound required several days hiking through rainforests, wetlands and mountain passes. Today, the Milford Trail is so busy with hikers the experience needs to be booked well in advance. The trek must be completed within three to four days regardless of weather. Hiking is allowed in one direction only and no tenting is allowed along the way. Overnights are spent in huts provided by the Department of Conservation. The rules may appear strict, but fourteen thousand hikers a year walk the trail.

It's astonishing that the hardships* experienced during construction of the tunnel were endured simply for the pleasure of tourists, but it's true. At the end of the road there is nothing but virgin forests, wilderness and quiet, except for the fifty buses that deliver three thousand people every day to experience the scenery and solitude.

Milford Sound is difficult to visit when it is not raining

---

* During construction of the Homer Tunnel, which required workers to live in tents in almost lightless conditions six months a year, rain and heavy snowfalls led to avalanches. At least three workers were killed. More often, snow and melting ice hampered progress. At those times, when men were unable to work, wages were suspended!

or at least drizzling. The stunning landscape of sheer granite cliffs and plunging waterfalls receives 8 metres (25 feet) of rain a year. Passengers wait for their pre-booked cruises in either a terminal building or a caféteria-style restaurant. Despite the number of people arriving at the site, the area has been kept remarkably wild.

We boarded the *Milford Mariner*, a small power/sailing passenger ship that offered breakfast, lunch and a buffet dinner to those staying in one of the thirty single, private sleeping cabins during an overnight tour of the Sound.

After leaving the wharf in a light drizzle of rain, and dropping anchor, we boarded one of the ship's tenders for an up-close look at shore while the ship's naturalist spoke about the wildlife and how the fjord was formed by glaciers. The guide announced that kayaking and swimming were optional but warned, that with water temperatures hovering around 7°C (44°F), "You may go in as Angus but you'll come out as Agnes."

The ship's bridge was often open to passengers and we would find the captain there, reclined in his navigation chair, his feet resting on the dash of the windshield, while two fingers guided the ship with a toggle switch. The good-humoured captain and the naturalist entertained us with facts while readily answering questions about the area.

We sailed the full length of the fiord, following the path of destructive glaciers that had gouged the Bush Clad Mountains, pushing them into vertical granite walls that now appeared like Goliaths standing above calm, serene water. After reaching the rougher waters of the Tasman Sea, the ship pivoted on its return route while dolphins swam just off the beam and fur seals stretched their slippery bodies over shoreline rocks. Arriving in Harrison Cove, the ship's crew attached the ship to a mooring. We enjoyed dinner and an informative slideshow of local wild-life before retiring. We woke in the morning to clear skies and a full view of Mitre Mountain comprising five prominent peaks. The previous day's rain gave strength to numerous vertical waterfalls and when the captain directed the ship's bow within metres of a cliff, the cascading run-off doused us with virgin water falling from heights of 1,800 metres (6,000 feet).

OUR PLANS WERE to drive up the West Coast, stopping whenever the urge struck us. Finding lodging would be a look-and-see experience, taking a chance on whatever we might find.

One of our first stops was Arrowtown, a quaint, historical gold-mining town established in the mid-1800s. When the valuable mineral was mined in the nearby Otago Goldfields, the town held over seven thousand inhabitants. Hundreds of Chinese immigrants were part of the population but discrimination forced them to establish their own communities outside the town; a few mud brick shacks, where immigrants often lived six or more to a shack, still exist.

With a main street named Buckingham, you would expect to see something royal and the grand old oaks and sycamores planted over a hundred years ago present the town in an old-fashioned but grand style.

Today there are only about two thousand people living in the town but seasonal festivities entice outsiders to visit when the townspeople celebrate the 'good old years'. A 1948 Austin truck, usually stored in a nearby hay barn, loads up annually with what locals term "the most mature band in New Zealand," the Arrow Miners Band. During fall celebrations, the town holds a Gold Panning Championship and a Pie and Pint Festival at which time lacy knickers flash from beneath colourful can-can skirts swished high by the not-so-young, 'Buckingham Belles'.

We walked to the Royal Oak, reputed to be one of the oldest watering holes in the area. Inside, a group of seniors, each wearing a red tartan Tam o' Shanter and holding a musical instrument, stood crowded together at the front of the one room tavern. The bulbous part of a tuba loomed over the heads of the others while bows slid across fiddles and a couple of musicians pumped air into small box accordions. We had in fact, stumbled on the one and only, Arrow Miner's Band! When we arrived, everyone was enjoying some real toe tapping music played on some of the most interesting instruments you would ever see. One musician, sitting on a chair, supported a long, wooden hand saw between his legs. To play the saw, the musician drew his bow across the back edge of the saw while bending the blade into various degrees of curvature. The result was the most eerie mix of vibrating pitches!

Our left hand lane driving abilities were seriously tested when we continued up the West Coast over narrow roads that had no shoulders and mountain passes 'sans' guard rails. As the rear wheels pivoted like luggage casters through near ninety degree turns, we both lacked a certain judgment on the passenger side and gained no pleasure torturing the other with multiple visions of cliff-side deaths.

The road between Haast and Wanaka, 122 km (76 mi.), took forty years to construct due in part to the geography of Haast Pass, which crosses the Southern Alps.

From Haast, the road climbed then dipped in plunging descents while following the winding Haast River in the valley below. Spanning it several times were single lane bridges, one that supported a railroad track down the middle. Charming, and narrow, the bridges were located in the lowest part of rugged, mountainous terrain and offered transport across dry, rocky riverbeds flowing with clear, bumpy flurry from melting glaciers. The bridges were nearly always preceded by tight, bending curves designed to slow vehicles upon approach.

Miles and miles of uninhabited scenery follows the West Coast's Heritage Highway presenting views of astonishing beauty. Cascading valleys flourish with impassible, dense forests while others are so dry and sparse they present dessert-like conditions. Massive rugged, dynamited passes, richly coloured with streaked minerals, looked even more brilliant in the sunshine. Rivers, white with rapids, spilled through tight gorges and often landed in pools of frigid, aqua blue water. While driving through valleys, we sped past long, rows of grape vines, acres of fruit orchards and fields of tall, golden, rippling grasses. On one road, grand beech trees spread their branches creating cathedral-high tunnels shading roads that separated fields of grazing, corralled deer and sheep gnawing grasses to their roots.

Fox Glacier and Franz Josef Glacier are located between the towns of Haast and Hokitika. Fox Glacier descends a steep, narrow valley and it can be reached at far lower altitude than most glaciers in the world. It was an easy walk along crunchy moraine to reach the base where we stood behind safety barriers to view the glacier.

Two hours north of Haast we stopped at a village located near the Franz Josef Glacier. The town lies along a single road where at the end our eyes came to rest on the grandeur of a snow-capped mountain; a piece of the Southern Alps so stately it dominates everything for miles. The town is small and you can walk from one end to the other in ten minutes. There are no banks or ATM machines, only a couple of motels, a restaurant or two, a bakery and two helicopter companies offering trips to the Franz Joseph Glacier. Every town, no matter how small, had a tavern. This one had a hot pink coloured van in their parking lot painted with the words, "I want to be just like Barbie, that bitch has everything."

Glaciers that form in the Southern Alps depend on moist, southwest winds known as the Roaring Forties. The winds blow across the Tasman Sea picking up moisture as they go, then dump it onto the West Coast. While the precipitation nurses the West Coast rainforest, it also helps to create glaciers. The Southern Alps form the highest land at that latitude and when the wind slams into them, moisture is forced higher, cooling as it rises to eventually drop in massive snow falls on the *neve* or plain of the glacier. Franz Joseph Glacier receives approximately 14 metres (45 feet) of snow a year. At high altitudes it doesn't melt, but instead piles up, compressing into glacier ice; ice that is far denser than the ice cubes in our freezers and appear blue in the sun.

With weather conditions changing rapidly in the mountains, helicopter trips to the glacier are dependent on a good forecast. One can never be sure the helicopter excursion booked the day before will actually take off, but after pulling on thick wool socks, cramming our feet into leather hiking boots and donning waterproof parkas, our chopper received clearance.

We began by flying low over a long valley bedded with miles of frozen, gravel moraine. This was the debris, glaciers swept out after weather and other natural forces broke down mountain rock. From the air, we could see vast ice sheets flowing like frozen rivers between perpendicular granite cliffs. Bending with swollen, cracked, jagged ice peaks, it erupted with protrusions that stood like frozen, white monuments.

We landed on the glacier and our guide offered us hobnailed cleats to clamp over our boots and suggested we walk using a broad gait stamping the picked boots into the ice to avoid hooking our own feet.

The silence of the ice field magnified the crunch and squeak of our cleats as we trod over compacted, granular crystals. We crawled through ice tunnels, hardly large enough for a single person, shuffled sideways through vertical crevasses and climbed around ice formations that could have won sculpture awards in a modern art gallery. We heard a groan, then a crack, and a tall chunk broke away, landing in an explosion of ice dust. The crash echoed eerily in the pure, crisp, cold air.

JUST outside Franz Joseph Glacier, two of New Zealand's highest peaks, Mt. Cook and Mt. Tasman, are reflected perfectly in the still waters of Lake Matheson. The unusual blue tinge to the water comes from the lake's natural organic filtering system and on a clear day the water can appear as blue as any sky. The sight is photographed and painted as often as Canada's Lake Louise.*

Rugged, coastal scenery continued to offer show-stopping ocean views all the way to Punakaiki. When the sea disappeared behind a blind of trees, a souvenir shop came into sight announcing our arrival at the Pancake Rocks at Dolmite Point in Punakaiki. Layered formations of limestone, sculpted by weather and sea, ripple like a pile of stacked pancakes creating a spetacular looking shoreline. Interrupted by hundreds of monolithic, wrinkled looking monuments, the shore is a labyrinth of windblown rock where incoming ocean swells, trapped within deep chasms, unleash their fury in violent crashings which then gush with forceful upward spurts through blowholes.

We contemplated driving across the island to Christchurch, but instead, continued to move northward to a small town where a sailing friend was holidaying with his parents. Westport is a coal town where generations of hard working families might never leave. Our friend Paul was an exception

---

* Lake Louise is located in Banff National Park in the province of Alberta. The alpine lake lies at the foot of the Canadian Rockies, part of the North American Rocky Mountain range.

and had left many times, even captaining a boat around the world. But there's no stronger call than a beloved family and now he was back for a break from his skippering duties. Our guide book stated the best thing about Westport was getting there but the directory could not do justice to the warm welcome we received from Paul and his mother, who kindly offered us a lunch of spaghetti on toast with egg. If we had really wanted to do something touristy, we could have taken a tour of the Cape Foulwind cement plant.

Our last stop, before returning our rental car and catching a plane back to the North Island, was the town of Nelson. I had my hair cut in Nelson and had a dream that same night in which I was sitting beside a man in a restaurant who asked me if I was a man or a woman. Since leaving England, my hair had been hacked at, spiked, and coiffured as if falling through a time machine to the swing and boogie-woogie era. I'd been scissored to resemble a shaggy haired dog, my hair styled like a coon pelt and once walked out of a salon looking like there was a sloth lying across my forehead. Now I was butchered to the point that my own subconscious wasn't even sure what gender I belonged to.

We returned to Gulf Harbour and spent several days checking repairs and improvements that had been carried out on *Baccalieu III* while we were away. The mainsail had been reinforced along the foot, but now it didn't run smoothly into the mast furling system. We had updated the navigation computer but now it wasn't communicating with the outside monitor. A new AIS (Automatic Identification System), which would identify ships by their registered names and note their intended direction, had been installed. The dinghy steering had been repaired, the generator had a new water pump and the autopilot had new brushes. A new SSB aerial was, we hoped, going to solve our communications problem. The updates all needed testing before we left the boat to return to Canada. If the process of certifying the propane tank, which was required before refilling it, was any indication of the expected speed of progress, we were in for a long haul. It had taken three visits to a dive shop to get the UK tank certified for filling in New Zealand.

We flew home to a Toronto winter to wait out the southern hemisphere cyclone season. In April, we returned to New Zealand and prepared *Baccalieu III* for another season of adventure. On average, each time we left the boat for an extended period, it took a week or more to prepare her to go to sea again.

While exploring the Yasawa Islands last season, we had nothing but continuous rain. Therefore, we decided to return to the outlying islands in Fiji. In the back of our minds was this New Zealand to Fiji passage that had the potential of another difficult trip.

During the next five months it would be just the two of us sailing *Baccalieu III* over which time we planned to travel from New Zealand to Australia making stops in Fiji, Vanuatu and New Caledonia. But first we had some local New Zealand cruising to do before we took on the passage to Fiji and we spent a few wonderful days at Great Barrier Island, New Zealand's fourth largest island.

Less than a thousand people live on Great Barrier Island and most are involved in general farming and raising oysters. In the 1800s, New Zealand's North Island was almost entirely covered by kauri forests. Trees in these forests towered 50 metres high (160 feet) and had girths spanning 16 metres (52 feet). Even though settlers had deforested much of the

North Island for making ships' masts and the construction of housing, Great Barrier Island continued to be a source of kauri gum. The island employed thousands of immigrants from Serbia, Croatia and Slovenia, as gum diggers.

The early Māori tribes used the gum for igniting fires. They chewed it for pleasure while people in the New World used it to produce varnish. In swamps and thick, shrub-covered kauri fields, gum had formed over a thousand years ago when resin leaked from ancient kauri trees, hardened on exposure to the air, then fell to the forest floor in clumps, eventually fossilizing. By using hooked spears, diggers could excavate to a depth of 12 metres (39 feet) locating further reserves of gum.

The gum was found in a variety of earth tones but the most valuable shades were pale gold and translucent. Gum remained Auckland's main export during the mid 1800s and was distributed as far as England and America. As synthetics were discovered for use in varnish, the demand for it diminished and it came to be utilized in the manufacturing of linoleum flooring, and eventually only in the making of jewelry and violins.

Today, the heavily forested island offers several walking trails through bush, canyons and old forestry dams that had provided the water needed to float kauri logs to the sea. Great Barrier Island remains the home of the rarely seen chevron skink and is, so far, free of unwanted stoats, possums and feral cats.

Domestic cats in New Zealand are about as desirable as a heel spur. If you really want to make your life miserable, try travelling with your kitty while in New Zealand. Our dock neighbours in Opua had left Victoria B.C. with two cats onboard. Upon arrival, they discovered the felines were welcomed with as much enthusiasm as a case of small pox.

As for travelling freely around the islands with a cat onboard, that's a no-can-do. Boats with cats on board are required to report to customs at every port to confirm they have not tired of owning Angel Cake and ditched her.

One cat story we heard involved an 8 kg (17.5 lb.) cat named Adolphus, who many people suggested might better have been called Ballast. The sailors who owned the creature needed to sign a waiver promising that if the big guy got off the boat, they would forfeit the $1,000 NZ ($800 US) bond they had been required to post with the government. The inspectors came to the boat three times a week to ensure Adolphus was still onboard. The sailors were never free to travel without worrying that the inspectors might drive out to wherever they were located and then charge the owners $60 NZ ($50 US) for their travel time. If the customs officers decided to check up on Adolphus while he travelled to Great Barrier Island, it was possible that the Ministry and Agriculture and Forestry inspectors could fly out and leave a $500 NZ ($400 US) expense charge beside his milk bowl.

GREAT Barrier Island offers several good bays in which to anchor. At Port FitzRoy (Port Fitzroy), rugged rock formations fall deep into the sea to resurface again, threatening the sailor's approach. The entrance to the bay is hidden among shore rock with Kaikoura Island in the backdrop. Once in, it spreads open to a large bay offering several smaller bays in which to drop anchor.

There are two entrances to Port FitzRoy, the widest being 100 metres where the New Zealand and British navies once anchored their ships. Port FitzRoy was named after the captain of the HMS *Beagle*, the ship Charles Darwin sailed during his famous voyage to the Galápagos Islands. FitzRoy was a pioneering meteorologist who helped make accurate weather forecasting a reality. He became governor of New Zealand in the mid-1840s.

They say New Zealand has the greatest variety of ferns in the world and Kaikoura Island is a mass of tropical ferns coloured in a palate of a thousand greens. Ferns with brown, curled underbellies blanket the forest floor while others, sprout over ten feet tall and have grand, spreading canopies as large as patio umbrellas.

Paths thickened and softened by scented, brown pine needles lead through dense forests where hills and gullies are protected from hiker's erosion with wooden stairs. Simple yet romantic bridges span deep gorges where streams trickle slowly downward filling a series of pools, each pond lower than the other like organized botanical gardens.

The air, sweetened with dampened vegetation, was intoxicating.

Smoke House Bay, named for the smoke shack standing among the trees just back from the beach, offers visitors a chance to smoke the day's catch over a fire of fallen branches. A wood fired water tank awaits a sailor's hankering for a bath and can be heated with a little patience and the help of an outdoor wood stove. The full-size bathtub rests inside a shack behind a large picture window overlooking the bay. Candles left by previous bathers sat on a shelf. And if an outdoor bath is preferred, there is one of those too. There are also five clothes washers with old-fashioned wringers available for those who need to do laundry. The washing machines are connected to a water well and sit near picnic tables that overlook the bay. A long rope-swing dangles from a tall branch nearby.

Before returning to Opua where we would clear customs and leave for Fiji, we visited the Bay of Islands. This group of one hundred and forty-four islands is one of the most popular cruising grounds in New Zealand.

Heading South
NEW ZEALAND

Our last anchorage was at Roberton Island, a long narrow island consisting of kānuka native shrub hardwoods and stands of maritime pine introduced by Europeans for the extraction of turpentine. The island offers an inviting beach and a bay wide enough to handle several day-cruisers. There were only two small yachts in the bay when we arrived but the occasional tour boat cruised past with announcers onboard who, while pointing to our Canadian flag, stated over loud hailers that people from all over the world travelled great distances just to cruise the Bay of Islands. I would often give a wave to the tourists and then watch while thirty arms shot into the air in response. But after the third tour boat had interrupted our peaceful surroundings with yet another announcement that we were Canadians in search of the Bay Islands, I rammed my middle finger into the air then watched as they all enthusiastically waved back. This at least provided my warped little mind with some degree of satisfaction.

After gathering green lipped mussels from below the tide line, day boats from the city left the anchorage to return home with their dinner catch. The sun was setting when we took our dinghy to shore and followed a path to a set of stairs which took us to the top of the cliff. Ocean swells smashed with fury against the rugged windward coast while *Baccalieu III* sat peacefully awaiting our return in the sheltered waters on the lee side of the island. In my back pack was a bottle of wine and two glasses. It was the perfect place to say goodbye to New Zealand and all the wonderful experiences she had given us.

BEFORE returning to Opua, Mike replaced the exhaust elbow on the Perkins engine. The company, who built Perkins engines, had admitted to having some problems with the elbows as they corroded prematurely due to the hot circulating saltwater. By now, Mike had become a competent mechanic. Transitioning from finance to mechanic was quite the reach and he did it all from reading manuals, listening to other sailors' experiences and a good deal of trial and error.

We had to check out with New Zealand customs before leaving for Fiji. Once checked out, customs officials expected boats to leave within the hour. Our plan was to wait for a weather window while at dock in Opua.

Arriving in the marina at Opua, we were given directions over the VHF radio to our assigned berth. As we backed the boat into the designated dock, a Māori family was fishing off the wharf above us, their lines dropped into the water in the middle of our berth. I gave a wave so as not to appear too inconsiderate but received in return an aggressive response. "What are you doing?" a stout man demanded. Hollering back, while standing on the stern, I explained the marina had assigned us the berth. Annoyed, the largest of the group shouted, "Ask a Māori if you can dock here!"

Keeping in mind that the Māori once ate their enemies, I trekked up to the office to request another berth. It was obvious our present location was going to be a point of contention with the locals. The attendant in the office rolled her eyes. When I returned and told the Māori fisherman we were moving to another dock, he grumbled unenthusiastic thanks. Later while connecting the power cord to our stern outlet at the new location, we found a yellow gob of spit clinging to the transom.

WHILE waiting for a weather window for the seven day passage to Fiji, I took advantage of the facilities in the marina knowing that it would be the last laundry room I would see for several weeks. Marina Laundromats are far more than just a place to wash and dry your clothes; they offer an important centre of communication. No matter what direction you're travelling, you will often meet someone who has arrived from that very destination and you can receive an update of local knowledge. The Laundromat is also a place where boaters leave items that are no longer needed. You might find mechanical and hardware parts or even a galley item like an old frying pan. The Laundromat acts as a hub where messages are left on the bulletin board such as "Crew Wanted," or "Casual Work Wanted." Someone looking for a crew position left this one, "Looking to crew — British female hoping to crew on a yacht heading just about anywhere beyond New Zealand. Contact Susie, thirty year old, English, neat and tidy. susiejuicy@nzmail."

People also advertise items for sale such as boats and cars. Someone had posted — "Wanted — Dead or alive fishing reels."

IT WAS MAY 13 when we set sail from Opua. It was even a Friday! It is thought by many sailors to be unlucky to start a voyage on a Friday, let alone on the 13th, and with a woman yet! But Friday has not always been thought unlucky. Friday was named after the Norse goddess Frigg, the goddess of love and fertility, thereby giving to Friday the sign of good luck, and an even more enhanced status when the Friday was to be one's wedding day. However, early Christians came to regard Frigg as a witch and the good luck day became known as an unlucky day.

Leaving on Friday the 13th will not put a hex on a sailor any more than a woman on board a ship will cause the sea to be angry. This had in truth, been another earlier belief until sailors decided that a naked woman would calm the sea. That is why ships in the early 1800s began to place seminude figureheads on the bow of their ships. The custom probably began in ancient times when seamen carried the head of a sacrificed animal onboard to offer the gods of the sea. Fishermen on Failaka Island, in the Persian Gulf, tied the head of a gazelle to the bows of their boats.

By the 1600s, wooden engraved heads depicting unicorns, lions, and even dragons, began to grace the bows of ships. Then knights in armour appeared under bow-sprits, followed by groups of knights in armour followed by groups of knights in armour riding horses! Figureheads got so weighty that the bows of ships became too heavy to take to sea. By the late 1800s, mermaids began to take their place up front (even though mermaids were thought to be dangerous seductresses). But around the same time, another myth suggested a seminude woman would calm turbulent seas. See how easy it is for a woman to manipulate a man's mind simply by taking off her blouse?

WHEN a high-pressure system settles between 25 and 30 degrees south latitude, light winds are the flavour of the day. I was glad I had placed precooked soups and casseroles in the freezer and I wasn't forced to cook in the rock and roll conditions we had started out into.

Light winds in such conditions were our enemy. We needed a good amount of wind power to punch through heaving, sloppy seas left from several days of high winds. But all day long the wind continued to stay just on the edge of useful. We turned the motor on and then we'd turn it off and then we'd turn it on again. The mainsail thrust to the right and then to the left, synchronizing its movements with the merciless roll of the boat. We felt every swell, every undulating heave, every crest, trough and peak in slow motion. The sheet of the relaxed genoa tapped its braid against the deck in uneven rhythms. Neither of us was sleeping well. At times like these, I understand why women confess to not liking long passages. What I don't understand are the men who volunteer for them. But with all the drawbacks, the sleepless nights, the bouncing, crashing, the unstoppable motion, the nauseous feelings and the challenge of staying upright while standing in the galley, the cold, the wet, the damn fishing vessels, I would still rather travel this way than on a luxury liner.

I don't understand myself either. I guess we're all complicated creatures.

That first day out I felt pukish. But I had a thought—a vision. With a little savvy, we could turn this route into a money maker; market the passage as a weight loss holiday and charge big bucks for it. The advertisement could read, "No more fat farms, no more skimpy meals. Come onboard, lose weight the natural way. Enjoy a sailing holiday with 'Weighty Waves' and watch the fat swim away. No calorie counting, no denying beloved iced cupcakes, Twinkies or even those delectable, chocolaty marshmallow Half-Moons. Call us at 'Weighty Waves' where you can have fun while losing weight."

Then we'd take them out and roll them around for six or seven days. We'd hardly need to spend any money at all on food!

The GRIB files Captain Mike had downloaded indicated we would run into some wind around 30° latitude. Then just like clockwork, ten miles from the thirty degree mark, we pulled out the Yankee and staysail. Thirty-six hours later we were still sailing without suffering any roll to our travel. I hadn't even taken a tablet for motion sickness.

I stood on the bow one morning, hovering over a pod of bottlenose dolphins. While darting across in front of our speeding hull, each slick body surfaced momentarily noisily sucking in breaths just before diving again, barely avoiding decapitation. Later that afternoon, while squalls coloured the horizon with thick ribbons of grey, I saw the most spectacular rainbow, a richly coloured, broad and full arc. Both ends were balanced on the sea, and a sister rainbow, smaller, but just as brilliant, lay underneath it.

I HADN'T slept much in the first three days. Neither of us had. We changed watches every five hours, allowing for a longer 'rest' period. During my off time, I often forced myself to stay in bed, not because the rest was enjoyable but because I believed lying horizontal was more beneficial for regaining strength than working the muscles needed to stay upright. I would lie there listening to the rush of the sea, the sounds of the wind and the workings of the boat. We both became proficient at cat napping while sailing long passages.

The watch system put Mike and I on entirely different timetables. He would be eating breakfast while I was having lunch. I never realized how much I depended on daily routines to guide me through necessary tasks. With no real 'before' bed time, when was I to floss my teeth or wash my face or use my Youth in a Bottle moisturizer? The hours converged and dictated no pattern at all.

On the fourth night we lost the wind and had to use the motor again. The night had an eeriness to it, almost ghostlike. The stern navigation light spilled a strong white light across the canvas-covered dinghy secured in the davits. At four o'clock in the morning I began to think it looked as if we were travelling with a coffin rather than a covered dinghy. Perhaps I have an over-active imagination, but in my mind's eye, it appeared as though someone was sitting upright in the coffin. The hump around the steering wheel suddenly resembled someone sitting straight-backed at the wheel. I got out my MP3 player hoping to mask my eerie thoughts with music. But instead the lyrics I heard seemed to accentuate them.

> There's not a soul out there
> No one to hear my prayer

I promptly removed the earbuds, turned my attention to

handling the boat, and avoided looking towards the stern for the rest of my watch.

On the fifth day the wind blew over the aft quarter, offering us the opportunity to set up the sails wing on wing. The air began to feel tropical again and we began to complain how warm it was when trying to sleep.

The waves built and the boat started to roll again. A macramé bag, full of fruit swung side to side like a pendulum on a clock. It smashed into the stairs pulverizing the bananas into goo that dropped in gobs beneath the stairs.

We took turns sleeping in the bunk cabin where there was less motion.

The next morning the wind was strong enough to frost the waves with whitecaps and put some serious power into the sails. It allowed for far more comfortable travel and we ate dinner that night like regular people; sitting at the cockpit table rather than choke-holding bowls of food.

Overnight the sea became a deeper colour of blue signaling we were back in the tropics.

The sun and stars have a profound effect on me no matter what the conditions. Seeing the sun or a host of glittering stars always lightens my spirits. That day the sun was out and the sky full of soft puffy clouds. I felt energized.

We began to feel less roll but now we were pitching nose first into long, sizable waves. I called the waves waist-benders because the motion caused us to nearly bend at the waist in order to maintain our balance. Not only did I handle the complexities of this motion well, I also survived the athletics required to take a shower. I felt like a million dollars after that shower.

With all my complaining, I knew the passage last fall, from Fiji to New Zealand had been much worse than this one. This day our log read: 12 knot wind SE on the quarter, blue skies—motor-sailing. Six months ago it read, "Wind 25 knots SE (headwinds) gusts to 40 knots, long, rough night, large seas, wet and cold."

Six months ago my head was in the toilet; this day I attempted to make some bread.

While standing watch, Mike took a VHF call from a skipper on a nearby catamaran. The boat was off to our port heading in the opposite direction. The skipper asked if we had any cigarettes onboard. While they were talking, Mike told him we were struggling with a mere ten knots of wind but the cat's skipper gleefully reported he was flying with fifteen. How could that be? He wasn't more than two miles away! I've always said you can't trust those multi hull guys. Thank goodness we didn't have any cigarettes on board. What kind of convoluted plan would he have suggested to retrieve them?

The final miles of that passage turned into a real tradewind sail. The winds blew fifteen knots but the seas showed much more activity than normal for that speed. Seas ran short and jerky, and the crests of waves were whipped to white bits of froth. Every now and again the bow dipped into a deep trough, spilling air from the poled Yankee and an audible whack in the cloth would signal a sudden interruption to our forward momentum as though someone had slammed on a brake. When that happened, I would brace myself to avoid pitching head-first.

As I lay in the bunkroom listening to the gurgle and swish of water rushing by the hull, I thought it quite remarkable that there was only 20 to 25 millimeters (less than one inch) of fiberglass between me and drowning. I should have been sleeping but since I couldn't, I decided to get up and treat myself to a novel, a frivolous, easy reading novel. Maybe even something a little naughty. But fat chance that was going to happen, the naughtiest book I had onboard was a sailing manual that warned that if I didn't pay attention while furling the mainsail, it might jam up within the mast. Every book that I had read while travelling was so serious; travel guides, pilot books, books about health. What was I doing way out there with books on health? I was definitely ready for something lighter.

I often browsed through the used books left in Laundromats. But I had never seen anything that interested me. All that ever seemed to be left on the shelves were books with titles like *Hannah Goes to the Mountain* or *True Confessions of a Prairie Wheat Farmer*. The truth of the matter was, Mike and I seldom had time to read.

That evening, we noted the time at which we lost the daylight. The sun set around 1730. It looked as if we would be arriving in Fiji the next evening after dark. We had navigated through the narrow passage in the reef twice before and felt confident we could do it in the dark. All we had to do was spot one undersized, lit reef marker on our portside and a naked stick on starboard.

Lautoka's harbour is Fiji's largest seaport for handling bulk cargo ships carrying sugar, molasses, petroleum and gas. There is not, however, enough ship traffic to warrant custom and immigration service twenty-four seven. We would need to stay in an anchorage overnight, although technically, visitors to the country are not allowed to remain in Fijian waters until they clear customs.

THAT night while approaching Fiji, we had near perfect weather. The sky was full of crisp, sparkling stars. Planets were even visible. Venus was so bright it left a white, glossy trail streaking for miles across the water. It was times like these, when the sails were full of wind and the seas steady, and *Baccalieu III* moved in a gentle yet powerful manner, that

I would feel at one with my surroundings. With only a whisper of water moving past the hull, the subtle rhythm of the sea crept into me by a kind of osmosis.

In the morning we were sailing on a starboard tack swooshing along at 7 and 8 knots as squall after squall came through, accompanied by horizontal rain. Mike was on duty taking the brunt of it and repeatedly changed sail configurations to deal with the variable conditions. I could hear him grinding reefs into the sails as I lay in my bunk. Letting them out, grinding them in. Grind, grind, grind, how was a girl ever to get her beauty sleep?

The skies were clear the following morning and the sun lifted my spirits with its brightness and warmth. The wind was blowing steadier. Now we were reveling in its strength, blasting through stirred up seas, port tacked and reefed. *Baccalieu III* loved that kind of weather.

The acceleration of wind got us to the reef in Fiji in the daylight. We dropped anchor in Momi Bay and hoisted our yellow Q flag to announce our arrival as a vessel from another country. We had already lowered New Zealand's British blue and four starred burgee and had hoisted the bright blue South Pacific colours of Fiji. Shortly after dropping anchor, two boats, filled with workers returning to their villages after night shifts, motored past. They all waved. We radioed customs but heard no response. No surprise there.

The next morning we sailed our salt encrusted boat into Lautoka. As I walked up the deck, I ran my hand along one short section of lifeline and gathered more salt between my fingers than I would use to prepare a month's worth of meals.

Lautoka is no place of beauty, but rather a working man's harbour equipped with cranes and high wharfs that accommodate container ships needing to off-load heavy freight. The sugar mill spews sugary black guck into the atmosphere that can quickly encase a boat like toffee on an apple. We hoped to check in and check out as quickly as possible.

The good news was that the sugar mill was closed. The bad news was that it was Sunday. We learned that customs would not process recreational boats on Sundays. Port Control informed us by radio that we were required to remain anchored in the industrial bay until the following day when they would check us in. "Could we wait in the adjacent bay and come back tomorrow?" we asked. "No," was the reply.

But soon someone radioed back saying that the custom officials would be in the office within fifteen minutes if we still wished to clear customs. We considered that a pretty fast turnaround considering it required four officers, including customs, immigration, quarantine and health to check us through. We wondered what this was going to cost.

Mike took the dinghy to the office where he filled out form after form with replicate information. At this point he had memorized the details needed on custom's forms, although each country had their differences. Fiji's peculiarity was to demand the eye colour and race of each person visiting the country.

Mike was asked to pay $240 FJ ($120 US), a higher rate than usual due to it being a Sunday. The previous year we had checked in during regular working hours and had paid $15 FJ.

After paying the required fee, the officials informed Mike he would need to return the next day for a cruising permit. We were stunned. It had made no sense for us to pay the exorbitant fee.

Mike declared twenty-five bottles of wine and was informed that they would not apply the usual tax as a special pardon for us. Nevertheless, we had declared thirty bottles the previous year without hearing anything about either a tax or a pardon. Legally visitors are allowed twelve bottles per person.

I heard the dinghy motor nearing the boat signaling that Mike was returning from customs. I was surprised to see he had a passenger with him. A young man named Nathan was coming to inspect the boat. This had not been necessary the last time we had checked into the country.

Nathan politely took off his shoes before going below and then walked through the salon to the forward cabin. That took him about ten seconds. He stood there shyly in the salon while Mike stood beside him, neither speaking to the other. No one knew what to do next. Nathan didn't seem to know and I didn't know. We had rarely been boarded for a custom's inspection. We learned that Nathan was mostly interested in bombs and firearms and since we said we didn't have any of those, the inspection appeared to be over. I thought of offering Nathan a soft drink but I felt the boat inspection was too superficial for an official check and I was concerned that he might ask for a personal gift of money. I decided not to detain him any longer than was necessary. Soon Nathan appeared to be satisfied with his inspection and indicated that he was ready to return to his office. Mike drove him back to shore.

I hope the security of the country is never dependent on Nathan.

OUR standard procedure for lifting or lowering the anchor requires one person to be at the wheel while the other is on the bow. It's common among sailing couples to have disagreements about how the procedure should be carried out. Many couples shout instructions to each other. Mike and I are remarkably quiet, using only hand signals to communicate. Although I have to admit that there have been a few times when my hand signal has been just one middle finger!

That day however, as we began taking up the anchor, Mike and I were on the same page but the anchor was good and stuck. Hazards for anchors include communication cables, coral or rocks, none of which suited the profile of this particular bay. But a dumping ground for junk? That could well be how the bay had been used for years. When the anchor came up, it lifted a flat piece of metal one and a half metres (five feet) long. It was fortunate we were able to break it loose from whatever held it. As Mike good humouredly said, he would have hated to see me dive into all that industrial waste to free it.

It was midafternoon by the time we were ready to move on. We motored a short distance to Saweni Bay and put down the anchor for the night. In the early morning, while the stars were still set in a coal black sky, I was woken by the morning ritual of a vocal rooster. I repositioned my head on my pillow, tuning an ear to a second sound that at first I couldn't identify. It was an amplified voice from shore that was riding the light morning breeze to our boat. It was probably an early morning religious service. I looked at the clock. It was 0430.

Shortly after the preaching ceased I heard several small boats passing through the anchorage, villagers on their way to work I suspected.

When I got up and went outside, it was still early. The warm, morning sun soon made the day cheerful. Petrels flittered about overhead and myna birds and finches quarreled in the nearby mango forest. I felt the same feeling of satisfaction that runs through your veins after disembarking from an airplane in an exotic country. It was the feeling of excited arrival.

FIJI—SECOND TIME AROUND
YASAWA ISLANDS

*In Fiji rugby is taken very seriously indeed—
second only, perhaps, to family. On meeting a
Fijian, often the first question asked of any male
visitor is, "Which position do you play?" The next
will be whether they prefer Sevens to Fifteens—
something of a running debate among the islanders
since the game was brought to the islands by British
soldiers in 1884, it's been the national obsession.*
TOM BRYANT

IT WAS THE end of May when we returned to Musket Cove, the same resort where we had spent so much time the previous fall with sailing regatta activities. This time we kept *Baccalieu III* on a mooring outside the marina. Our intention was to stay only a few days to catch up on rest before touring the outlying islands. We didn't want to get too comfortable at dock.

It was the end of a South Pacific summer and the beginning of a new tourist season for Musket Cove. The cyclone season had been kind to Fiji throughout the summer months and had now ended. But the Cove had not gone untouched by the seasonal weather; excessive amounts of rain had fallen in the Mamanuca Islands resulting in the flooding of the marina office, the dive shop and many of the bures. The good news was that the cisterns were overflowing with fresh water and the landscape was beautiful and green. Long brown bean pods hung from trees and a delicate scent of white frangipanis blossoms drifted in the breeze.

A few changes had taken place in the months we had been away. A new Mandara Spa had opened at the resort and the Three Dollar Bar was now the Four Dollar Bar.

Our radio call to the Cove announcing our arrival brought an instant reply, "Mike! *Baccalieu!* So nice to hear from you." We even received hugs from staff when we arrived. Dick Smith, the owner of Musket Cove, recalled the name of our boat when he saw us walking towards him. We were surprised by the warm welcome showered on us by so many.

The greetings to our return made us feel like *real* cruisers. On the other hand, the welcome was kind of scary. Had we really stayed that long last year?

During the summer, a coup had overthrown the Fijian government, apparently the result of unrest over former government corruption and the *qoi qoi* bill which would have given indigenous Fijians legal and exclusive water rights in front of their villages. The pending bill would have meant, among other things, that transient sailors and others who anchor in local bays, would need to pay fees for that privilege. It would have resulted in most cruisers finding another playground. As well, the bill would have given native Fijians the right to claw back land formerly owned by ancestors, which probably would have been all of it. This fact had the resort owners very nervous. Dick Smith was well aware of the consequences of such government policies. He had lost his entire estate in Vanuatu when the government declared independence in 1980.

Commodore Voreqe Bainimarama, a native Fijian, military leader and now self-proclaimed President, was working towards crushing the proposed bills and eliminating government corruption. We were pleased to find that this time when we applied for a cruising permit while in Musket Cove, that the permits were returned to us promptly with no hint from any official that the permit would be expedited if extra money were to change hands. That was impressive.

THE YASAWA ISLANDS offer small bays where boats can drop anchor for at least daytime pleasure if not for overnight stays. They sit on the northwestern limit of Fiji and run almost linear to the exposed sea. A north swell can ruin a night's sleep if your boat is not tucked into a protected bay.

Our first stop was Navadra, a small uninhabited island so near to its sister island that the two form a small bay between them. Local pilot books report that you can always expect a little roll in this bay and that once there, you are committed for the night because the distance to the next sheltered bay is not reachable by sundown. There is room for no more than two boats in this pretty little spot and we chose a location in deep water to avoid damaging the abundant collection of soft corals with our anchor. The water was as clear as a new piece of glass and we could easily see the coral stretching all the way from the shore to the middle of the bay.

Swimming with our snorkeling gear, we discovered hefty, perfectly formed brain corals, long, unbroken branches of stag horns and grand, colourful arrays of coral microbes. Fish, intensely coloured in florescent hues, were so well camouflaged we could hardly detect them until our fin kicks flushed them back into their coral hideaways. After swimming to the outer reef, the sighting of a lone shark sent us finning fearfully back to the shallows. We are far more comfortable diving among them in the deep than attracting their attention with our fin kicks on the surface.

Other than goats on the island, we were alone. Such solitude meant I could shower naked on the stern platform and then wind-dry myself carefree and unconcerned on deck.

There's something to be said for standing in the elements like a premium-fed plucked chicken. Although I would never be ready to join the crowds who frequent nudist beaches, it was always pleasant to savour such freedom and to feel the wind wafting over my body.

That night, a crescent shaped moon illuminated the island just enough so that it never fully disappeared. The fine, white sand on the beach turned silvery, and I could see the black silhouette of a lone goat standing on the narrow, nearly luminescent peninsula. Never had the sighting of a goat been so romantic.

The following morning, arriving in Blue Lagoon, we almost met with a submerged reef when we took one of those baffling reef markers on the wrong side. After anchoring, we calculated that if the wind were to increase, we'd be dangerously close to the reef. We moved the boat to where we thought it safer. But there, the anchor wouldn't take hold and when we hoisted it a second time the anchor chain jammed in the windlass. Admittedly, we were both a little tired due to poor sleeps from the night before and there was no doubt we had only ourselves to blame for the wedged chain links. We grabbed a screwdriver and set about dismantling the windlass while drifting towards the reef. We freed the chain in time to avoid a disaster and put down the anchor again. It was times like these that I can say that we lived on the edge.

DARYL, from *Cool Bananas*, another boat located in the anchorage, invited us to join him and his crewmembers for a *lovo* (Fijian dinner) that the island's chief had agreed to prepare the following evening. The cost was 15 Fijian dollars ($7.50 US). It was short notice for the Fijian family to prepare such a festive meal, but they were willing to do it if Daryl would take them in his dinghy across the bay, where they could obtain the required chickens and then up island to fetch other supplies.

The island was called Blue Lagoon by tourists but locally known as Nanuya Lailai. According to the locals, the island's former chief had recently passed away and the land had transferred to his son. It was the son, Sammy, and his family who were hosting the lovo. Sammy's family included his wife and child, his mother and her two-year old grandson from a daughter who had died the previous year. We had met the family the year before not long after the young mother had died. At our first meeting, the grandchild, who sat next to us on the ground, had been scooping fistfuls of sand into his mouth. The new parents had not reacted to the situation and I remember having been intrigued by the adoptive parents' passive response. Sammy's family simply figured the child would stop eating sand once he found it too gritty to swallow.

Daryl and Sammy obtained everything needed to host the lovo. We watched Sammy dig an underground oven and line it with firewood and stones. While Sammy prepared the bake oven, his wife and mother were sitting on a floor mat inside a hut absorbed in the tedious job of picking delicate meat from the cooked coconut crabs that had been captured the night before.

When we arrived for our evening meal around five-thirty in the afternoon, a hot loaf of white, aromatic bread was just being pulled from a propane oven. The food was set out buffet style with several freshly caught red snappers, sweet, roasted pumpkin and potato, taro root, platters of crabmeat in coconut sauce and two recently killed chickens. Each piece of food had been wrapped individually in palm fronds, placed into the earthen oven earlier in the day, and covered with sand. We ate Fijian style, sitting crossed legged on a woven coconut mat, while the yellow glow of a kerosene lantern illuminated our meal. We were offered knives and forks but our hosts, who ate after we had finished, used their fingers. Sammy and his wife delayed their meal even further to entertain us with Fijian folk songs while he strummed his guitar in accompaniment.

The next morning, we went diving with the Yasawa Dive Centre.

It's an entirely different world beneath the sea, a weightless world where divers can relax suspended and 'fly' with only the gentle kick of a fin; a place where you can lie weightlessly and explore unique, submerged land forms and the critters that stow away in them.

This dive site was a mysterious wasteland of overhanging cliffs and canyons. We maneuvered around small, twisted spaces and then emptied our lungs to descend deeper where, just metres from the ocean floor, giant plates of overhanging coral allowed us to swim beneath to inspect their undersides. While following a silvery sand bottom, between two submerged mountains, we swam amid canyon walls that bulged with grey, warty outcrops. We came to a cavernous tunnel where, in the tunnel's dark crevices, we came upon several good-sized rock lobsters. Other than the lobsters, the limestone cave was too dark for even microbes to survive and when our air bubbles wiggled upwards, they shimmered in the light of our flashlights like quivering, silver balls of mercury. Colliding with the rocky ceiling, they collected into piles like bowls of fragile, glittery, Christmas balls.

During the two days of diving, we also dove on vertical cliffs resembling sloping, planted rock gardens. Fiji waters create perfect conditions for the formation of carbonate foundations and are known for their spectacular display of soft corals. Patterns of coral vary not only between species but also within the specie itself. Sometimes imitating the grand head of stag antlers, they can also mimic the blooms of elegant, trumpet-like flowers. Fans of delicate, coral lace and long stemmed, dainty black ferns quiver in the slow motion sweeps of deep surges. There are times I think I could swim forever in this beautiful, unique world under the sea.

The bay where we had anchored was one of the most protected in the Yasawa Group. The local ferry *Yasawa Flyer*, brought visitors to the island but due to the lack of docking facilities, passengers needed to disembark into longboats that delivered them to a small holiday resort or a backpacker's camp.

It was possible to walk around the entire island if we walked on the beach during low tide but my favourite walk was a twenty-minute trek across the centre of the island where we often met backpackers staying at a resort on the other side. At the top of the hill, tall yellow grasses rippled and swayed in the breeze as it swept over the island. A paw paw tree, rooted in a hollow, had grown into a giant, sprawling shade tree. Sometimes we would hear the soft cackle of women's voices coming from this direction. Then one day we discovered the women sitting underneath the paw paw tree near the cassava patch that their husbands were tending. They issued cheerful greetings to us. The people of Fiji were like that. They seemed to always exude happiness. No matter how many times we made that walk, we were always met with friendly greetings of, "Bula!" Even the man and his son who were raking volcanic pumice from their shoreline and the grandmother sitting in a rickety old chair cradling her grandchild on her lap would call greetings to us.

Arriving on the windward side, we followed the path through the property of the Sunrise Resort. This Fijian-owned backpacker's resort, offered communal-style living where young tourists shared rooms with other travelers and ate at outdoor, covered picnic tables. The resort sat on the edge of a rocky shoreline paved with dead coral. This uninviting shoreline is the reason backpackers frequently crossed the island to reach the more desirable beach on the calmer shore.

We followed the beach past two thatch-roofed resort-camps and stopped at a turquoise painted teahouse. Inside, small pots of artificial flowers decorated two long, rough-hewn picnic tables sitting on a green-patterned, oil-cloth-covered floor. Tapa designed fabric enhanced the walls and a wind chime, crafted from a collection of seashells, hung from the ceiling over the tables. We decided on a cup of tea after noticing the coffee came from a jar of instant. It was fun to share a piece of chocolate cake because we least expected to find such a treat while exploring the island.

We returned to the beach where it appeared the shore was under siege from a host of darting, transparent crabs. We met a young couple from Germany, who were staying at the Sunrise Resort. We talked a while and shared each other's travel plans. Mike and I followed the shoreline in the opposite direction of the couple, but we met them again on the leeward beach. We were about to have lunch at another resort, we invited them to join us. Stella was intrigued by the geckos that were scurrying across the floor in the restaurant and two days later, we found one sitting on our boat between the instruments. I had rested my backpack on the floor at the restaurant and had accidently carried it aboard. Geckos are harmless and will even dry up if not returned to their habitat but it was the last time I ever put my bag on any floor. I could have easily carried a cockroach onboard instead.

We decided to head for Mantaray Bay, (Nanuya Balavu Is.), only four hours away. Before leaving, I caught the gecko I had days earlier carried onboard and placed him in a plastic container until I could set him free on the next island. The morning we left, a light rain shower doused the far end of the island creating a large, luminous rainbow with a secondary one underneath it. We needed to eyeball our way out through the shoals. Low light always made the task a little nerve-racking.

We were the first boat to arrive in the small, quiet anchorage. Anchoring alone always seemed to heighten the experience of being with nature. But not long after, a second, and then a third boat arrived, and by the following day we had the lime green-coloured *Awesome* party cruiser for a neighbour and then the cruise ship, *Spirit of Yasawa* arrived. Then the *Spirit of the Pacific* arrived and when she headed for the far side of the pass, she drove quite near to us, cutting between *Baccalieu III* and the *Awesome*. The passengers, mostly young tourists, leaned over the side waving and shouting friendly "Bula!" greetings to us.

We drove the dinghy to a backpacker's resort where we hoped to send a fax of a document that was needed at home. After pulling our dinghy onto the beach, a friendly employee welcomed us with a handshake and directed us to the office where the staff attempted to send the fax without success. I returned to the beach to wait for Mike and sat on the sand next to our dinghy. I was joined by another employee who was expecting a new group of backpackers to arrive. She sat beside me in the sand. She was a young Fijian girl in her teens. I enquired about the messy script tattooed on her arm. Sheepishly, she confessed that a friend had done it with a sewing needle.

We moved again in search of another resort that we had heard, from other cruising sailors, was worth a stop. We knew the Octopus Resort was located somewhere on the northwest corner of Waya Island, but we had no detailed information on how to get there and our electronic charts were of little help.

We finally located the resort in Likuliku Bay and took the dinghy to shore where the staff succeeded in sending our fax.

The manager of the Octopus Resort invited us to make use of the amenities of the resort. Besides the swimming pool, beach volley ball, and a Happy Hour that took place each evening, a Fijian lovo was being prepared and a seafood buffet would be featured the following night. It sounded like we might never want to leave. But that night, an ocean swell rolled into the open anchorage and rocked us without mercy. The following morning, we had to pry ourselves away from what we knew could have been a very nice retreat and head for a more protected bay.

ARRIVING at our next location, we dropped anchor between two islands off the southern shore of Wayasewa Island. There was another boat in the spacious bay but it left the following morning just after the roosters from all three villages cock-a-doodle-dooed their way into daylight.

We stayed there a few days and each morning were wakened by the rooster mania, although it could have been the beating of drums from one of the villages that had woken me. Or was it the church bells from the other village? I expect the beating drums woke the roosters, or maybe it was the squealing pigs being tormented by the dogs, but all of it took place before daybreak.

A school was located on the southwest corner of Wayasewa where each morning, the rising sun appeared to suddenly ripen shoulder height grasses to the colour of harvest-ready amber. Later in the morning, the familiar high-pitched squeals of young schoolyard voices would drift across the water to our boat.

Well before seven, I would watch a young boy carry a heavy pail from his village down the beach to where the village pigs were penned beneath a canopy of shade trees. Not yet in his school uniform of grey shorts or sulu and white shirt, he struggled to heft the pail onto his shoulder. He carried it until his arms and shoulders must have ached because I could see him shift it to his right hand then to his left while appearing to barely manage the load. After dumping the scraps carelessly into the pen, he shuffled his way back to the village looking as if in no hurry to get ready for school.

As the morning progressed, a string of children scuffled

along the beach towards the school; the girls in their blue, knee length dresses, and the boys in their greys. It was a strange sight to see children in uniforms way out there in the middle of nowhere.

Those who lived furthest from the school followed the sandy beach around a jutting rock face, thankful for the low tide on those mornings. They probably knew from tracing the same path so many times whether they would be wading in tidal deep water on the way home after school.

By eight-thirty all fell silent. School was in.

When we took the dinghy ashore, near the village of Namara, a five-year-old boy met us at the shoreline to help drag our boat out of the water. With no hesitation, he threw his meager weight into the job as if his childish strength could really make a difference. Dry, brown kava roots poked from the newspaper wrapped bundle I carried in my backpack.

Village chiefs always appeared to appreciate receiving kava root. A young Fijian woman that I had befriended in Musket Cove confided that in some villages, men often sat around kava bowls for an entire evening, sometimes not staggering home until the following morning. With a bit of disgust in her voice, she added that in her village, even a few women drank it in the afternoon.

WHEN we arrived at shore we could see only a single house, but almost immediately a woman, wearing a welcoming smile, came to greet us.

Natha invited us into her house to meet her father, the chief. Many Fijians do not wear shoes and we did not receive any guidelines on where to take our shoes off. It was not obvious because the loose sand on the beach ran straight into the house where it formed the floor.

When we entered, Natha's father and husband were busy constructing an addition to their three-room house but they stopped working when they saw they had visitors. I expect Natha's husband was home because he did not have a job outside his community. Village men are challenged to find employment, leaving their villages dependent on the earnings from the scattered resorts that lease their land. Resorts owned and managed by Europeans employ local islanders at a rate of 60 Fijian dollars ($30 US) a week. Local fishermen earn wages by supplying the resorts with their fresh, daily catch.

Following Natha to her sitting room, we passed through two small ante-rooms with sand floors and a spacious, but nearly bare, kitchen where water, from the nearby hills, was pumped to a sink. Natha said villagers found it necessary to collect rain water for drinking due to the occasional small, shrimp-like creatures found in the runoff supply.

A shelf over the sink supported four, two-gallon plastic containers. Two contained a small amount of flour and sugar they had purchased from a visiting coastal ship. The other two containers stood empty. For merchandise not delivered by ship or for other needs, it was necessary for them to travel by ferry to Lautoka at a cost of $45 FJ ($22 US) for a one-way ticket.

Cooking is customarily done on an outdoor fire, but Natha was one of the few villagers who owned a kerosene stove, which she used during inclement weather when she had fuel. The absence of modern technology explained why, when I took baking to a village, someone would invariably ask if I had baked it in an oven. Following my affirmative reply, the villagers always appeared to be in awe. Even the local men at the Yasawa Dive shop asked me if I had baked their cookies in an oven. Then while diving with them over a period of two days, one or the other would repeat his appreciation for the baked goods.

The room where we were invited to sit had a raised wooden floor covered in vinyl much like what we would use for a table cloth on an outdoor picnic table. A woven mat was spread in the centre of the room over the vinyl. The room was void of furniture except for an old 50 cm (20 in.) television set. Fabric hung like wallpaper on two of the four walls in patterns and colours totally unrelated to the other. A bare light bulb dangled from the ceiling and a curtain separated a bed from the sitting room. Electricity came from the village generator but at the time of our visit, it had run out of diesel. Natha hoped to collect enough money from the residents to enable her to purchase fuel when the next delivery ship stopped at the island.

Mike placed the kava on the floor in front of the chief while we both lowered ourselves to the cane mat, crossing our legs in traditional Fijian style. Natha and her husband sat behind us. The chief wore a bright yellow T-shirt advertising the local tourist cruiser, the *Awesome*. Neither of the men appeared happy. Perhaps they wished they had not been interrupted from their construction duties and were wishing it were not necessary to go through the traditional ceremony of accepting new friends. I could understand that. The chief picked up the kava and proceeded with some rambling ceremonial words. We were thankful he skipped the part of preparing and sharing it with us.

Once outside, Natha invited me to take a picture of her house and when I suggested we include her in the picture, she showed great enthusiasm and went inside to drag her husband and father away from their work again. She insisted on moving laundry aside that she had hung earlier so it would not be visible in the picture. Touching her black, tight short curls, she confessed to not having combed her hair that morning.

Natha invited us to visit the kindergarten where a small, rough-hewn box hung attached to the outside of the building. She mentioned that it was there in case someone might like to make a donation. We hadn't carried money ashore but during our second visit to the village, we remembered to deposit a donation into the box. The kindergarten teacher was not at the school but was hand washing her laundry in the front yard of her house, shouting distance from where we were located. She hollered back that she would join us shortly. Her name was Anita.

Anita had obtained her schooling in Lautoka after which she had been posted to Namara. We learned that when the former teacher left, she had taken the small amount of toys and puzzles with her. The room was void of furniture and school materials. There were no children in the classroom because Anita had sent them home early so that she could do laundry. She had been scrubbing her clothes on a washboard when we called to her from the school.

Natha took a seat on the floor by the door and invited Anita and Mike to sit beside her then requested that I take a picture of them. In preparation for the picture, Natha used a large, broad comb to poke and lift her snarled black curls. Following the picture taking, Natha mentioned that the previous boaters, who had just visited, had taken a picture of the children and then developed it on their boat before leaving the bay.

As we left the school, Anita offered me a small piece of paper from which she had torn from a pad. On it was the address of the school, just in case we wished to send a donation she said. Several months later after arriving home, we sent the village wooden puzzles, books and educational games.

THERE were about seventy children attending the primary school, including several from nearby islands who boarded Monday to Friday while attending grades one to eight. The parents of the boarders paid two dollars a semester per child, which included transportation by boat on weekends when they returned to their villages. The children slept in a two-room, brightly painted dormitory, one room for boys, a separate one for girls. If the generator had diesel fuel, the lights stayed on until eight in the evening.

The beds in the dormitory had been donated by a British boarding school in 2002. The cream coloured paint was peeling from the iron beds but the mattresses were covered in an array of colourful sheets, blankets and pillows, filling the room with a myriad of plaids, stripes and traditional roses. A single stuffed animal lay on one of the pillows.

It was almost lunchtime when two women lifted a large, heavy cauldron from the three concrete blocks that supported it over a smouldering fire. An assortment of well-worn, opaque plastic containers, round, square, oblong, anything capable of holding liquid food, lay spread over the long counter top awaiting the soup. It was a light lunch for active, growing children.

WE learned that a weekly rugby game was to take place the following day. Due to the death of a forty-year-old woman in the village across the bay, (a ten minute boat ride), no one was certain if the game was to be held there or in Namara. We were told that the elders of the affected village would make a decision that evening. Anita mentioned that if the game were to be held in the village across the bay, she and her children would like to attend. She had no transportation and she suggested that she and her children could ride with us in our boat. We replied that we would be happy to take them and we would check back in the morning to confirm the location of the game. Before we left, Natha reminded me that I had promised to print the picture that I had taken of the three of them in front of her house. I hadn't made any such offer but it was obvious that we should make an attempt to copy it. We had never printed a picture before but we had a small printer and suitable paper onboard.

We bounced all night with incoming swells but we decided to stay two more days. It was an opportunity to learn more about Fijian culture and to watch a village game of gritty Fijian rugby. The next day, we took the dinghy to the village where Natha met us on the beach.

We arrived with a gift of T-shirts and a few other tokens including some home baked cookies that Natha could distribute among the villagers. We had succeeded in printing the photograph Natha had expressed such interest in, and she was very pleased to receive it. But the following day I was puzzled when she reported, with a broad smile, that one of her uncles had seen the picture and he would be hanging it in his house. Natha's strong desire to have the picture and her willingness to give it up perplexed me throughout the day. But then I recalled that happiness to a Fijian is not due to what one owns, but to how much one can share with others.

Guests from a backpackers resort arrived to watch the rugby game but there was still confusion as to where the game was to be held. It was the first time we had seen young men in the village and while they stood debating the location of the game, Natha took us to the meeting hall where several women, sitting on floor mats, displayed simple handmade shell jewelry they hoped to sell to the backpackers.

Mike and I received special treatment with an additional tour of the Free Methodist church which consisted of a large, empty room furnished with a single, red fabric-draped altar. A child, who had been following us, knew precisely the next move when she ran to pick up the wooden offering bowl and stood before us with a wide smile. Our donation resulted in being blessed several times as we strode back through the village and Natha announced to her friends, in local dialect, that we had just supported the church. Natha was evidently a good fund-raiser.

When we returned to the beach, the gathering of men, ranging in age from their mid-twenties to thirties, had decided that the match would be held in the village across the bay. Natha would have liked to come, but her father was continuing to work on the house and she needed to be there to serve him his customary five o'clock tea and sweet.

The players piled into the village's small longboat. Soon the shallow boat overflowed with twelve strapping rugby players and a few passengers that were so tightly squeezed together, many were forced to sit on the gunwale. It was easy to understand why Anita wouldn't have wanted to add another body to an overloaded boat, and not knowing how to swim, she hoped for a safer way of travel. But in fact, we surprised her when she learned we were taking our inflatable dinghy rather than our sailboat across the bay.

Mike carried her three-year-old and five-year-old children through the water and set them on the dinghy's front seat. Anita hiked up her sulu, waded into the water and swung her leg over the pontoon while Mike climbed in to man the motor. I pushed the boat out past the shallows.

We were still having problems with our outboard motor. Because of the motor's quirky behaviour, we often started it with the accelerator pressed further forward than recommended.

After leading the dinghy over the reef, I quickly climbed in, and while fending off the coral with an oar, Mike pulled several times on the starter-cord. When the motor showed signs of life, he pushed the throttle forward into super high revs to keep it from stalling, then immediately into gear. The dinghy took off at break neck speed, nearly causing us all whiplash. It's a wonder I didn't topple off the pontoon. It had taken so much time to get the motor in operation that by now the bow had turned and we were headed straight for the beach. Mike rammed the steering handle to port. The dinghy spun 'round with the G-force of a Six Flags roller coaster. God only knows what the long-boat full of spectators were thinking. Poor Anita must have wondered if she had chosen the right boat.

When we landed on the beach across the bay, several children from that island's boarding school were waiting for their village boats to arrive to take them home for the weekend. Several different dialects might be spoken in any given village but schooling is taught in a universal Fijian language.

As soon as I stepped onto the beach, I sensed a difference in the attitude of the children. It was the end of the week, and perhaps they were anxious to get home, but there were none of the happy smiles like we saw in the attractive Fijian children in the Namara village, and no one offered to help pull our boat ashore as they did on the other island. Anita noticed the difference too and was the first to mention it. Surprisingly, Anita had never been to this island before even though it was only a kilometre across the bay. She even had several cousins and relatives who boarded there. I wondered what she thought of people like us who had travelled thousands of miles to reach secluded villages like hers.

As we watched the rugby game Anita introduced us to several children who came to greet her: her mother's sister's child's child, her grandfather's daughter's son's child, her father's mother's brother's grandchild. I was impressed she could track the linage of all these people, although sometimes she needed to give her family tree some deep thought.

There was a noticeable difference in the upkeep of the village bures and the school looked tired and drab. One morning, while gazing towards this village from our boat with my binoculars, I thought I saw a man chasing a young boy along the beach with a machete in his hand, although perhaps it was a stick. In any case, the dogs knew enough to keep their distance and the kid was a pretty good runner.

I think Anita had been right when she said her village

had been blessed with good fortune. But as well, they had Natha—a fund raising guru.

Anita had brought several little bags of homemade fudge and a sweet Indian snack that she boasted no one else in the village knew how to make. She had mixed portions of flour and water together, fried them, then dipped the small crunchy pieces into sugar. She sold them at the game for twenty cents a bag and said she always set these earnings aside as savings. She liked living in Namara because she could save more money than when she lived in the city of Lautoka.

The rugby game was interesting but I can't say that I found much pleasure while watching it. When I learned the nearest medical facility was a very, very long walking distance from where we were located, I was seized with fear for the players.

In this part of the world, women don't often see a medical person during their pregnancy and Anita confessed that the red sores on her youngest child's legs should have been seen by the nurse but it meant walking a great distance and she had put the visit off. If a major injury occurred during the rugby game it would be necessary for the injured player to be transported to Lautoka 80 kilometres (50 miles) away, a two-hour long and uncomfortable ride in a small, jostling boat. But this fact did not in the least minimize the energy or enthusiasm of the local team players. Instead, each man fought for ownership of the rugby ball as if competing for the World Cup. Over and over again they crashed and collided with one another while running full speed down the field throwing endless lateral passes. Fast paced and fiercely competitive, the game saw each player throwing himself mercilessly into the action.

In Fiji's world of geographically dispersed peoples, the game of rugby has united the country's diverse cultures and, in a move to reconcile and unify ethnic tensions, the government has come to recognize the power the game has to offer.

After a Fiji team won the Melrose Cup in 2005, and the country had faced three coups, a government spokesman stated the "Sevens Rugby World Cup heroes ... [captivated] the hearts of the different peoples of Fiji, uniting them as one nation and one people in the course of supporting our national team."

And the enthusiasm didn't stop there; Fijian musician and composer Daniel Rae Costello recruited a group of musicians to donate their time and expertise to the making of the upbeat feel-good song, *We Are Fiji*. The song's lyrics encourages Fijians to live together in harmony, walk together "side by side," and to "put our differences behind us."

In 1977, Fiji's Sevens won the international Hong Kong Sevens tournament, one year after the tournament, had been introduced. As of 2011, the Sevens team had won eight more Hong Kong Seven tournaments and two World Cups. Rugby is widely believed to have introduced Fiji to the rest of the world, and today players in the National League and on the Sevens team continue to capture the hearts of people around the world with their infectious enthusiasm while acting as ambassadors for their country.

And here, way out in the Yasawa Islands, in a tiny village, this same infectious spirit was evident. Injured players grimacing with pain limped off the playing field, sometimes supported by teammates, only to quickly rejoin the play even though they should have been benched with a pack of ice. Players, so exhausted they could hardly catch their breath, remained on the field, ruthlessly pushing their bodies while playing on bare feet.

We returned Anita and her children to her home shore just before dark and told them we would be leaving the following morning. She gave me an affectionate kiss goodbye. Before leaving I promised she would hear from us in the future. I hope the games and puzzles reached her school.

We pushed our dinghy into the water where a young boy, standing knee deep in water, had just helped a fisherman move his longboat away from shore. The boy and I had not met before and he asked my name as I waded past him. In the palm of his hand he held a small, extraordinarily beautiful mollusk shell. It was brown with darker bands winding around the body. White, squiggly lines ran from the tightly twisting apex towards the opening; in the shell's orifice, sat a round, hard shiny plug. It looked like an eye. He turned it over and over in his hand and perhaps is why it was so highly polished. He stretched his hand towards me and pressed the beautiful piece into my hand. I was astounded that he would give up something so special to a stranger. But he did. And he did it with a smile.

His name was Eli and we had known each other for less than a minute. I shall never forget this act of friendship or the cheerfulness of all the Fijians we had met while travelling throughout those islands.

THE next morning I felt some sadness about leaving. Having the opportunity to meet people and learn more of their culture was a highlight of our travels. I left wishing we could have given them more. Their needs are basic. They only wish for better medical care, improved nutrition, better hygiene and education for their children.

While motoring out of the bay, I turned for one last look at the village. Lost in the velvet greenery of the hills, it was already gone from sight.

LEAVING MUSKET COVE

WHEN WE RETURNED to Musket Cove, I learned more about Fijian life style when I visited the newly opened spa. Varra, a young Fijian woman, recounted the story of how she had left her village to work in the spa at the resort.

Her story began when she and her best friend were eighteen years old and had just completed high school. They came from the same village and sometimes would go into the nearby city of Nandi to see a movie. One day, while in town, they noticed an advertisement for employment at a spa. Embarrassed, Varra confessed they had no idea what the word 'spa' meant, but they envisioned it to be a store that sold native artifacts. When the girls returned the following day with their school certificates they were accepted as trainees. They began their training without knowing what they were about to learn. While walking through the spa that first day, Varra recalled hearing soft music and catching glimpses of waiting rooms with cane furniture and lovely plants. The interviewer, whom they were following, opened a door to a room where a female employee lay on a salon table, positioned face down. Naked from the waist up, she had a towel draped over her lower half and an instructor was teaching the art of massage. The sight of such nakedness shocked Varra. She refused to enter the room proclaiming it would not be proper for her to see or be part of whatever was taking place in the room. She had no idea what massage was but seeing someone naked was unacceptable in her culture. Realizing the girls had applied for jobs they knew nothing about, the instructor offered an explanation. Varra and her friend hovered near the back of the room while watching in horror as the instructor placed her hands on the girl's back and began kneading her muscles

After that first session, Varra and her friend decided not to continue with the training, but by morning had changed their minds and returned for a second class. They completed the full two months of training and graduated as certified masseuses. Their parents had not been aware of how the girls were spending their time and when Varra finally told them, Varra's father immediately refused to let her continue and questioned why she would ever want to see people while they were naked. It could only lead to bad things, he said. Hoping to convince her father that partial nakedness played only a small part of her job, Varra cleared the family dinner table, covered it with a mattress and gave her father his first massage. Her father loved it and even fell asleep.

Her parents were farmers who grew pineapples, paw paw, kava and taro root on the plateau of the Sleeping Giant Mountain. They worked hard but they could never earn enough money to help Varra reach her ambition as a schoolteacher. When Varra told her parents she hoped to work at the spa to earn enough money to attend school, her parents gave their consent. But it still perplexes her father why his daughter would want to "look at other people's bums."

DUE to the political situation within Fiji, the resort had few guests and I would visit the girls during their idle times. Since leaving home, they had both learned that not everyone shared the same customs as *they* did and laughed at their earlier innocence.

Josephine, Varra's friend, was twenty-four. After high school she had trained as an esthetician. Many of her friends had married as soon as they finished high school but several were already divorced after only two years of marriage and now living with their parents with their babies. Josephine wanted to travel before she married, although she had never been far from her home except when she had gone to school in Nadi, and now to work on the island at Musket Cove. She paused a moment before confiding she would never be having this conversation with her parents because it was disrespectful to disagree with their views which were focused on her marrying and having their grandchildren before they passed on. Her dream was to travel to England. She could save money while living at the resort due to not having to pay for lodging or food. She made $4.50 FJ ($2.25 US) an hour. Before we left the island, I left her a small donation tucked inside a note of encouragement.

AFTER four enjoyable weeks in Fiji it was time to leave. We spent our last few days completing small maintenance jobs in preparation for the upcoming passage to Vanuatu. We played one last round of golf. Oddly, the course was covered in a mass of hopping toads!

My last few walks around Malolo Lailai began at daybreak when first light spread in soft, pastel colours throughout the sky. I'd ramble around rocky headlands stumbling over stony beaches until one morning, I found myself sloshing knee deep between mangrove trees and steep rocky shoreline because I had mistimed an incoming tide. I was doing exactly what Mike and I had warned each other not to do, walk alone in areas where an escape route to shore was not possible when the water level rose.

It was far wilder on the windward side where scrub brush and woodlots ran right to the edge of the ocean. Tangled fishing line, frayed rope and plastic bottles intertwined with driftwood, rested in wavy lines along the shore. I never saw another person at any time that I was ever there and sometimes I'd look back to see only my footprints pressed into the sand. I would often feel a certain loneliness come over me, yet I liked walking there alone. Sometimes on my homeward journey I would cut across the island through waist-high grasses and small, dark wooded patches. One day I came across a single grave marked 'Ken Carter, Remembered Forever, Over and Out.'

On returning to the boat, I would often walk down the sandy airstrip where the resort had recently installed new lights after the driver of the lawnmower had ripped the lights off during a careless runway manicure. It would be around seven o'clock when I reached the vicinity of the employee's residences. I would always hear the laughter of men's voices come from where they were playing volleyball before leaving for work.

I loved those walks.

The night before leaving, we shared drinks at the Four Dollar Bar with fellow cruisers. We cooked two steaks on the barbeque and ate our supper beneath the stars on a wooden picnic table. The weather was perfect.

We wanted to be in Australia by August and it was now the middle of June. Our plans were to stop in Vanuatu and New Caledonia en route to Australia. In the morning, when the tide was high, we untied the stern lines to shore. We were about to say goodbye to our Fijian utopia one last time.

In some situations, it can be challenging for two people to untie the lines from shore and manage the boat without leaving the other behind on the dock. When we left during unfavourable conditions, we would always note where the pickup point would be if one of us had to go back for the other. It had only happened once and I can tell you, boarding a boat while it's moving is like jumping onto an elevated carousel.

LEAVING MUSKET COVE

The morning we left the wind was light and boarding was not the problem, instead the windlass jammed while pulling up the anchor just metres from the reef.

With the anchor off the bottom, but not yet on deck, we were free to drift onto the reef or into boats behind us. But that's not all. The dangling anchor had the potential to hook and dislodge the anchors of the surrounding boats. Those in peril might view our vessel as the forked bucket on a front-end loader.

Suddenly people appeared from nowhere. With fenders in hand and scowling faces, those with boats near to us took up positions on their bows. Within seconds our status changed from friend to menacing hazard. Then there were the onlookers on shore, there to witness the big screw up. We did it too, sit in our cockpit watching people anchor while clucking our tongues at their ineptitude. Or would watch them bring their yacht in and keep an eye to see how well they were meeting the challenge. Will they scrape the boat beside them or ram one of the posts? We mean no harm; it's all in the name of entertainment. Sometimes we might even sit with a drink while the action carries on in front of us. Maybe someone will do something really, really stupid like the guy who tried to pull away from the dock while his electrical cord was still plugged in. Oh wait, that was Mike. Well, I remember the time a woman stepped ashore with a line in her hand thinking it was attached to the boat, but it wasn't. That was really irresponsible. Oh yeah…, that was me. Ok this is the one… I also remember seeing a boat almost at dock that had apparently forgotten to take in their mainsail! O.K., O.K. that was us too. We believed in providing entertainment for our neighbours. What can I say?

By now the crowd really wanted to see if we would go up on the reef, maybe even take a few boats with us after snagging some anchor chains. Maybe the spectators were placing bets. How many would we take with us? I'm sure they were placing bets. All good naturedly of course.

But Mike knew exactly where to find the Allen key, a small hexagonal tool required to take the cover off the windlass. He grabbed it from his 'basket', a container resting on the navigation station. This basket had often been a bone-of-contention with me. Quite often an object I might have been looking for was not where it belonged, but buried somewhere in a pile of rubble in this basket: punches, flashlights, bolts, screws, bits of line, electrical connectors, florescent markers, a wrench because it was used once a week, a head lamp if it had been used in the past four weeks. There could even be a hat in there! It wouldn't be the first time I stood with my hands on my hips sighing heavily, clucking over not finding what I needed because it hadn't been put back where it belonged.

But that morning the basket yielded the right tool easily and Mike quickly lifted the top off the windlass, released the jam and we moved out of the marina with still enough tide beneath the keel to prevent grounding.

We didn't go far; we tied to a buoy outside the marina to wait for the sun to move higher in the sky when it could assist us in navigating through the surrounding reefs. When it came time to slip our mooring line from that old, faded number 24 buoy, it was goodbye to Musket Cove. We felt nostalgic as we left the place that had been so good to us.

As we pulled out of the bay, Sophie, from the Cove's radio room, thoughtfully called on the VHF radio to wish us a second goodbye. I responded with sincere thanks and closed the radio conversation with the standard, "This is *Baccalieu*, over and out."

This time those words carried far more weight than usual.

AFTERWORD

The following months we sailed over 14,000 miles, visiting exotic countries and remote islands (*Yes, The World Is Round, Part II: Fiji to the Caribbean*).

Vanuatu, a country comprising dense jungles, fiery volcanoes and tribes that honour witchdoctors, was our next stop.

On the island of Espiritu Santo, we took part in an extreme hiking adventure. We trekked through dense bush, clambered over boulders and teetered precariously on ladders spanning neck-breaking heights.

Espiritu Santo is home to one of the most famous shipwrecks in the world, the SS *President Coolidge*. The ship lies in approximately 125 feet of water and was one of the deepest, darkest, wreck penetrating dives we have undertaken.

We watched the sun set on Ayers Rock (Uluṟu) in Australia's outback and drove a 4x4 off-road vehicle over stony creeks and steep, slippery gravel roads to see the ancient forests of Cape Tribulation National Park.

Exploring 2,000 miles of Australia's coastline, we sailed the renowned Whitsunday Islands, Cape York Peninsula — the northernmost point of Australia, and the wild and remote Torres Strait.

Bali's countryside was awe-inspiring: panoramic views, volcanoes, waterfalls, bamboo forests and acres of sloping, terraced rice fields. Balinese are gentle, content people. So it came as a surprise, when officials detained us for two days, before allowing us to leave the island.

THE remote Cocos Keeling Islands lie 2,000 nm west of Darwin. These serene, tropical atolls were an idyllic stopover before undertaking the 2,300 nm passage across the Indian Ocean, one of the world's roughest bodies of water. Swells roll north from the Roaring 40s and brisk tradewinds create cross swells.

EN route to South Africa, we stopped at Mauritius, an island of lush, green tea plantations, sugarcane fields and exotic flora, and Réunion Island, home to one of the most active volcanoes in the world.

DURBAN was the point from where we left to round the Cape of Good Hope, one of the most dangerous stretches of coastline in the world. Timing our departure from Durban was crucial. We left on the edge of a passing low-pressure system, hoping to make the 700 nm passage to Cape Town before the next 'low', blasted us with headwinds and created chaos in the notorious Agulhas Current.

CAPE Town was our home while we waited for suitable weather in the South Atlantic Ocean. We were there six weeks. The layover gave us time to tour some of South Africa's most famous sites. Cape Peninsula's rugged coastline juts into the Atlantic Ocean where wind and seas, hammer into the continent. It was interesting to stand on land and view what we had, just days earlier, experienced by sea.

Cape Wineland is surrounded by striking mountain scenery, valleys running with fields of vine-supported wine grapes and working estates that produce world renowned wines. Some of the best chefs in the world are found here.

WHILE taking part in a Safari in Botswana, we had an up close and frightening experience with a herd of elephants. We travelled to Zimbabwe to view Victoria Falls.

FROM South Africa, we set our sights on Brazil, 3,500 nm distant. For the passage, we joined a fleet of international racing and cruising yachts for the annual, Heineken Cape to Bahia Race, the longest continent-to-continent race in the world. As part of the cruising division, we were allowed a forty-eight hour stopover on St. Helena Island, one of the most isolated islands in the world.

OUR arrival to Brazil was timed so that we could take part in two of Brazil's famous week-long Carnivals—the 'Mardi Gras' of the southern hemisphere. There are more reasons to be frightened during a Brazilian Carnival than there are while sailing oceans.

Checking in and out of the country with Brazil's customs and immigration officials was another nightmare.

LEAVING Brazil, we pointed *Baccalieu III*'s bow northward, towards the Caribbean. This is where we would complete our circumnavigation. After traveling thousands of miles, crossing oceans, battling high winds and unruly seas, we hit a wall. Not literally, but a wall all the same. It knocked the stuffing out of us.

PORTS, ANCHORAGES

*Dock (D), Anchorage (A), Mooring (M),
Med-Mooring (MED-MOOR)*

2004

ENGLAND (JUNE)
London: St. Katharine Docks (D)
Ramsgate, East Kent: Royal Ramsgate Marina (D)
Brighton, East Sussex: Brighton Marina (D)
Yarmouth, Isle of Wight (M)

CHANNEL ISLANDS (JUNE)
Guernsey: the Pool, St. Peter Port Marina (D)
Alderney: Braye Harbour (A)

ENGLAND (JULY)
Cowes, Isle of Wight: Cowes Yacht Haven (wharf) (D)
Studland Bay, Dorset (A)
Portsmouth, Hampshire: Trafalgar Wharf (D)
Dartmouth, Devon: Dart Marina Yacht Harbour (D)
Plymouth, Devon: Yacht Haven Quay (wharf) (D)
Falmouth, Cornwall: Falmouth Marina (D)

WEST COAST IBERIAN PENINSULA

SPAIN (JULY)
Baiona, Pontevedra: Baiona Marina (D)

PORTUGAL (JULY)

Leixões, Matosinhos: Porto Atlântico Marina (D)
Cascais, Greater Lisbon: Marina de Cascais (D)
Sines: Alentejo, Marina de Sines (D)
Lagos, Algarve: Marina de Lagos (D)

SPAIN (JULY)

Puerto Sherry, Andalusia, Cádiz: Puerto Sherry Marina (D)

GIBRALTAR (AUG)

Marina Bay, Gibraltar Harbour (D)

MEDITERRANEAN SEA (AUG-OCT)

SPAIN

COSTA DEL SOL

Estepona, Andalucia: Estepona Marina (MED-MOOR)
Benalmádena, Andalucia: (MED-MOOR)
Almerimar, Andalucia: El Ejido Marina, Puerto Deportivo (MED-MOOR)
Roquetas de Mar, Aguadulce, Andalucia: Aguadulce Marina, Puerto Deportivo Aguadulce (MED-MOOR)

BALEARIC ISLANDS

Espalmador Island (A)
Ibiza: Cala Jolanda (A), Puerto del Nuevo (A), Cala Bassa (A)
Majorca: Palma, Real Club Náutico de Palma (D)
Cabrera Island (A)

WESTWARD TO GIBRALTAR

Ibiza: Cala Boix (A)
Cabo de Gata, Nijar Natural Park, Andalucia (A)

COSTA DEL SOL

Almerimar, Andalucia: El Ejido Marina, Puerto Deportivo (MED-MOOR)
Sotogrande, Andalucia: Marina Marbella, Cádiz (MED-MOOR)

GIBRALTAR (OCT)
Queensway Quay Marina, Gibraltar Harbour (D)

CANARY ISLANDS, ATLANTIC OCEAN: (Oct /Nov)
Graciosa Island: Playa Francesca (A), Bahia del Salado (A)
Lanzarote: Marina Rubicón, Playa Blanca (D)
Gran Canaria: Las Palmas (D)

TRANS-ATLANTIC CROSSING (NOV/DEC)

2005

CARIBBEAN CRUISING: (Jan-May). *The following does not reflect islands revisited.*

St. Lucia: Rodney Bay Marina (D), Rodney Bay (A), Marigot Bay: The Moorings (D), Pitons (A)

Bequia Island: Admiralty Bay (A)

Mustique: Britannia Bay (A)

Tobago Cays Marine Park (A)

Union Island: Chatham Bay (A), Clifton Harbour (A)

Petit St. Vincent (A)

St. Vincent: Young Island Cut (A)

Palm Island (A)

HEADING NORTH

Union Island: Chatham Bay (A)

Tobago Cays Marine Park (A)

Mustique: Britannia Bay (A)

Martinique: Sainte-Anne (A), Fort de France (A); Petit Anse d'Arlet (A)

Schoelcher (A)

Dominica: Prince Rupert Bay (A)

Guadeloupe: Bas-du Fort Marina (D), Îles des Saintes (A); Deshaies (A)

Antigua: Falmouth Harbour, Catamaran Club (D), English Harbour (MED-MOOR)

Deep Bay (A), Ffryes Beach (A), Green Island (A), Jolly Harbour, Jolly Harbour Marina, (D)

Barbuda: Coco Point (A)

Nevis: Pinney's Beach (A)

St. Barts (Saint Barthélemy): Gustavia (A), Colombier Bay (A)

St. Martin: Simpson Bay (A)

BERMUDA (JUNE)

Hamilton Harbour: Royal Hamilton Amateur Dinghy Club (D), St. George's Harbour (A)

UNITED STATES (SEPT)

Rhode Island, NE: Brenton Cove, Goat Island, Newport, Oldport Marine (M), Portsmouth, New England Boatworks (D)

Annapolis, MD: Port Annapolis Marina (D), Solomons Zahniser's Yacht Center (D)

Little Creek Marina: Norfolk, VA (D)

2006

CARIBBEAN (NOV)

Antigua: Falmouth Harbour (D), Green Island (A), Jolly Harbour (D)

Barbuda, Antigua & Barbuda: Coco Point (A)

ABC ISLANDS (ARUBA, BONAIRE, CURAÇAO) (FEB)

Bonaire: Kralendijk (M)

Aruba: Renaissance Marina, Oranjestad (D)

PANAMA (FEB)

San Blas Islands: Sapibenega (A), Green Island (A), El Porvenir (A), Cayo Chichime (A)

Colón: Portobelo (A), Limon Bay (A)

Panama City: Flamenco Yacht Club and Marina (D)

PACIFIC OCEAN CROSSING: *(Mar)*

LAS PERLAS ARCHIPÉLAGO
Contadora Island (A)
Cana Island (A)
San José Island (A)

GALÁPAGOS ISLANDS *(MAR)*
Santa Cruz Island: Puerto Ayora (A)

FRENCH POLYNESIA (APR–JUNE)

MARQUESAS ISLANDS
Fatu Hiva: Hanavave (A)
Nuka Hiva: Taioa Bay (Daniel's Bay) (A)

THE TUAMOTUS
Kauehi (A)
Fakarava (A)
Toau: Anse Amyot (A)
Rangiroa: Motu Nao Nao (A), Motu Fara (A)

SOCIETY ISLANDS
Tahiti: Papeete (MED-MOOR)
Moorea: Cooks Bay (A)
Huahine: Fare (A), Avea Bay (A)
Raiatea: Tapuama Bay (A), Uturoa (wharf D)
Bora Bora: Bora Bora Yacht Club (M), Bloody Mary's (A)

COOK ISLANDS
Rarotonga: Avarua (MED-MOOR)

NIUE (JUNE)
Alofi (M)

KINGDOM OF TONGA (JUNE)

Vava'u Island Group

Vai'utukakau Bay (A)

Neiafu, Port of Refuge (M)

Unnamed anchorage (A)

FIJI ISLANDS (JULY-OCT)

VANUA LEVU

Savusavu: Copra Shed Marina, (M)

Coconut Point (A)

Bua Bay (A)

VITI LEVU

Vitogo Bay (A)

Mamanuca Islands

Malolo Lailai, Musket Cove (D)

VITI LEVU

Somosomo Bay (A)

Yasawa Islands

Naviti Island (A)

Nacula Island: Nacula Bay (A)

Nanuya Lailai Island (Blue Lagoon) (A)

Waya Island: South Waya Bay (A), Yalobi Bay (A)

DENARAU ISLAND

Port Denarau (MED-MOOR)

VITI LEVU

Momi Bay Battery Historic Park (A)

NEW ZEALAND (NOV)

Bay of Islands

Port Opua: Bay of Islands Marina (D)

Gulf Harbour, Whangaparaoa Peninsula (D)

2007

NEW ZEALAND

HAURAKI GULF
Kawau Island (A)
Great Barrier Island: Smoke House Bay (A), FitzRoy Harbour (A)
Northland: Tutukaka Harbour (A)
Kaikoura Island (A)

BAY OF ISLANDS
Roberton Island (A)
Port Opua: Bay of Islands Marina (D)

FIJI ISLANDS (JUNE)

VITI LEVU
Momi Bay (A)
Lautoka Harbour (A)

VLADI ISLANDS
Saweni Bay (A)

MAMANUCA ISLANDS
Malolo Lailai, Musket Cove (M)

YASAWA ISLANDS
Navadra Island (A)
Nanuya Lailai Island, (Blue Lagoon) (A)
Nanuya Balavu Island: Mantaray Bay (A)
Wayasewa Island (A)
Waya Island: Likuliku Bay (Octopus Resort) (A), Yalobi Bay (A)

DENARAU ISLAND, SAWENI BAY (A)

MILEAGE

Days documented for non-stop passages over 500 nm

DATE	PASSAGE	MILEAGE	DAYS
June/July 2004	South Coast UK and Channel Islands	500	
July 2004	Falmouth, UK to Baiona	500	3
July 2004	Cruise Atlantic Coast: Baiona to Gibraltar Baiona–Leixões... 200 Leixos–Cascais... 100 Cascais–Sines... 50 Sines–Lagos... 100 Lagos–Puerto Sherry... 100 Puerto Sherry–Gibraltar... 50	600	
Aug.–Oct. 2005	Gibraltar to Majorca to Gibraltar (cruising)	1,000	
Oct. 2004	Gibraltar to Gran Canaria, Canary Is.	600	4
Nov. 2004	Atlantic Ocean Crossing Gran Canaria to St Lucia	3,000	18
Dec. 2004–May 2005	Eastern Caribbean (cruising)	900	
May 2005	St. Martin to Newport St. Martin–Bermuda... 900 Bermuda–Newport RI., U.S.A. ... 700	1,600	5 5

Nov. 2005	Newport to Antigua *Newport, RI–* *Annapolis* ... 350 *Annapolis–Norfolk* ... 150 *Norfolk–Antigua* ... 1,650	2,150	10
Jan.–Feb. 2006	Antigua to Panama (cruising) *Antigua–Bonaire* ... 500 *Bonaire–Aruba* ... 100 *Aruba–San Blas Is.* ... 550 *San Blas Is.–Panama* ... 100	1,250	3 3
Feb.–June 2006	Pacific Ocean Crossing Panama to Fiji *Panama–Galápagos* ... 850 *Galápagos–* *Marquesas* ... 3,100 *Marquesas–Tuamotus* ... 500	6,800	5 19 3
Feb–June 2006 cont.	*Tuamotus–Tahiti* ... 250 *Tahiti–Bora Bora* ... 250 *Bora Bora–Cook* *Islands* ... 500 *Cook Islands–Niue* ... 600 *Niue–Tonga–250* *Tonga–Fiji–500*		4 4 3
Oct. 2006	Fiji to New Zealand	1,000	6
May 2007	New Zealand to Fiji	1,000	6

PLAYERS IN THE STORY

Andy Jones, *Baccalieu III*, Oyster 56, CAN

Arthur English, *Baccalieu III*, Oyster 56, CAN

Bernard and Jean Clark, *Golden Eye of Chichester*, Westerly Oceanlord 12.3 GBR

Bob Medland, *Baccalieu III*, Oyster 56, CAN

Brian and Doreen Long, *Chinook*, Oyster 56, CAN

Brian Norton Sn & Brian Norton Jr, *Four Freedoms*, Warrior 40, GBR

Brian Smith, *Baccalieu III*, Oyster 56, CAN

British Offshore Sailing School, *Ocean Wanderer*, Westerly Oceanlord 41, GBR

Christian Potthoff-Sewing, *Auliana II*, Faurby 424, DEU

Christina Bruguera, ESP, *Carpe Diem*, Oyster 65, BVI

Christoph Rassy *Bamsen*, Hallberg Rassy 62, SWE

Daryl and Laurel Fisher, *Cool Bananas*, Admiral 50, NZ

David and Betty Francis, *Sundance*, trawler, USA

David Hill, *Baccalieu III*, Oyster 56, CAN

David Pratt, *Jenard of Mersey*, Hallberg Rassy 43. GBR

Douglas, Robert Marika & Charlotte, *Cat Talo*, Prout Escale. GBR

Duncan & Inge Stewart, *Anna Caram*, Westerly Oceanmaster 48, GBR

Duncan & Inge Stewart, *Anna Caram*, Westerly Oceanmaster 48, GBR

Fred and Robin Kay, *Lady Menai*, Oyster 435, IRL

Glenn and Rebecca McMillan, *Onyva*, Hallberg Rassy 39, GBR

Henry & Estelle Vander Hoven ,*Moi Noi Jodine*, Oyster 56, ZAF

Jason Pickering, *Ciao*, Moody 39, GBR

Jennifer Hill, *Baccalieu III*, Oyster 56, CAN

John & Jenny Greenwood, *Tzigane*, Jenneau 54, GBR

John & Judy Thompson, CAN, *Entrada*

John & Marian Morse, *Saoirse K*, Legend 410, GBR

John & Jean McNeil, *Baccalieu III*, Oyster 56, CAN

John and Cheryl Ellseworth, *Baccalieu III*, Oyster 56, CAN

Julian & Anne Whitlock, *Freewheel*, Tayana, 16.7, GBR

Karl-Ludvig Mauland & Hedda Maria Harringtonson, *Glad*, Comfort 30, NOR

Keith and Rosemary Hamilton, CAN, *Carpe Diem*, Oyster 65, BVI

Klaus and Marlies Schuback, *White Wings*, Oyster 485, DEU

Lauren and John, *Velocity*, USA

Luigi Buras, *Marivel*, Sweden 45, ITA

Manuela Uribe, CAN

Mark Curtis, CAN

Michael Dixon, *Renee*, Oyster 56, GBR

Mike Cobbe, *Kellys Eye of Hamble*, De Vries Lentsch 38, GBR

Mike Rose AG/GRB, *Baccalieu III*, Oyster 56, CAN

Nick Pochin, *Festina Lente*, Discovery 55, GBR

Niels and Tove Jahren, *Blackbird*, Bavaria 14.6, NOR

Patrick Doran & Angela Butcher, *Autumn Breeze*, Fred Parker Ketch, 14m, GBR

Paul Fenn, NZL, *Carpe Diem*, Oyster 65, BVI

Pavlidis & Catherine Panayotis, *Pytheas*, Hallberg Rassy 43, FRA

Peter & Sally Turner, *Asolare*, Amel Super Maramu 2000, GBR

Peter & Val Newns, *Valhalla of Marlow*, Hallberg Rassy 352, GBR

Peter Turner & Sally Turner, *Asolare*, Amel Super Maramu2000. GBR

Philip & David Hitchcock, *Toutazimut*, Formosa 51, GBR

Philip (Hutch) & Gillie Hutchinson, *Fenella*, Jeanneau 14.1, GBR

Philipp Hiller & Stella Nottbrock (Mr & Mrs. Hiller), DEU

Ray Graham, *Baccalieu III*, Oyster 56, CAN

Rock Lenardic, SI, *Baccalieu III*, Oyster 56, CAN

Rolf Herlig, *Moana*, Oyster 53, DEU

Ron & Shirley Fabro, CAN

Susan & Peter MacKay, GBR, *Stella*, Amel Maramu 13.8, GBR

Tim and Beckie Brettell, *Tallulah of Falmouth*, Oyster 53, GBR

Tom and Diane Might, *Between the Sheets*, Hallberg Rassy 62, U.S.A.

SELECTED BIBLIOGRAPHY

ARCHIVAL SOURCES, SCIENTIFIC PUBLICATIONS, CRUISING GUIDES

National Maritime Museum, Greenwich, London.

Royal Observatory, Greenwich, London.

New Caledonia Museum, New Caledonia.

Auckland Museum, Auckland, Australia.

Brice, Graham. *Destination New Zealand, Blue Water Cruising Guide, New Zealand's Northern Water.* 1993, 4th edition 2002, Winston Brice Ltd.

Bradt. *Travel Guide, St Helena.* Steiner, Liston, Globe Peguot Press Inc., 2nd edition, 2007.

Calder, Michael. *A Yachtsman's Fiji.* The Cruising Classroom, Sydney Australia, 1993, 2nd edition.

Colfelt, David. *100 Magical Miles—Of the Great Barrier Reef, the Whitsunday Islands.* Windward Publications Pty Ltd. 8th addition.

Cornell, Jimmy. *World Cruising Handbook.* McGraw, 2001, 3rd edition.

Cornell, Jimmy. *World Cruising Routes.* International Marine/McGraw, 2002, 5th edition.

Dolye, Chris. *Leeward Islands 2004–2005.* Chris Doyle Cruising Guide.

Dolye, Chris. *Windward Islands 2005–2006.* Chris Doyle Cruising Guide Publications, 12th edition 2004

Doyle, Chris. *Windward Islands 2009–2010.* Chris Doyle publishing 14th edition.

Harewood, Jocelyn, Tione Chinula, Vincent Talbot. *Vanuatu & New Caledonia.* Lonely Planet, July 2006, 5th edition.

Carolyn Bain, Sandra Bao, Susannah Farfor, Alan Murphy, Nina Rousseau, Simon Sellars, Justine Vaisutis, Ryan Ver Berkmmoes, Meg Worby. *Lonely Planet, Australia 2005.* Lonely Planet Publications, 13th edition.

Lonely Planet, The South Pacific. Lonely Planet Publications 2nd edition.

Ryan Ver Berkmoes. Iain Stewart. *Lonely Planet, Bali and Lombok.* Lonely Planet Publications 2007.

Lucas, Alan. *Cruising the Coral Coast.* Alan Lucas Cruising Guides, 8th addition.

Patrick, Noel. *Noel Patrick's Curtis Coast.* L.M Kombrekke: Blue Water Books and Charts, 2003.

Patuelli, Jacques. *Grenada to the Virgin Islands.* Imray Laurie Norie & Wilson Ltd. 2003.

Jolly, Margaret, Professor in Anthropology, Gender and Cultural Studies and Pacific Studies in the School of Culture, *History and Language in the College of Asia and the Pacific.*1994

Rousseau, Benedicta, *The Achievement of simultaneity: Kaston in contemporary Vanuatu,* 2004

Russell, Joe. *Exploring the Marquesas Islands.* Fine Edge Productions.

Seaworthy Publications. *A cruising guide to the Isthmus of Panama.* The Panama Guide, 2nd edition.

Smith, Julian. *Ecuador, including the Galápagos Is.* Moon books, 3rd edition.

Stanley, David. *South Pacific Moon Handbooks.* Avalon Travel 8th edition.

Steiner, Susan, Robin Liston. *St. Helena, Bradt Travel Guide.* The Globe Pequot Press, U.S.A.

Stephenson, Marylee. *The Galápagos islands.* Mountaineers Books, 1989, 2000, 2nd edition, Edith Publishing.

Street, Donald M. Jr. *Anguilla to Dominica.* WW Norton & Company 2001.

BOOKS

Adkins, Roy and Lesley Adkins. *Jack Tar.* Little Brown 2008.

Allen, Dr. Gerald R. Allen, Roger Steene. *Indo Pacific Coral Reef Field Guide, Tropical Reef Research.*

Anderson, Dale. *Building the Panama Canal.* World Almanac Library 2005.

Baker, Ian. *St. Helena: One Man's Island.* Wilton 65, 2004.

Belich, James. *Making Peoples, A History of New Zealanders.* University Pressod Hawai'i Press, 1996.

Biturogoiwasa, Solomoni. *My Village, My World, Everyday Life in Nadoria, Fiji*. Institute of Pacific Studies, University of the South Pacific 2001.

Bunce, Pauline. *The Cocos (Keeling) Islands*. The Jacaranda Press.

Cole, Tom. *Hell West and Crooked*. Collins Publishers 1998.

Covarrubias, Miguel. *Island of Bali*, Routledge &Kegan Paul, Book Publishers (UK) Ltd.

Denholm, Ken. *From Signal Gun to Satellite*. Canister, Jamestown, Island of St. Helena.

Diamond, Jared. *Guns, Germs, And Steel: The Fates of Human Societies*. W.W. Norton & Company Ltd.

Eriksen, Ronnie. *St. Helena Lifeline*. Mallett & Bell Publications, 1994.

Flood, Josephine. *The Original Australians*. Allen & Unwin publishers, 2006

Godwin, Peter. *When a Crocodile Eats the Sun*. Picador Africa, an imprint of Pan Macmillan South Africa 2006

Gosse, Philip. *St Helena 1502–1938*. Anthony Nelson Ltd., England.

Harrison, Tom. *Savage Civilisation*. London Victor Gollancz Ltd., 1937, Camelot Press Ltd., London & South Hampton.

Hill, Ernestine. *The Territory*. Halstead Press Pty., Ltd., Sydney, 1951.

Howarth, David. *Tahiti, A Paradise Lost*. Viking Press 1983.

Horwitz, Tony. *Blue Latitudes*. Henry Holt and Co. 2002.

Howe, James. *A People Who Would Not Kneel*. Smithsonian Institution Press, 1998.

Heyerdahl, Thor, *Fatu-Hiva, Back to Nature*. Doubleday & Company, Inc.1974.

Heyerdahl, Thor, *Kon-Tiki*. Simon & Schuster.

Igesias, Marvel, Marjorie Vandervelde. *Beauty Is a Ring in My Nose*. Veld Press1978.

Jackson, EL. *St. Helena: The Historic Island From The Discovery To The Present Date*. Thomas Whittaker 1905.

Knox-Johnston, Robin. *The Cape of Good Hope, a Maritime History*. Hodder & Stoughton, 1989.

MacClancy, Jeremy. *To Kill a Bird With Two Stones, a Short History of Vanuatu*. Vanuatu Cultural Centre Port Vila 2002.

Mackay, Susan. *Stella Circles the World*, 2007.

McCullough, David. *The Path Between The Seas*. Simon and Schuster 1977.

Murdock, Lynas. *Four Years on St. Helena*. Arthur House UK. 2010.

Rothwell, Nicolas. *Another Country*. Black Inc. 2007.

Shineberg, Dorothy. *They Came For Sandalwood*. Melbourne University Press, Carlton, Victoria 1967.

Smith, Dennis. *The Prisoners of Cabrera, Napoléon's Forgotten Soldiers 1809–1814*. Four Walls Eight Windows, New York, 2001.

Sobel, Dava. *Longitude*. Penguin Books 1995.

Stevenson, Robert, Louis. *In the South Seas: Being an Account of Experiences and Observations in the Marquesas, Paumotus and Gilbert Islands in the Course of Two Cruises on the Yacht "Casco" (1888) and the Schooner "Equator."* (1889). New York, Charles Scribner's Sons 1896, Nabu Public Domain Reprints.

Stewart, Paul D. *Galápagos, The Islands That Changed The World*. Yale University Press, New Haven and London, 2006.

Stone, Peter, Allan Power, Reece Discombe. *The Lady and the President*. Ocean Enterprises 1943.

Treherne, John, *The Galapagos Affair*. Dr. J.E. Treherne Butler & Tanner Ltd., Frome & London 1983.

Von Mücke, Hellmuth. *The "Ayesha": Being the Adventures of the Landing Squad of the "Emden."* Reproduction of original before 1917, translated by Helen S. White, Ritter & Company.

Weaver, Tony. St. Helena, *500 Years of History—1502–2002*. Anchor Marine and associates UK

William Washburn Nutting. *The Track of the "Typhoon."* The Motor Boat Pub. Co. 1921.

Winchester, Simon. *Atlantic*, Harper Collins publishers.

Winchester, Simon, *Pacific*, Harper Collins publishers.

Zuill, W.S. *The story of Bermuda and her people*. Macmillan Publishers1999 3rd edition.

MUSIC

Abba, *Gimme, Gimme, Gimme, (A Man After Midnight)*, ABBA's Greatest Hits, Vol. 2 and Gold: Greatest Hits,1979.

Archies, *Sugar, Sugar*. Written and produced by Jeff Barry. 1969.

Burl Ives, *Holly Golly Christmas*. Decca Records.1965

Daniel Rae Costello, *We are Fiji*. 2005

Daniela Mercury, *Swing Da Cor*. Eldorado.1991

De Yarza, Carlos, Alberto Triay, Mike Romero, Antonio Ruiz, Rafael. *Macarena*. 1992

Neil Diamond, *Cherry, Cherry*. Produced by Jeff Barry & Ellie Greenwich. 1966, Bang records, 1966

Nessun dorma; Puccini—from the final act of Giacomo Puccini's opera *Turandot*.

MAGAZINES/NEWSPAPER/ARTICLES

Caribbean Compass, Compass publishing.

The Coastal Passage 30th addition, Fenny, Bob.

Cruising World magazine, Nicholson, Theresa, March of 2002: "Can Polynesia Survive Reality TV?", p. 14.

The Daily Harold. Everett WA. Posada, Janice. 2001

Dock Talk, the marine Publication of St. Marten/St. Martin, vo l2/issue no.11 April 15, 2005.

The Leewards Times. Saint Kitts, Nevis 8th year, Issue 353, April 29-May 5, 2005.

Sail Magazine "Daniel's Bay Lost", David Content, March, 2002, p. 16–17

The Nation, Murphy, Padraic.

The *Sydney Morning Herald*, Baker, Jordan, Au. 30, 2007.

The *Weekend Australian*, Toohey, Paul, June, 2008.

Yachting World, Kopeman, Mike. March 2005.

WEBSITES

ENGLAND

MacDonald, Janet, Feeding Nelson's Navy, *ageofsail.wordpress.com/2009/05/15/navy-cheese/*

CARIBBEAN

Seabreeze.com.au Cruising

seabreeze.com.au/News/Cruising/ARC-yacht-Auliana-II-loses

rudder-and-crew-had-to-abandon_3190727.aspx
The Government of Montserrat Information Service: Official Press Releases:
geo.mtu.edu/volcanoes/west.indies/soufriere/govt/monmedia/index.html
WIRED associated press 11/06/05 (drug statistics)
wired.com/science/discoveries/news/2005/11/69494
Red Frog Beach, redfrogbeach.com/news_departures.html
Mustique, travelwizard.com/caribbean/mustique/
Daily Mail Online: dailymail.co.uk/femail/article-1238582
Doyle for the Caribbean Compass April 2004 "\Ancient Customs in St. Lucia? caribbeancompass.com/luciarules.htm

BERMUDA

Bernews, Lilies:When Bermuda Was 'The Easter Isle', April 2011
hbernews.com/2011/04/lilies-trumpeting-a-bermuda-success-story/
The Gulf Stream: Joanna Gyory, A.J. Mariano, Edward H Ryan: Surface Currents in the Atlantic Ocean: oceancurrents.rsmas.miami.edu/atlantic/gulf-stream.html

GIBRALTAR

Graham Lawton, *Monsters of the Deep, New Scientist*: dieselduck.net
Posada, Janice: mindfully.org/.../Nike-Pacific-Dump-Ebbsmeyer.htm
Shipping containers: Aaron Saenz for SingularityHUB. *singularityhub.com/.../10000-shipping-containers*

SPAIN

Fainburg, Denise, A Pilgrim but a Tourist Too: santiago-compostela.net/contrib-dfainberg.html
Sacred Destinations: Cathedral Compestelo
sacred-destinations.com/spain/santiago-cathedral

KUNA INDIANS

Kuna Indians: Jacob Pritchard: *gsevenier.online.fr/kunacultureeng.html*
RedOrbit, Power, Mike, (Reuters), *Panama Indian Albinos a Revered Elite,* redorbit.com/news/health/425725/panamas_indian_albinos_a_revered_elite/
Internet Archive: Kuna ancestry

archive.org/stream/panamapersonalreoorobirich/
panamapersonalreoorobirich_djvu.txt

Do or Die magazine—Kunas, eco-action.org/dod/no10/kuna.htm

Cultural Survival, culturalsurvival.org/publications/cultural-survival-quarterly/panama/kuna-general-congress-and-statute-tourism

PANAMA CANAL

Lecture by Daniels Ammen

pbs.org/wgbh/americanexperience/features/transcript/panama

Panama Canal auction sites, Platts, New York, 17 Feb 2011:

platts.com/RSSFeedDetailedNews/RSSFeed/Shipping/8558535 or Bristol Voss, bristol_voss@platts.com

Catskill Archive Panama,: catskillarchive.com

Good Old Boat, issue 56, Sept/Oct, 2007

johnguzzwell.com/Home.html

Meditz, Sandra W & Hanratty, Dennis M., Panama, A Country Study, Washington: GPO for the Library of Congress,//countrystudies.us/panama/

Panama ship sizes:maritime-connector.com/wiki/ship-sizes

GALÁPAGOS

Natural History Museum, nhm.ac.uk/nature-online/evolution/how-did-evol-theory-develop/Galápagos-mockingbirds/index.html

TED case studies, Galápagos, 1.american.edu/TED/galapag.htm

Tuna Fisheries Status and Management in the Western and Central Pacific Ocean

hawsassets.panda.org/downloads/background_paper___status_and_management_of_tuna_in_the_wcpfc.pdf

Early Human Expansion and the Innovation in the Pacific: Thematic Study. Ian Lilley (co-ordinator) Dec. 2010

international.icomos.org/world...TS_Pacific_20101210_final.pdf

Oceanography and Marine Life of the Galapagos Islands

geol.umd.edu/~jmerck/galsite/research/projects/fitz/ocean2.html

Darwin: darwinonline.org.uk

Why can birds fly:.yalescientific.org/2013/03/qa-why-cant-humans-fly/

Magellan: books.google.com/books?id=FM7tAAAAMAAJ

Piailug: pvs.kcc.hawaii.edu/.../tributes_to_mau.ht.

Selected Bibliography   595

FRENCH POLYNESIA

Borte, Jason, *Surfline*, Tahiti's Teahupoo *surfline.com/surfing-a-to-z/teahupoo-history_925/*

Countries and Their Cultures: *everyculture.com/Cr-Ga/French-Polynesia.html*

Tahiti Traveler: *thetahititraveler.com/general/artdance.asp*

David Content, *Sail Magazine*, "Daniel's Bay Lost", March, 2002, p. 16–17 *sailmagazine.com*) *sailmag.com/html/NewsFeat/Danlsbay.html*

CoastalPolicyCaseStudy: *public.iastate.edu/~sws/coastalcase%20studies/nukuhiva.htm*

Cruising World magazine, March of 2002: "Can Polynesia Survive Reality TV?" Source: p. 14. *cruisingworld.com*

Lieutenant William Bligh, *A Voyage to the South Sea: William Bligh's Narrative of the Mutiny on the Bounty*, 1790 *law2.umkc.edu/faculty/projects/ftrials/bounty/blighnarrative.html*

TONGA

Peace Corp Journals, *peacecorpsjournals.com/?Country&country_id=80&full_page=1*

Peter Kinsey, *A Watery Kingdom, Tales of Tonga*, *gorp.com/weekend.../travel-ta-tonga-sidwcmdev_054953.html*

Survey Ship Penguin: *collections.rmg.co.uk/collections/objects/551566.html*

FIJI

Jennifer Cattermole, Shima: *The International Journal of Research. We Are Fiji shimajournal.org/issues/v2n2/h.%20Cattermole%20Shima%20v2n2%2099–115.pdf*

David Stanley, MoonHandbooks Fiji, *books.google.com/books?isbn=1566913365*

Fiji Times Online: Ernest Heatly Fact file: *fijitimes.com/story.aspx?id=304324*

NEW ZEALAND

Donna Yates: *Toi moko: Traffickingculture.org*

Eric Hoffman: *New Zealand Parrot Pranksters—Keas newzealandatoz.com/index.php?pageid=163* Eric Hoffman

John Vigor, *Unlucky Fridays, johnvigor.blogspot.ca/2009/02/sailing-on-friday.html*

Dead Media Archive: Nautical Figureheads *cultureandcommunication.org/deadmedia/index.php/Nautical_Figurehead*

Anita Brooks for the *New Zealand Herald*

nzherald.co.nz/travel/news/article.cfm?c_id=7&objectid=10657160

150 years of fish & chips: Ian Stuart for *New Zealand Herald: nzherald.co.nz/lifestyle/news/article.cfm?c_id=6&objectid=10685334*

Papunya Tula: Pintupi Trail 2011, papunyatula.com.au/news/141/

Australia Bureau of Statistics Government: *The Dreaming, australia.gov.au/about-australia/australian-story/dreaming*

habs.gov.au/Ausstats/abs@.nsf/0/75258e92a5903e75ca2569de0025c188?OpenDocumentGENERAL

travelwizard.com

BirdLife International

birdlife.org/datazone/userfiles/file/IBAs/.../Mauritius.pdf

FAO Fisheries & Aquaculture — Fishing Techniques

fao.org › FAO Home › Fisheries & Aquaculture

CREDITS

CHAPTER 1: **Toughening Up:** *London, Channel Islands*

"Life is either a great adventure or nothing," Helen Keller, *The Open Door*. Doubleday, 1957.

ENGLAND'S SOUTH COAST, IBERIAN COAST: *Spain, Portugal*

1811, approximately 1019 ships: Roy Adkins and Lesley Adkins, *Jack Tar*. Little Brown 2008.

John Guzzwell wore a British Columbia Indian sweater knitted from raw wool: Miles Smeeton *Once is Enough*. Hart Davis, 1959.

Da Gama took 161 days to complete the passage: Robin Knox-Johnston, *The Cape of Good Hope, A Maritime History*. Hodder & Stoughton, 1989.

CHAPTER 2: **Leaving The Mediterranean:** *Spain*

"There is nothing like lying flat on your back on the deck..." *My Wicked, Wicked Ways*; Errol Flynn. G.P. Putnam's Sons, Rowan & Littlefield, Aurum Press 1959.

"When you travel, remember that a foreign country is not designed to make you comfortable." Clifton Fadiman 1904-1999.

MAJORCA; RETURN TO GIBRALTAR

"The sea, vast and wild as it is...": David Thoreau; *Cape Cod* 1855-1865, in *The Writings of Henry Thoreau*, vol.4 Houghton Mifflin 1906.

Defeated French prisoners: Dennis Smith, *The Prisoners of Cabrera, Napoléon's Forgotten Soldiers 1809-1814*. Four Walls Eight Windows, New York, 2001.

3,500 hundred to 5,000 prisoners perished: Dennis Smith, *The Prisoners of Cabrera, Napoléon's Forgotten Soldiers 1809-1814*. Four Walls Eight Windows, New York, 2001.

Obelisk: Dennis Smith, *The Prisoners of Cabrera, Napoléon's Forgotten Soldiers 1809-1814*. Four Walls Eight Windows New York, 2001.

"The most beautiful thing we can experience is the mysterious." Albert Einstein, *Living Philosophies* World Publishers 1943.

CHAPTER 3: Crossing The Atlantic Ocean: *Preparation*

"Before anything else preparation is the key to success"; Alexander Graham Bell to a reporter, 1847-1922. *Sophia's Fire*, Sango Mbella.

Pound of bread, gallon of beer: Roy Adkins and Lesley Adkins, *Jack Tar*. Little Brown 2008.

DAYS LEADING UP TO DEPARTURE

"One cannot think well, love well, sleep well, if one has not dined well." An essay by Virginia Wolf, *Women and Fiction*; Forum 1929.

CROSSING THE ATLANTIC OCEAN

"Twenty years from now you will be more disappointed..."; Mark Twain, letters and writings 1853-1880.

Ocean Wanderer: Mike Kopeman, *Yachting World* magazine. March 2005.

CHAPTER 4: End Of The First Leg:

"Visual surprise is natural in the Caribbean..." Derek Walcott; Nobel Lecture; *The Antilles: Fragments of Epic Memory* 1992.

ANTIGUA AND BARBUDA

The island supported 500 slaves; *The History of the Island of Barbuda*; V. Langford Oliver. Mitchell and Hughs, London 1894.

Required a thousand new slaves per year: Mark Kurlansky, *Cod: A Biography of the Fish that Changed the World*: Penguin Books.

Eight thousand slaves imported annually: Mark Kurlansky, *Cod: A Biography of the Fish that Changed the World*: Penguin Books.

HOMEWARD

Oceanographer/beachcomber Curtis Ebbesmeyer: Janice Posada, *The Daily Harold*. Everett WA 2001.

CHAPTER 5: Embracing The New Lifestyle:

"I wish I could describe the feeling..." Steve Callahan, *Adrift*; Ballantine Books 1996.

ANTIGUA TO ARUBA

One of the five most difficult routes in the world: Jimmy Cornell: *World Cruising Routes*. International Marine/McGraw, 2002, 5th edition.

ARUBA TO THE SAN BLAS ISLANDS

A People Who Would Not Kneel: James Howe, Smithsonian Institution Press, Washington and London 1998.

Kunas wanted no part of it: James Howe, *A People Who Would Not Kneel*. Smithsonian Institution Press.

'Brothers of Satan': James Howe, *A People Who Would Not Kneel*. Smithsonian Institution Press..

Needed to learn writing and mathematics: James Howe, *A People Who Would Not Kneel*. Smithsonian Institution Press.

No written word: Marvel Igesias, Marjorie Vandervelde, *Beauty Is a Ring in My Nose*. Veld Press.

Many credit their nearly hairless bodies to not having used soap: Marvel Igesias, Marjorie Vandervelde, *Beauty Is a Ring in My Nose*. Veld Press.

Beauty has always been determined by the shape of the nose: Marvel Igesias Marjorie Vandervelde, *Beauty Is a Ring in My Nose*. Veld Press1978.

Kuna matriarchal society: James Howe, *A People Who Would Not Kneel*. Smithsonian Institution Press.

Basketball: Marvel Igesias Marjorie Vandervelde, *Beauty Is a Ring in My Nose*. Veld Press1978.

No windows or doors, an issue with missionaries: Marvel Igesias, Marjorie Vandervelde, *Beauty Is a Ring in My Nose*. Veld Press..

A deceased baby might be buried in the hut beneath the mother's hammock: Marvel Igesias, Marjorie Vandervelde, *Beauty Is a Ring in My Nose*. Veld Press.

Cleft lip: Marvel Igesias Marjorie Vandervelde, *Beauty Is a Ring in My Nose*. Veld Press.

'Brown the baby': Marvel Igesias, Marjorie Vandervelde, *Beauty Is a Ring in My Nose*. Veld Press.

"...at the very heart of creation": Marvel Igesias, Marjorie Vandervelde, *Beauty Is a Ring in My Nose*. Veld Press.

Stone used for breakwater during the construction of the Panama Canal: David Mccullough, *The Path Between the Seas*. Simon and Schuster.

TRANSITING THE PANAMA CANAL

Log book and frying pan: William Washburn Nutting, *The Track of the "Typhoon"*: The Motor Boat Pub.Co. 1921.

"Three tons": *Trekka Round the World*: John Guzzwell, Fine Edge Publishing.

95 percent of the ships in the world were less than 100 feet: David Mccullough, *The Path Between the Seas*, Simon and Schuster.

Early stages of the French canal excavation; Panama Canal: David McCullough, *The Path Between the Seas*, Simon and Schuster.

Working in the Canal Zone: David McCullough, *The Path Between the Seas*. Simon and Schuster.

Most were black: David McCullough, *The Path Between the Seas*. Simon and Schuster.

Wages: David McCullough, *The Path Between the Seas*. Simon and Schuster

Five million sacks of cement: McCullough, David, *The Path Between the Seas*. Simon and Schuster.

Gates:745 tons each: David McCullough, *The Path Between the Seas*. Simon and Schuster.

Steel from Pittsburg Illinois: David McCullough, *The Path Between the Seas*, Simon and Schuster.

THE GALÁPAGOS ISLANDS

Inventory of whales between the late 1700s and early 19th century: Stewart, Paul D, Patrick Morris, Andrew Murray, Joe Stevens, Richard Wollocombe, Godfrey Merlen, *Galápagos, The Islands That Changed The World*. Yale Press, New Haven and London.

200,000 tortoises taken: Marylee Stephenson: *The Galapagos Islands: The Essential Handbook for Exploring, Enjoying & Understanding Darwin's Enchanted Islands*. Mountaineers Books, 1989, 2000, 2nd edition, Edith Publishing.

HMS *Victory* (100): Roy Adkins and Lesley Adkins, *Jack Tar*. Little Brown.

Darwin's mockingbirds: Stewart, Paul D, Patrick Morris, Andrew Murray, Joe Stevens, Richard Wollocombe, Godfrey Merlen, *Galápagos, The Islands That Changed The World*. Yale Press, New Haven and London.

Storing tortoise meat: Roy Adkins and Lesley Adkins, *Jack Tar*. Little Brown.

Before all tortoises became extinct, the inventory of whales lessened: Stewart, Paul D, Patrick Morris, Andrew Murray, Joe Stevens, Richard Wollocombe, Godfrey Merlen, *Galápagos, The Islands That Changed The World*. Yale Press, New Haven and London.

In 1987 the government of Ecuador suggested restricting the annual number of visiting tourists to the Galápagos to 25,000: *Volcano and Geothermal Tourism*. Edited by Patricia Erfurt-Cooper and Malcolm Cooper, Earthscan publishing.

Ferdinand Magellan names Mare pacific: Antonio Pigafetta; English translation by James Alexander Robertson. Volume II; *Magellan's Voyage Around The World*, University of Michigan Libraries 1817. The Arthur H. Clark Co. 1906

Polynesians were capable of long distance voyages centuries before European explorers: *Pacific*, Simon Winchester, Harper Collins.

Chapter 6: Leaving The New World

You could drop the entire dry landmass of our planet…David Stanley, *Moon Handbooks South Pacific*; ATP Moon; 8th edition 2004.

CROSSING THE PACIFIC OCEAN

'liquid phosphorus': "the vessel drove before her bows two billows of liquid phosphorus": Rob Viens, *The Beagle Project: Reflections on Darwin's Voyage of Discovery*.

FRENCH POLYNESIA, MARQUESAS IALSNDS

The First Experience can never be repeated: R.L Stevenson: *In the South Seas: Being an Account of Experiences and Observations in the Marquesas, Paumotus and Gilbert Islands in the Course of Two Cruises on the Yacht "Caso" (1888) and the Schooner "Equator (1889)*.

Fully-modern humans: *ICOMOS* (international council on monuments and sites): *Thematic Study* Ian Lilley co-ordinator.

Linking first human colonization: Jared Diamond, *Guns, Germs, and Steel*: the Fates of Human Societies: W.W. Norton & Company Ltd.

Development of the canoe: Jared Diamond, *Guns, Germs, and Steel*: the Fates of Human Societies: W.W. Norton & Company Ltd.

Modern humans have always been seafarers: James Belich: *Making Peoples, A History of New Zealanders*, University Pressod Hawai'i Press.

Polynesian populations were weakened: Jared Diamond, *Guns, Germs, And Steel, The Fates of Humane Societies*: W.W. Norton & Company.

"Run away from bureaucracy, technology and twentieth century civilization," Thor Heyerdahl: *Fatu-Hiva, Back to Nature*. Doubleday & Company, Inc.

Captain Cook's crewmembers carry infectious diseases: Jared Diamond, *Guns, Germs And Steel: The Fates of Human Societies*. W.W. Norton Company, New York London.

Horrible slaughters took place: Thor Heyerdahl, *Fatu Hiva, Back to Nature*, Doubleday & Company, Inc.

Cleaning skulls: Thor Heyerdahl: *Fatu-Hiva, Back to Nature*. Doubleday & Company, In.

"Watching the yellow bulldozer…": David Content: *Sail* magazine *"Daniel's Bay Lost"*, March, 2002, p. 16-17.

Elephantiasis: Thor Heyerdahl: *Back to Nature*. Doubleday.

TAHITI, BORA BORA

"Tahiti was the fulfillment of a sailor's dream, a dream as old as the legend of the Sirens": David Howarth, *Tahiti, A Paradise Lost*, Viking Press

Polynesians settled near reef passes: Jared Diamond, *Guns, Germs, and Steel*: the Fates of Human Societies: W.W. Norton & Company Ltd.

"Tis impossible to describe the beautiful Prospects we beheld in this charming spot," Captain Samuel Wallis aboard HMS Dolphin 1767. John Hawkesworth, *An Account of the Voyages Undertaken by the Order of His Present Majesty for Making Discoveries in the Southern Hemisphere and Successively Performed by Commodore Byron, Captain Wallis, Captain Carteret, and Captain Cook, in the Dolphin, the Swallow, and the Endeavor*, Drawn Up from the Journals which were kept by the several commanders, and from the Papers of Joseph Banks, Esq. 3 vols. London, 1773.

"Conceived a heaven but not yet a hell." David Howarth, *Tahiti, A Paradise Lost*, Viking Press.

"Tahiti was the fulfillment of a sailor's dream...": David Howarth, *Tahiti, A Paradise Lost*, Viking Press.

Captain Cook on Point Venus: Roy Bishop: *Royal Astronomical Society of Canada*. Observer's handbook.

COOK ISLANDS: *Rarotonga; Niue, Tonga*

Culture is like an onion: a system that can be peeled, layer by layer, in order to reveal the content: Geert Hofstede: *Culture's Consequences: Software of the Mind* SAGE Publications.

Blood red colouring on their faces: *Captain Cook's Journal during his first voyage around the world made in H.M. Bark "Endeavour" 1768-71*. A literal Transcription of the Original Mss. with notes and Introduction edited by Captain W.J.L. Wharton, R.N., F.R.S. Hydrographer of the Admiralty; University of Adelaide.

Several Niueans left their island for the first time to fight in WWI: Tony Horwitz, *Blue Latitudes*: Henry Holt and Company.

They had to adjust to wearing shoes for the first time: Tony Horwitz, *Blue Latitudes*. Henry Holt and Company.

Tongans massacre visitors: *Tonga Islands, William Mariner's Account*, John Martin. Vava'u Press.

Partook in eating of their own kind: *Tonga Islands, William Mariner's Account*, John Martin, Vava'u Press.

"The greatness of a nation...": Mahatma Gandhi. Some believe the quote is taken from the *Collected Works of Mahatma Gandhi*, (98 volumes). Publications Division of the Government of India, 1999.

Chapter 7: Heading South

There are no foreign lands. It is the traveler only who is foreign: Robert Louis Stevenson; *The Silverado Squatters* (1883), The Works of Robert Louis Stevenson; Swanston edn vol ii (London Chatto and Windus, 1911).

FIJI, THE CANNIBAL ISLES, MUSKET COVE

"Yaqona is a good friend, but a bad master.": Solomoni Biturogoiwasa, *My Village , My World, Everyday Life in Nadoria*, Fiji, Institute of Pacific Studies, University of the South Pacific.

Preparing human flesh: Thor Heyerdahl, *Fatu-Hiva Back to Nature*. Doubleday & Company, Inc.

Wealth is determined by the ability to help others: Solomoni Biturogoiwasa, *My Village, My World, Everyday Life in Nadoria*, Fiji, Institute of Pacific Studies, University of the South Pacific.

Early Fijians built houses using their enemies as supporting posts: Solomoni Biturogoiwasa, *My Village , My World, Everyday Life in Nadoria Fiji*, Institute of Pacific Studies, University of the South Pacific.

Resembles the family system of the North American Iroquois Indian: Solomoni Biturogoiwasa, *My Village, My World, Everyday Life in Nadoria Fiji*, Institute of Pacific Studies, University of the South Pacific.

Spirit of Urubuta: Solomoni Biturogoiwasa, *My Village, My World, Everyday Life in Nadoria Fiji*, Institute of Pacific Studies, University of the South Pacific.

Shipwreck or even death: Solomoni Biturogoiwasa, *My Village, My World, Everyday Life in Nadoria*. Fiji, Institute of Pacific Studies, University of the South Pacific.

Prawns found in only two locations in Fiji: Solomoni Biturogoiwasa, *My Village, My World, Everyday Life in Nadoria*. Fiji, Institute of Pacific Studies, University of the South Pacific.

PASSAGE TO NEW ZEALAND

Sunshine almost always makes me high: John Denver, *Sunshine on my Shoulders* from the album *Poems, Prayers & Promises*, 1971.

NEW ZEALAND

The first colonies to settle New Zealand, arrived there approximately eight hundred years ago. *Sapiens*, Yuval Noah Harari: McClelland & Stewart, 2014.

Native Hawaiians, Samoans, the peoples of Easter Island and the Maori of New Zealand, share the same ancestry...: James Belich: *Making Peoples, A History of New Zealanders*, University Pressod Hawai'i Press, 1996.

Sharing the same ancestry: Thor Heyerdahl: *Kon-Tiki*, Simon &Shuster.

It took until 1642: James Belich: *Making Peoples, A History of New Zealanders*, University Pressod Hawai'i Press.

Tied the head of a gazelle to their bows: Thor Heyerdahl, *The Tigris Expedition*, Doubleday & Company.

FIJI—SECOND TIME AROUND

In Fiji rugby is taken very seriously indeed...Tom Bryant; *The Guardian* 2007

INDICES

~ ACCOMMODATIONS, RESORTS ~

Canary Islands
  Hotel Volcan 108
Fiji
  Musket Cove Island Resort 546

Nanuya Island Resort 553
Octopus Resort 554
Sunrise Resort 553

~ ATTRACTIONS ~

Bonaire
  scuba diving 251
Bora Bora
  scuba diving 407
Canary Islands
  Cueva de los Verdes 110
Caribbean
  Antigua
    Classic Yacht Regatta 203
    Concours d'Elégance 203
    Fort Berkeley 205
    Montserrat helicopter tour 249
    Nelson's Dockyard, (UNESCO) 205
    Shirley Heights 205
    Superyacht Cup 202
  Guadalupe
    Carbet Falls 199
    hiking 199

Mustique
  Colin Tennant statue 170
  Kawasaki cart rentals 171
St. Barthélemy
  Gutavia Marine Park 222
  shopping (designer fashions) 221
St. Lucia
  Anse La Raye 163
  hiking 168
  Roseau Valley Distillery 162
Union Is.
  Happy Is. 184
England
  Greenwich 13
  London
    Covent Garden 12
    St. Paul's Cathedral 62
    Tower Bridge 9
    Trafalgar Square 12

Portsmouth Historic
  Dockyard 29, 30
St. Katharine Docks 9
Fiji
  red prawn tour,
    Naweni Village 472
  scuba diving 551
French Polynesia
  Anse Amyot 376
  Daniel's Bay 362
  hiking 351, 365, 405, 421
  Hikoku'a Tohua 361
  Moorea island tour 402
  scuba diving 382
  shopping
    (artisan crafts) 351
    (pottery) 401
  Tahiti
    Arahurahu marae 397
    Le Truck Circle Is.
      Tour 394
    Point Venus 394
    Teahupoo 394
    Vaiete Square 393
  Tuamotus
    black pearl oyster farm 382
Galápagos Islands
  cruise ship Explorer II 299
  lava tunnels 311
  scuba diving 305
Gibraltar
  Cable Car 65
  Cathedral Cave 64
  Grand Casemates Square 63
  Trafalgar Cemetery 64
New Zealand
  Auckland Museum 516
  Bob's Peak 517
  Chinese settlement
    (historic) 523
  cruise ship Milford
    Mariner 522

Fox Glacier 525
Franz Josef Glacier 525
hiking 518, 521, 532
hot springs 513
Lake Matheson 527
Milford Road 520
Red River jet boat ride 517
Skyline Gondola 517
Sky Tower 515
West Coast Heritage
  Highway 525
Panama
  Black Christ 270
  Historic District of Panama,
    (UNESCO) 285
  Portobelo Museum 270
Panama Canal
  Miraflores Observation
    Pavilion 277
Portugal
  Graham's Port Wine
    Lodge 48
  Igreja de São Francisco 49
  Palácio Nacional da Pena,
    (UNESCO) 54
  Praça da Ribeira 47
  St. Clérgios Church
    Tower 49
Spain
  Alhambra 71
  Fortress Monterreal 41
  hiking 43, 99
  Santa María de Afuera 39
  Santiago de Compostela
    Cathedral 43
  shopping 80, 93

~ EARLY EXPLORERS & HISTORY MAKERS ~

Bligh, William, (1754–1817) 358, 434, 465
Bougainville, Louis-Antoine de (1729–1811) 392
Charles V (1500–1558) 71
Chichester, Sir Francis, (1901–1972) 15, 385
Churchill, Sir Winston (1874–1965) 66
Codrington, John & Christopher, (1600s) 205
Columbus, Christopher, (1451–1506) 13, 41, 42, 58, 117, 216, 269
Cook, James, (1728–1779) 32, 35, 63, 243, 347, 395, 425, 432, 465
da Gama, Vasco, (1469–1524) 56
Darwin, Charles, (1809–1882) 296, 297, 531
Drake, Sir Francis, (1540–1596) 269
FitzRoy, Robert, (1805–1865) 531
Guzzwell, John, (1930–) 42, 275
Halley, Edmond, (1656–1742) 396
Hardy, Sir Thomas (1769–1839) 31
Heyerdahl, Thor, (1914–2002) 347, 370

Huggins, W.J. (1781–1845) 31
King Consort Dom Fernando II (1816–1885) 54
King Henry VIII (1491–1547) 29
Magellan, Ferdinand, (circa-1480–1521) 313
Manrique, César, (1919–1992) 109
Montcalm-Gazon, Louis-Joseph de (1712–1759) 392
Morgan, Henry, (1635–1688) 269, 285
Nelson, Horatio, (1758–1805) 205, 219
Piailug, Mau (1932–2010) 320
Pinzón, Martín Alonso, (1441–1493) 42
Queen Dona Maria II (1819–1853) 54
Smeeton, Miles, (1906–1988), Beryl, (1905–1979) 42
St. James the Apostle (-AD44) 43, 45
Tasman, Abel, (1603–1659) 432, 465, 507
Tennant, Colin, (1926–2010) 169
Wallis, Samuel, (1728–1795) 391, 395

~ HISTORY ~

Barbuda 205, 210
Bermuda 232
  Easter Lily Island 232
Caribbean
  Antigua 204
  Arawaks & Caribs 163
  British navy (1715–1800s) 204
  Mustique 169

Navigation Act 205
Nevis 218
slavery 218
St. Barthélemy 221
St. Martin, Sint Maarten 227
England
  Battle of Trafalgar 27
  Cutty Sark, the 14

Endeavour, HMS 35, 243
London Missionary Society
   (*1795*) 396
Lord Sandwich, the 243
Mayflower, the 35
mutiny, HMS Bounty 358
St. Katharine Docks 10
Victory, HMS 26
Fiji 465, 470, 488
French Polynesia
   Fatu Hiva 353
   Marquesans 360
   Marquesas Islands 343, 345
   Nuka Hiva 357
   Tuamotus 371
Galápagos Islands 296
Gibraltar
   Battle of Trafalgar 62, 64
   Great Siege, the 64
   Siege Tunnels 64
   WW II 64
Kingdom of Tonga 435
New Zealand 507, 529
   Otago Goldfields 523

Niue 425
   WW I 427
Panama
   Colón 280
   Kuna Indians 259
   Panama Canal Yacht
      Club 274
   Panama City 285
   Panamá Viejo 285
   Portobelo 269
Portugal
   Porto 50
Spain 70, 71
   Baiona 41
   Barbary pirates 94
   Battle of Trafalgar 95
   Napoleonic War 95
   Nasrid Kings 71
   Niña, the 42
   Pinta, the 42
   Santa María, the 42
   Spanish Armada 53
Tahiti 391
   London Missionary
      Society 396

～ MEMORABLE MEALS ～

Bora Bora
   Bloody Mary's 406
Caribbean
   Antigua
      Abracadabra
         Restaurant 204
      Catherine's Cafe 204
      Shirley Heights 205
      Trappas Bar &
         Restaurant 204

Mustique
   Basil's Bar 172
   Cotton House 172, 196
   Firefly 173
Nevis
   Sunshine's 219
Petit Martinique
   Palm Restaurant 190
Petit St.Vincent
   Petit St. Vincent
      Resort 186

St. Lucia
   Rainforest Café, Marigot Bay 168
Union Is.
   Chatham Bay, Shark Attack 180

England
   J. Sheekey 11
Tahiti
   Roulettes, Vaiete Square 393

~ PLACE NAMES ~

ABC Islands
   Aruba 255
   Bonaire 250
   Curaçao 252
Bay of Biscay 35, 37
Bermuda 229, 230, 231
   St. George's Harbour 234
Canary Islands 105, 117, 120
   Graciosa Island 105, 106
   Gran Canaria, Las Palmas 112, 128
   Lanzarote, (UNESCO) 105, 108
Caribbean
   Antigua 202
      English Harbour 203, 204
      Falmouth Harbour 204
   Barbuda 210
      Codrington 210
   Bequia Is. 192
   Guadalupe 199
   Îles des Saintes 201
   Martinique 196
   Mustique 169, 170
   Nevis 215, 219
      Charlestown 216
   Petit Martinique 188, 189
   Petit St. Vincent 184, 188
   St. Barthélemy 220
      Gustavia 221

   St. Lucia 130, 151, 152, 161
      Anse La Raye 163
      Marigot Bay 166
      Rodney Bay 151
      Soufrière 168, 195
   St. Martin 226
      Simpson Bay Lagoon 226
   St. Vincent 192
   Tobago Cays 176
   Union Is. 179
      Chatham Bay 179, 190
      Clifton Harbour 182, 184
      Clifton Village 181
Cook Islands
   Rarotonga 412, 415, 416, 417
   Avarua 415, 417
England
   Cowes 24, 28, 30
   Dartmouth 34
      Dartmouth Harbour 35
   English Channel 17, 19
   Falmouth 35, 37
   Ipswich 5
   Plymouth 35
   Poole 32
   Portsmouth 26
      Portsmouth Harbour 28
   Solent 17, 19, 20, 25
England/Channel Islands
   Channel Islands 19, 21, 22

Guernsey 22
  St. Peter Port 21
Isle of Jersey 23
Fiji 457, 490
  Mamanuca Islands
    Beachcomber Is. 485
    Malolo Lailai 479
    Musket Cove 479, 480, 546, 567
  Vanua Levu 465, 467
  Viti Levu 465
    Lautoka 491, 541
    Momi Bay 542
    Port Denarau 491, 493
    Saweni Bay 545
  Yasawa Islands 489, 548
    Blue Lagoon/Nanuya Lailai Bay 490
    Likuliku Bay 554
    Namara Village 556
    Navadra 548
    Wayasewa Is. 555
French Polynesia
  Bora Bora 395, 409
  Fatu Hiva 340, 348
    Hanavave 348
  Huahine 402, 403
    Fare 404
  Marquesas Islands 320, 341
  Moorea 400
    Cook's Bay 400
  Nuka Hiva 357
    Baie des Vierges 342
    Daniel's Bay 362
    Taiohae Bay 357, 361
  Raiatea 404
    Uturoa 404
  Tahiti 286, 390, 391
    Papeete 391
    Papeete, Port of 399
  Tuamotus 370
    Anse Amyot 376
    Fakarava 375
    Kauehi Is. 371, 374
    Rangiroa 381, 385
Galápagos Islands 286, 295
  Bartolomé Is. 301
  Fernandina Is. 303
  James Is. 302
  Santa Cruz 298, 302
    Puerto Ayora 310, 312
  Santiago Is. 299
Gibraltar 61, 96, 101, 102, 103
  Gibraltar, Strait of 66
Kingdom of Tonga 415, 427, 432, 433
  Neiafu 438
  Port of Refuge 433
  Vai'utukakau Bay 433
  Vava'u 433, 446
Mediterranean 61, 68
New Zealand 507
  Arrowtown 523
  Auckland 515
  Bay of Islands 532
    Roberton Is. 533
  Glenorchy 402
  Great Barrier Is. 529, 531
    Port FitzRoy 531
    Smoke House Bay 532
  Gulf Harbour 528
  Haast 524
  Kaikoura Is. 532
  Punakaiki 527
  Queenstown 513, 517
  Te Anau 518
  Westport 527
Niue 425, 426
  Alofi 429
Panama
  Cayo Chichime 267

El Porvenir 268
Las Perlas Archipélago 287
Playón Chico 262
Portobelo 269
Port of Cristóbal 272
San Blas Islands 256, 258
Sapibenega 259
Portugal 40, 46, 48
  Cascais 46, 52, 53
  Leixões 46
  Porto 46, 47, 48, 51
  Porto de Pesca 56
  Sines 46, 56, 57
  Sines, Port of 56
  Sintra 53
Spain 21, 28, 79
  Aguadulce 83
  Almerimar 82, 98, 100
  Baiona 41
  Cíes Islands 43
  Balearic Islands 83
  Benalmádena 70, 82
  Cabo de Gata 98
  Cabrera Is. 94
  Cala Jolanda 84
  Espalmador 96
  Estepona 68, 69
  Formentera 87
  Granada 70
  Ibiza 84, 89
    Ibiza Town 89
  Majorca 84
    Palma 92
  Marbella 69
  Santiago de Compostela 43
  Sotogrande 101
United States
  Rhode Island 230, 234
    Narragansett Bay 242

~ SUBJECTS ~

medical supplies 123
provisioning 117, 179
  Canary Islands 128
  Caribbean
    Antigua 287
    Nevis 217
    Union Is. 182
  Galápagos Islands 319
  Nuka Hiva 362
  Panama City 286
  Spain 79
  Tahiti 398
safety equipment 122
spare parts 121

ABOUT THE AUTHOR

RAISED IN A rural southwestern Ontario tobacco town where local watering holes went by the names of Big Creek and Quance's Dam, Donna took up sailing with her husband Mike in the 1970s on Lake Simcoe, located an hour north of Toronto.

Never having sailed before, Mike and Donna purchased an 18 foot Nova Scotia built day sailor which they used to discover the basics of sailing. Their interest in the sport, lead them to exploring the Great Lakes, Georgian Bay, the North Channel, Vancouver's Gulf Islands and Newfoundland's North Atlantic Ocean. Weekends and holidays were often an adventure for the family of four while visiting forts located around Lake Ontario and roasting marshmallows on White Cloud Island in Georgian Bay.

They continued to purchase larger boats to make longer journeys and in 2004, they set off from England in an Oyster 56 with no real plans other than to explore the Mediterranean Sea. But discovering travelling by sea was to their liking, they adopted a lifestyle of water gypsies and eventually visited the five continents of the world. Now having completed seven ocean passages and 50,000 nm, Donna shares the couple's experiences while circumnavigating the world.

Donna is the author of articles for both magazines and newspapers. She is one of thirty-seven female members of the Cruising Club of America and is the recipient of the John Parkinson Memorial Trophy awarded for Transoceanic Passage.

Yes, The World Is Round, Part I: England to Fiji; *Part II: Fiji to the Caribbean,* are her first books.

Made in the USA
Columbia, SC
04 March 2018